FIVE HUNDRED THOUSAND

STROKES FOR FREEDOM.

MNEMOSYNE PUBLISHING CO., INC.
MIAMI, FLORIDA
1969

975603

Lamar State College of Technology
Beaumont, Texas

 PRINTED IN U.S.A.

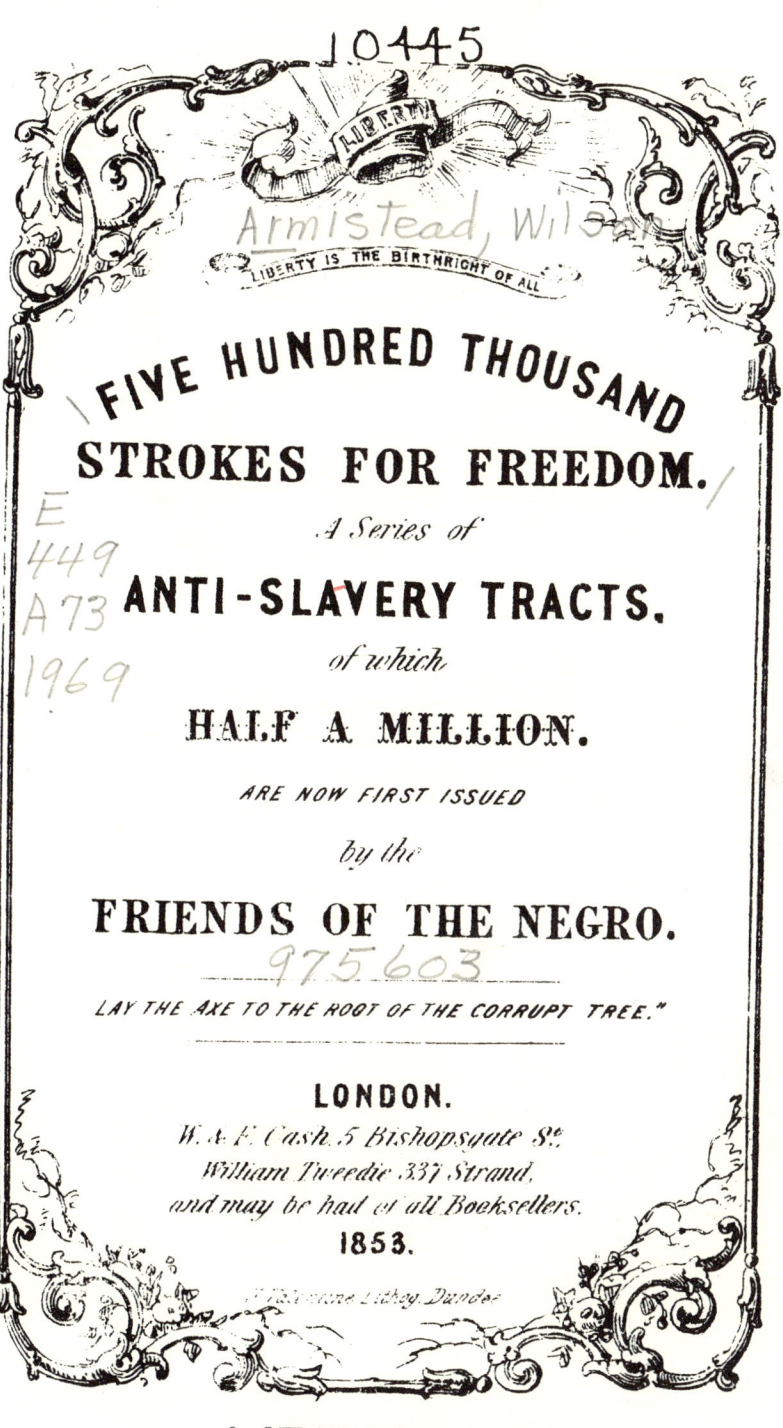

LIBERTY IS THE BIRTHRIGHT OF ALL.

FIVE HUNDRED THOUSAND STROKES FOR FREEDOM.

A Series of

ANTI-SLAVERY TRACTS,

of which

HALF A MILLION.

ARE NOW FIRST ISSUED

by the

FRIENDS OF THE NEGRO.

"LAY THE AXE TO THE ROOT OF THE CORRUPT TREE."

LONDON.
W. & F. Cash, 5 Bishopsgate St.
William Tweedie, 337 Strand,
and may be had of all Booksellers.
1853.

First Mnemosyne reprinting 1969

**Reprinted from a copy in the
Fisk University Library Negro Collection.**

Copyright © 1969 Mnemosyne Publishing Co., Inc. Miami, Florida

Library of Congress Catalog Card Number:

77-83953

Printed in the United States of America

PREFACE.

Whilst millions of our oppressed and manacled fellow-creatures are still groaning under the cruelties of slavery, and panting for deliverance from thraldom, no apology is thought requisite in presenting anything calculated to increase a feeling of sympathy for that portion of suffering humanity whose own voice has but little chance of being heard, and when it *has* an opportunity of being raised in self-defence, is too often but little regarded.

It must be evident to the most superficial observer, that recent events have excited an awakened interest universally in behalf of the down-trodden slave. It is exceedingly desirable that this feeling should not be allowed to pass hastily away, but that the public mind should be kept alive to the great subject of the negro's wrongs, till such time as they are effectually redressed.

It has been thought, that an extensive distribution of Anti-Slavery Tracts would be very opportune at the present moment, and assist more than any other means in maintaining this feeling; for, in the days in which we live, more is to be effected by public opinion, and by appeals to the great sympathies of mankind, than by force or by statute laws. The want of a cheap variety of well-written, judiciously-selected, and popular Anti-Slavery Tracts, has long been felt, for distribution after public meetings, lectures, and on all suitable occasions. We have abundance of **Tracts** on Peace and on Temperance, &c., in extensive circulation —*Olive Leaves* are scattered the wide world over. Why should we not have something equally available for diffusing information on the question of Slavery, when it is admitted to be one of the greatest calamities that afflict mankind? something calculated to excite an interest in a subject so intimately connected with the happiness or misery of a very large portion of the human family?

Thoughts like the above have long occurred to the writer, but the difficulties of effectually supplying the want have appeared considerable. The idea not being lost sight of, however, plans have become gradually developed for carrying out the design; and it has been eventually resolved to issue a series of half a million of Tracts. The subject was first communicated to a few well-known friends of the cause, who not only expressed approbation, but soon furnished a handsome nucleus of contributions for carrying out the design forthwith. Circulars were struck off and distributed, and although the undertaking was deemed by many to be somewhat Herculean, and by a few of the more timid, altogether Utopian, the call has been very generally responded to. Indeed the result has proved that the quantity originally contemplated, 500,000, is quite inadequate to the requirements of Anti-slavery friends; for whilst the first impression is passing through the printer's hands, the demand for these Tracts has been so great, that a second Half Million are already in the press. Many contributions have been received for a gratuitous circulation, which alone will provide for the distribution of 300,000 Tracts.

By this means a scattering of Anti-slavery missiles will be effected to an extent not hitherto attempted, which cannot fail to assist in increasing the lively interest already excited on this question ; and create among a large class who are still ignorant of the evils of Slavery a feeling for suffering humanity of which they are at present wholly unconscious.

The series prepared for the first half million, consists of eighty-two distinct Tracts, varying from 1 to 28 pages each, a list of which will be found at the end of this volume, which also contains one of each of the series in rotation. The compiler claims no merit for originality in these Tracts. Though many of them are expressly written for the occasion, they consist chiefly of reprints from American, or other publications adapted to the present purpose. They will be found admirably suited for general circulation ; and those who employ themselves in the distribution of tracts, will find them an efficient means of maintaining a renewed interest in the oppressed. Without advocating any particular plan of emancipation, they point out the facts and iniquities of the foul system, in such a manner as cannot fail to arouse an Anti-slavery feeling—deep, strong, and practical—and assist in promoting the abolition of an "institution" involving such complicated distress.

It is an appalling fact, that all the efforts of philanthropists, to arrest the progress of slavery, have hitherto proved ineffectual. Still,—

" ——— hideous Slavery,
Full fraught with horror, reigns ; and wild despair
Binds to the earth his victims."

Not only so, but the accursed system of oppression has for some years steadily advanced. There are now seven to eight millions of our fellow-creatures in servile bondage, nearly half of that number being held by professedly free and Christian America—a caricature to its institutions, and a fact palpably turning its boast of religion and liberty into a lie.

Thanks be to God, England has freed herself from the taint of slavery. "On the page of history," says Hugh Stowell, "one deed shall stand out in bold relief—one consenting voice pronounce—that the greatest honour our country ever attained, was when, with her sovereign at her head, she proclaimed—*The Slave is Free!* In the pages of history this act will stand out the gem in our diadem." No more is heard within our borders the cracking of the torturing whip, the clanking of the accursed chain:—

> " Long time has past
> Since first our English soil with magic touch,
> Ithuriel-like, transmuted bond to free;
> The fetters from the wretches' limbs dropt off,
> And he, who erst by fell oppression's yoke
> Bent down enslaved, now lifts his head in hope,
> And feels himself a MAN!"

But having rid *ourselves* of the sin, let us not think we are at liberty to rest. Whilst a single brother or sister continues to endure the chains of slavery, it is our duty to raise our voices to demand their release; and if we remain silent, our brother's blood will be upon us. Christian philanthropy and love know nothing of geographical limitations. We must not confine our sympathies within the narrow sphere of our own country, but extend them throughout the whole habitable globe. As children of Him who hath made of *one* blood all the nations of the earth, we must recognize in the human form, wheresoever it presents itself, a man and a brother, a woman and a sister, each and every one entitled to the blessed privilege of liberty, and the pursuit of happiness—

> " Blest privilege!
> Nay, rather say, *inalienable right!*
> Which every son of earth may justly claim;
> No less the native of the torrid zone
> Of darkest hue, than they who dwell beneath
> More temperate skies, and every shade between—
> This sacred right, alike possessed by all,
> By lawless force or fraud alone withheld."

Seven to eight millions of our fellow-beings, deprived of this rightful liberty, demand our exertions for their emancipation from this unrighteous thraldom; our brother's blood crieth from the ground, craving our help and our protection.

Duties are ours—*consequences* are in the hands of the Omnipotent. Our duty is to sow the seed—the great Husbandman can alone give the increase. Though no immediate success may seem to crown our efforts, they may be as bread cast upon the waters, which shall one day return to yield a rich harvest.

Angelina J. Knox, in the *Pennsylvania Freeman*, Oct. 1852, relates the following circumstance, illustrating the beneficial results of Tract distribution:—

" A slaveholder in Alabama, who had almost become a disbeliever in the Christian religion, had a little son who returned delighted from school, with a prize which his teacher had given him. The father called his happy child to his side to examine his gift. It was a tract. For a moment he looked at it, and then resolved he would read it.

Its perusal led him to reflection, and then to his conversion to the religion of Jesus. In looking at his slaves, he felt that he had no right to retain them longer in bondage, and at once formed the noble resolution of liberating them. True to his principles, he faltered not; but, with trust in God for his future necessities, he removed with them to Kentucky (not being able to liberate them in Alabama), and there, after much instruction and kindest care over them, he made them free. His property, which wholly consisted in his slaves, was estimated at a hundred thousand dollars. At once he sacrificed it all, and became poor for conscience sake. For years he was ridiculed by the name of 'abolitionist,' but it moved him not from his purpose. He has been mobbed and insulted, even in the free states, yet never did he dodge a single missile hurled at him. The decided Christian, the great philanthropist, the uncompromising abolitionist, we now see in him all the fruits of that little tract! What a blessing followed that teacher's gift! Who can tell all the happy influences arising from that one Christian act? 'In the morning, sow thy seed, and in the evening withhold not thy hand; for thou knowest not whether shall prosper, this or that, or whether they both shall be alike good.'"

What abundance of good might be effected, if packages of Anti-slavery Tracts were distributed amongst emigrant ships, bound for foreign lands where slavery prevails, or is advocated! America should be deluged with these missiles. They should be wafted over the vast stronghold of slavery, like the leaves of autumn. Pamphlets, embodying facts, arguments, and appeals, calculated to arouse the reader to a sense of the sinfulness of slaveholding; exhibiting briefly, yet cogently, its enormous evils, its inherent cruelties, and its repugnance to Christianity; contrasting it with the benefits of emancipation, and showing that the holding of men in abject bondage, subjected every moment to all the liabilities attaching to any other description of property, is utterly opposed to those inalienable rights with which God has invested every human being—to all the principles of truth and justice—to the provisions of all righteous government—and to the laws of God; and that it therefore becomes our duty, as men and Christians, to seek its eternal overthrow.

If persons corresponding with, or sending goods to America, made a point of inclosing some of these tracts, it would be like scattering seed in the now-prepared soil. We ought, also, to endeavour to derive the full benefit from our cheap postage at home, by making up the weight prescribed with something likely to do good. Tracts might be inclosed in every letter, without increasing the postage. Let them be sent in faith, a blessing asked upon them, and we know not how many may take root, and what a fruitful harvest will result. We must not be silent or inactive so long as a single fellow-creature bleeds in chains. So long as one man holds property in another, an Anti-slavery feeling needs to be created and kept alive—society must be saturated with it; it must be preached everywhere, and to the great work of emancipation every assistance must be summoned.

Let us not then fear the voice of ridicule or censure, but follow the dictates of those sympathies which the God of nature hath implanted in our bosoms; defend the defenceless, succour the oppressed; plead the cause of the innocent; manifest our allegiance to Him, the distinctive badge of whose disciples is *love*—love to the whole human family; and prove that we joyfully exchange the admiration of the world for the blessing of the perishing. Then, in solemn anticipation of that day when the negro, his friends, and his foes, shall stand before the one Judge and Father of all, we may be found worthy to receive the approving sentence, " Ye have done what ye could." " Inasmuch as ye did it unto one of the least of these my brethren, ye did it unto me. Enter into the joy of your Lord."

WILSON ARMISTEAD.

Leeds, 6*th Month*, 1853.

VALEDICTION;

WRITTEN FOR THE HALF MILLION ISSUE OF ANTI-SLAVERY TRACTS;

BY JANE BRAGG.

"Five hundred thousand strokes for freedom!"
Freedom from the galling chain!
Freedom from the cruel bondage,
Slavery's fetters, slavery's pain—

Noble is the cause ye plead for—
Glorious will the triumph be—
Fearlessly ye intercede for
Human rights and liberty!

Strike with courage, strike in earnest,
Strike! till every blow shall fall
On the hearts of human feeling,
Tell them we for mercy call!

Raise a cry, most loud and fervent,
Far and wide through earth's domain,
Till oppression quails beneath it—
Shamed of its polluted stain!

Tell the world that "man's a brother;
Tell the world that God, who gave
Black and white to love each other,
And in each a soul to save,

Never meant that man should shackle,
Lash and mangle, brand and sear,
Buy and sell a fellow-being
Whom he holds, by nature dear!

God be with you! grant your mission
May be heard and blessed be,'
Speed ye onward, heavenly Father!
Till the wretched shall be free!

Leeds Anti-slavery Series. No. 1.

BRIEF DEFINITION OF NEGRO SLAVERY.

"Negro Slavery is the sum of all villanies."—WESLEY.
"Slavery is a mass, a system of enormities."—WM. PITT.

NEGRO slavery is truly what it ever was, "the sum of all villanies." It reduces a human being as much as possible to the position of a beast, depriving him of all power to act for himself, excluding all knowledge from his mind, robbing him of the rewards of his labours, and working him so severely for gain, as greatly to shorten his life. It deprives him of any redress for ill-usage, as he is not allowed to give any evidence in a court of justice.

Negro slavery is beyond all question the most gigantic system of oppression and iniquity which has ever disgraced our fallen world or degraded our fellow-men ;—the most appalling enormity and outrage ever committed under the stimulus of a vicious self-interest. In whatever light we view it, it is entirely at variance with the genius and spirit of Christianity ; and whilst millions of our oppressed and manacled brethren are still groaning under its cruelties, and panting for deliverance from its thraldom, it is our duty to expose, by all possible means, a system so contrary to every principle of justice, humanity, and religion.

" Enslaving men," says Theodore Weld, an American writer, "is reducing them to articles of property—making free agents chattels—converting *persons* into *things*. A slave is one held in this condition. In law, ' he owns nothing, and can acquire nothing.' His right to himself is abrogated. If he say, *my* hands, *my* body, *my* mind, *myself* ; they are figures of speech. To use *himself* for his own good, is a *crime*. To keep what he

---

Sold by W. and F. G. CASH, 5, Bishopsgate Street, London; and by JANE JOWETT, Friends' Meeting Yard, Leeds, at 1s. 2d. per 100.

carns, is *stealing*. To take his body into his own keeping, is *insurrection*. In a word, the profit of his masters is made the end of his being, and he a mere means to that end—a mere means to an end into which his interests do not enter, of which they constitute no portion.

" *Man*, sunk into a thing! the intrinsic element, the principle of slavery;—*men*, bartered, leased, mortgaged, bequeathed, invoiced, shipped in cargoes, stored as goods, taken on executions, and knocked off at public outcry! Their *rights*, another's conveniences; their *interests*, wares on sale; their personal, inalienable ownership, a serviceable article, or a plaything; their deathless nature, conscience, social affections, sympathies, hopes, marketable commodities! This is slavery. The eternal distinction between a person, and a thing trampled under foot—the crowning distinction of all others—alike the source, the root, and the measure of their value; the rational, immortal principle, consecrated by God to universal homage in a baptism of glory and honour, by the gift of His Son, His Spirit, His Word, His presence, providence, and power; His shield, and staff, and sheltering wing; His opening heavens, and angels ministering; and a great voice in heaven proclaiming eternal sanctions, and confirming the Word with signs following."

Trade suggests ideas of national civilization and enterprise; but the *trade in man* is a violent outrage upon its legitimate meaning, and is, in fact, a moral anomaly. It is an unsightly, hideous excrescence upon the great body of commerce, which mars its beauty, shades its advantages, and vitiates its honours.

Some idea may be formed of the conflict sustained by a rational and susceptible being when forced from his country, his kindred, and all that renders life most dear; but it is impossible for language to convey a tithe of the agonies or of the unparalleled distress to which the hapless negroes are doomed. The bare recital of facts connected with their original capture, their being driven in gangs, chained together, over the burning sands of Africa, and then stowed into those frightful receptacles of human woe, the slave ships, to endure the incalculable horrors of the middle passage, and, lastly, put up like beasts at the auction-block—the bare recital of such facts fills the mind with horror.

And what is the condition of the hapless victims of this nefarious system in the last stage to which they are reduced by their iron-hearted oppressors, which is a hopeless, endless state of slavery?

Reader, listen again! " The slave is unprotected by the laws of his country, and stands without one recognized right, fully exposed to the storms of passion, the venom of prejudice, and the scorn of pride. Left almost entirely to the caprice of his owners, he may be abused and even murdered with impunity. If he escapes from his detested bondage, he is advertised in the public papers by his ' cropped ears,' or his ' scars from iron collars,' &c., &c. Letters are branded with hot iron on his feet, and the law of his country is silent; he is hunted by blood-hounds—the law is silent; his weeping child is forcibly separated from him for ever—the law is silent; the woman whom he loves (to call her his *wife* is a cruel mockery) is torn from his hands and sold—the law is silent; she is sometimes compelled—*compelled by the lash*—(would to heaven this were a lie, and not the awful truth) to submit to the polluting embraces of her crime-loving master—the law is silent still—silent even *here*. When, then, does it speak, and what does it say? Let us hear.

" A man wants money; he looks at another man, and calculates *the value* of his sinews. Then, the law says, sell him. He sends him to the market—to the shambles. He may, perchance, feel some small wish to escape, and *betray himself*—the law says, chain him. He has received a deep personal injury—the law says I will not take, shall not even *hear* his evidence. He is found on a road, with six other coloured persons, but with ' no white person'—the law says let him receive twenty lashes! He meets together with a few more of his unfortunate class for religious purposes—the law says, disperse and lash *them!* A 'free man' teaches a slave to read—the law says, lash *him* too. A slave has taught *himself* to read, or has been taught by stealth, and attempts to teach his child to read the Bible—the law still cries out too, lash *him;* and Louisiana says, if he dare commit this *offence* a *second* time, the penalty I inflict is—death !"

Such are the tender mercies of slavery! Justly, indeed, has it been termed the " Crowning Crime of Christendom." How long shall its barbarities continue to affright, and its pollutions sicken the soul?

Seven and a half millions of our fellow-creatures are yet suffering from its unparalleled atrocities! Held as goods and chattels, the property of other human beings, transferred from one owner to another, like beasts that perish! The contemplation is as awful as it is true. Seven and a half millions of our fellow-creatures! Seven and a half millions of men, women, and children, with tearful eyes, and with uplifted hands, with branded and bleeding bodies, with lacerated feet and clanking chains, supplicate on bended knees for the restoration of their rights.

Reader! assist, I implore thee, in the great contest for liberty, that the full blessings of Christianity may be bestowed, and " the dew of kindness distilled, upon the most helpless and injured portion of the human family." " Laurels more fair, victory more glorious, never yet graced the annals of Christian warfare, than would be won and worn by thee, if clad in the armour of God, thou wouldst assail the battlements and bulwarks of oppression till they should totter and fall. Proudly as they lift their summits to the skies, exulting in having stood long as conspicuous and lofty as they stand now, yet vain is their glory, deceptive is their strength. The very citadel of slavery is founded upon 'hay and stubble,' and the frail edifice is no better prepared to resist a steady vigorous charge from a mighty phalanx of united Christians, than is the house of sand which the child erects upon the shore to withstand the force of the overwhelming billow. Even as the vestiges of that fragile toy are borne away into the sea, so would the onward march of those great conquerors, religion and virtue, sweep away every trace of an institution which mars the beauty of God's moral creation, by interrupting the happiness and defiling the purity of mankind."

> " Alas! that such a beauteous land,
> So vast, so fertile, so sublime,
> Should wear upon her front the brand
> And impress of so dark a crime!"

Leeds Anti-slavery Series. No. 1.

Sold by W. and F. G. CASH, 5, Bishopsgate Street, London; and by JANE JOWETT, Friends' Meeting Yard, Leeds, at 1s. 2d. per 100.

Leeds Anti-slavery Series. No. 2.

SLAVERY DESCRIBED

BY A MEMBER OF CONGRESS.

"To what depths of degradation can slavery reduce the immortal mind. It blots out the intellect, and reduces man, created in the image of his God, to the level of the brutes. In Alabama no one dare teach his slaves to read the Word of God. It would subject him to punishment in the penitentiary, were he to do it. Nor need we go to Alabama to find such laws. If, Sir, you pass over the river (Potomac) lying before our windows, and on its southern bank attempt to kindle in the dormant intellect of a slave the hope of a future life, by teaching him to read the Scriptures, you will be liable to an incarceration in the penitentiary. Yes, it is regarded as a *crime* to teach a slave to read the Bible in this Christian land —this land of Sabbaths, and ministers, and Bibles, and slaves.
.... What is slavery, and what are its effects? A gentleman, once a member in the other end of the Capitol, and a slaveholder, of accurate information, some years since stated, that the average life of slaves, after entering the sugar plantations, was only five years, and upon the cotton plantations only seven years. That is to say, they are driven so hard at labour as to destroy the lives of the whole of them every five and seven years upon an average. Now, is it not as much murder to destroy the life of our fellow-man, by a torture of five or seven years, as it would be to strike him down at a blow? Yea, is not this prolonged torture a refinement in cruelty? I have no time to refer to the licentiousness, or indeed to the almost total obliteration of moral sentiment, to be found not only among slaves, but among all slaveholding communities.

"It is said, and I believe with perfect truth, to be no unusual thing for slaveholders to sell their own children as slaves. Brothers traffic in the bodies of their fathers, sons, and daughters. Such crimes have no names. Well might Wesley denounce slavery as the sum of all villanies; for it is so in fact."

Leeds Anti-slavery Series. No. 2.
Sold by W. and F. G. CASH, 5, Bishopsgate Street, London; and by JANE JOWETT, Friends' Meeting Yard, Leeds, at 6*d.* per 100.

Leeds Anti-slavery Series. No. 3.

STARTLING FACTS,

RELATIVE TO SLAVERY AT THE PRESENT TIME.

THERE are now, in various parts of the world, SEVEN AND A HALF MILLIONS of our fellow-creatures in SLAVERY!
Four Hundred Thousand human beings are annually torn from their homes and friends. Nearly THREE HUNDRED THOUSAND of this mighty host perish by fire and sword in their capture, or from privation and suffering. The remainder are transported over the wide sea, sold by public auction to the highest bidder, and consigned to endless slavery; husbands, wives, and families being separated from each other, probably never to meet again in this world.

Upwards of *three millions* of slaves are held in the United States of America. They are kept in the greatest ignorance, and subjected to the most cruel treatment in that professing Christian country, ever boasting of its *freedom!*

The imagination cannot picture a system which could produce more evil fruit than negro slavery *has* produced, and *is* producing, wherever its horrid aspect is exhibited. Does it not outrage every human right—crush every lofty aspiration—rupture every lovely tie? Is it not, in a word, the total subversion of the law of right for the lawless principle of force? How long shall its barbarities continue to affright, and its pollutions sicken, the soul?

Seven and a half millions of our fellow-creatures are now suffering from its unparalleled atrocities;—held as goods and chattels; the property of other human beings; transferred from one owner to another, like beasts that perish. The contemplation is as awful as it is true.

Reader, hast thou any sympathy and Christian feeling for these millions of thy brethren and sisters in cruel bonds? Consider speedily what thou canst do to hasten their freedom.

Leeds Anti-slavery Series. No. 3.
Sold by W. and F. G. CASH, 5, Bishopsgate Street, London; and by JANE JOWETT Friends' Meeting Yard, Leeds, at 6*d.* per 100.

Leeds Anti-slavery Series. No. 4.

THE SLAVE-TRADE,
ITS EXTENT AND HORRORS.

"Africa beholds her tribes, at home,
In battle slain; abroad, condemned to roam
O'er the salt waves, in stranger isles to bear
(Forlorn of hope, and sold into despair),
Thro' life's slow journey, to its dolorous close,
Unseen, unwept, unutterable woes."

THANK God, this is not what it was. There was a time when it was carried on by means of British industry, and capital, and skill. That time has for ever gone. The slave-trade now is principally confined to the supply of slaves from Africa to Cuba and Brazil. During the last session of Parliament, James Wilson procured a "return, as nearly as the same can be furnished, of the number of slaves embarked on the coast of Africa, and landed in Cuba and Brazil in each year, from 1842 to the latest date to which the accounts extend." The return extends from 1842 to 1851, and though, of course, anything like accuracy is hardly attainable in such a case, the numbers, towards the close of the period in question, are, in the case of the greatest supporters of this accursed traffic, such as to encourage our highest hopes :—"From 1842 to 1850 there were imported successively, year by year, into Brazil, from Africa, the following batches of slaves :—17,435, 19,095, 22,849, 10,453, 50,324, 56,172, 60,000, 54,000, and 23,000. Such a result is, in every aspect and bearing of it, most gratifying, and the more so, that it is said to be mainly due to a resolution, at length sincerely taken on the part of Brazil herself, to make the suppression of the trade a reality. The case as regards Cuba is not so satisfactory; but the numbers imported into that island are much more limited; and the variations, during the ten years embraced in the return, are of an extreme

Sold by W. and F. G. CASH, 5, Bishopsgate Street, London; and by JANE JOWETT, Friends' Meeting Yard, Leeds, at 2s. 3d. per 100.

and altogether capricious character. But the trade is firmly planted there, owing to the wealth and intelligence of the slave-traders. Should the scandalous project, on the part of a portion of the inhabitants of the United States, symbolized by the "lone star," be prosecuted to a successful result, the extinction of the slave-trade to Cuba from Africa will be one result, although the rivetting of the chains of the black population of the island, it is to be feared, will be another. It is calculated that Africa is annually robbed of FOUR HUNDRED THOUSAND of her population, to glut the cupidity, or to minister to the pride and luxury, of nominal Christians and the followers of Mahomet; from two to three hundred thousand of this number perish by fire and sword in their original capture, by privation and fatigue in their transit to the coast, and by disease and death, in their most horrible forms, crossing the middle passage. When the contest against the slave-trade first commenced, half a century ago, it was calculated there were from two to three millions of slaves in the world. There were recently, according to documents quoted by Sir T. F. Buxton, six to seven millions, now probably increased to seven and a half millions.

That the slave-trade is equally cruel as every other part of the abominable system, the following instances show. In the memoirs of Granville Sharp we read:—

"March 9, 1783. Gustavus Vasa called on me with an account of 132 negroes being thrown alive into the sea, from on board an English slave-ship.

"The circumstances of this case could not fail to excite a deep interest. The master of a slave-ship trading from Africa to Jamaica, and having 440 slaves on board, had thought fit, on a pretext that he might be distressed on his voyage for want of water, to lessen the consumption of it in the vessel, by throwing overboard 132 of the most sickly among the slaves. On his return to England, the owners of the ship claimed from the insurers the full value of those drowned slaves, on the ground that there was an absolute necessity for throwing them into the sea, in order to save the remaining crew, and the ship itself. The underwriters contested the existence of the alleged necessity; or, if it had existed, attributed it to the ignorance and improper conduct of the master of the vessel. This contest of pecuniary interest brought to light a scene of horrid brutality, which had been acted during the execution of a detestable plot. Upon the trial, it appeared that the ship *Zong*, Luke Collingwood, master, sailed from the island of St. Thomas, on the coast of Africa, September 6, 1781, with 440 slaves and fourteen whites on board, for Jamaica, and that, in the November following, she fell in with that island ; but instead of proceeding to some port, the master mistaking, as he alleges, Jamaica for Hispaniola, ran her to leeward. Sickness and mortality had by this time taken place on board the crowded vessel ; so that, between the time of leaving the coast of Africa and the 29th of November, sixty slaves and seven white people had died; and a great number of the surviving slaves were then sick and not likely to live. On that day the master of the ship called together a few of the officers, and stated to them that, if the sick slaves died a natural death, the loss would fall on the owners of the ship ; ' but, if they were thrown alive into the sea, on any sufficient pretext of necessity for the safety of the ship, it would be the loss of the underwriters,' alleging, at the same time, that it would be less cruel to throw sick wretches into the sea, than to suffer them to linger out a few days under the disorder with which they were afflicted. To this inhuman proposal the mate, James Kelsal, at first objected ; but Collingwood at length prevailed on the crew to listen to it. He then chose out from the cargo 132 slaves, and brought them on deck, all or most of whom were sickly, and not likely to recover, and he ordered the crew by turns to throw them into the sea. ' A parcel' of them were accordingly thrown overboard, and, on counting over the remainder in the morning, it appeared that the number so drowned had been fifty-four. He then ordered another parcel to be thrown over, which, on a second counting on the succeeding day, was proved to have amounted to forty-two.

" ' On the third day the remaining thirty-six were brought on deck, and, as these now resisted the cruel purpose of their masters, the arms of twenty-six were fettered with irons, and the savage crew proceeded with the diabolical work, casting them down to join their comrades of the former days.' Outraged misery could endure no longer; the ten last victims sprang disdainfully from the grasp of their tyrants, defied their power, and, leaping into the sea, felt a momentary triumph in the embrace of death."

A faithful abstract, drawn up by Mr. Stokes, of the evidence taken before a committee of the House of Commons, in 1792, gave the following results, which may afford some idea of the horrors attending the slave-trade:—Every slave, whatever his size might be, was found to have only five feet and six inches in length, and sixteen inches in breadth to lie in. The floor was covered with bodies stowed or packed according to this allowance ; but between the floor and deck, or ceiling, were often platforms or broad shelves in the midway, which were covered with bodies also. The height from the floor to the ceiling, within which space the bodies on the floor and those on the platform lay (two tiers of human beings), seldom exceeded five feet eight inches, and in some cases it did not exceed four feet. The men were chained two and two together by their hands and feet, and were chained also by means of ring-bolts, which were fastened to the deck. They were confined in this manner at least while they remained on the coast, which was from six weeks to six months, as it might happen. Their allowance consisted of one pint of water a-day to each person, and they were fed twice a-day with yams and horse-beans. After meals they jumped up in their irons for exercise. This was so necessary for their health that they were whipped if they refused to do it, and this jumping was termed dancing. They were usually fifteen or sixteen hours below deck out of the twenty-four. In rainy weather they could not be brought up for two or three days together. If the ship was full, their situation was then distressing ; they drew their breath with anxious and laborious efforts, and some died of suffocation. Then, with respect to the loss of life, from papers laid on the table of the House of Lords, in 1799, it appears that in the year 1791 (three years after the passing of the Slave-Carrying Act), of 15,754 slaves carried from the coast of Africa, 1378 died during the middle passage, the average length of which was fifty-one days, making a mortality of $8\frac{3}{4}$ per cent. in that time, or of $62\frac{1}{2}$ per cent. per annum, a rate of mortality which would depopulate the earth in a year and seven months. The amount of the mortality in 1792 was, however, still more enormous ; of 31,554 slaves carried from Africa, no fewer than 5413 died in the passage, making somewhat more than 17 per cent. in fifty-one days. Had the voyage been prolonged, and the slaves continued to die in the same proportion, the whole number would have been swept away in about ten months.

We have given facts where America is concerned—we must be equally honest when speaking of our own countrymen. The following extract from a Parliamentary Blue Book, shows the connection of Englishmen abroad with the horrible slave-trade: —Evidence given before the slave-trade committee, 1848, by Capt. R. H. Stopford, R.N.—"I was lying in Rio harbour, as senior officer, for the two months that I was in Rio, and I used to attempt to get information on shore with regard to vessels expected across with slaves, that I might send cruisers to intercept them. I was told by several persons, among others English merchants, 'You cannot expect information from us, because unless those slaves are landed we cannot be paid for our merchandize.' Therefore you cannot expect information from any of the English merchants there. The only way we had of getting information was this: we had a spy, who was paid out of the proceeds of the slaves taken."

Another extract, from the same source, exhibits the awful destruction of human life which resulted from the landing of a single cargo of goods:—

"Lieut. Barnard to the Commander, dated *Thunderbolt*, August 15, 1846.—'Whilst we were at Zanzibar, the American barque *Lucy Penniman*, brought out a cargo for the purchase of 5000 slaves, for which the dealers have been making a great rush ever since. In May, 1844, 700 of them were drowned in a barque called the *Julia*, on the Barsas da India, 300 were burnt in a baracoon, and 200 died of sickness in a small schooner, which attempted to get away, but was obliged to put back with half her miserable cargo; 1500 were got off from Inhambane and Delagoe Bay, through the agency of Paulo Roderique, who had again returned from Rio; 420 were found on board a brig which we drove on shore, and about 350 were taken or driven on shore by the *Mutine*, which accounts for a great proportion of them."

The way in which the trade is at present carried on is as follows:—When the slaves are stolen, or purchased, or made captives, as the King of Dahomey makes them by marauding expeditions, they are taken to permanent slave-factories, called barracoons, where they are kept ready for shipping at any moment. In these the slaves are much in the same condition as when at rest on a sugar plantation, and the slave-dealer is interested in keeping them in perfect health. The moment the slave-vessel appears, the slaves are shipped, and in an hour or two she is under sail on the return voyage. The fastest sailing vessels in the world are now employed in the trade, so that the voyage only lasts about half as long as formerly, and the previous confinement on board is entirely prevented. The models best adapted for fast sailing admit only of one deck or tier, and these being close to capacious hatchways, the slaves breathe a far purer air than could penetrate to the holds of such vessels as were used formerly, and would be used again if the trade were thrown open.

The Rev. Pascoe Grenfell Hill, in a little work published in 1848, entitled *Fifty Days on Board a Slave-Vessel in the Mozambique Channel,* gives an account of the heart-sickening horrors of the middle passage, that we must fain make an extract or two here. After boarding the vessel, he says:—

" During the first watch our breeze was light and variable, the water smooth, the recently-liberated negroes sleeping, or lying in quietness about the deck. Their slender supple limbs entwine in a surprisingly small compass; and they resembled, in the moonlight, confused piles of arms and legs, rather than distinct human forms. They were, however, apparently at ease, and all seemed going on as fairly as could be desired. But the scene was soon to undergo a great and terrible change. About one hour after midnight, the sky began to gather clouds, and a haze overspread the horizon to windward. A squall approached, of which I and others who had laid down on the deck received warning by a few heavy drops of rain. Then ensued a scene, the horrors of which it is impossible to depict. The hands having to shorten sail suddenly, uncertain as to the force of the squall, found the poor helpless creatures lying about the deck, an obstruction to getting at the ropes and doing what was required. This caused the order to send them all below, which was immediately obeyed. The night, however, being intensely hot and close, 400 wretched beings thus crammed into a hold twelve yards in length, seven in breadth, and nly three and a half feet in height, speedily began to make an effort to re-issue to the open air. Being thrust back, and striving the more to get out, the after-hatch was forced down on them. Over the other hatch-way, in the fore-part of the vessel, a wooden grating was fastened. To this, the sole inlet for the air, the suffocating heat of the hold, and, perhaps, panic from the strangeness of their situation, made them press, and thus great part of the space below was rendered useless. They crowded to the grating, and clinging to it for air, completely barred its entrance. They strove to force their way through apertures, in length fourteen inches, and barely six inches in breadth, and, in some instances, succeeded. The cries, the heat—I may say, without exaggeration, 'the smoke of their torment'—which ascended can be compared to nothing earthly. One of the Spaniards gave warning that the consequence would be 'many deaths.'

"Thursday, April 13th.—(Passion Week).—The Spaniard's prediction of last night this morning was fearfully verified. Fifty-four crushed and mangled corpses lifted up from the slave-deck have been brought to the gang-way and thrown overboard. Some were emaciated from disease; many bruised and bloody. Antonio tells me that some were found strangled, their hands still grasping each other's throats, and tongues protruding from their mouths. The bowels of one were crushed out. They had been trampled to death for the most part, the weaker under the feet of the stronger, in the madness and torment of suffocation from crowd and heat. It was a horrid sight, as they passed one by one—the stiff distorted limbs, smeared with blood and filth—to be cast into the sea. Some, still quivering, were laid on the deck to die; salt water thrown on them to revive them, and a little fresh water poured into their mouths. Antonio reminded me of his last night's warning, 'Ya se lo dixè anoche.' He actively employed himself with his comrade Sebastian in attendance on the wretched living beings now released from their confinement below; distributing to them their morning meal of 'farinha,' and their allowance of water, rather more than half a pint to each, which they grasped with inconceivable eagerness, some bending their knees to the deck, to avoid the risk of losing any of the liquid by unsteady footing, their throats doubtless parched to the utmost with crying and yelling through the night.

A heavy shower having freshened the air, in the evening

most of the negroes went below of their own accord, the hatchways being left open to allow them air. But a short time, however, had elapsed when they began tumultuously to re-ascend, while persons above, afraid of their crowding the deck too much, repelled them, and they were trampled back, screaming and writhing, in a confused mass. The hatch was about to be forced down on them, and, had not the lieutenant in charge left positive orders to the contrary, the catastrophe of last night would have been re-enacted."

Such was the slave-trade when the above was written in 1848; and though some abatement of its activity to the Brazils is said to have taken place recently, it is yet carried on to an enormous extent, and its *horrors* are increased rather than diminished.

Mr. Hill says, " While we boast the name of Wilberforce, and the genius and eloquence which enabled him to arouse so general a zeal against the slave-trade; while others are disputing with him the claim of being the true annihilator of the slave-trade ; that trade, far from being annihilated, is at this very hour carried on under circumstances of greater atrocity than were known in his time."

Lord Denman has well said, " The slave-trade is by far the greatest evil, with its revolting horrors, that ever afflicted mankind."—" In no species of merchandise," observes Sir T. F. Buxton, " is there such a waste of the raw material as in the merchandise of men. Two-thirds of the goods perish, in order that one-third may reach the market! The vast amount of suffering, and the waste of human life, is but a part of the evils of the slave-trade. It stands as a barrier excluding everything that can soften, or enlighten, or elevate the people of a vast continent. It suppresses all other trades, creates endless insecurity, kindles perpetual war, banishes commerce, knowledge, and social improvement, and, above all, Christianity, from one quarter of the globe, and from hundreds of millions of mankind."

Leeds Anti-slavery Series. No. 4.

Sold by W. and F. G. CASH, 5; Bishopsgate Street, London; and by JANE JOWETT, Friends' Meeting Yard, Leeds, at 2s. 3d. per 100.

Leeds Anti-slavery Series. No. 5.

STATISTICS OF THE COLOURED RACE.

THE number of the people of colour in the New World cannot be exactly ascertained, but the following statement of particulars will be found to approximate near to the truth, viz.:—

United States .	. 3,650,000	Haïti . . .	850,000
Brazil . . .	. 4,050,000	French Colonies	. 270,000
Spanish Colonies	. 1,470,000	Dutch Colonies	. 50,000
South American		Danish Colonies	. 45,000
Republics .	. 1,130,000	Mexico . . .	70,000
British Colonies	. 750,000	Canada . . .	35,000

Total 12,370,000

Of these, seven millions and a-half are in slavery in the United States, Brazil, and the Spanish and Dutch colonies; one quarter of a million in process of emancipation in the South American republics; and the remainder, four millions six hundred and twenty thousand, are free. In the United States, the coloured population is increasing at the rate of one hundred thousand a-year, notwithstanding the greater portion of them are subject to the rigours of slavery; and in the several countries where they are now free, and an equality of the sexes exist, they are increasing more or less rapidly. In the Spanish colonies and Brazil, the number is kept up by constant importations of slaves from the coast of Africa, otherwise there would be a considerable annual decrease in the coloured populations of those countries until the sexes became equalised, as in the United States. Here, then, we have the important fact that there are, at the present time, upwards of TWELVE MILLIONS of Africans, and their decendants, in the New World, united together in suffering, in sympathy, in hope, or in despair. The following statement of the number of slaves held by professing Christians, of various denominations, may be relied on:—

Sold by W. and F. G. CASH, 5, Bishopsgate Street, London; and by JANE JOWETT Friends' Meeting-Yard, Leeds, at 7d. per 100.

Denominations.	Ministers.	Members.	No. of Slaves.
Methodists	5,080	1,178,637	219,563
Presbyterians	3,264	333,458	77,000
Baptists	6,598	812,921	125,000
Campbellites	—	—	101,000
Episcopalians	1,404	67,550	88,000
Other Denominations	—	—	50,000
Total number of Slaves held by Ministers of the Gospel, and Members of the different Protestant Churches			660,563

The denominations above cited have under their control 89 colleges, with 5495 students, and 26 theological seminaries, with about 700 students. Some of these colleges and seminaries have been built and endowed partly by the sale of slaves, and all are looking for slaveholding patronage.

What ought these religious slaveholders to do? Some will say, immediately, and at all hazards, Emancipate their slaves. Others will say, Go to work immediately, and with earnestness, as citizens of the country, to procure the repeal of the laws. Others will say, Commence immediately and sincerely the work of giving instruction to the slaves, to prepare them for freedom. But will any intelligent Christian say, that these 60,000 slave-holders are discharging their duty, while eating and wasting the earnings of their slaves, and making no effort in any way to give them their freedom?

It has been contended that these men are degraded so as often to be incapable of amelioration—that as savages they could be more easily civilized than as slaves. Out of the worst of systems, or the most deplorable of events, Providence may often brings results full of promise. But let not the planter who holds the slave, or the minister of religion who supports him in it, imagine that the wrong he does is any the less wrong because good may sometimes arise out of it. Let him not flatter himself that even if God did pronounce a curse on Canaan and so make slavery the inevitable lot of the negro (a question which we do not care to argue), he will look with a gracious eye on those who make themselves the ministers of his will that they may promote their own selfish interests. " Offences will come, but woe to those by whom they come."

Leeds Anti-slavery Series. No. 5.

Sold by W. and F. G. CASH, 5, Bishopsgate Street, London; and by JANE JOWETT, Friends' Meeting-Yard, Leeds, at 7d. per 100.

Leeds Anti-slavery Series. No. 6.

WORKINGS OF AMERICAN SLAVERY
AS REGARDS CASTE AND PREJUDICE.

THE great object of leading American statesmen is to get rid of the free people of colour—quietly if they can—forcibly if they must. Their increase is viewed with serious apprehension in the Slave States, and with displeasure throughout the whole Union. Many of the states have prohibited the admission of free blacks or mulattoes within their borders, and have authorized their sale into slavery; some of the Slave States threaten to expel the free coloured people by force, and, with the aid of the American Colonization Society, to transport them to Africa. In 1849, the House of Representatives of Georgia passed a bill to remove all free negroes then in the State to Liberia. In Virginia, the sum of 30,000 dollars has been appropriated, by an Act of the Legislature, annually for five years, to transport the same class to Africa, and another act has been passed to induce the free negroes of the State to emigrate therefrom, by which an annual tax of one dollar each is levied upon every free negro between the ages of twenty-one and fifty-five years, to raise a fund to be added to the above appropriation. There are 30,000 free coloured persons in that State. Kentucky, in great measure through the influence of the President of the Colonization Society, Henry Clay, has followed the example of Virginia in proscribing the people of colour. The same course has been pursued by Maryland, and even by the free states of Indiana and Illinois. One example will suffice. By the new constitution of Indiana, negroes and mulattoes are excluded from hereafter settling in that state; and it has been decided that all contracts with these people are void, and that any one employing them or encouraging them to remain in the State shall be liable to a fine. By the laws of South Carolina, for

---

Sold by W. and F. G. CASH, 5, Bishopsgate Street, London; and by JANE JOWETT Friends' Meeting Yard, Leeds, at 1s. 2d. per 100.

seriously scalding or burning a slave, either by boiling water or fire, for cutting out a slave's tongue, for destroying an eye or breaking a limb, the penalty is one hundred dollars! For killing a slave in a moment of excitement, or by excessive punishment, tne penalty is five hundred dollars and six months' imprisonment! So that there, for five-and-twenty pounds, you may enjoy the pleasure of cutting out a man's tongue or breaking his leg; or for one hundred and twenty pounds—luxuries are expensive—you may kill him outright, provided only that his skin is black and yours white. North Carolina is even more indulgent to those who have an amiable weakness for homicide, for its laws enact that any fugitive slave "being outlawed, and who hides himself in the woods or marshes, is regarded as dangerous, and offending against the laws, and *may be lawfully killed.*" In Mississippi, as well as in Virginia and Kentucky, a justice of the peace may inflict as many lashes as he pleases on any slave found abroad without his master's permission. If a slave, found beyond his master's plantation unaccompanied by a white man, refuses to answer the question of any white person whatever, the latter may seize him and administer *a moderate correction*, and if the negro defends himself and strikes the white, he may *lawfully be killed!* These laws denote the extent of slavery feeling—they show how prejudices against the slave have eaten into the heart of the white population. Actually to this very day, America persists in refusing to acknowledge the free governments of Liberia and Hayti.

For proof of the prejudice existing against colour in the United States, we refer to the proceedings of the American Colonization Society. This society is justly open to the charge of fostering the feeling which gives rise to cruel and unjust legislation against the coloured people, and to the persecutions and insults they are compelled to endure. In its last report, read at its annual meeting in January last, over which the Hon. Daniel Webster, Secretary of State, presided, we find its Executive Committee saying—"We perceive with pleasure that, in several of the States, the chief executive officers, in their communications to the Legislatures, have strongly recommended the American Colonization Society, as the only organized agency which has contributed to produce practical results beneficial to the African race; and, consequently, as worthy of approval and support.'' One of the principal speakers at this meeting, Mr. Stanton, said—"The free negro in this country is almost always a degraded being. He communicates this degradation to the slave, and generally exerts his influence in misleading and corrupting him. . . The fact remains undisputed, that in vice, crime, and degradation, the condition of the negro in the non-slaveholding states, is immeasurably below that of any other part of the population. . . In the very nature of things—from the constitution of society, and the natural instincts of man—the general condition of the free blacks, in any portion of this country, must be one of inevitable degradation. . . The unconquerable repugnance—the instinctive repulsion between the white and black races—that prejudice, if you choose to call it so—renders utterly impossible a social intercourse upon a footing of equality. . . Already they are fast being driven from profitable employment, in all parts of the country, by the competition of the whites. They are going down in the scale of prosperity, and they must necessarily sink in the scale of civilization by the continued operation of the same cause. The only remedy for this antagonism, which must exist as long as the races remain together, is, in my humble judgment, SLAVERY. *Like the alkali which causes the oil and water to combine, slavery neutralises the antagonism of the whites and the blacks, for the mutual interest of both.*'' Another orator, the Rev. Philip Slaughter, said—"There are some visionaries who profess to entertain the expectation and the hope that these persons will, some day or other, be brought to stand upon the same platform with the white race. Sir, no dream in the *Arabian Tales* was ever more vain, mischievous, and visionary. It is utterly impossible. Almighty God has placed between us and them, by a visible mark, an impassable gulf. No human power or wisdom can bridge over that gulf, so that they can come over and stand on the same platform of political and social equality with us.'' In the present relation of the Indians, the whites, and the negroes in America, this profound theologian discerns the fulfilment of the prophecy of Noah—"God shall enlarge Japhet, and he shall dwell in the tents of Shem, and Canaan shall be his servant.'' Mr. Webster, in concluding the proceedings of the meeting, said—"I believe it to be right, I believe it is expedient, to follow the example of the Patriarch, and say to these, our black fellow-citizens, 'Take the right hand, and we the left.'" Thus slavery eats into the heart of American society. The more we see of the institution, the more we shall see how it corrupts the heart, how it degrades the victims, how it fills the land with blood, and misery, and tears.

De Beaumont, a French traveller, justly observes, "the prejudice against colour, in the United States, haunts its victim wherever he goes,—in the hospitals, where humanity suffers,—in the churches, where it kneels to God,—in the prisons, where it expiates its offences,—in the graveyards, where it sleeps the last sleep." It is a lamentable fact that the sin of slaveholding in the South, and the scarcely less unchristian system of caste in the North, find their stronghold and support in the institutions and teaching of the church in all its branches. It is not beneath the presidential chair, nor in the halls of Congress, nor in the seats of learning, that these enormities find their chief shelter and protection, but in the synods and solemn assemblies of the church,—under the very altars of God, and the most sacred but abused sanctions of religion. And until the church boldly testifies against these evils,—until she denounces the guilty dogma, that man may hold property in man, or may treat him as an alien and an outcast on account of the colour of his skin, so long will she be chargeable with giving her countenance to all the immorality, irreligion, and misery, that spring from the system of caste and slavery in that land.

Let Christians everywhere earnestly pray for the hastening of the day, when the cry of the oppressed shall enter into the ears of the Lord of Sabaoth; when he will arise to break every yoke, and proclaim liberty to the captive,—liberty from the manacles which bind the body, as well as those which *enslave the soul.* Then, and not till then

"The long scorned African,—
His Maker's image radiant in his face,—
Among earth's noblest sons shall find his place."

Leeds Anti-slavery Series. No. 6.

Sold by W. and F. G. CASH, 5, Bishopsgate Street, London; and by JANE JOWETT, Friends' Meeting Yard, Leeds, at 1s. 2d. per 100.

Leeds Anti-slavery Series. No. 7.

SLAVERY A SYSTEM OF INHERENT CRUELTY.

FLOGGING A SLAVE FASTENED TO THE GROUND.

THIRTY HUNDRED THOUSAND PERSONS in the United States of America, men, women, and children, are in SLAVERY. Is slavery, as a condition for human beings, good, bad, or indifferent? We submit the question without argument. You have common sense, and conscience, and a human heart—pronounce upon it. You have a wife, or a husband, a child, a father, a mother, a brother, or a sister—make the case your own, make it theirs, and bring in your verdict. The case of human rights against slavery has been adjudicated in the court

Sold by W. and F. G. CASH, 5, Bishopsgate Street, London; and by JANE JOWETT, Friends' Meeting Yard, Leeds, at 3s. 6d. per 100; or 6d. per doz.

of conscience times innumerable. The same verdict has always been rendered—" Guilty ;" the same sentence has always been pronounced—" Let it be accursed !" and human nature, with her million echoes, has rung it round the world in every language under heaven—" Let it be accursed ! Let it be accursed !" His heart is false to human nature who will not say " Amen." There is not a man on earth who does not believe that slavery is a curse. Human beings may be inconsistent, but human *nature* is true to herself. She has uttered her testimony against slavery with a shriek, ever since the monster was begotten; and, till it perishes amidst the execrations of the universe, she will traverse the world on its track, dealing her bolts upon its head, and dashing against it her condemning brand. We repeat it—every man knows that slavery is a curse. Whoever denies this, his lips libel his heart. Try him; clank the chains in his ears, and tell him they are for *him;* give him an hour to prepare his wife and children for a life of slavery; bid him make haste and get ready their necks for the yoke, and their wrists for the coffle chains, then look at his pale lips and trembling knees, and you have *nature's* testimony against slavery.

At least thirty hundred thousand persons in the United States are in this condition. They were made slaves, and are held such by force, and by being put in fear, and this for no crime ! Reader, what have you to say of such treatment ? Is it right, just, benevolent ? Suppose I should seize you, rob you of your liberty, drive you into the field, and make you work without pay as long as you live, would that be justice and kindness, or monstrous injustice and cruelty ? Now, everybody knows that the slaveholders do these things to the slaves every day, and yet it is stoutly affirmed that they treat them well and kindly, and that their tender regard for their slaves restrains their masters from inflicting cruelties upon them. We shall go into no metaphysics to show the absurdity of this pretence. The man who *robs* you every day is, forsooth, quite too tender-hearted ever to cuff or kick you ! True, he can snatch your money, but he does it gently, lest he should hurt you. He can empty your pockets without qualms, but if your *stomach* is empty, it cuts him to the quick. He can make you work a life-time without pay, but loves you too well to let you go hungry. He fleeces you of your *rights* with a relish, but is shocked if you work bareheaded in summer, or in winter without warm stockings. He can make you go without your *liberty*, but never without a shirt. He can crush, in you, all hope of bettering your condition, by vowing that you shall die his slave; but, though he can coolly torture your feelings, he is too compassionate to lacerate your back—he can break your heart, but he is very tender of your skin. He can strip you of all protection, and thus expose you to all outrages; but if you are exposed to the *weather*, half clad and half sheltered, how yearn his tender bowels! What! slaveholders talk of treating men well, and yet not only rob them of all they get, and as fast as they get it, but rob them of *themselves* also; their very hands and feet; all their muscles, and limbs, and senses; their bodies and minds; their time, and liberty, and earnings; their free speech and rights of conscience; their right to acquire knowledge, and property, and reputation; and yet they, who plunder them of all these, would fain make us believe that their soft hearts ooze out so lovingly toward their slaves, that they always keep them well housed and well clad, never push them too hard in the field, never make their dear backs smart, nor let their dear stomachs get empty.

But there is no end to these absurdities. Are slaveholders dunces, or do they take all the rest of the world to be, that they think to bandage our eyes with such thin gauzes? Protesting their kind regard for those whom they hourly plunder of all they have and all they get! What! when they have seized their victims, and annihilated all their *rights*, still claim to be the special guardians of their *happiness?* Plunderers of their liberty, yet the careful suppliers of their wants? Robbers of their earnings, yet watchful sentinels round their interests, and kind providers for their comfort? Filching all their time, yet granting generous donations for rest and sleep? Stealing the use of their muscles, yet thoughtful of their ease? Putting them under *drivers*, yet careful that they are not hard pushed? Too humane, forsooth, to stint the stomachs of their slaves, yet force their *minds* to starve, and brandish over them pains and penalties, if they dare to reach forth for the smallest crumb of knowledge, even a letter of the alphabet!

It is no marvel that slaveholders are always talking of their *kind treatment* of their slaves. The only marvel is, that men of sense can be gulled by such professions. Despots always insist that they are merciful. The greatest tyrants that ever dripped with blood have assumed the titles of "most gracious," "most clement," "most merciful," &c., and have ordered their crouching vassals to accost them thus. When did not vice lay claim to those virtues which are the opposites of its habitual crimes? The guilty, according to their own showing, are always innocent, and cowards brave, and drunkards sober, and harlots chaste, and pickpockets honest to a fault. Every body understands this. When a man's tongue grows thick, and he begins to hiccough and walk cross-legged, we expect him, as a matter of course, to protest that he is not drunk; so when a man is always singing the praises of his own honesty, we instinctively watch his movements, and look out for our pocket-books. Whoever is simple enough to be hoaxed by such professions, should never be trusted in the streets without somebody to take care of him. Human nature works out in slaveholders just as it does in other men, and in American slaveholders just as in English, French, Turkish, Algerine, Roman, and Grecian. The Spartans boasted of their kindness to their slaves, while they whipped them to death by thousands at the altars of their gods. The Romans lauded their own mild treatment of their bondsmen, while they branded their names on their flesh with hot irons, and, when old, threw them into their fish-ponds, or, like Cato "the Just," starved them to death. It is the boast of the Turks that they treat their slaves as though they were their children, yet their common name for them is "dogs;" and, for the merest trifles, their feet are bastinadoed to a jelly, or their heads clipped off with a scimitar. The Portuguese pride themselves on their gentle bearing towards their slaves, yet the streets of Rio Janeiro are filled with naked men and women yoked in pairs to carts and waggons, and whipped by drivers like beasts of burden.

Slaveholders, the world over, have sung the praises of their tender mercies towards their slaves. Even the wretches that plied the African slave-trade tried to rebut Clarkson's proofs of their cruelties, by speeches, affidavits, and published pamphlets, setting forth the accommodations of the "middle passage," and their kind attentions to the comfort of those whom they had stolen from their homes, and kept stowed away under hatches, during a voyage of four thousand miles. So, according to the testimony of the autocrat of all the Russias, he exercises great clemency towards the Poles, though he exiles them by thousands to the snows of Siberia, and tramples them down by millions at home. Who discredits the atrocities perpetrated by Ovando in Hispaniola, Pizarro in Peru, and Cortez in Mexico, because they filled the ears of the Spanish court with protestations of their benignant rule? While they were yoking the enslaved natives like beasts to the draught, working them to death by thousands in their mines, hunting them with bloodhounds, torturing them on racks, and broiling them on beds of coal, their representations to the mother country teemed with eulogies of their parental sway! The bloody atrocities of Philip II., in the expulsion of his Moorish subjects, are matters of imperishable history. Who disbelieves or doubts them? And yet his courtiers magnified his virtues, and chanted his clemency and his mercy, while the wail of a million victims, smitten down by a tempest of fire and slaughter let loose at his bidding, rose above the *Te Deums* that thundered from all Spain's cathedrals. When Louis XIV. revoked the edict of Nantes, and proclaimed two millions of his subjects free plunder for persecution—when, from the English Channel to the Pyrenees, the mangled bodies of the Protestants were dragged on reeking hurdles by a shouting populace—he claimed to be "the father of his people," and wrote himself, "His most *Christian* Majesty."

That the slaves in the United States are treated with barbarous inhumanity; that they are over-worked, under-fed, wretchedly clad and lodged, and have insufficient sleep; that they are often made to wear round their necks iron collars armed with prongs, to drag heavy chains and weights at their feet while working in the field, and to wear yokes, and bells, and iron horns; that they are often kept confined in the stocks day and night for weeks together, made to wear gags in their mouths for hours or days, have some of their front teeth torn out or broken off, that they may be easily detected when they run away; that they are frequently flogged with terrible severity, have red pepper rubbed into their lacerated flesh, and hot brine, spirits of turpentine, &c., poured over the gashes to increase the torture; that they are often stripped naked, their backs and limbs cut with knives, bruised and mangled by scores and hundreds of blows with the paddle, and terribly torn by the claws of cats drawn over them by their tormentors;

BARBAROUS MODE OF PUNISHING A SLAVE WITH THE PADDLE.

that they are often hunted with bloodhounds, and shot down like beasts, or torn in pieces by dogs; that they are often suspended by the arms, and whipped and beaten till they faint, and, when revived by restoratives, beaten again till they faint, and sometimes till they die; that their ears are often cut off, their eyes knocked out, their bones broken, their flesh branded with red hot irons; that they are maimed, mutilated, and burned to death over slow fires; are undeniable facts.

The enormities inflicted by slaveholders upon their slaves will never be discredited, except by those who overlook the simple fact, that he who holds human beings as his *bona fide* property, regards them as property, and not as *persons;* this is his permanent state of mind toward them. He does not contemplate slaves as human beings, consequently does not treat them as such; and, with entire indifference, sees them suffer privations, and writhe under blows, which, if inflicted upon whites, would fill him with horror and indignation. He regards that as good treatment of slaves, which would seem to him insufferable abuse if practised upon others; and would denounce that as a monstrous outrage and horrible cruelty, if perpetrated upon white men and women, which he sees every day meted out to black slaves, without perhaps ever thinking it cruel. Accustomed all his life to regard them rather as domestic animals, to hear them stormed at, and to see them cuffed and caned; and, being himself in constant habit of treating them thus, such practices have become to him a mere matter of course, and make no impression on his mind. True, it is incredible that men should treat as *chattels* those whom they truly regard as *human beings;* but that they should treat as chattels and working animals those whom they *regard* as such, is no marvel. The common treatment of dogs, when they are in the way, is to kick them out of it; we see them every day kicked off sidewalks, and on Sabbaths out of churches; yet, as they are but dogs, these do not strike us as outrages; yet if we were to see men, women, and children—our neighbours and friends— kicked out of stores by merchants, or out of churches by the deacons and sexton, we should call the perpetrators inhuman wretches.

Slaveholders organize themselves into a tribunal to adjudicate upon their own conduct, and give us, in their decisions, their estimate of their own character; informing us with characteristic modesty, that they have a high opinion of themselves; that in their own judgment, they are very mild, kind, and merciful gentlemen! In these conceptions of their own merits, and of the eminent propriety of their bearing towards their slaves,—slaveholders remind us of the Spaniard, who always took off his hat whenever he spoke of himself, and of the Governor of Schiraz, who, from a sense of justice to his own character, added to his other titles those of "Flower of Courtesy," "Nutmeg of Consolation," and "Rose of Delight."

When men speak of the treatment of others as being either good or bad, their declarations are not generally to be taken as testimony to matters of *fact,* so much as expressions of *their own feelings* towards those persons or classes who are the subjects of such treatment. If those persons are their fellow-citizens; if they are in the same class of society with themselves; of the same language, creed, and colour; similar in their habits, pursuits, and sympathies; they will keenly feel any wrong done to them, and denounce it as base, outrageous treatment; but let the same wrongs be done to persons of a condition in all respects the reverse, persons whom they habitually despise, and regard only in the light of mere conveniences, to be used for their pleasure, and the idea that such treatment is barbarous will be laughed at as ridiculous.

We have said that slaveholders regard their slaves not as human beings, but as mere working animals, or merchandise. The whole vocabulary of slaveholders, their laws, their usages, and their entire treatment of their slaves, fully establish this. The same terms are applied to slaves that are given to cattle. They are called "stock." So, when the children of slaves are spoken of prospectively, they are called their "increase;" the same term that is applied to flocks and herds. So the female slaves that are mothers are called "breeders," till past child-bearing; and often the same terms are applied to the different sexes that are applied to the males and females among cattle. Those who compel the labour of slaves and cattle have the same appellation—"drivers;" the names which they call them are the same, and similar to those given to their horses and oxen. The laws of slave states make them property, equally with goats and swine; they are levied upon for debt in the same way; they are included, in the same advertisements of public sales, with cattle, swine, and asses; when moved from one part of the country to another, they are herded in droves like cattle, and, like them, urged on by drivers; their labour is compelled in the same way. They are bought and sold, and separated like cattle; when exposed for sale, their good qualities are described as jockeys show off the good points of their horses; their strength, activity, skill, power of endurance, &c., are lauded, and those who bid upon them examine their persons just as purchasers inspect horses and oxen; they open their mouths to see if their teeth are sound; strip their backs to see if they are badly scarred, and handle their limbs and muscles to see if they are firmly knit. Like horses, they are warranted to be "sound," or to be returned to the owner if "unsound." A father gives his son a horse and *slave;* by his will he distributes among them his race-horses, hounds, game-cocks, and *slaves.* We leave the reader to carry out the parallel which we have only begun. Its details would cover many pages.

That slaveholders do not practically regard slaves as *human beings*, is abundantly shown by their own voluntary testimony. In a recent work, entitled, *The South Vindicated from the Treason and Fanaticism of Northern Abolitionists*, which was written, we are informed, by Colonel Dayton, late member of Congress from South Carolina, the writer, speaking of the awe with which the slaves regard the whites, says, " The northerner looks upon a band of negroes as upon so many *men*, but the planter or southerner *views them in a very different light!*"

Extract from a speech of Mr. Summers, of Virginia, in the legislature of that state, January 26, 1833. See the *Richmond Whig*:—" When, in the sublime lessons of Christianity, he (the slaveholder) is taught to ' do unto others as he would have others do unto him,' HE NEVER DREAMS THAT THE DEGRADED NEGRO IS WITHIN THE PALE OF THAT HOLY CANON."

President Jefferson, in his letter to Governor Coles of Illinois, dated August 25, 1814, asserts that slaveholders regard their slaves as brutes, in the following remarkable language:— "Nursed and educated in the daily habit of seeing the degraded condition, both bodily and mental, of these unfortunate beings (the slaves), FEW MINDS HAVE YET DOUBTED BUT THAT THEY WERE AS LEGITIMATE SUBJECTS OF PROPERTY AS THEIR HORSES OR CATTLE."

. Having shown that slaveholders regard their slaves as mere working animals and cattle, we now proceed to show that their actual treatment of them is *worse* than it would be if they were brutes. We repeat it—SLAVEHOLDERS TREAT THEIR SLAVES WORSE THAN THEY DO THEIR BRUTES. Whoever heard of cows or sheep being deliberately tied up and beaten and lacerated till they died? or horses coolly tortured by the hour, till covered with mangled flesh? or of swine having their legs tied, and being suspended from a tree, and lacerated with thongs for hours? or of hounds stretched and made fast at full length, flayed with whips, red pepper rubbed into their bleeding gashes, and hot brine dashed on to aggravate the torture? Yet, just such forms and degrees of torture are *daily* perpetrated upon the slaves. Now, no man that knows human nature will marvel at this. Though great cruelties have always been inflicted by men upon brutes, yet incomparably the most horrid ever perpetrated, have been those of men upon *their own species.* Any leaf of history, turned over at random, has proof enough of this. Every reflecting mind perceives that, when men hold *human beings* as *property,* they must, from the nature of the case, treat them worse than they treat their horses and oxen. It is impossible for *cattle* to excite in men such tempests of fury as men excite in each other. Men are often provoked if their horses or hounds refuse to do, or their pigs refuse to go where they wish to drive them, but the feeling is rarely intense, and never permanent. It is vexation and impatience, rather than settled rage, malignity, or revenge. If horses and dogs were intelligent beings, and still held as property, their opposition to the wishes of their owners would exasperate them immeasurably more than it would be possible for them to do with the minds of brutes. None but little children and idiots get angry at sticks and stones that lie in their way or hurt them; but put into sticks and stones intelligence, and will, and power of feeling and motion, while they remain as now, articles of property, and what a towering rage would men be in, if bushes whipped them in the face when they walked among them, or stones rolled over their toes when they climbed hills! and what exemplary vengeance would be inflicted upon door-steps and hearth-stones, if they were to move out of their places, instead of lying still where they were put for their owners to tread upon! The greatest provocation to human nature is *opposition to its will.* If a man's will be resisted by one far *below* him, the provocation is vastly greater than when it is resisted by an acknowledged superior. In the former case, it inflames strong passions, which, in the latter, lie dormant. The rage of proud Haman knew no bounds against the poor Jew who would not do as he wished, and so he built a gallows for him. If the person opposing the will of another be so far below him as to be on a level with chattels, and be actually held and used as an article of property, pride, scorn, lust of power, rage, and revenge, explode together upon the hapless victim. The idea of *property* having a will, and that, too, in opposition to the will of its *owner,* and counteracting it, is a stimulant of terrible power to the most relentless human passions; and, from the nature of slavery, and the constitution of the human mind, this fierce stimulant must, with various degrees of strength, act upon slaveholders almost without ceasing. The slave, however abject and crushed, is an intelligent being: he has a *will*, and that will cannot be annihilated, *it will show itself;* if for a moment it is smothered, like pent-up fires, when vent is found, it flames the fiercer. Make intelligence *property*, and its manager will have his match; he is met at every turn by an *opposing will*, not in the form of downright rebellion and defiance, but yet, visibly, an *ever-opposing will*. He sees it in the dissatisfied look, and reluctant air, and unwilling movement; the constrained strokes of labour, the drawling tones, the slow hearing, the feigned stupidity, the sham pains and sickness, the short memory; and he *feels* it every hour, in innumerable forms, frustrating his designs by a ceaseless, though perhaps invisible countermining. This unceasing opposition to the will of its "owner," on the part of his rational "property," is to the slaveholder as the hot iron to the nerve. He raves under it, and storms, and gnashes, and smites; but the more he smites the hotter it gets, and the more it burns him. Further, this opposition of the slave's will to his owner's, not only excites him to severity, that he may gratify his rage, but makes it necessary for him to use violence in breaking down this resistance—thus subjecting the slave to additional tortures. There is another inducement to cruel inflictions upon the slave, and a necessity for it, which does not exist in the case of brutes. Offenders must be made an example to others, to strike them with terror. If a slave runs away and is caught, his master flogs him with terrible severity, not merely to gratify his resentment, and to keep him from running away again, but as a warning to others. So in every case of disobedience, neglect, stubbornness, unfaithfulness, indolence, insolence, theft, feigned sickness, when his directions are forgotten, or slighted, or supposed to be, or his wishes crossed, or his property injured or left exposed, or his work ill-executed, the master is tempted to inflict cruelties, not merely to wreak his own vengeance upon him, and to make the slave more circumspect in future, but to sustain his authority over the other slaves, to restrain them from like practices, and to preserve his own property.

A multitude of facts, illustrating the position that slaveholders treat their slaves *worse* than they do their cattle, will occur to all who are familiar with slavery. When cattle break through their owner's inclosures and escape, if found, they are driven back and fastened in again; and even slaveholders would execrate, as a wretch, the man who should tie them up, and bruise and lacerate them for straying away; but when *slaves* that have escaped are caught, they are flogged with the most terrible severity. When herds of cattle are driven to market, they are suffered to go in the easiest way, each by himself; but when slaves are driven to market, they are fastened together with handcuffs, galled with iron collars and chains, and thus forced to travel on foot hundreds of miles, sleeping at night in their chains. Sheep, and sometimes horned cattle, are marked with their owners' initials, but this is generally done with paint, and of course produces no pain. Slaves, too, are often marked with their owners' initials, but the letters are stamped into their flesh with a hot iron. Cattle are suffered to graze their pastures without stint; but the slaves are restrained in their food to a fixed allowance. The slaveholders' horses are notoriously far better fed, more moderately worked, have fewer hours of labour, and longer intervals of rest, than their slaves; and their valuable horses are far more comfortably housed and lodged, and their stables more effectually defended from the weather, than the slaves' huts.

When we hear slaveholders say that their slaves are *well treated*, we have only to remember that they are not speaking of *persons*, but of *property;* not of men and women, but of *chattels* and *things;* not of friends and associates, but of *vassals* and *victims;* not of those whom they respect and honour, but of those whom they *scorn* and trample on; not of those with whom they sympathize, and co-operate, and interchage courtesies, but of those whom they regard with contempt and aversion, and disdainfully set with the dogs of their flock. Reader, keep this fact in your mind, and you will have a clue to the slaveholder's definition of "*good treatment.*"

Leeds Anti-slavery Series. No. 7.

Sold by W. and F. G. CASH, 5, Bishopsgate Street, London; and by JANE JOWETT, Friends' Meeting Yard, Leeds, at 3s. 6d. per 100, or 6d. per dozen.

Leeds Anti-slavery Series. No. 8.

SLAVERY CONSIDERED

IN ITS

VARIOUS RELATIONS AND CONSEQUENCES.

WHY DISCUSS THE SLAVE QUESTION?

BECAUSE it is a question of vast importance, and the great diversity of sentiment respecting it is evidence that it needs to be discussed.

I am bound to examine and to understand the subject of slavery, because I am *a man*, and whatever concerns the condition, the character, and the destiny of human beings concerns *me*.

I am bound to know the *facts* in relation to this subject, because they are within my reach. I am bound to know the *principles* upon which this question is to be settled, because God has revealed them, and because they are the principles by which *all* my actions and aims are to be regulated.

I am bound to *apply* correctly those principles to those facts, and govern my activities accordingly; because I am bound to do this on all great moral questions, and cannot otherwise discharge the duties growing out of the varied relations in which the providence of God places me.

The question of slavery, as a moral question, involves the question of a pure or of a corrupted religion, so that all the reasons why I should understand the subject of religion, and be able to discriminate between religious truth and religious error, are reasons why I should understand, and therefore investigate, the subject of slavery.

Sold by W. and F. G. CASH, 5, Bishopsgate Street, London; and by JANE JOWETT, Friends' Meeting Yard, Leeds, at 7s. 6d. per 100; 1s. per doz.; or 1½d. each.

The question of slavery or emancipation is the question of freedom or of chains to millions of my fellow-creatures. It involves, therefore, the question of free or of despotic institutions for ages to come. *Can* I blink the discussion of such a question?

The question of abolishing slavery is the question of education and enlightenment, of civilization and human progress. On these vital subjects I cannot take an interest, or become intelligent, without earnestly and successfully investigating the slave question.

The question of slavery and of its abolition is a question of political economy, involving one of the most important financial and commercial problems ever propounded in any nation, and bearing directly and irresistibly upon all the pecuniary interests of the countries in which it exists—agricultural, mechanical, manufacturing, mercantile, and monetary. On these subjects I must content myself to be profoundly ignorant, unless I make myself acquainted with the slave question, including a knowledge of the comparative workings and effects of free and slave labour upon the productive industry of such countries.

Within the last twenty or thirty years, the discussions of the ablest theologians, moral philosophers, political economists, statesmen and philanthropists in the civilized world; the consequent action of civil governments, in both hemispheres, and especially, the grand experiments and the practical workings and results of abolition, in different parts of the globe, have unitedly thrown a flood of new light on the whole subject; correcting old mistakes, revising old theories, and compelling the most profound observers and experienced statesmen to confess their former mistakes. Not to avail myself of these important advances in knowledge, by a careful study of these discussions and experiments, would be to fall, disgracefully, behind the times, to live in the darkness of past generations, rather than in the light of the present, to linger on the confines of ancient barbarism, instead of filling an appropriate place in the existing stage of human progress.

The slave question not only *ought* to be, but has actually *become*, and must *continue* to be (until it is settled), one of the leading questions of the age, especially in a land of boasted Christianity and freedom, where the existence of slavery constitutes an anomaly too glaring to be overlooked; and where the antagonistic influences of such diametrically opposite elements cannot fail to secure an agitation that cannot possibly be quelled, but by the disappearance of either the one or the other of the belligerent forces leaving its opponent in possession of the field. The experiment of combining two such elements in the same religion, and under the same government, has proved a manifest failure, and the nostrums once employed to produce temporary quietness can no longer answer the ends of those who employ them.

Christianity enjoins inquiry on this subject by commanding us to do unto others as we would have others to do unto us; to "remember them that are in bonds as bound with them;" declaring that "the righteous considereth the cause of the poor, but the wicked regardeth not to know it." It admits of no excuse or apology, on the ground of ignorance, when the necessary information is within our reach. "If thou forbear to deliver them that are drawn unto death, and those that are ready to be slain; if thou sayest, Behold, we knew it not; doth not he that pondereth the heart consider it, and he that keepeth thy soul, shall he not know it? And shall he not render to every man according to his works?"

WHAT IS SLAVERY?

"The slave is one who is in the power of a master to whom he belongs."—*Louisiana, Civil Code, Art.* 35. "Slaves shall be deemed, sold, taken, reputed, and adjudged in law to be *chattels personal*, in the hands of their owners and possessors, and their executors, administrators, and assigns, to all intents, constructions, and purposes whatsoever."—*Law of South Carolina,* 2 *Brev. Dig.* 229, *Prince's Digest,* 446, &c.

"The cardinal principle of slavery, that the slave is not to be ranked among sentient beings, but among *things,* as an article of property, a chattel personal, obtains as undoubted law in all these [slave] states."—*Stroud's Sketch,* p. 23.

This, then, is slavery as it exists in America. God created man in his own image. He made him a little lower than the angels, crowned him with glory and honour, and gave him dominion over the beasts of the field. But slavery reduces him to a thing, a commodity, an article of merchandise!

This is no flourish of rhetoric—no idle abstraction. So far as the power of man can accomplish such a result, it is accomplished by slavery. If it cannot take away the immortal soul of man, it deems, reputes, and adjudges him to have none! It ranks him, not a little lower than the angels, but on a level with the beasts that perish!

GOOD TREATMENT.

What do those mean, who tell us of the *good treatment* of slaves? Is it, or can it be, good treatment of a *man*, a *woman*, or a *child*, to account, to repute, to deem, to adjudge them to be on a level with beasts, and articles of property? Do those who talk of the "good treatment" of slaves, intend to say or imply this? We may charitably presume that they do not. What, then, *do* they mean? The idea they have in mind, perhaps, may be this: Considering that these poor creatures *are* slaves, their treatment is as good as it could be expected to be —as good as the treatment of a *slave can* be. But the question again returns whether it *is* good treatment of a man, a woman, or a child, to treat them *as slaves?* If not, then the plea of good treatment is illusory, and meets not the proper question to be considered, in disposing either of the claims of slavery, or of the practice of slaveholding, or the conduct of slaveholders.

INTEGRAL PARTS OF THE SLAVE SYSTEM.

These are such as are involved, of necessity, in the cardinal principle of slavery, viz.: *human chattelhood.* We enumerate the following:—

1. The unlimited authority of the slave master or owner.
2. The abrogation of marriage, and the family relation, among slaves.
3. The power to enforce labour without wages.
4. The incapacity of the slave to acquire or hold property.
5. His incapacity to make contracts or bargains.
6. His incapacity to enjoy civil, domestic, or political rights.
7. The liability of the slave to be sold, like other chattels, and separated from relatives. The authorized prosecution of the SLAVE-TRADE!
8. The absence of any adequate legal protection for the slave.

9. The power of the master to forbid education and social religious worship, at his own discretion.

10. The power of the legislatures of slave states to prohibit education, even by the masters, and to prohibit or restrict free social worship.

11. The power of legislatures of slave states to abolish freedom of speech and of the press to citizens in general.

A beautiful system—is it not? for a free, Christian country!

INCIDENTS, OR PRACTICAL WORKINGS OF SLAVERY.

These are just such as might be anticipated by a study of the cardinal principle and integral parts of the slave system.

As the various parts of the system, drawn out in detail upon the statute-books of the slave states, assure us that the cardinal principle of slavery (*human chattelhood*) is no empty abstraction, so a collection from authentic sources of information, of the practical workings and incidents of the system in actual operation, assures us that those statutes are not a dead letter, and that the cardinal principle of human chattelhood is not obsolete, inoperative, or dissevered from the daily activities and ordinary scenes of life, in slaveholding communities. Among these matter-of-fact incidents and results, we may notice the following:—

1. Habits of despotism, haughtiness, and lawlessness, on the part of the master—habits of servility and vice on the part of the slaves.

2. Habits of brutality among the slaves—congenial habits of licentiousness among the slaveholders—both resulting from the absence of the family relation, and of the safeguards of female chastity among the slaves, "in the power of their masters."

3. General hatred of labour. Industry despised by the free as degrading, and rendered impossible to the slave from the absence of motive. Consequent thriftlessness, bad tillage, want of economy, loose management, poverty, debts, bankruptcy, exhausted soil, no healthful tie of interest or of attachment between the employed and the employer; a miserable peasantry, a beggarly aristocracy, one-half of the community impoverished by the other half, and all impoverished together by an insane system imported from the depths of African barbarism.

4. The slave-trade, accordingly, in brisk operation, among

Americans, who brand the heathen tribes of *Africa* as brutes, just fit to be enslaved, because they tolerate the piratical traffic on their benighted continent!

5. The *producers* of what wealth there is in the community, literally forbidden to *possess* any portion of it, and actually inventoried as constituting a large portion of the property themselves! For slavery, true to nothing but to its own incomparable falsehood (the chattelhood of humanity), contradicts all legitimate right to property—the right of a man to himself and to his own earnings, that it may maintain its pretended right to property in man!

6. Another characteristic incident of slavery, is the dense pall of ignorance and heathenism it spreads over the land cursed by its presence. The labouring population, for the most part, unable to read or write, and laws forbidding them to be taught disgracing the statute-book, with the exception of two states, where public sentiment, for the most part, is found sufficient, without law, to compass the same object. The consequent absence of any adequate system of common schools for the benefit of the whites, and the corresponding prevalence and growth of ignorance among a majority of the free, without distinction of colour.

7. Patrols to prevent husbands from visiting their wives too frequently, or without written leave from their masters, to restrain the free exercise of religion, and free social worship; colporteurs arrested for attempting to distribute Bibles among slaves!

8. Cruelties authenticated by the "testimony of a thousand witnesses," many of them slaveholders, at the mention of which humanity recoils. Men hunted with bloodhounds for attempting their escape to a land of freedom; babes wrenched from their mothers to be sold by the pound; their parents separated from them and from each other, to be dragged into returnless exile. High prices claimed for some of these chattels because they are exemplary Christians, and for the same, or others, because their youth and beauty fit them for victims of licentiousness, and a place in a harem!

9. The existence and the efficient administration of laws in America, forbidding the public discussion, by the tongue or by the press, of the self-evident truths of the National Declaration

of Independence, in their application to millions of the native inhabitants, descendants, in many instances, of the framers and supporters of that Declaration, and connected by blood (as attested by colour), to a great and growing extent, with the race that thus despoils and oppresses them.

10. Laws excluding the testimony of all coloured persons against white persons, forbidding free people of colour to be taught reading and writing, even the teaching of children by parents! These laws efficiently administered and advocated as necessary and proper.

11. To this we may add the despotic control over the entire nation, the nominally free states not excepted, of a petty oligarchy of less than three hundred thousand slaveholders in a population of seventeen millions, dictating all national measures for the support of the slave system, waging wars for the recovery of fugitive slaves, and for opening a new market for human chattels on territory where it has been once abolished.

These facts, and others like them, too notorious to be questioned, too familiar to create excitement, assure us that slavery in theory, on the statute-book or in prospect (as inferred from such statutes), is not more fiendish or frightful, more disgraceful or debasing, more criminal or demoralizing, more insane or destructive, than it is in actual operation and exercise at the present time. America can present to the world no exception to the time-tested maxim, that "no people are ever found to be better than their laws, though many have been known to be worse." Were it otherwise, there would be neither necessity nor occasion to draw such humiliating pictures, nor to urge on a free people the duty of rising up at once, as one man, and putting a stop to such atrocities.

CONSISTENCY AND UNITY OF THE SLAVE SYSTEM

The *theory* of American slavery agrees with its *practice*. The whole system of slave legislation grows legitimately out of the chattel principle upon which slavery is founded. And the most revolting usages and practices, to be detected among the incidents and workings of the system, are to be found in perfect keeping and harmony both with the principle of human chattelhood and with the slave code.

1. The very idea of human chattelhood involves the idea of

the unlimited control of the master, and the absolute defencelessness of the slave. Habits of tyranny and of servility must follow of course, with all the insecurity and outrage that grow out of them.

2. The absence of legal marriage, and of the protected family relation, is manifestly essential to the idea of human chattelhood. Chattels are not married, and cannot constitute families. Chattels may be transferred, bought, sold, and *used*. The promiscuous intercourse of the sexes, especially at the bidding of the master, follows, of course, and is not to be censured by those who consent to the system, or to the practice of slaveholding.

3. Chattels never receive wages, or acquire or hold property. The deep poverty of the slave, and all the effects of that poverty, with the absence of a motive to labour, follow, of course.

4. Chattels can make no contracts, not even the contract of marriage. And this is the law of the slave.

5. Chattels can have no rights, and hence the slave can have none.

6. Chattels may be bought and sold. Hence the existence of slavery involves, of necessity, the slave-trade, as Henry Clay testifies.—*Speech in the U. S. Senate*, 1839.

7. Chattels can claim no legal protection, and therefore the slave can have none. And all the cruelties of slavery must be tolerated.

8. Chattels are not to be educated, or instructed in religion! The idea is an absurdity. If the slaveholders are right in holding slaves as chattels, they cannot be blamed for withholding education and religious privileges from them. If the government may sanction or permit slaveholding, it must, to be consistent with itself, prohibit literary and religious instruction.

9. The same may be said of the laws forbidding freedom of speech and of the press. Such freedom is manifestly impracticable and unsafe in the presence of chattel slavery. The entire south attests this; and thus far the testimony is truthful. If slavery is to be maintained, or even tolerated, then liberty, of course, is to be relinquished. This is self-evident.

These brief statements show the consistency and unity of the slave system. If this idea can be properly conveyed and impressed, it will settle many controversies in respect to the subject in general, the manner of treating it, and the duties of slaveholders and their fellow-citizens.

HALF-WAY ABOLITIONISM.

Since the slave system, in its theory and its practice, its code and its workings, is symmetrical, consistent, and compact in its unity, we may perceive the futility and folly of all attempts to wage a desultory and piecemeal warfare with it. It must stand as a whole, or fall as a whole. The hideous picture cannot be transformed into a beauty by obliterating one feature at a time. The tree cannot be destroyed, or rendered sightly or innoxious, by lopping off some of its branches, while sparing the trunk or the roots. It is absurd and mischievous to talk of the *abuses* of such a system in distinction from the system itself.

"ABUSE OF OUR SOUTHERN BRETHREN."

It is manifestly unjust and abusive, to fellow-citizens of the slave states, to berate them for particular *results* of the system that may happen to be inconvenient or annoying *to us,* but which are inevitable during the existence of slavery, while we fail to protest earnestly against the continuance of the system, and perhaps frame apologies for their support of it!

If we concede to them the innocency of slaveholding, it is preposterous and insulting to deny them the right of doing that which slaveholding manifestly involves and requires.

If they are to hold men as chattels, then they must be tyrants, and act and appear like tyrants, and compel their chattels to be degraded and servile! If they have a right to hold human beings in slavery, then they have a right to keep them in absolute subjection, to deny them the exercise of any rights, for this is necessarily involved in the right to hold slaves. If they fail to do this, they fail of *holding* their slaves at all, and let them *go free!* In order to hold them as chattels they *must* blot out the family relation, they *must* introduce promiscuous sexual intercourse, or prevent it altogether, and so run out their breed of slaves. They *must* permit and practice the slave-trade, or give up the principle and the practice of human chattelhood. If they have a right to hold slaves, then they have a right to deny them legal protection, to exclude their access to civil courts as witnesses or plaintiffs, to prohibit their education, free social worship, and choice of avocation and locomotion, their capacity to make contracts, to earn wages, to hold property—for everybody knows that, in the present age of the world, under the light of the gospel, in the existing state of society, and with their facilities for emigration and self-support, they *could not* be permitted to enjoy these privileges, and yet be held as slaves.

"RIGHTS OF THE SOUTH."

The right to hold slaves and maintain slavery, in the United States, involves the right to prohibit free discussion, freedom of speech, and of the press. "If 'our southern brethren' have a right to hold slaves," writes an American, "they have a right to maintain the slave system. This they cannot do without overturning civil and religious liberty, and wielding all the powers of the government, state and national, in support of slavery. This is proved by the facts of the case. The direst necessity compels them to attempt all this, or cease to be slaveholders. And hence the struggle we now witness. Let us be just and honest to our fellow-citizens, both of the south and of the north. Let us concede to the south the right to overthrow the liberties of the country, and tyrannize over us all, as completely as they have ever attempted to do, or else let us tell them distinctly that they have no right to hold slaves."

DESPOTISM OF SLAVERY.

"Despotism.—Absolute power; authority unlimited and uncontrolled by men, constitution, or laws, and depending, alone, on the will of the prince, as the despotism of a Turkish sultan."—*Noah Webster* (the American lexicographer).

"It is plain that the dominion of the master is as unlimited as that which is tolerated by the laws of any civilized country, in relation to brute animals, to *quadrupeds,* to use the words of the civil law."—*Judge Stroud, Slave Laws,* p. 23.

"The slave is one who is in the power of a master, to whom he belongs."—*Louisiana Civil Code,* Art. 23.

"The slave is ENTIRELY subject to the WILL of his master." —*Ib.,* Art. 273.

"The whole commerce between master and slave is a perpetual exercise of the most boisterous passions, *the most unre-*

mitting despotism on the one part and degrading submissions on the other."—*Jefferson.*

"And with what execration should the statesman be loaded, who, permitting one-half the citizens thus to trample on the rights of the other, transforms those into *despots* and these into enemies, destroys the morals of the one part and the *amor patriæ* of the other."—*Jefferson.*

The Declaration of Independence affirms it to be "the right" and "the duty" of a people to *throw off* a government that "evinces a design to reduce them under *absolute despotism.*"

SLAVEHOLDERS ARE TYRANTS.

"Tyrant.—A monarch, or other ruler or master, who uses power to oppress his subjects ; a person who exercises unlawful authority, or lawful authority in an unlawful manner ; one who, by taxation, injustice, or cruel punishment, *or the demand of unreasonable services, imposes burdens and hardships upon those under his control,* which law and humanity do not authorize, or which the purposes of government do not require." " A despotic ruler, a cruel master, an oppressor."—*Noah Webster.*

Says Paley :—" Slavery is a dominion and system of laws the *most merciless* and *tyrannical* that were ever tolerated on the face of the earth."

The American Declaration of Independence denominates the king of Great Britain, George III., "a tyrant," though he never attempted to reduce his subjects to chattelhood, and all his oppressive measures were light in comparison with slaveholding. The general fact is stated by a slaveholder in the following terms :—

"The parent storms, the child looks on, catches the lineaments of wrath, puts on the same airs in the circle of smaller slaves, gives loose to his worst passions, *and thus nursed, educated, and daily exercised in* TYRANNY, cannot but be stamped by it with odious peculiarities."—*Jefferson.*

If slaveholding be not tyranny, what practice can be deserving of that name ? The definition of Webster applies to many usages less oppressive and cruel.

Can American *liberty* be safe in the hands of tyrants ? The Declaration of Independence answers the question—

"A prince whose character is thus marked by every act

which may define a TYRANT, is *unfit* to be the ruler of a free people."

Can it be safe, then, or right, to vote for a slaveholder?

SLAVERY versus MARRIAGE.

" Slaves are not entitled to the rights and considerations of matrimony, and therefore have no relief in cases of adultery," &c.—*Stroud*, p. 21.

" A slave cannot even contract matrimony."—*Stroud*, p. 61.

" A slave has never maintained an action against the violator of his bed."—*Opinion of D. Dulaney*, Attorney-General of Maryland.

In Connecticut, during the existence of slavery there, it was held that the consent of a master to the *marriage* of a slave was equivalent to *manumission*.

In 1835, the Savanna River Baptist Association of ministers decided that slave members of churches, cohabiting together as husband and wife, but afterwards separated by sale, were not to be subjected to *church censure* for contracting new connections, though both the parties were still living. Among the reasons assigned, one was, that in contracting such new connections, they would be "*acting in obedience to their masters.*" —" Such separation," said they, "among persons situated as our slaves are, is *civilly* a separation by *death*, and they (the association) believed that in the sight of God it would be so viewed." .... "*The slaves are not free agents*, and a dissolution by death is not more entirely without their consent and beyond their control, than by such separation."

Yet the members of this association were doubtless themselves slaveholders, and opposed to the abolition of the slave laws. The Charleston Baptist Association, the same year, addressed a memorial to the legislature of South Carolina in defence of the right of slavery! Thus do men abrogate the laws of their Maker, to establish their own!

" Shall I not visit for these things? saith the Lord!"

LICENTIOUSNESS INSEPARABLE FROM SLAVERY.
TESTIMONY OF THE PRESBYTERIAN SYNOD OF KENTUCKY.

" The system produces general licentiousness among the slaves. Marriage, as a civil ordinance, they cannot enjoy.

Our laws do not recognize this relation as existing among them, and of course do not enforce, by any sanction, the observance of its duties. Indeed, until slavery waxeth old, and tendeth to decay, *there cannot be* any legal recognition of the marriage rite, or the enforcement of the consequent duties. For all regulations on this subject *would limit the master's right of absolute property in the slaves.* In his disposal of them, he would no longer be at liberty to consult merely his own interest. He could no longer separate the wife and the husband, to suit the convenience or interest of the purchaser, no matter how advantageous might be the terms offered."—" Hence, all marriages allowed to them would be a mere contract, voidable at the master's pleasure. Their present *quasi marriages* are continually thus voided. They are, in this way, brought to consider their matrimonial engagements as a thing not binding, and they govern themselves accordingly."—" We are then assured by the most unquestionable testimony, that *licentiousness is the necessary result of the system."—Synod of Kentucky,* Address, pp. 15, 16.

"Chastity is no virtue among them (the slaves), its violation neither injures female character, in their own estimation, nor in that of their master or mistress. No instruction is ever given —no censure pronounced. I speak not of the world. I speak of *Christian families generally."—Lexington, Ky., Luminary.*

This licentiousness notoriously extends to the whites.

IGNORANCE INSEPARABLE FROM SLAVERY.

"Slavery dooms thousands of human beings to *hopeless ignorance."—"* If slaves are educated, it must involve some outlay on the part of the master."—" It is inconsistent with our knowledge of human nature to suppose that he will do it for them. The present state of instruction among this race answers exactly to what we might thus naturally anticipate. Throughout the whole land, so far as we can learn, there is *but one* school in which, during the week, slaves can be taught. The light of three or four Sabbath schools is seen glimmering through the darkness that covers the black population of a whole state. *Here and there,* a family is found where humanity and religion impel the master, mistress, or children, to the laborious task of private instruction."—"Nor is it to be expected that this state of things will become better, unless it is determined that slavery shall cease."—*Synod of Kentucky.* Address, p. 8.

If such be the condition of the slaves in Kentucky, where, as in Maryland, the *laws* do not prohibit their instruction, what must be their condition in the other slave states, in all of which, we believe, the laws rigidly *forbid* even the masters to instruct them?

The motive for withholding instruction, alluded to by the Synod of Kentucky, might suffice, perhaps, to account for the state of things they describe, even in the absence of any other motive. But the prohibitory laws of all the slave states, except two, afford evidence that there are other and stronger motives. This is confirmed by the known fact that in Maryland and Kentucky, a large portion (probably a great majority) of slaveholders will not permit their slaves to be gratuitously taught to read or write, even in the Sabbath-schools. An educated population could not long be held in slavery. Their qualifications would be above their condition, and increase their discontent. The knowledge of their rights could not be kept from them, nor the means of regaining the exercise of those rights. Any adequate system of instruction would amount to manumission, and imply or include it. This, the slaveholders well understand. And hence the idea of persuading them to *prepare* their slaves for freedom, by *previous education,* has always proved to be visionary and delusive. The slaveholders better understand their position. Whenever they determine to *educate* their slaves, they will determine to *set them free.*

HEATHENISM INSEPARABLE FROM SLAVERY.

Christianity cannot coexist with ignorance, concubinage, promiscuous sexual intercourse, and the absence of the family relation. To suppose the possibility of this would be to suppose Christianity an impure and worthless religion.

The Synod of South Carolina and Georgia said in 1834:—

"The negroes are destitute of the gospel, and *ever will be,* under the present state of things."—"The coloured population may justly be considered *the heathen* of this Christian country, and will bear comparison with heathen in any country in the world."—*Report,* in *Charleston Observer.*

"Generally speaking, the slaves appear to us to be without God in the world, *a nation of heathen* in our very midst. We cannot cry out against the Papist for withholding the Scriptures from the common people, and keeping them ignorant of the way of life; for we withhold the Bible from our servants, and keep them in ignorance of it; while we will not use the means to have it read and explained to them."—*Rev. C. C. Jones,* of Georgia.

"There are" ("within the bounds of our Synod") "at least one hundred thousand slaves, speaking the same language as ourselves, who *never heard* of the plan of salvation by a Redeemer."—*Charleston Observer.*

"*Heathenism is as real in the slave states* as it is in the South Sea Islands, and our negroes are as justly objects of attention to the American and other Boards of Missions, as the Indians of the western wilds."—*Western Luminary,* Lexington, Ky.

"Thousands amongst us cannot read the Word of God, and but seldom hear it, and whose instruction in the truth is *little concern* to their owners, to *God's ministers,* or to any other persons whatsoever." "I am utterly amazed, and I ask, can the pure love of God, and of the lost souls of men, animate the Christian ministers of our land?"—*Bishop Meade,* of Virginia.

"Slavery deprives its subjects, in a great measure, of the privileges of the gospel."—"It is evident that, as a body, our slaves do not enjoy the public ordinances of religion. Domestic means of grace are still more rare among them."—*Synod of Kentucky.*

The Synod proceed to say that the proposal to employ missionaries among them will never be sustained by the community, *until they are* "*ripe for measures of emancipation.*"

These general statements are not to be invalidated by the fact that there are some pious slaves, nor by the fact that some religious denominations enrol large numbers of slaves among their communicants; while, as slaveholders, they are neither prepared to give them the Bible, to teach them letters, or to instruct them in the sanctities of the family relation.

Whenever American Christianity undertakes, in earnest, the enterprise of educating and Christianizing the labouring population of the slave states, it will undertake the enterprise of abolishing American slavery.

RELIGIOUS PERSECUTION INSEPARABLE FROM SLAVERY.

"Great efforts have been made to abolish this practice," *i. e.*, the preaching of negroes), "but they have been attended with *the usual effects of religious persecution*, secrecy and nocturnal meetings in old fields and plantations where no white persons reside."—*Bishop Meade,* of Virginia.

In 1838, Rev. Mr. Turpin, a missionary of the South Carolina Methodist Conference, undertook to labour among the slaves. A remonstrance addressed to Mr. Turpin, signed by 353 citizens, was published in *The Greenville* (S. C.) *Mountaineer*. In this address it was said, "Intelligence and slavery can have no affinity for each other." The fear was expressed that "a progressive system of improvement will be introduced" .... "that will ultimately revolutionize our civil institutions." It was added, "We do not think that a reasonable abolitionist could desire a more auspicious commencement."—*Signed by James S. Pope and* 352 *others.*

The publication of this remonstrance in *The Mountaineer* was accompanied by the following statement of the editor:—

"The opposition to the late home mission among us composed the great body of the people."

The enterprise was promptly abandoned, and we hear of no counter remonstrance from the Methodist Conference.

This religious persecution is authorized by the law of slavery, and constitutes an essential feature of "the peculiar institution."

"The owners of human beings among us may *legally* restrain them from assembling to hear the instructions of divine truth, or even from ever uniting their hearts and voices in social prayer and praise to Him who created them."—*Address, Synod of Kentucky.*

In many of the states the laws not only sanction but *require* the religious persecution of slaves and free negroes assembling "for purposes of mental instruction or religious worship."—

See Laws of Georgia, South Carolina, North Carolina, Louisiana, &c.

But why multiply proofs? Who does not know that in most of the slave states it is not safe, if even practicable, to "preach the gospel of deliverance to the captives," to reprove the sin of oppression, to attempt giving religious instruction to the slaves, or to furnish them with Bibles? We talk of "the times of persecution" as though they had gone by, and point to pagan or popish countries for specimens of religious persecution! But if the Christians of America are ready to suffer persecution for the cause of Christ, they have only to enter upon the work of preaching *Christ's* Christianity in our own slave states!

SLAVEHOLDING IDENTICAL WITH, AND INSEPARABLE FROM, THE SLAVE-TRADE.

"The moment that the incontestable *fact* is admitted that the slaves are *property*, the law of movable property *irresistibly* attaches itself to them, and secures the right of carrying them from one state to another."—*Henry Clay, Speech U. S. Senate, February* 7, 1841.

This argument shows, as it was designed to do, that the slave-trade between the states cannot be abolished while slaveholding continues. This agrees with the fact that the governments of Great Britain and of other countries, have never been able to put a stop to the African slave-trade. So long as there is a market for human chattels, so long as humanity is held in chattelhood, so long (as Mr. Clay says) the law of chattelhood must "irresistibly" attach to them.

And this justifies the sentiment of Wesley:—" Men-buyers are exactly on a level with men-stealers." And the General Assembly of the Presbyterian Church, in 1794, adopted a note on the eighth commandment (which was retained till 1818), embracing the following :—" Stealers of men are all those who bring off slaves or freemen, and *keep*, sell, or buy them."

Thomas Jefferson Randolph, in a speech in the Virginia Legislature, in 1832, compared the African slave-trade, which the United States' *laws* denominate "piracy," with the internal American slave-trade, and showed wherein the latter is "*much worse!*" In 1828, about 1100 citizens of the district of

Columbia, including the Hon. Judge Cranch, in a petition to Congress against slavery and the slave-trade in the district, instituted a similar comparison, declaring the "domestic slave-trade scarcely less disgraceful in its character" (than the foreign), "and even more demoralizing in its influence."

Let the people ponder this testimony, and then consider that if Henry Clay understood the nature of slave law, and if the abortive efforts of the British and other governments to abolish the African slave-trade convey any instruction, then there is no way to stop the American slave-trade but by abolishing American slavery. When shall it be done?

SLAVEHOLDING IS ROBBERY.

Of course it can be nothing else, if, as United States' laws declare, the African slave-trade be "piracy," and if Henry Clay, John Wesley, and the General Assembly of the Presbyterian Church (from 1794 to 1818), were correct in identifying *slavery* with the *slave-trade*. The slave-trade introduced slavery. The atrocity of the *former* consisted chiefly in its facilitating the *latter*. If the slave-traders had never *held* their emigrants as slaves, and had never so disposed of them as to put them into the hands of *slaveholders*, nobody would ever have dreamed of denouncing the importation of the Africans as piracy! It is the fact of *slaveholding*, and nothing else, that gives to the *slave-trade* its unparalleled atrocity and infamy. How absurd to execrate the slave-*trade*, and yet palliate or apologize for slave*holding!*

But dropping the comparison between the two, let us examine the character of slave*holding*, and see whether or no it be *robbery*. What *is* it to *rob?*

"*Rob*, to take from the person of another feloniously, by putting him in fear; to plunder, to strip, unlawfully; *to take away by oppression and violence*. 'Rob not the poor, because he is poor.'—Prov. xxvi. *To withhold what is due.*—Mal. iii."—*Webster's Dictionary.*

This definition is sustained by innumerable expressions of Scripture:—"Trust not in oppression, and become not vain in robbery."—Psal. lxii. "The robbery of the wicked shall destroy them, because they refuse to do judgment."—Prov. xxi. "He meaneth this chiefly of judges and princes."—*Scott's*

Commentary. "The people of the land have used oppression and exercised robbery."—Ezek. xxiii.

How does the practice of slaveholding correspond with these definitions and uses of the terms *rob* and *robbery?* We cite the testimony of the Rev. Robert J. Breckenridge, D.D., of Baltimore:—

"The man who cannot see that involuntary domestic slavery, as it exists among us, is founded on the principle of taking *by force* that which is *another's*, has, simply, NO COMMON SENSE."

A bitter pill for the northern people, who cannot bear to hear their dear southern brethren accused of robbery! If the forcible and unjust taking of liberty, of personality, and of the wages of labour (the essence of all property) be not robbery, there is left no definite or intelligible meaning to the word. We might as well blot it out from our dictionaries, our Bibles, our commentaries, and the common literature of our language. If we cannot call slaveholding robbery, then we cannot describe it as it *is*, we cannot show *wherein* its criminality consists, nor tell slaveholders of *what* they must repent, or lose their souls. We cannot be faithful to God and his truth. We cannot maintain the honest testimony of the wise and good, of former times, against slaveholding. We cannot stand by the side of Wesley, who said, "Man-stealers! the worst of thieves! in comparison with whom highway robbers and housebreakers are innocent; and men-buyers are exactly on a level with men-stealers." Nor by the side of Jonathan Edwards, who said, "It is really as wicked to rob a man of his liberty as to rob him of his life; and it is much *more* wicked than to rob him of his property. To *hold* a man in slavery, is to be, *every day*, guilty of robbing him of his liberty, or of man-stealing."—"To steal a man," says Grotius, "is the highest kind of theft." This statement, the General Assembly of the Presbyterian Church could once repeat, and add that all who "*keep*" slaves are men-stealers.

These are "words of truth and soberness," not of abusive and angry vituperation. They fasten upon *the consciences* of the slaveholders and torment them, and this is the true reason why a clamour is raised by them, and they cry out, "Let us alone."

THE AMERICAN SLAVE-TRADE AND THE CHURCHES OF THE SOUTH.

If it *were* true, as some claim, and as a general public sentiment has seemed, until recently, to concede, that slave*holding* is vastly more respectable, or less infamous than slave-*trading*, the distinction would avail little or nothing for the mass of the slaveholding community, including the membership of the churches of most sects, in the American slave states.

The Rev. James Smylie, A.M., of the Amite Presbytery, Mississippi, in his defence of slavery, says:—

"If slavery be a sin, and advertising and apprehending slaves, with a view to restore them to their masters, is a direct violation of the Divine law, and if the *buying, selling, or holding* of a slave, FOR THE SAKE OF GAIN, is a heinous sin and scandal, then verily, *three-fourths* of all the Episcopalians, Methodists, Baptists, and Presbyterians, in eleven states of the Union, are of the devil. They hold, if they do not buy and sell slaves, and with few exceptions they hesitate not to apprehend and restore runaway slaves, when in their power."

Mr. Smylie, it will be noticed, disdains to make the frivolous distinction between slaveholding and the slave-trade, and he spurns also the pretence, sometimes set up, that slaves are held by professors of religion, for benevolent purposes, and not for the sake of gain. Of the *fact* of an existing slave-trade, with all its attendant cruelties and atrocities, participated in by church members, we have other testimony at hand.

"Brutal stripes, and all the various kinds of personal indignities, are not the only species of cruelty which slavery licenses. The law does not recognize the family relations of the slave, and extends to him no protection in the enjoyment of domestic endearments. The members of a slave family may be forcibly separated, so that they shall never more meet until the final judgment. And cupidity often induces the master to practise what the law allows. Brothers and sisters, parents and children, husbands and wives are torn asunder, and permitted to see each other no more. *These acts are daily occurring in the midst of us.* The shrieks and the agony often witnessed on such occasions, proclaim, with a trumpet tongue, the iniquity and cruelty of our system. The cries of these sufferers go up to the ears of the Lord of Sabaoth. *There is not a neighbourhood where* *these heart-rending scenes are not displayed. There is not a village or road* that does not behold the sad procession of *manacled outcasts, whose chains* and mournful countenances tell us that they are exiled, by force, from all that their hearts hold dear. Our church, years ago, raised its voice of solemn warning against this flagrant violation of every principle of mercy, justice, and humanity; yet we blush to announce to you and to the world, that this warning has been often disregarded by those who hold to *our communion.* Cases have occurred in our own denomination where *professors of the religion of mercy have torn the mother from her children, and sent her into a merciless and returnless exile.* Yet acts of discipline have rarely (*never**) followed such conduct."—*Address, Synod of Kentucky.*

There is every reason to think that the statement of the Synod of Kentucky does not convey an exaggerated account of the extent to which church members have been and still are engaged in the traffic, and of the general apathy of the church in respect to it. In the General Assembly of the Presbyterian Church in 1835, Mr. Stewart, of Illinois, a ruling elder, made the following statement, without contradiction, yet without being able to procure any testimony against the practice!

"*Tens of thousands* of our fellow-creatures are writhing under the lash, often inflicted too by *ministers and elders* of the Presbyterian Church."—"In this church a man may take a free-born child, force it away from its parents, to whom God gave it in charge, saying, 'Bring it up for me,' and sell it as a beast, or hold it in perpetual bondage, and not only escape corporeal punishment, but really be esteemed an excellent Christian. Nay, even ministers of the gospel and *doctors of divinity may engage in this unholy traffic, and yet sustain their high and holy calling.*"—"*Elders, ministers, and doctors of divinity are, with both hands, engaged in this practice.*"

It is known that, within a few years past, itinerating preachers have carried handcuffs in their pockets, wherewith to confine the slaves they might purchase; have actually made the pur-

---

* This correction from the pen of James G. Birney (formerly of Kentucky), in 1836, has never been called in question. The Address of the Synod was published in 1834.

chases, and procured their shipment to the far south, for sale on speculation!

The testimony of Thomas Jefferson Randolph in the legislature of Virginia, and of Judge Cranch and numerous citizens of the Federal District (cited in a previous article) confirm, in general terms, the account of the Kentucky Synod concerning the nature of the traffic.

MAGNITUDE OF THE AMERICAN SLAVE-TRADE.

"It was stated in the *Natchez Courier*, that, during the year 1836, no less than two hundred and fifty thousand slaves were carried into Mississippi, Alabama, Louisiana, and Arkansas." The value of slaves imported into Mississippi alone, during the same year and a portion of the next following, was estimated at ninety millions of dollars! All these were, of course, exported from the more northerly slave states, Virginia, Maryland, Kentucky, &c. The *Virginia Times*, as quoted by *Niles' Register*, computed the exports from Virginia alone, during the year 1836, to be forty thousand slaves, at an average of six hundred dollars each, and amounting to TWENTY-FOUR MILLIONS OF DOLLARS! This was a year of unusual briskness in the traffic. But in 1831 the imports coastwise into New Orleans alone were estimated at twenty thousand persons, besides importations into Mobile, and overland supplies received into the states above mentioned, amounting, as has been estimated, to fifty thousand in all, which, at the reduced price of five hundred dollars each, would have amounted to *twenty-five millions of dollars.*

All this corroborates the statements frequently made on southern authority, that in Maryland, Virginia, Kentucky, and some portions of North Carolina and Tennessee, the practice of slave*holding* is continued, chiefly, for the purpose of *breeding* slaves for the *market!* The exhausted state of the soil, and the comparatively lean statistics of *other* exported products confirm the statement, and illustrate the speech of Mr. Gholson in the legislature of Virginia, in which he said: "Why, really, I have been under the impression that I *owned* my slaves. I lately purchased *four women and ten children,* in whom I thought I had obtained a great bargain, for I really supposed they were my own property, *as were my brood mares !*"

Thus the *slaveholding* of the older slave states is identified with slave-*selling*, and that of the newer slave states with slave-*buying*. What avails, then, the broad line of distinction attempted to be drawn between *slaveholding*, and the slave-*trade?* And what, in the middle of this nineteenth century, are we to think of the Christianity that either *practises* these enormities, or *apologizes* for them.

DEFENDERS AND APOLOGISTS OF SLAVEHOLDING.

The Synod of South Carolina and Georgia, whose testimony concerning the essential heathenism of the slave population is given in a previous article, "Resolved, unanimously (in 1836), that in the opinion of this Synod, abolition societies, and the principles on which they are founded, in the United States, are inconsistent with *the rights of slaveholders,* and the great principles of our political institutions."

The Charleston Union Presbytery (7th April, 1836), "Resolved, that in the opinion of this Presbytery, the holding of slaves, so far from being a SIN in the sight of God, is nowhere condemned in his holy Word: that it is in accordance with the example and consistent with the precepts of patriarchs, apostles, and prophets," &c. &c.

The Missionary Society of the South Carolina Conference of the Methodist Episcopal Church, by their board of managers, said, "We denounce the principles and practice of the abolitionists, *in toto.*" * * * * * * "We believe that the Holy Scriptures, so far from giving any countenance to this delusion, do, unequivocally, authorize the relation of master and slave."

The Hopewell Presbytery of S. Carolina issued a document affirming that "Slavery has always existed in the Church of God, from the time of Abraham to this day."—"That this relation is not only recognized, but its duties are defined clearly, both in the Old and New Testaments," and that "emancipation is not mentioned among the duties of the master to the slave."

The Presbyterian Synod of Virginia " Resolved, unanimously, that we consider the dogma, that slavery as it exists in the slaveholding states is necessarily sinful, and ought to be immediately abolished, and the conclusions which naturally follow from that dogma, as directly and palpably contrary to the plainest principles of common sense and common humanity, and the clearest authority of the Word of God."

The *General Conference of the Methodist Episcopal Church*, in 1836, "Resolved, that we are decidedly opposed to modern abolitionism, and wholly disclaim any right, *wish*, or intention to interfere in the civil and political relation of master and slave, as it exists in the slaveholding States in this Union."

Prof. Hodge, of Princeton (N. J.), Theological Seminary (Presbyterian), in April, 1836, published an article in the *Biblical Repertory*, which contained the following :—

"At the time of the advent of Jesus Christ, *slavery* in its worst forms prevailed over the world. The Saviour found it around him in Judea, the apostles met with it in Asia, Greece, and Italy. How did they treat it? Not by the denunciation of *slaveholding*, as necessarily *sinful*. The assumption that slaveholding is, in itself, a crime, is not only an error, but it is an error fraught with evil consequences."

The *Quarterly Christian Spectator, New Haven, (Ct.)*, Congregational, in 1838, said, "The Bible contains no explicit prohibition of slavery; it recognizes, both in the Old Testament and in the New, such a constitution of society, and it *lends its authority to enforce* the mutual obligations resulting from that constitution."

Rev. E. Hedding, D.D., Bishop in the Methodist Episcopal Church, said, "The right to hold a slave is founded on this rule, —Therefore, all things whatsoever ye would that men should do to you, do ye even so unto them, for this is the law and the prophets."—*Christian Advocate and Journal*, Oct. 20, 1837.

Several Methodist ministers, in reply to an appeal of certain Methodist abolitionists, issued a counter appeal, March 27, 1837, in which they said, "The general rule of Christianity not only *permits*, but in supposable cases *enjoins*, a continuance of the master's authority."—"The New Testament enjoins obedience upon the slave as an obligation *due to a present rightful authority*."—*Signed by Willbur Fisk, John Lindsley, B. Otheman, H. S. Ramsdell, E. T. Taylor, Jacob Sanborn, H. H. White.*

Dr. Dalcho, of S. Carolina (Episcopalian), said, "Slavery is not forbidden in the divine law, so it is left to our own judgment whether we will have slaves or no."

T. R. Dew, Professor in William and Mary College (Episcopalian), said, "Slavery was established by divine authority among even the elect of heaven, the children of Israel."

Rev. G. W. Freeman (Episcopalian), said in a sermon, Nov. 1836, "No man nor set of men, in our day, are entitled to pronounce it wrong; and we may add that *slavery*, as it exists at the present day, is agreeable to the order of *Divine Providence.*"

D. R. Furman (Baptist), in an exposition of the views of the Baptists, addressed to the Governor of South Carolina, in 1833, said, "The right of holding slaves is clearly established in the Holy Scriptures, both by precept and example."

Prof. Moses Stuart, of the Theological Seminary, Andover (*Mass.*), in response to a letter of Pres. Fisk, of the Wesleyan University, in 1836, said, " The precepts of the New Testament respecting the demeanour of slaves and of their masters, beyond all question, recognized the existence of slavery. The masters are, in part, 'believing masters,' so that a precept to them how they are to behave as *masters*, recognizes that the relation may still exist, *salva fide, salva ecclesia* (*i. e.*, without violating the Christian faith or the Church).'' In the same letter, Prof. Stuart represents Paul, as "sending him (Onesimus) back, to be a servant for life." Forgetful that the request was, that he should be received "*not* now as a servant, but *above* a servant, a *brother beloved,*" "both in the flesh, and in the Lord."

Query.—"What have northern Christians to do with slavery," in view of its connection with the Church?

MORAL INFLUENCES OF SLAVERY.

Slavery imbrutes and heathenizes its immediate victims. It hardens the hearts and depraves the morals of those who wield and administer it. The contagion of this moral disease affects surrounding communities, and poisons the moral atmosphere of whole nations.

By undermining *industry*, it assails the foundations of *virtue*, as effectually as it does the elements of individual prosperity and national wealth.

By making labour the badge of degradation, it discourages the labour of the free. It makes men ashamed of the industry that should have ennobled them, and proud of the idleness that depraves them, and of which they should be ashamed! Without industry there can be no sound moral character—no moral improvement—no moral progress, in individuals, families, communities, or nations. Instead of moral and intellectual advancement, among the idle, there must be decrepitude and decline.

These influences, so powerful in slaveholding communities, cannot be confined to the geographical boundaries of the slave states.

Gambling is, proverbially, among the vices of slaveholders. They need its excitements—they need the relief it yields them from the *ennui* of unemployed time. This spirit spreads into the surrounding states. It becomes fashionable to gamble, for slaveholders give shape to the customs and habits of those who emulate their idleness, and who associate and sympathize with them. Transplanted into the soil of the free states, or engrafted upon the thrifty tree of northern enterprise, this spirit of gambling takes the form of commercial and monetary speculation. It converts cotton bales into dice, and harvest-fields into chess-boards. It gambles with bank capital and the public stocks. The speculations in cotton, commencing in New Orleans, and marching with rapid strides, like the cholera, through all our commercial cities, has, more than once, sent bankruptcy into hundreds of counting-houses, and poisoned a larger number with the mania of commercial gambling. While this mania prevails, there is an embargo upon legitimate enterprise, a paralysis upon patient industry, a suspension of the healthful functions of sober and honest commerce. And the storm, when it has spent itself, is found to have devastated, without having fertilized, to have riven with its thunderbolts without having cleansed the moral atmosphere—nay, to have sown the salt of barrenness in all its track, to have generated a moral miasma that is not to be readily expelled.

As the idleness engendered by slavery is the parent of the vices in general, it is especially so of the vice of licentiousness in particular. Idleness, by its physical and its moral tendencies, combined, becomes the prompter to lawless indulgence, it furnishes the hot-bed of unbridled desire, "the cage of every unclean and hateful bird." In a state where female chastity, in one-half of the population, and *that* the dependent and servile portion, is virtually proscribed by the statute, it cannot be credible that the idleness of the other and the domineering portion would fail to plunge them into the depths of defilement and pollution. It cannot be credible that chastity, with the male portion of such a community, could be so prevalent, as to constitute anything more than exceptions to the general rule. Nor can it be credible that the infection of this licentiousness should not spread into the surrounding communities. A nation, in one-half of which the family relation has become an abstraction, can hardly be expected to retain a high tone of social morality and virtue. " We are dignified with the title of wives," said the sister of a prominent southern statesman, " but we are only mistresses of seraglios." Yet, at the seat of our national government, the masters and the mistresses of these seraglios are " the observed of all observers," the centres of attraction in the highest circles of social intercourse, to which the elegance and wealth of the nation resorts, to take lessons in refinement and manners.

Where habits of idleness, gaming, unchastity, and brutal domination are prominent characteristics of a community, it cannot be supposed that there can be witnessed the spirit and the habit of quiet subordination to the restraints of social order and the reverenced administration of *law!* Nor could it be supposed that a nation in one-half of which these features were prominent would escape the contaminating influences of so bad an example. If murders, assassinations, bloody encounters, lynchings, and duels, should not be witnessed frequently in slave states—if manifestations of disorganization, mob violence, and arrogant dictation and menace should not have appeared among those, in the non-slaveholding states, who sympathize with slaveholders, it must be because the common tendencies of moral causes acting upon human nature are, in this instance, turned aside ; or because the moral character of slaveholding is widely different from what abolitionists have supposed. On the other hand, if *the facts are* such as have been described, the inherent wickedness of slaveholding is confirmed, for " the tree is known by its fruit."

THE REMEDY OF SLAVERY—WHAT IS IT?

What *can* it be but the *abolition* of slavery ? If slaveholding be wrong, it ought to be abandoned. If the slave laws are iniquitous, they ought to be repealed. Can any remedy be more simple, more obvious, more effectual, more unobjectionable than this? Could any *other* remedy reach the disease? What other remedy can be conceived, or proposed, that would not betray, upon the very face of it, absurdity and folly, to mention nothing worse!

God's remedy for transgression is repentance, and works meet for repentance.

God's remedy for the sin of oppression is—"Break every yoke! Let the oppressed go free."—" Bring the poor that are cast out to thine own house, and hide not thyself from thine own flesh."

WHEN SHOULD SLAVERY BE ABOLISHED?

When should *sin* be repented of, and abandoned? " Behold! now is the accepted time. Behold! now is the day of salvation."—" To-day, if ye will hear his voice, harden not your hearts."—" Execute judgment *in the morning*," (*i. e.*, timely, early), "and deliver the spoiled out of the hand of the oppressor."

There are no reasons that can be urged against the abolition of slavery now, that were not urged, in substance, fifty years ago. There are none that could not be urged with equal plausibility, fifty years hence, should slavery be continued so long, as it must be, unless abolished peacefully, or overthrown by violence.

" Procrastination is the thief of time." The grand adversary of mankind asks nothing but the *delay* of repentance and obedience. Nations, as well as the individual souls of whom nations are composed, are always ruined by *delay*. The signs of the times indicate that the guilty nation has received more faithful warnings on this subject than it is likely to receive again. " He that being often reproved hardeneth his neck, shall suddenly be destroyed, and that without remedy." " Proclaim liberty, then, throughout all the land, unto all the inhabitants thereof."—" Let him that stole steal no more, but rather let him labour, working with his hands."

Leeds Anti-slavery Series. No. 8.

Sold by W. and F. G. Cash, 5, Bishopsgate Street, London; and by Jane Jowett, Friends' Meeting Yard, Leeds, at 7s. 6d. per 100; 1s. per doz.; or 1½d. each.

Leeds Anti-slavery Series. No. 9.

SALES BY AUCTION OF MEN, WOMEN, AND CHILDREN,

WITH HOUSES, LANDS, AND CATTLE, &c.

Husbands, Wives, and Families sold indiscriminately to different purchasers, are violently separated—probably never to meet again.

"See the poor victim torn from social life,
The shrinking babe, the agonizing wife!"

The following is from the *Christian Index*, published at Penfield, Ga.:—

"EXECUTORS' SALE.—Will be sold at the late residence of Jesse Perkins, deceased, late of Greene county, on Wednesday, the 1st of March next, the following property, viz.:

"Allen, about 30 years old; Claiborn, 25; Dick, 25; Anderson, 20; Asa, 15; Israel, 14; Harrison, 13; Nathan, 13; Sirena, 14; Adaline, 12; and Wesley, 10.

"Also, stock of hogs, stock of cattle, horses, corn, fodder and oats, plantation-tools, &c.

"All sold as the property of the said Jesse Perkins, deceased, under his last will, in order to make a division among the legatees of said estate. Terms on day of sale.

VINCENT SANDFORD, } Ex'rs.
NICHOLAS PERKINS,

"Jan. 15, 1848."

"The sale of about one hundred and sixty negroes, 44 mules and horses, 250 or 300 pork hogs, stock hogs, cattle, corn, fodder, oats, plantation-tools, cooking utensils, &c., &c., will commence on Friday, the 10th of December, at the plantation of John Jones, deceased, near Warsaw, Sumter county.

"The sale will be continued on Monday, 13th of December, at the late residence of John Jones, deceased, in Greene county —say, *one hundred and fourteen or fifteen negroes*, 33 mules and horses, 7 yoke of oxen, pork hogs, stock hogs, cattle, road-waggon, ox-waggon, horse-carts, cart-wheels, cotton-gins, corn, fodder, oats, plantation-tools, &c.

"The terms of sale, twelve months' credit. Notes with two approved securities—interest to be added from sale. All sums under 20 dollars, cash.

WILLIAM JONES, JR., } Adm'rs."
JOHN P. EVANS,

—*Eutaw (Ala.) Whig.*

The Rev. Dr. Furman, of North Carolina, addressed a lengthy communication to the Governor of that State, expressing the sentiments of the Baptist church and clergy on the subject of slavery. This brief extract contains the essence of the whole:—" The right of holding slaves is clearly established in the Holy Scriptures, both by precept and example."

Not long after, Dr. Furman died. His legal representative thus advertises his property:—

"NOTICE. On the first Monday of February, will be put up at *public auction*, before the *court-house*, the *following property*, belonging to the estate of the late Rev. Dr. Furman, viz:—

"A plantation or tract of land, on and in the Wataree Swamp. A tract of the first quality of fine land, on the waters of Black River. A lot of land in the town of Camden. A Library of a miscellaneous character, chiefly theological. *Twenty-seven Negroes*, some of them very prime. Two mules, one horse, and an old waggon."

SALE OF A YOUNG FEMALE SLAVE AT CLINTON, GEORGIA.

An Englishman, passing through Clinton, observed, opposite his hotel, a sale of negroes, and, on approaching the auctioneer's stand, discovered a young female negro for sale, who had just been married to a young man, a slave in the same town. The reason of her being sold was to pay her master's debts, who was then in embarrassed circumstances. The poor creature seemed in the wildest grief; her hysterical screams and sobs were most heart-rending; in fact, so exciting was the scene, that it seemed to affect even the callous-hearted slaveholders around, who were accustomed to such exhibitions. The young man, her husband, was not to be sold. The party who wished to buy his wife, was a trader from the far South, and in all probability she would be separated from him for ever, many hundreds of miles. A person in the town, with more humanity than the rest, wishing to prevent this separation, bought her in, much to the satisfaction of the by-standers. Thus, by a mere accident, was the nearest and dearest tie of life prevented being sundered. No thanks, however, to the inhuman system of slavery. The screams of ecstasy uttered by the young woman, as she rushed into the arms of her husband, who was standing near, were affecting to all who witnessed them.—*Report of a respectable English Traveller.*

A SCENE IN BALTIMORE.

" I send you a few incidents that have occurred here during the past week, which may prove of some interest to your readers. Hope H. Slatter, the notorious dealer in God's image, has made a shipment of a large number of *men, women, and children,* for the rich swamps of the far South.

" The *General Pinkney,* the vessel which took this freight of bodies and souls, cleared several days previously to sailing, and lay anchored off the Point, and in real slave-trading style, at the appointed time weighed anchor, dropped into her berth, took in her cargo, and immediately sailed. Slatter's slave-prison is about two miles from the Point. He generally, as in this case, treats his *goods* to an omnibus ride from their public house to the vessel; and in the free, enlightened, *Christian* city of Baltimore, third city of the *only republican and free country on earth,* on Tuesday, Jan. 19th, 1847, might have been seen a train of omnibuses crowded with human beings, 'made but a little lower than the angels,' torn from all that makes life desirable, without crime or offence, and hurried off to toil beneath the burning sun of a Southern plantation, without reward, with no man to care for their souls. Following the train, was a tall, gray-headed old man, of sixty, on horseback.

"The trader's heart was callous to the wailings of the anguished mother for her child. He heeded not the sobs of the young wife for her husband. The sister, whose grief was insupportable, as she heard the last farewell, faintly uttered, from an only brother, as he was hurried on board that accursed vessel, moved not the adamantine heart of this human trafficker. These connections may not have existed as I have stated them; but friendship in every relation is severed by these horrible transactions. I saw a mother whose very frame was convulsed with anguish for her first-born, a girl of eighteen, who, notwithstanding her master was under bond, to the amount of two thousand dollars, not to sell any of the family out of the State, had been sold to this dealer, and was among the number then shipped. I saw a young man who kept pace with the carriages, that he might catch one more glimpse of a dear friend, before she was torn for ever from his sight. As she saw him, she burst into a flood of tears, and was hurried out of his sight, sorrowing most of all that they should see each others' faces no more.

"'These are not uncommon occurrences in this city. The last Tuesday in December, there was a much larger number shipped than on last Tuesday. This is about all that we see of slavery here in the city. Humanity is not shocked, as on our plantations, with the frequent floggings of the slave; or, at least, it does not fall under observation, as in the other case. The effects of slavery, however, are to be seen on every hand; and marks of this blighting system will be visible after slavery has been abolished."—*Anti-Slavery Reporter.*

Leeds Anti-slavery Series. No. 9.

Sold by W. and F. G. CASH, 5, Bishopsgate Street, London; and by JANE JOWETT, Friends' Meeting Yard, Leeds, at 1*s*. 2*d*. per 100.

Leeds Anti-slavery Series.   No. 10.

THE FAREWELL
OF A VIRGINIAN SLAVE-MOTHER TO HER DAUGHTER, SOLD INTO SOUTHERN BONDAGE.

EVERY Slave State in America has its peculiar enormity; that of Virginia, *sending slaves to the southern market*, proceeds from its position being such, that slave-labour no longer bears a high value within the State. It happens, hence, that those who are born and reared in the Old Dominion are frequently sold south; where the extensive cotton, sugar, and rice plantations give a constant demand for coloured labourers.

Heart-rending separations of families are of very frequent occurrence, and even masters otherwise humane, when placed in difficulties, resort to it as a means of raising funds. In elucidating the following poem, which owes its deep pathos to those separations, we shall take a tale of recent and fearful interest, that of Emily Russel.

Nancy Cartwright, the mother of this slave-girl, was and is a respectable coloured woman, and has been for several years resident in New York. She had purchased her own freedom, and redeemed a part of her children from slavery by her own industry, aided by the liberality of friends. In January, 1850, Emily, still in slavery, wrote to her mother from the slave-pen of Bruin and Hill, in Alexandria, to inform her that she, Aunt Sally, with all her children, and Aunt Hagar, with all hers, were in Bruin's jail waiting purchasers, and grandmother almost crazy. "My dear mother," she adds, "will you please to come on as soon as you can; I expect to go away very shortly. O! mother, dear mother! come now and see your distressed and heart-broken daughter once more. Mother! my dear mother! do not forsake me, for I feel desolate. Please to come now. Your daughter—Emily Russel."

In reply to this appeal, Bruin and Hill were written to by the Editor of the *New York Tribune*, requesting to know at what price Emily would be sold to her mother, and how much time would be given the latter to make up the amount; also the prices at which they held the other members of the family. In the answer to this, Hagar and her seven children were valued at 2500 dollars; Sally and her four at 2800 dollars; while for Emily, the slave-dealer added, he could not take less than 1800 dollars. In his own words—" This may seem high to you, but cotton

---

Sold by W. and F. G. CASH, 5, Bishopsgate Street, London; and by JANE JOWETT, Friends' Meeting Yard, Leeds, at 1s. 2d. per 100.

being very high, slaves are high also. We have two or three offers from gentlemen in the south for Emily, who is said to be the finest-looking woman in the country. We expect to start with the negroes on the 8th of February, and if you intend doing anything, you had better do it soon."

The enormous sum placed on Emily was quite beyond the means of the afflicted mother; yet anxious to make a further effort, by her request a gentleman called at the slave-pen in Alexandria. He was received, he tells us, with a suavity of manners which would eclipse Lord Chesterfield, by Bruin himself, whom he describes as a middle-aged man, all smiles and politeness; very intelligent, and altogether wofully belying his profession. The conversation, during this interview, was heartless beyond expression on the part of the slave-dealer, and led to no arrangement. To raise 1800 dollars was to the mother impossible; when told this, and also that the friends had abandoned the hope of raising it, " I am glad of it," said he, " I don't want to send her north; I prefer that she should go to the south."

The mother, when compelled to give up all hope of redeeming her from the dreadful doom, and when she learned that the coffle had actually departed for the south, drooped like a stricken woman. Her mind was with her daughter—" Gone, gone, sold and gone," on her way to her frightful destiny. By a merciful dispensation of Providence, Emily Russel was spared the degradation and misery to which she seemed destined. She died in Georgia, according to the announcement of Bruin and Hill, before reaching the far southern market from which her soul so deeply revolted. The nature of her disease, and her sufferings in early dissolution, are alike a secret to us, but known well to Him who took her from the evil to come.

The news of her premature death was received by her mother with fervent thankfulness.

The narratives from which these facts are briefly stated, may be found more at length in the *North Star* newspapers for February 15, March 8, and May 10, 1850. They were current events of the year; Emily's first letter bearing date January 22, and her death being the news of the day in the last-mentioned paper.

———

" Behold and see if there is any sorrow like unto my sorrow"
(Lam. i. 12).

GONE, gone, sold and gone,
 To the rice-swamp dank and lone,
Where the slave-whip ceaseless swings,
Where the noisome insect stings,

Where the fever demon strews
Poison with the falling dews,
Where the sickly sunbeams glare
Through the hot and misty air.
>   Gone, gone, sold and gone,
>   To the rice-swamp dank and lone,
>   From Virginia's hills and waters,
>   Woe is me, my stolen daughters!

>   Gone, gone, sold and gone,
>   To the rice-swamp dank and lone.

There no mother's eye is near them,
There no mother's ear can hear them;
Never, when the torturing lash
Seams their back with many a gash,
Shall a mother's kindness bless them,
Or a mother's arms caress them.
>   Gone, gone, sold and gone,
>   To the rice-swamp dank and lone,
>   From Virginia's hills and waters,
>   Woe is me, my stolen daughters!

>   Gone, gone, sold and gone,
>   To the rice-swamp dank and lone,

O! when weary, sad, and slow,
From the fields at night they go,
Faint with toil, and rack'd with pain,
To their cheerless homes again,
There no brother's voice shall greet them,
There no father's welcome meet them.
>   Gone, gone, sold and gone,
>   To the rice-swamp dank and lone,
>   From Virginia's hills and waters,
>   Woe is me, my stolen daughters!

>   Gone, gone, sold and gone,
>   To the rice-swamp dank and lone,

From the tree whose shadow lay
On their childhood's place of play,
From the cool spring where they drank,
Rock, and hill, and rivulet bank,
From the solemn house of prayer,
And the holy counsels there.

Gone, gone, sold and gone,
To the rice-swamp dank and lone,
From Virginia's hills and waters,
Woe is me, my stolen daughters!

Gone, gone, sold and gone,
To the rice-swamp dank and lone,
Toiling through the weary day,
And at night the spoiler's prey.
O, that they had earlier died,
Sleeping calmly, side by side,
Where the tyrant's power is o'er,
And the fetter galls no more.
Gone, gone, sold and gone,
To the rice-swamp dank and lone,
From Virginia's hills and waters,
Woe is me, my stolen daughters!

Gone, gone, sold and gone,
To the rice-swamp dank and lone.
By the holy love He beareth,
By the bruised reed He spareth,
O, may He, to whom alone
All their cruel wrongs are known,
Still their hope and refuge prove,
With a more than mother's love.
Gone, gone, sold and gone,
To the rice-swamp dank and lone,
From Virginia's hills and waters,
Woe is me, my stolen daughters!

Americans!—We plead with you on behalf of three millions and a half of immortal beings whom you hold in bondage. We plead for the removal of the curse from their brow, the gall from their earthly cup, the chain from their limbs, the iron from their souls. We plead for the immediate, unqualified, and entire abolition of slavery throughout your land.

Leeds Anti-slavery Series. No. 10.

Sold by W. and F. G. Cash, 5, Bishopsgate Street, London; and by Jane Jowett, iends' Meeting Yard, Leeds, at 1s. 2d. per 100.

Leeds Anti-slavery Series. No. 11.

TRAFFIC IN HUMAN AFFECTIONS,

WITH REFLECTIONS THEREON.

EXTRACT FROM THE "REFLECTOR," DATED NASHVILLE, TENNESSEE, FROM AN EYE-WITNESS.

"This is a fine city, but it is a devoted slavery city. I witnessed a sale, a few days ago, of twelve negroes at auction, men, women, and children; husbands sold to go one way, and wives the other. One woman had four children; the oldest, eight years of age, a boy, who was to go off to one place, and his sister, six years old, to another. The other sister, only three years old, was sold to a slave-trader to go anywhere that he might sell her. The mother and infant were sold together—she wailing in agony for her children, and staying in the square all day, pleading for her child, only three years old, to go with her. By the interposition of several individuals, among whom was myself, this barbarian of a slave-trader was induced to let her go to the man who bought the mother, by being paid fifteen dollars for his bargain. Such is the cruelty of slavery. I can never forget the wails of that mother! Some that were sold were half white, and the auctioneer dwelt long upon the circumstance, *to get a better price.* There are plenty of slaves here whiter than I am."

A HARD-HEARTED PRESBYTERIAN.

An American paper relates the following case:—
"A Presbyterian elder, in *good and regular standing* (!), among his goods and chattels, owned a young female, who is a member of the Congregational Baptist Church. This female displeased her master in some way, as a punishment for which

---

Sold by W. and F. G. CASH, 5, Bishopsgate Street, London; and by JANE JOWETT, Friends' Meeting Yard, Leeds, at 1s. 2d. per 100.

offence he forthwith gave her into the hands of the slave-traders, who took her over to Alexandria, and incarcerated her, with others, in a slave-pen, where she was to remain until a full drove was made up for the southern market. When spoken to upon the subject, the elder excused himself by charging her with crime. The girl protested her innocence, and desired, and even begged for a trial. This poor slave had a mother, who was also in bonds. When apprized of the situation of her daughter, she flew to the pen, and with tears besought an interview with her only child, but she was cruelly repulsed. She then tried to see the elder, but failed. Although she was a slave, she was a woman of no ordinary power of mind. Failing to see the master of her child, she addressed to him a letter, the concluding paragraph of which we subjoin:—

"'Suppose now, for a moment, that *your* daughter, whom you love, instead of mine, was, in these hot days, incarcerated in a *negro-pen*, subject to my control, eaten by vermin, fed on the coarsest food, committed to the entire will of a brute, denied the privilege commonly allowed even to the murderer, that of seeing the face of his friends—O! then you would FEEL! Feel now, then, for a poor slave-mother and her child, and do for us as you shall wish you had done when we shall meet before the Great Judge; and when it shall be your greatest joy to say, "I *did* let the oppressed go free." 'ELLEN BROWN.'

"Ellen Brown had almost sufficient money to purchase her daughter's freedom, but her owner would listen to no terms of compromise, as the elder said he wanted her out of his sight, as far south as she could be got."

EXTRACTS FROM THE LIFE OF FREDERICK DOUGLASS.

"My mother and I were separated when I was but an infant. It is a common custom in the part of Maryland from which I ran away, to part children from their mothers at a very early age. I never saw my mother, to know her as such, more than four or five times in my life, and each of these times was very short in duration, and at night. She was a field hand, and lived some miles from my home. A whipping being the penalty for not being in the field at sunrise, she made her journey to see me in the night, travelling the whole distance on foot, after the performance of the day's work. She would lie down with me, and get me to sleep, but long before I waked she was gone. I was not allowed to be present during her illness, at her death or burial. She was dead long before I knew anything about it."

REFLECTIONS ON THE ABOVE, DESIGNED FOR A MOTHER.

In the above extracts, we are presented with a few of the affecting circumstances attached by a *cruel necessity* to the condition of slavery, but few as they are, they make a direct and powerful appeal to the heart of a mother. Surely those among us who have hitherto bestowed no attention upon this subject, would act a kind part toward their coloured sisters, to enter at once upon the consideration of their wrongs. They would be undoubtedly pained, and deeply pained, at the information they would thus gain; but be it remembered, that if we did *not* fix our attention upon social evils, even though it gives pain to do so, they would flow on for ever, swelling and deepening the tide of human corruption and misery. Let each mother, then, ask herself these questions: Can I do nothing, *absolutely nothing*, to stem this tide, either by taking direct action upon moral questions, or by the honest expression of a lively concern for the sufferers from man's cruelty ? Ought I not, at least, to cultivate most assiduously that genuine love of my kind, and of social order and virtue, which would dictate earnest prayer to the Great Ruler of all events, to expand that virtue, to establish that order, and to deepen that love ? These questions cannot be deemed idle and unimportant, for they bear directly upon the heart-sickening system of slavery. I have here before me a touching instance of the strength of maternal love, in the great physical exertion which it enabled a mother to undergo, in order to obtain brief and hasty intercourse with her child. To pass it by with indifference would only prove me to be cold and unsympathising in regard to the most tender and powerful yearnings of nature. I am a mother; and I cannot look upon my own child, love its caresses, rejoice in its smiles, and pray for its welfare, without feeling the treasured privileges of the maternal position. When these privileges are outraged, and a mother is forcibly separated, not only from her child, but from her husband, how deep is the wrong, and how intense the agony that must be endured. Yet how frequently is this wrong perpetrated. Infants are torn from their mother's arms, and they see them no more. Let me reflect, also, horrible as it sounds, that it is a fact, *incapable of refutation*, that they have been, and still are, sometimes sold to PURCHASE BIBLES! Yes, in the name of that Saviour who came to establish a *kingdom of love* (and who would have allowed no cruel prejudice against colour to have obstructed the comprehensive benevolence of his invitation, "Suffer little children to come unto me, and forbid them not"), the holiest tie of nature is ruptured without one pitying thought of the being whose bosom that rupture tears. Is *this* a system in the utter destruction of which a Christian mother should show no interest, and take no part? Her duties may indeed present a barrier to her bestowing much, either of time or work, for promoting its overthrow; but she may watch the cause of emancipation, and collect information upon it, with feelings of interest. Her sympathies are at least unfettered; these let me, as a mother, exercise and strengthen, inasmuch as we are commanded "to weep with those who weep, as well as to rejoice with those that rejoice." While I gladly do the one, let me not evade the other, or imagine that genuine concern for the distressed, felt and expressed, does no good, even where we have nothing else to offer.

> "The slave, the slave hath many wrongs,
> Where might her pleader be?"

Our opinions, our sympathies influence our friends; and it should *never* be forgotten, that the whole gigantic mass of wrongs connected with slavery is, under Providence, destined to fall by the roused and indignant force of enlightened humanity. May those who are enabled to engage *actively* in this righteous cause be strengthened from above, and fixed with a holy constancy upon accomplishing the abolition of that system, which as unquestionably lays the burden of *sin* upon the *enslaver* as that of suffering upon the enslaved.

Leeds Anti-slavery Series. No. 11.

Sold by W. and F. G. CASH, 5, Bishopsgate Street, London; and by JANE JOWETT, Friends' Meeting Yard, Leeds, at 1*s*. 2*d*. per 100.

Leeds Anti-slavery Series. No. 12.

ALLEGED EXAGGERATIONS

OF SLAVERY CONSIDERED.

It is often remarked by those who *hear much*, but *know little* of slavery, "that its atrocities are over-stated; that it is against the interest of the masters to overtask their slaves (be it remembered that, under overseership, many a brutal deed is committed of which the master knows nothing); that they are as well off as many of the labouring classes elsewhere," &c.

With such off-hand assertions do the unthinking supply sedatives to their consciences in regard to this momentous subject. But where is the ground for such lulling and quieting conclusions? Consider what man *is*, and *has been*. Hear what the Inquisition says: The rack—the wheel—the burning pile! Do they not all tell us that, when entrusted with irresponsible power over others, he has proved himself a savage? Do not let us be misunderstood. God forbid that we should think so ill of human nature, as to believe that where a man has the power he has *always* the *inclination* to work unrighteousness, or to do the cruel and atrocious deed. No doubt, in some kind and compassionate natures, this power may have been exercised for at least the *temporal* good of its object. So far it is well, but let us never lose sight of this point—that whereas in regard to many *other* institutions, customs, and practices in society, their *abuse* may be said to afford no argument against their *use*, yet with regard to *irresponsible power over man*, the *good* use to which the master may *occasionally* apply it, ought not to close our eyes to the truth that it is *inherently* a fearful and vicious principle of legislation. Passionate, cruel, and vindictive, as man too often is, even when the restraining hand of the law is upon him, what must we not expect where this power is *not in force, not in existence;* and this *is* the case in many a deep wrong committed against the person of the slave. It argues a childish ignorance of human nature, not to know that instead of *overstatement* of the slave's wrongs, there must be a long catalogue of unrighteous and ferocious acts *not* revealed to public view, unrolled to that Eye alone who "marks the man that treads his fellow down." Go into the details of what slavery *was* in our own colonies, and, while the accounts are such as to freeze the blood with horror, and to "interpose a shade between the eye of piety and heaven," ask yourselves whether the vicious and ungoverned, be they where they will, make a better use of irresponsible power over man now than they did then. Alas! there are but too many proofs that they do not, proofs already before the British public, and which, therefore, need not be given in any great number here. The awakened and repentant sympathy of that public snapped asunder the chain which bound the limbs of their fellow-man, and Britain received, in return, the tribute of eight hundred thousand grateful and loving hearts. This example, however, should never be quoted by us without modesty, since it was but the late reparation of a deep wrong—which wrong, America tells us, and with too much truth, entailed the guilt of slavery upon *her*. Let the penitent mother, therefore, ask pardon of her child, who is yet in her sin, nor let that child turn away unmoved, while she tells of the joys of an approving conscience, and a bosom unburdened of heavy guilt. Americans! we repent of our sin, and repent of having made you partakers of it. Refuse not companionship with us in the better way, but, listening to the voice of humanity, manifest, in a manner *still nobler*, the power of its appeal. The number of slaves which *we* liberated at a distance from our shores, was small compared with the number whom you behold shackled with chains in the land of your birth, and frequently passing by the doors of your habitations. *Three millions* speak to you of wretchedness, of thraldom, and of death. Listen to them, we beseech you. Summon to your aid all that is great and good within you (and we gladly own that you have much of both), to enable you to forego unrighteous gain. Break their bonds, and prove to an admiring and applauding world, that not in *theory* but in *practice* you grant to every man "life, liberty, and the pursuit of happiness."

Leeds Anti-slavery Series. No. 12.

Sold by W. and F. G. Cash, 5, Bishopsgate Street, London; and by Jane Jowett Friend's Meeting-Yard, Leeds, at 7*d*. per 100.

Leeds Anti-slavery Series. No. 13.

THE NEGRO OUR BROTHER MAN.

WE are told, on the highest authority, that "God hath made of one blood all the nations of men;" and that all are equally regarded by the Almighty, who is no respecter of persons. "I am fully convinced," says Mungo Park, the great African traveller, "that whatever difference there is between the European and the Negro in conformation and colour, there is none in the genuine sympathies and characteristic feelings of our common nature." Hence the appropriateness of the following lines of the poet Montgomery:—

HERE dwells the Negro, nature's outcast child;
Scorned by his brethren; but his mother's eye,
That gazes on him from her warmest sky,
Sees in his flexile limbs untutored grace,
Power on his forehead, beauty in his face;
Sees in his breast, where lawless passions rove,
The heart of friendship and the home of love;
Sees in his mind, where desolation reigns,
Fierce as his clime, uncultured as his plains,
A soil where virtue's fairest flowers might shoot,
And trees of science bend with glorious fruit;
Sees in his soul, involved with thickest night,
An emanation of eternal light,
Ordained, 'midst sinking worlds, his dust to fire,
And shine for ever when the stars expire.
Is he not *man*, though knowledge never shed
Her quickening beams on his neglected head?
Is he not *man*, though sweet religion's voice
Ne'er made the mourner in his God rejoice?
Is *he* not man, by sin and suffering tried?
Is *he* not man, for whom the Saviour died?
Belie the negro's powers:—in headlong will,
Christian! *thy* brother thou shalt prove him still:
Belie his virtues; since his wrongs began,
His follies and his crimes have stamp'd him man.

Leeds Anti-slavery Series. No. 13.

Sold by W. and F. G. CASH, 5, Bishopsgate Street, London; and by JANE JOWETT, Friends' Meeting Yard, Leeds, at 6*d.* per 100.

Leeds Anti-slavery Series. No. 14.

THE DEATH OF THE SLAVE.
BY MARIA LOWELL.

In a low and ill-thatched hut,
   Stretched on a floor of clay,
With scanty clothing round her wrapped,
   The dying woman lay.

No husband's kindly hand,
   No loving child was near,
To offer her their aid, or shed
   A sympathizing tear.

For now the ripened cane
   Was ready for the knife,
And not a slave could be spared to aid
   His mother or his wife.

She is struggling now with death,
   Deep was that dying groan,
For a corpse now lies on the cold clay floor,
   The soul, set free, has flown.

The planter, walking by,
   Chanced at the door to stop,
And he cursed his luck, "there was one hand less
   To gather in the crop."

O, Jesus! thou hast said,
   "The poor your care shall be:
Who visit not the poor and sick,
   They do it not to me."

Leeds Anti-slavery Series. No. 14.

Sold by W. and F. G. CASH, 5, Bishopsgate Street, London; and by JANE JOWETT, Friends' Meeting Yard, Leeds, at 6d. per 100.

Leeds Anti-slavery Series. No. 15.

AUCTIONEERING ADVERTISEMENTS.

"AUCTION SALES.
" Slaves !   Slaves !   Slaves !
" BY BEARD, CALHOUN, & Co. J. A. Beard, Auctioneer.
"Thursday, May 10th, 1849, will be sold at auction, at 12 o'clock, at Banks' Arcade, 15 SLAVES, comprising cooks, washers, ironers, nurses, labourers, field-hands, mechanics.
" Full particulars of each Slave will be given at the sale.
" *Credit Sale of choice Servants.*
"Thursday, 10th May, 1849, at 12 o'clock, at Banks' Arcade, will be sold at auction, the following valuable servants, belonging to a family in the city, namely:—MARY, aged 15½ years, a valuable house-girl, nurse, and excellent serving-girl. SOPHIA, aged 20 years, a washer, ironer, American cook, and superior house-servant. JOHN, aged 35 years, an excellent ostler and driver.
" *Terms:*—One-fourth cash, balance in a note, payable the 1st December, 1849, endorsed to the satisfaction of the vender, with interest at 6 per cent. per annum from date till paid.
" Also, the negro man HARRISON, aged about 30 years, a first-rate finishing plasterer.
" *Terms:*—One-fourth cash; balance six and twelve months' credit, for notes endorsed to the satisfaction of the vender, bearing mortgage on the property, with 6 per cent. interest from date to maturity. Should any note not be paid promptly, to bear interest at the rate of 8 per cent. per annum.
" The above Slaves are fully guaranteed against the vices and maladies prescribed by law."—*New Orleans Paper*, 1849.

Advertisements, similar to the above, both of purchasers and venders of men, women, and children, abound in the most respectable newspapers in the Slave States of America ; and heart-rending scenes, arising from the separation of family ties, are of daily occurrence. What a scandal upon a professedly civilized Christian country !

Leeds Anti-slavery Series. No. 15.
Sold by W. and F. G. CASH, 5, Bishopsgate Street, London; and by JANE JOWETT, Friends' Meeting Yard, Leeds, at 6*d.* per 100.

Leeds Anti-slavery Series. No. 16.

A SLAVE AUCTION IN A SOUTHERN CITY.

"I TURNED to look for the doomed. She stood upon the auction stand. In stature she was of the middle size, slim, and delicately built. Her skin was lighter than many a northern *brunette*, and her features were round, with thin lips. Indeed, many thought no black blood coursed in her veins. Now, despair sat on her countenance. O! I shall never forget that look. 'Good heavens!' ejaculated one of the two fathers, as he beheld the features of Helen, 'is that beautiful lady to be sold?'

"Then fell upon my ear the auctioneer's cry, 'How much is said for this beautiful healthy slave-girl—a real albino—a fancy girl for any gentleman? How much? How much? Who bids?' 'Five hundred dollars,' 'Eight hundred,' 'One thousand,' were soon bid by different purchasers. The last was made by the friends of the merchant, as they wished to assist him to retain her. At first, no one seemed disposed to raise the bid. The crier then read from a paper in his hand, 'She is intelligent, well-informed, easy to communicate, a first-rate instructress.' 'Who raises the bid?' This had the desired effect—'Twelve hundred,' 'Fourteen,' 'Sixteen,' quickly followed. He read again—'She is a devoted Christian, sustains the best of morals, and is perfectly trusty.' This raised the bids to two thousand dollars, at which she was struck off to the gentleman in favour of whom was the prosecution. Here closed one of the darkest scenes in the book of time.

"'This was a southern auction—an auction at which the bones, muscles, sinews, blood, and nerves, of a young lady of nineteen, sold for one thousand dollars; her improved intellect for six hundred more; and her Christianity—the person of Christ in his follower—four hundred more."—*Letter in Anti-Slavery Reporter.* How long shall these things be tolerated?

Leeds Anti-slavery Series. No. 16.
Sold by W. and F. G. CASH, 5, Bishopsgate Street, London; and by JANE JOWETT, Friends' Meeting Yard, Leeds, at 6*d.* per 100.

DEPOSITING THE ASHES OF GENERAL NAPOLEON IN THE CHURCH OF THE INVALIDES AT PARIS.

Leeds Anti-slavery Series. No. 17.

SALE OF AGED NEGROES.

"I WAS staying a few days at Winnsboro', South Carolina, and, on the sale day, had the curiosity to walk to the auction stand, where I saw an aged negro and his wife exposed for sale. They were almost worn out with stripes and hard usage; and the woolly heads of both were nearly white. The old negro was more than 70, his wife a year or two younger. They were knocked down for 13 dollars. This sum appears, indeed, trifling as the price of two human beings; but the fact is, they would (commercially speaking) have been dear at a gift."—*Report of an English Traveller.*

A WOMAN SOLD FOR A JACKASS.—"Mr. Moore, sometime ago, was a citizen of Todd County, Kentucky. He was, and is still a local preacher in the M. E. Church, in good standing. A short time before he left Todd County, he sold a *woman* for a jackass. He then traded the jackass to Mr. J. H. Robins of Trigg County, Kentucky, for a house and some land in Woodford County, Illinois. Moore told Robins that he gave a woman and a child for the jack; but when Robins inquired into the matter, he found that Moore traded on Saturday, and that the child was born on Monday afterwards! So the child was sold for a jackass, before it was born, and by a professed preacher of the Gospel!!"—*Western Citizen.*

"A person informs the Christian people of St. Louis, that he will sell a superior *Maltese Jack*, and receive in payment goods or NEGROES! Said Jack is said to be 14 hands high, and therefore, in the estimation of his owner, equivalent to several of God's living images. O humanity! Give this proposition a sober thought. 'How much better is a man than a sheep?' asked he who lived and died for man. How much better is an ass than a man? asks the owner of the one, of the owner of the other, in the market of a Christian city."

Leeds Anti-slavery Series. No. 17.
Sold by W. and F. G. CASH, 5, Bishopsgate Street, London; and by JANE JOWETT, Friends' Meeting Yard, Leeds, at 6d. per 100.

Leeds Anti-slavery Series. No. 18.

BUSINESS LETTER FROM A SLAVE-TRADER
OF NORTH CAROLINA.

SINCE the discontinuance of the African slave-trade, some parts of America have become great breeding districts, in which human cattle are raised for the southern market. The following is a specimen of the style of correspondence of gentlemen engaged in this commerce. It is from a North Carolina merchant to his consignee at New Orleans:—

"Halifax, North Carolina, Nov. 16, 1839.
"DEAR SIR,—I have shipped in the brig, *Addison*, prices as below:—

No.		Dollars.	No.		Dollars.
1.	Caroline Ennis,	650	4.	Maria Pollock,	475
2.	Silvy Holland,	625	5.	Emeline Pollock,	475
3.	Silvy Booth,	487·50	6.	Delia Averitt,	475

"The two girls that cost 650 and 625 dollars, were bought before I shipped my first. I have a great many negroes offered to me, but I will not pay the prices they ask, for I know they will come down. I have no opposition in market. I will wait until I hear from you before I buy, and then I can judge what I must pay. Goodwin will send you the bill of lading for my negroes, as he shipped them with his own. Write often, as the times are critical, and it depends on the prices you get, to govern me in buying.—Yours, &c., G. W. BARNES.
"Mr. THEOPHILUS FREEMAN, New Orleans."

The above was a small, but choice invoice of wives and mothers. Nine days before Mr. Barnes advised Mr. Freeman of having shipped a lot of 43 men and women, Mr. Freeman, informing one of his correspondents of the state of the market, writes (*Sunday*, 21st Sept., 1839)—

"I bought a boy yesterday, 16 years old, and likely, *weighing* 110 lbs., at 700 dollars. I sold a likely girl, 12 years old, at 500 dollars. I bought a man yesterday, 20 years old, six feet high, at 820 dollars; one to-day (*Sunday*), 24 years old, at 850 dollars, black and sleek as a mole."

Thus do the brokers in human flesh, and butchers of human hearts,
"Guage and span,
And buy the muscles and the bones of man!"

The American government prohibits the trading of slaves from Africa, yet makes it lawful to buy a fellow-countryman, and possibly a fellow-Christian, in North Carolina, and sell him in New Orleans. What wicked inconsistency!

Leeds Anti-slavery Series. No. 18.
Sold by W. and F. G. CASH, 5, Bishopsgate Street, London; and by JANE JOWETT, Friends' Meeting Yard, Leeds, at 6d. per 100.

Leeds Anti-Slavery Series. No. 19.

UNFAVOURABLE

INFLUENCE OF THE AMERICAN CHURCHES

ON THE PROGRESS OF EMANCIPATION.

If anywhere the slave should find a friend, it should be in the person of a minister of religion. He at least should be ready to extend to all the blessings of civil and religious liberty, and to do to others as he would have others to do to him. Unfortunately in America this is not the case. Men assume the name of Christ in that country, and sanction slavery, and are often slave-owners themselves. Nearly the whole American church is tainted in this respect. So late as September 11, we read, in the *Watchman* of that date—" Slavery in America is not only the danger of the Union, but the peril of the churches. It is lamentable to observe, that the Methodist Episcopal churches of the northern States have come to no unanimous opinion on the relation of slaveholding to Christian membership. The Erie Conference respectfully requests the next General Conference to amend its decisions on the subject, so as to decide that ' no slaveholder shall be eligible to membership in our church hereafter—where emancipation can be effected without injury to the slave.' But how is this exception to be defined and applied? The Black River and Oneida Conferences are for the exclusion of all slaveholders from the church, without any regard to their peculiar situation, circumstances, and difficulties. The resolutions of the former of these Conferences are characterised as being so violent, that the presiding bishop declined to sign the journal of proceedings, unless he might be permitted to enter his individual protest against them." Not only have many of the churches failed to protest against the sin and shame of slavery, but actually many of the pastors of American churches have

---

Sold by W. and F. G. CASH, 5, Bishopsgate Street, London; and by JANE JOWETT, Friends' Meeting Yard, Leeds, at 2s. 3d. per 100.

lifted their voice in its defence. Evidence of this character we present without comment:—In some of the older slave States, as Virginia and South Carolina, churches, in their *corporate* character, hold slaves, who are generally hired out for the support of the minister. The following is taken from the *Charleston Courier* of February 12, 1835 :—" Field Negroes, by Thomas Gadsdon.—On Tuesday, the 17th instant, will be sold, at the north of the Exchange, at ten o'clock, a prime gang of ten negroes, accustomed to the culture of cotton and provisions, belonging to the Independent Church in Christ Church Parish. . . . . . February 6."

At Charleston, South Carolina, where, in 1835, the abolitionists became active, a public meeting was held to complete, in the same spirit in which they were commenced, preparations for excluding anti-slavery publications from circulation, and for ferreting out persons suspected of favouring the doctrines of the abolitionists, that they may be subjected to Lynch law. At this assembly, the *Charleston Courier* informs us, " The clergy of all denominations attended in a body, lending their sanction to the proceedings, and adding, by their presence, to the impressive character of the scene." It was there resolved, " That the thanks of this meeting are due to the reverend gentlemen of the clergy in this city, who have so promptly and so effectually responded to public sentiment, by suspending their schools in which the *free coloured population* were taught; and that this meeting deem it a patriotic action worthy of all praise, and proper to be imitated by other teachers of similar schools throughout the State."

The alarm of the Virginia slaveholders was not less, nor were the clergy in the city of Richmond, the capital, less prompt than the clergy in Charleston to respond to " public sentiment;" accordingly, on July 29, they assembled together and resolved, unanimously, " That we earnestly deprecate the unwarrantable and highly improper interference of the people of any other State with the domestic relations of master and slave." We now turn to the testimony of ministers :—

The Rev. N. Bangs, D.D., Wesleyan minister, New York, says, " However much the apostles might have deprecated slavery, he did not feel it his duty to disturb those relations which subsisted between master and servant, by denouncing slavery as a mortal sin." Rev. E. D. Simms (Wesleyan), says, "Holy Writ unequivocally asserts the right of property in slaves; whether we consult the Jewish polity, or the New Testament and the moral law, it is evident that slavery is not immoral. The slavery which exists in America is founded in right."— Rev. W. Winans (Wesleyan), says he has become a slaveholder on principle; "Presbyterians, Baptists, Methodists, should be slaveholders; yes—he repeated it boldly—there should be members, and *deacons*, and ELDERS, and BISHOPS, too, who were slaveholders."—Rev. J. H. Thornwell (Wesleyan), says, "Slavery is no evil, and is consistent with the principles of revealed religion; all opposition to it arises from fiendish fanaticism." —Rev. George W. Langhorne (Wesleyan), writes, "that he would as soon be found in the ranks of banditti, as numbered with the slavery abolitionists."—Rev. J. C. Postell (Wesleyan), argues that "slavery, so far from being a moral evil, is a merciful visitation, and subsists by Divine appointment." The same reverend gentleman, in a letter to *Zion's Watchman*, subscribes himself "the friend of the Bible and the opposer of abolitionists."—Rev. Mr. Crowder (Wesleyan), of Virginia, says, "Slavery was not only countenanced, permitted, and regulated by the Bible, but it was positively instituted by God himself; he, in so many words, enjoined it."—The Rev. Lucius Bolles, D.D. (Baptist), says, "There is a pleasing degree of union among the multiplying thousands of Baptists throughout the south, both ministers and people are generally slaveholders."—Rev. Dr. Furman, (Baptist), says, "the right of holding slaves is clearly established in the Holy Scriptures, both by precept and example."—In the memorial, addressed by the Charleston Baptist Association to the legislature of South Carolina, the following remarks occur :—" The Divine Author of our holy religion found slavery a part of the existing institutions of society, with which, if not sinful, it was not his design to intermeddle, but to leave them entirely to the control of men. The question of slavery is purely one of political economy; whether the operatives of a country shall be bought and sold, and themselves become property, as in this State; or whether they shall be hirelings, and their labour only become property, as in other States. The right of a master to dispose of the time of his slaves has been distinctly recognised by the

Creator of all things, who is surely at liberty to invest the right of property over any object in whomsoever he pleases."—Dr. Gardiner Spring (Presbyterian), says, "If by one prayer I could liberate every slave in the world, I would not offer it."— Rev. Dr. Parker (Presbyterian), says, "Abolition might be pronounced a sin as well as slavery."—The late Rev. Dr. Rice said he was fully convinced that slavery was the greatest evil in the country, except *whisky*.—Speaking of the abolition movement, Rev. Dr. Plummer (Presbyterian), says, "Let the character of the abolitionist be what it may in the sight of the Judge of all the earth, it is my belief that the movement is the most meddlesome, impudent, reckless, fierce, and wicked excitement I ever saw."—Rev. T. Witherspoon (Presbyterian), says, "I draw my warrant from the Old and New Testament to hold the slave in bondage. I go to the Bible for all my warrantries in moral matters. Lynch law is one of the most wholesome and salutary remedies for the malady of the abolitionists, and if they dare to venture across the Potomac, I cannot promise that their fate will be less than Haman's."—Rev. R. Anderson says, "If there be any stray goat of a minister among you, tainted with the blood-hound principles of abolitionism, let him be ferreted out, silenced, excommunicated, and left to the public to dispose of him in other respects."—"What effect," asks the Right Rev. Bishop Hopkins, of Vermont, "had the Bible in doing away with slavery? *None whatever.*" Bishop Bowen, of Charleston, denounces the abolition movement as "malignant philanthropy." Rev. W. Rogers says, "If resistance to the carrying out the Fugitive Slave Law should lead the magistracy to call the citizens to arms, their duty was to obey; and if ordered to take human life, in the name of God to take it."—Rev. Orwille Dewey, a distinguished Unitarian Divine, declares "that he would send his own brother or child into slavery, if needed, to preserve the union between the free and slaveholding states." W. S. Seabrooke, of South Carolina, says, "In the judgment of my fellow-citizens, slavery is not inconsistent with the laws of nature and of God. The Bible informs us that it was established and sanctioned by Divine authority, even among the elect of heaven."—Edward Brown, of the same place, says, "Slavery has been the stepladder by which civilized countries have passed from barbarism to civilization. It appears, indeed, to be the only state capable of bringing the love of independence and ease, inherent in man, to the discipline necessary to the supply of food, raiment, and shelter necessary to his physical wants."—Dr. Dalcho assures us, that " as slavery is not directly forbidden by the Divine law, it is left to our own judgment whether we hold slaves or not." —The *Charleston Courier* says, "We confidently pronounce that he must wilfully shut his eyes against the broad and palpable light of truth, who will not acknowledge that the Old Testament conclusively shows that slavery was not only not condemned, but received the *express sanction* of the God of Abraham, of Isaac, and of Jacob."—" We deny," says the Episcopalian Dr. Duer, " that it is a crime to retain in slavery those ignorant and helpless beings who have been cast upon American protection, as well as thrown into American power, by no act of their own."—Rev. G. W. Freeman says, "No man, or set of men in our day, are entitled to pronounce it wrong. Slavery, as it exists at the present day, is agreeable to the order of Divine providence."—Professor Whedon (Methodist), says, " There were Christian or believing slaveholders in the primitive Christian church, who were brethren, faithful and well-beloved, partakers of the gospel benefit."—Governor Macduffie says, " God forbid that my descendants, in the remotest generations, should live in any other than a community having the institution of domestic slavery."—The editor of the *Washington Telegraph* says, "As a man, a Christian, and a citizen, we believe that slavery is right; that the condition of the slaves, as it now exists in the slaveholding states, is the best existing organisation of civil society."—The Rev. James Smylie, A.M., a Presbyterian minister in Mississippi, says, in a pamphlet he has recently published in favour of American slavery, "If slavery be a sin, and if advertising and apprehending slaves, with a view to restore them to their masters, is a direct violation of the Divine law, and if the buying, selling, or holding a slave for the sake of gain is a heinous sin and scandal, then, verily, three-fourths of all the Episcopalians, Methodists, Baptists, and Presbyterians, in eleven states of the Union, are of the devil. They 'hold,' if they do not buy and sell slaves, and, with few exceptions, they hesitate not to 'apprehend and restore' runaway slaves when in their power."

Thus we see slavery corrupting and blighting the American church everywhere. The societies formed for the spread of the gospel of the free have actually succumbed to the monster evil. If we turn to the Tract, Missionary, and Bible Societies, Sunday School Union, &c., we find all these bodies have slaveholding members.

The Tract Society employs seven steam-presses, but refuses to print any tract on the slavery question.

The Board of Commissioners for Foreign Missions, throughout its extensive operations, never treats slavery as a sin.

The Parent Sunday School Union, at the requirement of the slave power, suppressed one of its volumes because it contained a paragraph descriptive of slavery.

The Home Mission Society, though sustained chiefly by the north, has been active in planting slaveholding churches in the south.

The Baptist Home Mission Society has planted slaveholding churches in the south, and refuses to treat slavery as a sin.

The American Baptist Missionary Union was organised for the purpose of fraternizing with slaveholders; they are members of the body, and of the mission churches in the Cherokee Territory. To the extent of its power, this " Union " crushes anti-slavery energy and sympathy.

The American Bible Society, and the American and Foreign Bible Society, make no appeal in behalf of the slave's destitution, and Bible-withholding despots are members of both bodies.

The American Bible Union is controlled by its slaveholding members, so are the societies to convert the Jews, the Indians, &c.

Well may we exclaim, " Alas, how is the gold become dim!" nay, indeed, it is changed, it is not gold now. The slaveholding, slave-countenancing religion of America has lost its resemblance to Christianity proper. We recognise between these religions the widest possible difference; so wide, that to receive the one as good, pure, and holy, is, of necessity, to reject the other as bad, corrupt, and wicked. To call the slaveholding, slavery-countenancing religion the religion of Christianity, must be looked upon as the climax of all misnomers, the boldest of all frauds, and the grossest of all libels.

" 1 am filled with unutterable loathing," says Douglass, the fugitive slave, "when I contemplate the religious pomp and show, together with the horrible inconsistencies, which coexist in the slave states. They have men-stealers for ministers, women-whippers for missionaries, and cradle-plunderers for church-members. The man who wields the blood-clotted cowskin during the week fills the pulpit on Sunday, and claims to be a minister of the meek and lowly Jesus. The man who robs me of my earnings at the end of each week, meets me as a class-leader on Sunday morning, to show me the way of life and the path of salvation. He who sells my sister for purposes of prostitution, stands forth as the pious advocate of purity. He who proclaims it a religious duty to read the Bible, denies me the right of learning to read the name of the God who made me. He who is the religious advocate of marriage, robs whole millions of its sacred influence, and leaves them to the ravages of whole-sale pollution. The warm defender of the sacrednesss of the family relation, is the same that scatters whole families, sundering husbands and wives, parents and children, sisters and brothers, leaving the hut vacant and the hearth desolate. We see the thief preaching against theft, and the adulterer against adultery. We have men sold to build churches, women sold to support the gospel, and babes sold to purchase Bibles for the *poor heathen! all for the glory of God and the good of souls!* The slave auctioneer's bell and the church-going bell chime in with each other, and the bitter cries of the heart-broken slave are drowned in the religious shouts of his pious master. Revivals of religion and revivals in the slave-trade go hand in hand together. The slave prison and the church stand near each other. The clanking of fetters and the rattling of chains in the prison, and the pious psalm and the solemn prayer in the church may be heard at the same time. The dealers in the bodies and souls of men, erect their stand in the presence of the pulpit, and they mutually help each other. The dealer gives his blood-stained gold to support the pulpit, and the pulpit, in return, covers his infernal business with the garb of Christianity. There we behold religion and robbery the allies of each other."

The Christianity of America is a Christianity of whose votaries it may be truly said, " Ye bind heavy burdens and grievous to be borne, and lay them on men's shoulders, but ye yourselves will not move them with one of your fingers." Professing much love for the heathen on the other side of the globe, they pray for him, pay money to have the Bible put into his hand, and missionaries to instruct him, while they despise and totally neglect the heathen at their own doors.

"*Heathenism*," says the *Western Summary*, a Kentucky paper, "*is as real in the slave states* as it is in the South Sea Islands, and our negroes are as justly objects of attention to the American and other boards of missions, as the Indians of the western wilds." The synod of South Carolina and Georgia said in 1834:—"The negroes are destitute of the gospel, and *ever will be,* under the present state of things."—"The coloured population may justly be considered *the heathen* of this Christian country, and will bear comparison with heathen in any country in the world."—" There are" ("within the bounds of our Synod") "at least one hundred thousand slaves, speaking the same language as ourselves, who *never heard* of the plan of salvation by a Redeemer."—*Charleston Observer.*

So long as this state of things continues, ought not the language to be, "Cry aloud and spare not!" When abolitionists are asked why they denounce the churches, justly do they answer, "Because they are teaching a horrible doctrine, and sustaining horrible crimes. When the church buys, sells, and heathenizes God's children, and blasphemously appeals to the name of Christ as its sanction, no language is strong enough to describe it. Talk of their piety! Though their prayers were longer than the Pharisees, and their praises were solemn and unceasing, it is all a mockery while they trample on God's image. Judge ye therefore what is Christianity, and give not the holy name to that which violates its laws, and has none of its spirit.

———— " Just God, and holy!
Is that church, which lends
Strength to the spoiler, Thine?"

Leeds Anti-Slavery Series. No. 19.

Sold by W. and F. G. CASH, 5, Bishopsgate Street, London; and by JANE JOWETT, Friends' Meeting Yard, Leeds, at 2s. 3d. per 100.

Leeds Anti-Slavery Series. No. 20.

EXPURGATED AMERICAN LITERATURE.

MUTILATION AND SUPPRESSION OF WORKS CONTAINING ANTI-SLAVERY SENTIMENTS.

COMMON literature is antagonistic to slavery. There is something that must not be allowed to enter the mind, which must not be admitted into educational courses, which it is dangerous to allow even to a general reader—in nearly all the writings of the good and great. America needs, and is expressing her need of, an expurgated literature, in which dangerous sentiments shall all have been carefully eschewed. The obliterating of portions of the reprints of works which contain anti-slavery sentiments is carried to a great extent, as well as the entire suppression of similar works.

A *History of the American Church* (see Tract No. 22), written by the Bishop of Oxford, a dignitary of the mother church, distinguished alike by his honoured name and elevated rank, is almost unknown in America. The concealment of Dr. Wilberforce's work is obviously intentional, and not accidental. The tracts and volumes issued by theological writers in England are republished and eagerly perused in America. Yet here is a history of themselves, in no small degree eulogistic, and, on various accounts, claiming their attention, which has been virtually suppressed. The very title of the book, and the name of the author, would have secured a rapid sale for a reprint. But it contained certain statements on the subject of slavery and caste in the church, which could not be admitted without sealing the condemnation of almost every sect in the state, and overwhelming them with shame and confusion.

In 1832, the American Sunday-School Union published a series of small books, containing an account of some of the most interesting persons and principal events mentioned in the Old

Sold by W. and F. G. CASH, 5, Bishopsgate Street, London; and by JANE JOWETT, Friends' Meeting Yard, Leeds, at 1s. 2d. per 100.

Testament; written in a style adapted to the comprehension of children, and calculated to impress the young mind with a knowledge of the history of the Israelites from Abraham to the birth of the Saviour. One of these volumes, *The Story of Isaac,* and of *Jacob and his Sons,* was stereotyped, and for more than seventeen years was one of the most popular of the series. But, during 1848, a slaveholding Vice-President of the American Sunday-School Union, residing in South Carolina, discovered that a certain passage in *Jacob and his Sons* was discourteous towards the 'peculiar institution,' and immediately wrote to head-quarters, and demanded that the circulation of the offensive book be instantly stopped; and, strange to say, the executive committee of the American Sunday-School Union, at the demand of the slave-power, dropped from its catalogue a book which had run through many editions, and was a great favourite with the people. Thus, in America, the *thought* that could lead to emancipation is if possible suppressed. The only light that can free the slave is kept out. The principle, the admission of which sets the captive free, is jealously excluded. This is slavery in its worst form.

An anti-slavery convention, of great interest and power, has lately been held at Ravenna, Ohio. It was composed mainly of Presbyterians, Congregationalists, Wesleyans, and Moravians, and the discussions and resolutions clearly indicate an advanced step among the churches. The discussion of the first resolution brought out "some most startling facts, showing that the publishing houses of the large religious denominations have carefully excluded, from all their issues, every paragraph which had the slightest reference to slavery."

Mr. Longley, of Chatham, a Congregationalist minister, stated that he was ashamed of their hymn-books, and also that of the Presbyterians. Occasionally he wanted to sing a freedom song, but could find none in the book. Slavery had torn them all out. A beautiful hymn, once familiar to all, had the stanza that hinted at slavery torn out—all else was retained. Here are the missing lines which the *northern churches,* at the bidding of the southern overseers, have expunged. Read it—think of it —good friend!

"Thy neighbour! yonder toiling slave!
Fettered in thought and limb,

"Whose hopes are all beyond the grave,
Go thou and ransom him."

Rev. Mr. Torrey, of East Cleveland, said that he had laboured under the same difficulty. Within a few years all the liberty songs had disappeared from his hymn-book. He had recently purchased a new one, neatly printed by the Tract Society, with the hymns on one page and the music on another. At a monthly concert, a short time since, he thought proper to remember the slave, and turned to the 72d of Watt's hymns, and commenced to read, when, to his amazement, he found that the *verse* which he most wanted *had gone.* Here it is,—

"Blessings abound where'er He reigns,
The joyful prisoner bursts his chains,
The weary find eternal rest,
And all the sons of want are blest."

The editor of the *Southern Literary Gazette* demands expurgated editions of such school-books as the *National Reader, Scott's Lessons,* and the *American First Class Book.* And why? Because they contain extracts from the writings of the greatest English and American authors, praising liberty and denouncing slavery. One of these extracts is that noble passage from Cowper, in which he says he would not have a slave—

"To carry me, to fan me while I sleep,
And tremble when I wake, for all the wealth
That sinews bought and sold have ever earned.
No; dear as freedom is, and in my heart's
Just estimation prized above all price,
I had much rather be myself the slave,
And wear the bonds, than fasten them on him."

This the editor sneers at, calls it "sickly sentimentality," and speaks of it as "stamping its infectious poison" upon the pages of school-books! He goes further than this, and objects to the following passage from one of Daniel Webster's speeches:—

"That ocean which seems to wave with a gentle magnificence, to waft the burdens of an honest commerce, and to roll its treasure with a conscious pride—that ocean which hardy industry regards, even when the winds have ruffled its surface, as a field of grateful toil—what is it to the victim of oppression, when he is brought to its shores, and looks forth upon it for the first time from beneath chains, and bleeding with stripes? What is it to him but a wide-spread prospect of suffering, anguish, and death? Nor do the skies smile longer, nor is the air fragrant to him. The sun is cast down from heaven. An inhuman and cursed traffic has cut him off in his manhood or in his youth from every enjoyment of his being, and every blessing which his Creator intended for him."

Will it be believed, in after times, that men, professing to be republicans, denounced such sentiments as these, and refused to teach them to their children!

The editor of the *South Carolinian* says, respecting a re-issue of the works of Professor Longfellow:—" We are *not* rejoiced to see the *complete* works of this author presented to the reading public of the United States—*the poems on slavery disgrace the fair fame of the writer.* These poems were written at sea—were the bile which concentrated in his mind during his European tour. This is all the excuse he can avail himself of at southern hands—at the hands of that portion of his fellow-citizens whom he has outraged and vilified—singing the woes and feelings of a class of whom he knows nothing."

But where shall this work of expurgation cease? The literature of the world is against slavery, because slavery is abhorrent to the dictates of civilized humanity. The greatest poets, orators, and historians have denounced slavery, because they could not do otherwise and be true to their great mission. Alas! for our editor; what poet can be safely put into the hands of his children? Is there none that will tell them, in inspired voice, of the divinity of slavery? No, not one! What is left for him but an 'expurgated' literature? He and his children cannot drink of the pure wells of English literature; there is an 'infectious poison' in them that will destroy their peace! They cannot wander at their will among its beds of flowers; a serpent is ever ready to sting them!

"What an accursed system is this of slavery, when it thus perverts the moral vision of men, and makes them shun, as 'poison,' the noblest sentiments of the human heart."

Leeds Anti-Slavery Series. No. 20.

Sold by W. and F. G. CASH, 5, Bishopsgate Street, London; and by JANE JOWETT, Friends' Meeting Yard, Leeds, at 1s. 2d. per 100.

Leeds Anti-slavery Series. No. 21.

CLERICAL OPPRESSORS.

THE opposition of a large body of the American clergy to *all* abolition movements, is to us extremely curious and unaccountable ; but, not to dwell on the occurrences of 1835, when this indignant invective was poured forth, we take for illustration the conduct of a large number of the Northern clergy, in 1850, in reference to the Fugitive Slave Law. This law requires, under heavy penalties, that the citizens of the Free States shall not only refuse food and shelter to a hunted, starving human being, suspected of no crime but that of endeavouring to gain his freedom, but if called on by the authorities, he is commanded to assist in sending him back to hopeless slavery.

Numerous indignant protests have issued from the Northern press against this tyrannical edict ; nevertheless the advocates for submission are also numerous, and among them very many of the most distinguished and most popular of the clergy.

By these the solemn day of thanksgiving, in 1851, was made use of to preach the duty of enforcing this law, and, in doing so, all that is sacred in heaven and earth, God, Christ, and his apostles, the Bible, Christianity, and patriotism, have been blasphemously paraded in support of slavery, and in justification of obedience to this concentration of infernal cruelty.

"What effect," asked the Right Rev. Bishop Hopkins, of Vermont, "had the Bible in doing away with slavery? *None whatever.*" If by one prayer he could liberate every slave in the world, Dr. Gardiner Spring assures his hearers he would not dare to offer it.

The Rev. W. M. Rogers, an orthodox minister of Boston, affirms—If this resistance to the carrying out the Fugitive Slave Law should lead the magistracy to call the citizens to arms, their duty was to obey, and "if ordered to take human life, in the name of God to take it."

Sold by W. and F. G. CASH, 5, Bishopsgate Street, London; and by JANE JOWETT Friends' Meeting Yard, Leeds, at 1*s.* 2*d.* per 100.

The Rev. Orville Dewey, a distinguished Unitarian divine, declares that he would send his own brother or child into slavery, if needed, to preserve the Union between the free and the slaveholding States. This preservation of the Union is the Moloch to which every better feeling is to be sacrificed; and for the sake of it the Rev. Moses Stuart, of Andover, one of the most distinguished theologians in the States, forgets his knowledge of the sacred volume so far as to aver, that "though we may pity the fugitive, yet the Mosaic law does not authorize the rejection of the claims of the slaveholders to their stolen property."

Were this true, it proves nothing against Christianity; but the following texts show how much the assertion maligns the Hebrew prophet:—" Thou shalt not deliver unto his master the servant which is escaped from his master unto thee; he shall dwell with thee, even among you, in the place which he shall choose in one of thy gates, where it liketh him best: thou shalt not oppress him " (Deut. xxiii. 15).

May we not say of such men, "they build up Zion with blood, and Jerusalem with iniquity?" Yet they lean upon the Lord, and say, "Is not the Lord among us? None evil can come upon us."

> Just God! and these are they
> Who minister at Thine altar, God of right!
> Men who their hands with prayer and blessing lay
>   On Israel's Ark of Light!
>
> What! preach and kidnap men!
> Give thanks—and rob Thy own afflicted poor!
> Talk of Thy glorious liberty, and then
>   Bolt hard the captive's door!
>
> What! servants of Thy own
> Merciful Son, who came to seek and save
> The homeless and the outcast—fettering down
>   The task'd and plunder'd slave!
>
> Pilate and Herod friends!
> Chief priests and rulers, as of old, combine!
> Just God and holy! is that church which lends
>   Strength to the spoiler, Thine?

> Paid hypocrites, who turn
> Judgment aside, and rob the Holy Book
> Of those high words of truth which search and burn
> In warning and rebuke!
>
> Feed fat, ye locusts, feed!
> And, in your tassel'd pulpits, thank the Lord
> That from the toiling bondsman's utter need,
> Ye pile your own full board.
>
> How long, O Lord! how long
> Shall such a priesthood barter truth away,
> And, in Thy name, for robbery and wrong
> At Thy own altars pray?
>
> Is not Thy hand stretch'd forth
> Visibly in the heavens, to awe and smite?
> Shall not the living God of all the earth,
> And heaven above, do right?
>
> Woe, then, to all who grind
> Their brethren of a common Father down!
> To all who plunder from th' immortal mind
> Its bright and glorious crown!
>
> Woe to the priesthood! woe
> To those whose hire is with the price of blood,
> Perverting, darkening, changing as they go,
> The searching truths of God!
>
> Their glory and their might
> Shall perish, and their very names shall be
> Vile before all the people, in the light
> Of a world's liberty.
>
> O! speed the moment on,
> When wrong shall cease, and liberty, and love,
> And truth, and right throughout the earth be known,
> As in their home above.

"Is it conceivable that a true Christian could regard or treat his own brother, the child of his own parents, as his *slave?* Surely it may be safely and confidently affirmed that *slavery* must cease to exist upon the earth, as soon as men shall introduce into the great family of God that domestic morality which, even in the present imperfect state of society, prevails for the most part in their private families ; as soon as they shall learn to feel towards their heavenly Father as they actually do feel towards their earthly parents ; as soon as they shall regard their brethren of mankind with an affection in any degree resembling that which, with rare exceptions, they cherish towards the beloved inmates of their homes, the dear fraternal band ; as soon as they shall have realized the truth, which they so often idly and vainly take upon their lips, when they say, ' Our Father !' "—*Rev. Joseph Hutton,* **LL.D.**

It is not a subject of the slightest doubt for the philosopher, statesman, historian, and Christian of our day, that slavery is to be condemned. It has been maintained that the Bible and the Christian religion nowhere prescribe its abolition. But the existence of slavery among the Jews furnishes no model whatever for imitation in our times. How the command, "Whatsoever ye would that men should do to you, do ye even so to them," is to be reconciled with slaveholding, it is not easy to conceive.

It was the common opinion of the ancient world, that the greater the freedom possessed by some, the less must be that enjoyed by others. But with Christianity, the right and the recognition of personal freedom in the state, and of equality in the sight of God, were brought forward in so decisive a manner, that slavery can only continue to exist in opposition to the new doctrine that claims a release from it.

"It is a fair conclusion, therefore," says the Rev. Albert Barnes, "that if Christianity would abolish slavery, it is sinful. It demonstrates the point before us, that it is contrary to the Bible, and cannot be defended from the Word of God." "It is for the Christian church to cease all connection with slavery." "There is no power *out* of the church that could sustain slavery an hour, if it were not sustained *in* it."

Leeds Anti-slavery Series. No. 21.

Sold by W. and F. G. CASH, 5, Bishopsgate Street, London ; and by JANE JOWETT, Friends' Meeting Yard, Leeds, at 1*s.* 2*d.* per 100.

Leeds Anti-slavery Series. No. 22.

REPROOF OF THE AMERICAN CHURCH,

BY THE BISHOP OF OXFORD.

THE Bishop of Oxford, a dignitary of the Church of England, distinguished alike by his honoured name and elevated rank, published, a few years ago, a " History of the Protestant Episcopal Church in America," in which he offered a faithful and Christian rebuke to his American brethren for their participation in the sin of slavery.

An American churchman, in alluding to this well-timed reproof, makes the following observations on the subject :—" Our church has hitherto erred in no small measure from ignorance and inadvertence. Such a plea can no longer avail her. A voice from abroad—a voice she can neither stifle nor deride —calls her to repentance and reformation. The reproof of Bishop Wilberforce must and will be heard. The sensibilities of Christians in our land are awakening to the momentous questions to which we have referred. The various denominations around us are daily breaking the ties which have hitherto bound them to the cause of the oppressor. Numerous churchmen among ourselves are complaining of the league which their clergy and representative bodies have formed with human bondage; and the Church of England is marking and lamenting the delinquencies of her daughter."

The following are the remarks of the Bishop of Oxford on the subject of slavery, and they are commended to the serious attention of every member of that church of which the writer

Sold by W. and F. G. CASH, 5, Bishopsgate Street, London; and by JANE JOWETT, Friends' Meeting Yard, Leeds, at 3s. 6d. per 100; or 6d. per doz.

is so worthy a prelate, especially if they be in any way connected with, or implicated in the evil.

"In forming an estimate of the moral influence of the Episcopalian body, we cannot fail to notice its bearing on the treatment of the coloured race. This is, in America, the great question of the present generation: socially, politically, morally, religiously, there is none which can compare with it. Never in the history of any people was the righteous retribution of the holy and living God more distinctly marked than in the manifold evils which now trouble America for her treatment of the African race. Like all other sinful courses, it has brought in, day by day, confusion and entanglement into all the relations of those contaminated by it. It is the cause which threatens to disorganize the Union; it is the cause which upholds the power of mobs and 'Lynching!' it is the occasion of bloodshed and violated law; it is, throughout the south, the destroyer of family purity, the hinderance to the growth of civilization and refinement; it is the one weak point of America as a nation, exposing her to the deadliest internal strife, that of an internecine war, whenever a foreign enemy should find it suit his purpose to arm the blacks against their masters. Further, like all other great and established evils, it is most difficult to devise any escape out of the coils which it has already wound around every civil and social institution; whilst every day of its permitted continuance both aggravates the evil and increases the difficulty of its ultimate removal.

"This, then, is exactly one of those sore evils of which the church of Christ is the appointed healer. She must, in His name, rebuke this unclean spirit; she who has been at all times the best adjuster of the balance between the rich and poor, between those who have and those who want; she who has redressed the wrongs of those who have no helper; she who, wherever she has settled, has changed slaves or serfs, by whatever title they are known, into freemen and peasants;—she must do this in the west, or the salt of the earth hath lost its savour, and is given over, with all things around, to the wasting of that utter and extreme corruption which she should have arrested.

"Now, to see how far the church has fulfilled this her vocation, we must have distinctly before us the real posture of this question in America. Of the twenty-six states, thirteen are slave states; admitting, that is, within their own borders, the institution of slavery as a part of their institutions; and of these, five—Maryland, Virginia, Kentucky, Missouri, and, in part, Tennessee—are slave-selling, whilst those south of them are slave-buying states.

"It will, therefore, be seen at once, that in the various districts of the Union widely different parts of the system are at work. But its curse is upon all. Chiefly does it rest upon the South. There, to his own, and little less to his master's degradation, the slave is held in direct personal bondage, and accounted merely as a chattel. Hence, at the caprice of his owner, he is treated not unfrequently with fearful cruelty: though these, it may be granted, are not the ordinary cases; since, except under the impulses of passion, no rational owner will misuse his own chattels. It is not, therefore, for these instances of cruelty, fearful as they occasionally are, that the system will be chiefly odious in the Christian's eyes.* Nor will it be from any notions of the abstract and inalienable rights of man. On these, in their common signification of the possession of political power, we do not touch; it is with the want of personal freedom we are concerned. Nor is it needful to assert, that slavery is, under all circumstances, directly forbidden by the

---

* Not to quote any of those occasional barbarities which may be turned in some measure aside as extreme cases, it is impossible to deny the ordinary cruelty of the system, when every Southern newspaper abounds in such advertisements as these:—" Ten dollars reward for my woman Siby, very much scarred about the neck and ears by whipping." —*Mobile Commercial Advertiser.* " Committed to jail, a negro slave; his back is very badly scarred."—*Planter's Intelligencer*, Sept. 26, 1838. " Run away, negress Caroline; had on a collar with one prong turned down."—*Bee*, Oct. 27, 1837. " Detained at the police-jail the negro wench Myra; has several marks of lashing, and has irons on her feet." —*Bee*, June 9, 1838. " Run away, a negro woman and two children; a few days before she went off, I burnt her with a hot iron on the left side of her face: I tried to make the letter M."—*Standard*, July 18, 1838. " Brought to jail, John ———, left ear cropt."—*Macon Telegraph*, Dec. 25, 1837. " Run away, a negro named Humbledon; limps on his left foot, where he was shot a few weeks ago, while a runaway."—*Vicksburg Register*, Sept. 5, 1838. " Run away, a black woman; has a scar on her back and right arm, caused by a rifle-ball."—*Natchez Courier*, June 15, 1832.

law of God. It is enough for our purpose, that, as administered in America, it is a violation of the Christian precept, ' Honour all men ;' that by its denial of all family life, its necessary irreligion, and its enforced ignorance, it deprives the slave of the privileges of redeemed humanity, and is directly opposed to the idea of the Christian revelation.

" To maintain this ground it is not necessary to assert that no slaves are happy in their servitude. For the happiest slave in American servitude is the greatest proof of the evil of the system. He is most utterly debased by it who can be happy in such a state. What that state is, is plain enough. The common language of the slave states, which has given to all those who labour the title of ' mean whites,' is abundant proof of their own estimate of slavery. But, further, as a general rule, the slave is not happy. The advocates of the system confess this in a thousand ways. Their columns of advertisements for runaways, their severe laws against those who aid or harbour fugitives, their occasional gifts of liberty to slaves who have wrought some great act of public good, their fierce jealousy of all speech or action which threatens ever so remotely their property in man, all bespeak the same secret conviction :—they do know the misery of slavery. The testimony of the Canadian ferryman,[*] who described the leap of the escaped slave, when the boat reaches the British shore, as unlike any other, is not more directly to the point.

" Accordingly, the master-evil of the South is, that the slaves are not treated as having souls ; they are often petted, often treated like spoiled children, never as men. On this point there is no dispute. ' Generally speaking, they are a nation of heathen in the midst of the land. They are without hope and without God in the world.'[†] ' They have no Bible to read by their own firesides ; they have no family altars ; and when in affliction, sickness, or death, they have no minister to address to them the consolations of the gospel.'[‡] ' They are destitute of the privileges of the gospel, and ever will be, under the present state of things. They may justly be considered the heathen

[*] *Retrospect of Western Travel (in America)*, vol. i., p. 114.
[†] Sermon by Rev. C. C. Jones, preached in Georgia before two associations of planters, 1831.
[‡] *Report in Synod of South Carolina and Georgia*, 1833.

of this country, and will bear a comparison with heathen in any country in the world.'* 'Throughout the bounds of the Charleston synod there are at least one hundred thousand slaves, speaking the same language as the whites, who have never heard of the plan of salvation by a Redeemer.'† And this is the fruit of no accident—it is inherent in the system. The black must be depressed below the level of humanity to be kept down to his condition. On this system his master dare not treat him as a man. To teach slaves to read is forbidden under the severest penalties in almost every slave state. In North Carolina, to teach a slave to read or write, or give him any book (the Bible not excepted), is punished with thirty-nine lashes or imprisonment, if the offender be a free negro; with a fine of 200 dollars if he be a white. In Georgia this fine is 500 dollars; and the father is not suffered to teach his half-caste child to read the Scriptures?‡

" The moral state of such a population need not be depicted. The habit of despising the true redeemed humanity in those around them grows always upon the licentious and the covetous, as they allow themselves to use their fellows as the mere instruments of their gain or pleasure: and in the slave states this evil habit reigns supreme. The Quadroon girls are educated in the South to live in bonds of shame with their white masters. With the slave-population itself the licentiousness of the whites is utterly unbridled: and by this, all the ties of nature are dissolved. Family-life amongst the slaves cannot exist; its fountains are always liable to be poisoned by arbitrary power. White fathers view their own slave-born children as chattels. They work, they sell them. By law they cannot teach them, or set them free; for the jealousy of slave-state legislation lays it down as a first principle, that every slave must have a master ' to see to him.'

" Here, then, in brief, is the curse of the southernmost or slave-buying states;—the holding of property in man, keeping men in servile bondage, using persons as things, redeemed

* *Report of the Synod of South Carolina and Georgia*, to whom was referred the religious instruction of the coloured population, 1834.

† *Charleston S. C. Observer.*

‡ *Caste and Slavery in the American Church*, p. 27. A noble and heart-stirring protest.

men as soulless chattels;—this is its essence. Here the testimony of the church must be against this first vicious principle. This has been the example set to God's witnesses in this generation by their fathers in the faith. They protested against such dominant iniquities, and they delivered their own souls, and saved us their children from the eating canker of a bloodstained inheritance. 'Let no man from henceforth,' said the Christian Council of London, in 1102,* 'presume to carry on that wicked traffic, by which men in England have been hitherto sold like brute animals.' This must be the church's rule on the banks of the Mississippi, as it was on those of the Thames. So much for the extreme south.

"As we come one degree northward, other features meet us. In the slave-selling states there is added to the evils of the South the execrable trade of breeding slaves for sale. By it 'the "Ancient Dominion" is converted into one grand menagerie, where men are reared for the market like oxen for the shambles.'† This is no figure of speech. The number of slaves exported, from Virginia alone, for sale in the Southern states, in one year, 1835-36, amounted to forty thousand;‡ whilst those imported from all quarters into the states of Louisiana, Mississippi, Alabama, and Arkansas, were reckoned in the year 1836 as not less than 25,000.§ 'Dealing in slaves,' says a Baltimore newspaper‖ of 1829, 'has become a large business; establishments are made in several places in Maryland and Virginia, at which they are sold like cattle: these places of deposit are strongly built, and well supplied with iron thumb-screws and gags.'

"The abominations of this trade must not pollute these pages. They may be readily conceived. But as a necessary part of such a traffic, an internal slave-trade, with its well-known horrors, recommences. Here are slave-auctions, with all their instant degradation, and all their consequent destruction of family and social life. Here are droves of chained negroes

---

* "Concilium Londinense, A.D. 1102, reg. Angliæ Hen. I. 3, statutum est: xxviii. Nequis illud nefarium negotium, quo hactenus homines in Angliâ solebant velut bruta animalia venundari, deinceps ullatenus facere præsumat."—Wilkins, *Concilia*, vol. i., p. 383

† Speech of Thomas Jefferson Randolph in Virginia Legislature, 1832.

‡ *Virginia Times.*   § *Natchez Courier.*   ‖ *Baltimore Register.*

marched under the whip, two and two, from the breeding district of Virginia to the labour-markets of Georgia and Alabama.

" Here, then, as in the farther South, the testimony of the church must be uncompromising and explicit. No motives of supposed expediency, no possible amount of danger, can justify her silence. She is set to bear a witness ; a witness against the evils around her ; a witness at all hazards ; a witness to be at any time attested, if so it needs must be, by bearing any amount of persecution. She, and she only, can do this. The exceeding jealousy of the several states makes them resent with peculiar warmth any interference from without. The regulation of its internal concerns, and so the whole continuance and system of Southern slavery, is solely under the jurisdiction of the several states. Congress cannot mitigate, much less abolish it. It can come before Congress only incidentally —as, for instance, on the question of admitting a new slave state into the Union. Even moral influence from without is bitterly resented by the South. This is its ground of quarrel with the abolition societies ; with which the general government has so far sympathized as to leave unredressed the violation of the Southern post-office, whereby abolition-papers are uniformly excluded from the South. Thus, at this moment, improvement can only arise from a higher standard of internal principle on this great question. This, it is the business of the church to create. She must assert her catholic character on behalf of these unhappy cast-aways. In other respects, there is no country upon earth so fitted by predisposing elements for uniting in one visible body all the company of Christ's redeemed. Gathered, as they are, from all countries, Americans are made partakers, even from natural causes, of a common, political, and social life. The strong lethargic common sense of the Dutch, and the gay vivacity of the French, the phlegm of the German, and the buoyant thoughtlessness of the Irish, the shrewd money-getting temper of the Yankee, and the hospitable elegance of the Southern gentleman—are all here fused into one common mass. From this universal brotherhood the African alone is shut altogether out. Him the church must take by the hand, and owning him as one of Christ's body, must lead him into the family of man. Not that she is bound to preach insurrection and rebellion. Far from it. It is quite easy to enforce upon the slave his duties, under a system, the unrighteousness of which is, at the same time, clearly stated. His bonds are illegal; but it is God's arm, and not his own violence, which must break them. Let the clergy of the South preach submission to the slave, if at the same time they declare to his master that these, for whom Christ died, are now no longer slaves, but brethren beloved;* and that a system which withholds from them their Christian birthright is utterly unlawful; that it is one which the master, not the slave, is bound to set himself honestly to sweep away. Above all should they, at any cost and by any sacrifice, protest in life and by act against this grievous wrong. The greater the cost, and the more painful the sacrifice, the clearer will be their testimony, and the more it will avail: to them it is given not only to believe in Christ, but also to suffer for His sake.

"What witness, then, has as yet been borne by the church in these slave states against this almost universal sin? How has she fulfilled her vocation? She raises no voice against the predominant evil; she palliates it in theory; and in practice she shares in it. The mildest and most conscientious of the bishops of the South are slaveholders themselves. Bishop Moore of Virginia writes to Bishop Ravenscroft :† ' The good and excellent girl presented to my daughter by Mrs. Ravenscroft paid the debt of nature on the 4th.' She was treated, it is true, with all the indulgence which she could receive, but still, favourite as she was, she was a slave; and, after her death, was laid ' in the coloured burial-ground, which is not enclosed, and therefore much exposed, and where the grave was liable to be disturbed.' This is no rare instance. The Bishop of Georgia has openly proposed to maintain ' The Montpelier Institute' by the produce of slave-labour; and *The Spirit of Missions,* edited with the sanction of the church, and under the eye of the Bishop (Onderdonk) of New York, proposes to endow a mission-school in Louisiana with a plantation to be worked by slaves, who should be encouraged to redeem themselves by extra hours of labour, before day in the morning, and after night in the evening; and should, when thus redeemed, be

---

* "Not now as a servant (lit., a slave—$\delta o\tilde{v}\lambda o\varsigma$), but above a servant, a brother beloved."—Philemon 16.

† *Life of Bishop Moore,* p. 282.

transported to Liberia, and the price received for them laid out in 'purchasing in Virginia or Carolina a gang of people who may be nearly double the number of those sent away.'*

"Nor are these merely evil practices into which, unawares and against their principles, these men have fallen. In a sermon preached before the Bishop of North Carolina in 1834, and published with his special commendation, it is openly asserted, that 'no man or set of men are entitled to pronounce slavery wrong; and that as it exists in the present day it is agreeable to the order of Divine Providence;' whilst the Bishop of South Carolina, in an address to the convention of his diocese, denounced 'the malignant philanthropy of abolition.'

"Such are the fearful features of the life of churchmen in the South. Nor is it any real lessening of this guilt to say that it is shared by all the Christian sects. The charge is, indeed, far too nearly true. There is no doubt that the evils of the system may be found still ranker and more gross amidst the prevailing sects of Baptists, Independents, Methodists, and Presbyterians.† But this is no excuse. It is the first duty of the church to reprove the sins of others, not to adopt them into her own practice; to set, and not to take the tone. The cruelty of their tender mercies should lead her to speak out more plainly; it should force her zealously to cleanse herself from their stain, and then fearlessly leave the issue to her God. But she is silent here; and to her greater shame it must be added, that there are sects ‡ which do maintain the witness she has feared to bear.

"But further, as has been already said, this clinging curse reaches even to the free states of the North, though it assumes

* *Caste and Slavery*, p. 34.
† Vide *Slavery and the Internal Slave-trade in America*, pp. 133–145, for horrors with which these pages shall not be polluted.
‡ The Quakers, and four small sects, the Reformed Presbyterians, United Brethren, Primitive Methodists, and Emancipation Baptists.—*Slavery and the Internal Slave-trade in America*, p. 132.
The annual conference of the United Brethren of Maryland and Virginia passed, in 1839, the following resolution:—"It appeared in evidence that Moses Michael was the owner of a female slave, which is contrary to the discipline of our Church. Conference therefore resolved, that, unless brother Michael manumit or set free such slave in six months, he no longer be considered a member of our Church."—*American Churches the Bulwark of Slavery*, p. 3.

in them another form. In them it leads to the treatment of the coloured race with deep and continual indignity. They cannot be held in personal bondage, but they are of the servile class; they may be claimed as runaways, and thus dragged, if not kidnapped, to Southern slavery.

"A mingled scorn and hatred of the coloured man pervades every usage of society. In the courts of law his testimony is not equally received with the white man's evidence; republican jealousy forgets its usual vigilance, in order to deny him his equal vote; he may be expelled with insult from the public vehicle; he must sit apart in the public assembly; and though no tinge of remaining shade may darken his cheek, yet a traditional descent from coloured blood will make it impossible for him to wed with any of the European race. Even in the fierce heat of the 'revivals,' this supreme law of separation is never or a moment overlooked. There are different 'pens' for the white and coloured subjects of this common enthusiasm. On all these points feeling runs higher in the free North than in the slave states of the South. There the dominion of the master is supreme, and he can venture when it pleases him to treat his slave with any degree of intimacy; for the beast of the field might, with as high a probability as he, claim equal rights with man. But in the North, where the coloured race are free and often rich, the galling insults of caste are needful to keep up the separation between blood and blood; and here therefore, more than anywhere, its conventional injustice is supreme; here, too, by an enforced silence as to the crimes of Southern slavery, a guilty fellowship in its enormities is too commonly established.

"Against these evils, then, the Church must here testify; she must proclaim that God hath made of one blood all nations of the earth; she must protest against this unchristian system of caste; her lips must be unsealed to denounce God's wrath against the guilty customs of the South. And what has been her conduct? If we seek to test her real power over men's hearts by asking what her influence has been, we shall rate it low indeed. No voice has come forth from her. The bishops of the North sit in open convention with their slaveholding brethren, and no canon proclaims it contrary to the discipline of their church to hold property in man and treat him as a chattel. Nay, further, the worst evils of the world have found their way into the church. The coloured race must worship apart ; they must not enter the white man's church ; or if they do, they must be fenced off into a separate corner. In some cases their dust may not moulder in the same cemetery. Whilst all classes of white children voluntarily attend the Sunday-schools on terms of perfect equality, any mixture of African blood will exclude the children of the wealthiest citizen. Recent events have shown that all this is not the evil fruit of an old custom slowly wearing itself out ; but that it springs from a living principle which is daily finding for itself fresh and wider developments.

"The General Theological Seminary, founded, as we have seen, at New York, under the superintendence of the whole church, was designed to secure a general training for all its presbyters. 'Every person producing to the faculty,' so ran its statutes, ' satisfactory evidence of his having been admitted a candidate for holy orders, with full qualifications, according to the canons of the Protestant Episcopal Church in the United States, shall be received as a student of the seminary.'* Curiosity once prompted the question to Bishop Hobart, the founder of the seminary, 'whether this wide rule embraced *coloured* candidates ?' 'They would be admitted,' was his answer, ' as a matter of course and without doubt.' Such, alas ! is not the rule of his successor in the bishop's seat. In June, 1839, Alexander Crummell applied for admission ; he came from three years' study at the Oneida Institute, from sharing equal rights with one hundred white students ; he brought with him a character which, it was conceded, would warrant his admission if it could be right to admit a *coloured* man at all : he was rejected for this single fault ; one Bishop (Doane) alone being found to protest against the step. Three years before, a similar injustice had been wrought. Both remain to this day unredressed. The church fears to lose the contributions of the South ; she fears to raise the mobs of Philadelphia; she dare not stand between the dead and living: she cannot therefore stay the plague. Even when admitted to the sacred functions of the priesthood, the coloured man is not the

* *Statutes of the General Theological Seminary*, chap. vii., sec. 1.

equal of his brethren. The Rev. Peter Williams, for years a New York presbyter, of blameless reputation, was, for this one cause, allowed no seat in the convention of his church. Thus, again, a special canon of the diocese of Pennsylvania forbids the representation of the African church at Philadelphia, and excludes the rector from a seat.

" Tried, then, by this test, what can we esteem the present influence of this body? It plainly has not been conscious of possessing power to stand up in God's name and to rebuke the evil one ; it has not healed this sore wound, which is wasting the true social life of America. It is a time for martyrdom; and the mother of the saints has scarcely brought forth even one confessor.

" It is not enough that the distinctive features which mark this communion should be kept clear and plain. There must also be a high tone on those great moral and social questions which are rising daily, and on which mere politicians have no utterance of principle. There must be no timid silence as to great enormities. In those mighty issues which indeed try the spirits of men, her voice must be clear. Thus, for example, the treatment of the negro population must be her care : the equal worth of the coloured race must be unequivocally held and asserted by her. It must no longer be the reproach of the Protestant Episcopal Church, that it is only in the Romish cathedral at New Orleans that whites and blacks are seen to kneel together, as those who were made of one blood by one Father, and redeemed from common death through the cross of one only Saviour. Timid, compromising conduct on these great subjects, safe as it may seem at present, will, more than anything besides, weaken through the whole nation the moral weight of any religious body. By an universal law of God's providence, it is in doing battle for His truth that men exercise and train their own spirits, and subdue the herd of weaker minds to their rule and government. By its courage or unfaithfulness on this one question, the Church, as far as we can see, is fixing now for good or ill its true weight and standing in the coming generation."

Leeds Anti-slavery Series. No. 22.
Sold by W. and F. G. CASH, 5, Bishopsgate Street, London; and by JANE JOWETT, Friends' Meeting Yard, Leeds, at 3s. 6d. per 100; or 6d. per doz.

Leeds Anti-slavery Series   No. 23.

SLAVE-BRANDING.

A LETTER from an officer on board the "Amphitrite," in the Bight of Benin, which recently appeared in the daily papers, revives in the public mind a recollection of the revolting cruelties to which a portion of our race is subjected, through the enormities of the slave-trade. He states, that six hundred slaves were lately murdered by the chiefs at Palma, who were unable to dispose of them.

It is evident, by the accounts received from all sources, that, in spite of the enormous cost at which England is keeping up a blockading squadron on the coast of Africa, this horrible traffic is carried on with as much activity, and with more cruelties, than ever; the risk which the slavers run of being taken, being just enough, and no more, to induce them to adopt certain measures of precaution, which involve increased sufferings and horrors to the poor wretches, who are being carried from their native shores. All the dreadful horrors that imagination can picture, fall short of the appalling reality of this nefarious trade.

Sold by W. and F. G. CASH, 5, Bishopsgate Street, London; and by JANE JOWETT, Friends' Meeting Yard, Leeds, at 1s. 2d. per 100.

The great markets for the traffic are on the Brazilian coasts; and it is stated, upon credible authority, that from 50,000 to 60,000 negroes have been annually imported into Rio Janeiro alone. Three other ports are stated to trade, to nearly, if not quite, the same extent, while many smaller places smuggle the unhappy wretches ashore. One chief mart is the island of Sanctos, or Santos, a large section of land dovetailed in with the continent, and affording not only great facilities for landing the slaves, but also for secreting them afterwards, till they are marched off and buried in the gold-mines of San Paulo, for the remainder of their lives.

The extent to which the slave-trade is prosecuted, may be, in some degree, judged of, when it is stated, that the slaves carried into the Brazils, since the treaty made with Great Britain for the suppression of the trade, exceed two millions and a half. In fact, when we take into consideration the trade carried on with the Brazils, Cuba, the Southern States of America, Morocco, Tunis, Tripoli, Egypt, Turkey, Persia, Arabia, and the borders of Asia, it is no exaggeration to say, that this frightful drain of human beings from the African shores, includes no fewer than from 300,000 to 400,000 souls a-year. Upwards of 8000 of these poor heart-broken slaves are *known* to have been landed in Cuba and Brazil alone, during the year 1851.

These unfortunates are collected in the interior of Africa, and are generally prisoners captured in some marauding affray of one nation upon another; or they are persons kidnapped secretly in the midnight assault. They are attached to a strong chain, by iron collars placed round their necks, and are thus marched down to the barracoons near the coast, where the cargoes are made up. Previous to embarkation, the poor creatures are mustered, and certain figures or numbers are branded on their naked flesh, by means of a hot iron. This practice is truly soul-sickening. Some of the victims undergo the torture in dogged and sullen silence; others are overcome by pain and terror; and it is often necessary to bind and gag them before the deed can be done.

We were long unwilling to believe that the branding of slaves with hot irons was still practised, but we blush to state that this is done in the United States of America, where there are upwards of three millions of slaves. Read the following advertisement copied from an American newspaper:—

"TWENTY DOLLARS REWARD.—Run away from advertiser, a negro girl named MOLLY, 16 or 17 years of age; *lately branded on the left cheek, thus, 'R,'* and a piece cut off her ear on the same side; the same letter on the inside of both legs."

The following is from an advertisement, quoted, amongst many others, in *Goodell's American Slave Code:*—

" Mary has a small scar over her eye, a good many teeth missing, the letter A branded on her cheek and forehead."

The following is from the *North Carolina Standard:*—

"TWENTY DOLLARS REWARD.—Run away from the subscriber, a negro woman and two children. The woman is tall and black, and a few days before she went off, *I burnt her with a hot iron on the left side of her face.* I tried to make the letter M; and she kept a cloth over her head and face, and a fly bonnet on her head, so as to cover the burn. Her children, &c.—MICAJAH RICKS."

On calling at the City of London News Room, 66 Cheapside (where, for a penny, papers can be seen from all parts of the world), we took up the *New Orleans Bulletin,* dated April 17, 1852, and glancing over its pages, we soon saw that American slaves are looked upon like the " beasts which perish," rather than as fellow immortal beings, for whom the Saviour died. From an advertisement of a public auction by Messrs. Palfrey & Co., in which a plantation, with buildings, is described, we copied the following sentence:—

"There are upon, and belonging to the place, fifty slaves, with mules, horses, oxen, sheep, hogs, and corn in abundance.

"A catalogue, with a description of the slaves, &c., may be had of the auctioneers."

Many pages might be filled with similar advertisements, which appear in the most respectable Southern journals, with the names of the advertisers, many of them prominent citizens, and sometimes respectable ladies ! The seventh Report of the American Colonization Society makes this acknowledgement : " We have never heard of slavery in any country, ancient or modern, Pagan, Mahometan, or Christian, so terrible in its character as the slavery which exists in the United States." And the Presbyterian Synod of Kentucky says : " They (the slaves) suffer all that can be inflicted by wanton caprice, by grasping avarice, by brutal lust, by malignant spite, and by insane anger. Their happiness is the sport of every whim, the prey of every passion that may occasionally or habitually infest the master's bosom."

Rev. James A. Thome, now of Ohio City, a native of Kentucky, and son of a slaveholder, says, "Slavery is the parent of more suffering than has flowed from any one source since the date of its existence. Such sufferings, too! sufferings inconceivable and innumerable; unmingled wretchedness from the ties of nature broken and destroyed; the acutest bodily tortures, groans, tears, and blood; lying for ever in weariness and painfulness, in watchings, in hunger, and in thirst, in cold, and in nakedness."

We forbear citing further witnesses. It is manifest that human chattels must be worse treated than brutes, in order to be kept in chattelhood. Other working animals are not punished as examples to their fellows. Other animals are not the objects of suspicion, jealousy, lust, or revenge. They are not hated; they are not threatened; they are not conversed and quarrelled with. They cannot be regarded guilty, or proper subjects of censure or punishment. They have no aspirations above their condition. They have no keen sense of being injured by being imbruted. They can utter no provoking language, nor retort, nor retaliate. All these items are bulwarks of defence to the brute, but inlets and avenues of attack upon the slave. The individuals and classes of men most wronged are proverbially most hated by the wrong-doer. This is the dreadful doom of the poor negro, and he is completely under the power of his tyrant. As the exercise of despotic power over the defenceless makes men hard-hearted and cruel, it is evident that the more absolute any despotism becomes, the more cruel will the persons become who administer it. And the most absolute form of despotism known among men is that human chattelhood in the United States of America.

Leeds Anti-slavery Series. No. 23.

Sold by W. and F. G. CASH, 5, Bishopsgate Street, London; and by JANE JOWETT, Friends' Meeting Yard, Leeds, at 1s. 2d. per 100.

Leeds Anti-slavery Series. No. 24.

SECRETS OF THE PRISON-HOUSE.

A CORRESPONDENT of the *Lowell Courier* writes from Charleston, South Carolina, as follows :—

" Since I have been here, I have visited what is called the workhouse, but, more properly speaking, slave-prison. Here are deposited for safe keeping those that are brought to market for sale; also, those that have run away and are brought here to be punished—some are put to breaking stones, others on the tread-mill. When I was in, there were three men and one woman on the wheel, and a driver standing by, with whip in hand; this wheel is attached to mill-stones, and in this way they grind their hominy. In a room in the building is the whipping apparatus—while I was examining this, there was a boy brought in by his master to be whipped. It appears to be the custom here, when slaves are to be punished, to bring them to this place, for which they pay one dollar. The boy was stripped naked, his feet fastened to the floor, his hands placed in a rope overhead, and then drawn straight by means of blocks, then a cap drawn over his head and face. The boy, I should think, was not over 13 years of age. He was whipped very hard—*the skin flying at every blow*. After he was let down and had gone out, I asked his master what he had been doing? He said he had run away the day before, and gone to the races. I thought it rather severe, considering how popular races are here. I was told that quite a number had been brought there that day, to be punished for the same offence."

" We were taken from Vicksburgh to New Orleans, where we were to be sold at any rate. We were taken to a trader's yard, in a slave-prison, in the corner of St. Joseph Street.

Sold by W. and F. G. CASH, 5, Bishopsgate Street, London; and by JA E JOWETT, Friends' Meeting-Yard, Leeds, at 7*d.* per 100.

This was a common resort for slave-traders, and planters who wanted to buy slaves; and all classes of slaves were kept there for sale, to be sold in private or public—young or old, males or females, children or parents, husbands or wives.

"Every day, at two o'clock, they were exposed for sale. They had to be in time for showing themselves to the public for sale. Every one's head had to be combed, and their faces washed; and those who were inclined to look dark and rough, were compelled to wash in greasy dish-water, to make them look sleek and lively.

" When spectators would come into the yard, the slaves were ordered out to form a line. They were made to stand up straight, and look as sprightly as they could; and when they were asked a question, they had to answer it as promptly as they could, and try to induce the spectators to buy them. If they failed to do this, they were severely paddled after the spectators were gone. The object for using the paddle in the place of the lash, was to conceal the marks which would be made by the flogging. And the object for flogging under such circumstances is to make the slaves anxious to be sold."—*Narrative of Henry Bibb, published at New York,* 1849.

It is difficult for any one who feels and reasons rightly, to dwell on the peculiar enormities of American slavery, without the utmost indignation being excited, that such horrible indignities should be perpetrated.

Slavery in the nineteenth century—in the bosom of a Christian country—in the full blaze of constitutional theory, historic tradition, and republican light, is an anomaly, and a horror which has no precedent in the universe, and to which nothing can reconcile a thinking and a feeling man.

Man held as a thing, and sold with as little concern, and often in the same lot as a Berkshire sow, or a Sussex boar! This is the indignity put upon our kind—an outrage committed on the world's liberty, which no sophistry can disguise, no expediency can palliate, and no language can hold up to sufficient execration.

Leeds Anti-slavery Series. No. 24.

Sold by W. and F. G. CASH, 5, Bishopsgate Street, London; and by JANE JOWETT, Friends' Meeting-Yard, Leeds, at 7*d.* per 100.

Leeds Anti-slavery Series. No. 25.

NEGRO BOY SOLD FOR A WATCH.

An African prince having arrived in England, and having been asked what he had given for his watch, he replied, "What I will never give again; I gave a fine boy for it."

How deeply has civilized humanity sinned against Africa. The produce of our arts and manufactures—everything that can please the eye or minister to the sensual gratification of the untutored savage—has been offered to him in return for slaves; and the positive premium to crime thus held out has, no doubt, done much to cause a continuance of the barbarism with which the slaveholder taunts the African.

The exchange of the negro boy for a watch, as above related, suggested to the poet Cowper the following lines:—

> WHEN avarice enslaves the mind,
>   And selfish views alone bear sway,
> Man turns a savage to his kind,
>   And blood and rapine mark his way.
> Alas! for this poor simple toy,
> I sold the hapless negro boy.
>
> His father's hope, his mother's pride,
>   Though black, yet comely to the view,
> I tore him helpless from their side,
>   And gave him to a ruffian crew,—
> To fiends that Afric's coast annoy,
> I sold the hapless negro boy.
>
> From country, friends, and parents torn,
>   His tender limbs in chains confined,

Sold by W. and F. G. CASH, 5, Bishopsgate Street, London; and by JANE JOWETT Friends' Meeting Yard, Leeds, at 7d. per 100.

I saw him o'er the billows borne,
   And marked his agony of mind;
But still, to gain this simple toy,
I gave the weeping negro boy.

In isles that deck the western wave,
   I doomed the hapless youth to dwell,
A poor, forlorn, insulted slave,
   A beast that Christians buy and sell!
And in their cruel tasks employ
The much-enduring negro boy.

His wretched parents long shall mourn,
   Shall long explore the distant main,
In hope to see the youth return;
   But all their hopes and sighs are vain:
They never shall the sight enjoy
Of their lamented negro boy.

Beneath a tyrant's harsh command,
   He wears away his youthful prime;
Far distant from his native land,
   A stranger in a foreign clime.
No pleasing thoughts his mind employ,
A poor, dejected negro boy.

But He who walks upon the wind,
   Whose voice in thunder's heard on high,
Who doth the raging tempest bind,
   And hurl the lightning through the sky,
In His own time will sure destroy
The oppressor of the negro boy.

Leeds Anti-slavery Series. No. 25.

Sold by W. and F. G. CASH, 5, Bishopsgate Street, London; and by JANE JOWETT Friends' Meeting Yard, Leeds, at 7*d.* per 100.

Leeds Anti-slavery Series. No. 26.

THE BLIND SLAVE BOY.

A few years ago, in the State of Kentucky, a slaveholder offered to sell a negro woman and her blind child to a slave-trader. The trader declined taking the boy, stating that he wanted slaves to stock a plantation, and that blind ones would be of no use to him. The master, who was desirous to sell the woman, did not want to be troubled with the helpless child after the sale of his mother. Thus both parties were much perplexed, until finally a third person stepped forward, and offered a dollar for the boy, and the bargain was closed. Mrs. Dr. Bailey, of Cincinnati, who was acquainted with the circumstance, wrote the following lines upon this touching incident:—

> COME back to me, mother! why linger away
> From thy poor little blind boy, the long weary day!
> I mark every footstep, I list to each tone,
> And wonder my mother should leave me alone!
> There are voices of sorrow and voices of glee,
> But there's no one to joy or to sorrow with me;
> For each hath of pleasure and trouble his share,
> And none for the poor little blind boy will care.
>
> My mother, come back to me! close to thy breast,
> Once more let thy poor little blind one be pressed;
> Once more let me feel thy warm breath on my cheek,
> And hear thee in accents of tenderness speak!
> O mother, I've no one to love me, no heart
> Can bear like thine own in my sorrows a part;
> No hand is so gentle, no voice is so kind!
> O! none like a mother can cherish the blind!

Sold by W. and F. G. CASH, 5, Bishopsgate Street, London; and by JANE JOWETT, Friends' Meeting Yard, Leeds, at 7d. per 100.

Poor blind one! no mother thy wailing can hear,
No mother can hasten to banish thy fear;
For the slave-owner drives her o'er mountain and wild,
And for one paltry dollar hath sold thee, poor child!
Ah! who can in language of mortals reveal
The anguish that none but a mother can feel,
When man, in his vile lust of mammon, hath trod
On her child, who is stricken and smitten of God!

Blind, helpless, forsaken, with strangers alone,
She hears in her anguish his piteous moan,
As he eagerly listens, but listens in vain,
To catch the loved tones of his mother again!
The curse of the broken in spirit shall fall
On the wretch who hath mingled this wormwood and gall,
And his gain, like a mildew, shall blight and destroy,
Who hath torn from his mother the little blind boy!

KIDNAPPING CHILDREN.

"Two men, from Kentucky, rented a tavern-stand at Fallstown, Beaver County, and, having expressed a desire to procure two coloured boys to perform little services about the house, a widowed coloured woman, residing in or near Hookstown, hired to them two of her children, four and seven years old. Soon after, the scoundrels absconded, taking with them the two children, as has been ascertained, for the purpose of selling them into slavery. The affair produced great excitement in Fallstown, and a reward of 100 dollars was offered there; but they have not yet been traced."—*Pittsburgh Gazette*, 1847.

"The *Village Register*, published at Salem, Ohio, says that a little girl (coloured) has been kidnapped in that town. The kidnapper pretended to come from a man with whom a brother of the child lived, with directions to take her there; and no suspicion was excited till sometime after he had gone. Pursuit was made as soon as the real state of the case was known; but the scoundrel had crossed the line, and was safe in Virginia with his prey."—*Ram's Horn*, May, 1847.

Leeds Anti-slavery Series. No. 26.

Sold by W. and F. G. CASH, 5, Bishopsgate Street, London; and by JANE JOWETT, Friends' Meeting Yard, Leeds, at 7d. per 100.

Leeds Anti-slavery Series. No. 27.

SCENE ON BOARD A STEAM-BOAT
AT WILMINGTON.

"BRUTAL stripes, and all the various kinds of personal indignities, are not the only species of cruelty which slavery licenses. The law does not recognise the family relations of a slave, and extends to him no protection in the enjoyment of domestic endearments. The members of a slave family may be forcibly separated, so that they shall never more meet till the final judgment; and cupidity often induces the masters to practise what the law allows. Brothers and sisters, parents and children, husbands and wives, are torn asunder, and permitted to see each other no more. These acts are daily occurring in the midst of us. The shrieks and the agony often witnessed on such occasions proclaim, with a trumpet-tongue, the INIQUITY AND CRUELTY OF OUR SYSTEM."—*Synod of Kentucky.*

" As I went on board the steam-boat at Wilmington, I noticed eight coloured men, handcuffed and chained together in pairs, four women, and eight or ten children—all standing together in the bow of the boat, in charge of a man standing near them. Coming near them, I perceived they were all greatly agitated, and, on inquiring, I found that they were all slaves who had been born and raised in North Carolina, and had just been sold to a speculator, who was now taking them to the Charleston market. Upon the shore was a number of coloured persons, women and children, waiting the departure of the boat. My attention was particularly arrested by two coloured females, who stood together a little distance from the crowd, and upon whose countenances was depicted the keenest sorrow. As the last bell was tolling, I saw the tears gushing from their eyes— they were the wives of two of the men in chains. There, too, were mothers and sisters, weeping at the departure of their sons

---

Sold by W. and F. G. CASH, 5, Bishopsgate Street, London; and by JANE JOWETT, Friends' Meeting-Yard, Leeds, at 7*d.* per. 100.

and brothers; and there, too, were fathers, taking the *last look* of their wives and children. My eyes now turned to those in the boat, and, although I had tried to control my feelings amidst my sympathy for those on shore, I could conceal them no more, and found myself literally weeping with those that wept. I stood near them, when one of the husbands saw his wife on the shore wave her hand for the last time; his manly efforts to restrain his feelings gave way, and, fixing his watery eyes upon her, he exclaimed, ' This is the most distressing thing of all—my dear wife and children, farewell !' Of the poor women on board, three of them had husbands whom they left behind. Sailing down Cape Fear River twenty-five miles, we touched at the little village of Smithport, on the south side of the river. It was at this place that one of the slaves lived, and here were his wife and five children. While at work on Monday last, his purchaser took him away from his family, carried him in chains to Wilmington, where he remained in jail. As we approached the wharf, a flood of tears burst from his eyes. The boat stopped but a moment, and, as she left, he espied his wife on the stoop of a house some rods from the shore, and with one hand, which was not in the handcuff, he pulled off his old hat, and, waving it towards her, he exclaimed, ' Farewell !' After a few moments' silence, conflicting passions seemed to tear open his breast, and he exclaimed, ' What have I done, that I should suffer this ? O ! my wife and children—I want to live no longer.' "—*Christian Advocate and Journal.*

" Still," observes Professor Raymond, " the terrible *fact* remains. Still *the tears and blood of the enslaved are daily dropping on our country's soil.* Throw over it what veil of extenuation and excuse you may, the essential crime and shame remain. Believe as kindly as you can of the treatment which the slaves receive of humane and Christian masters, it is only on condition that they first surrender their every *right* as men. Let them dare demur to that, and their tears and blood must answer it. That is the terrible fact ; and our country [America] is the abettor, the protector, and the agent of the iniquity."

Leeds Anti-slavery Series. No. 27.

Sold by W. and F. G. CASH, 5, Bishopsgate Street, London; and by JANE JOWETT, Friends' Meeting-Yard, Leeds, at 7*d.* per. 100.

Leeds Anti-slavery Series. No. 28.

KIDNAPPING A MAN OUT OF SLAVERY INTO FREEDOM.

" WE have heard, from a gentleman in Canada, a story of an exhibition of courage and generalship by a fugitive slave, which, had it been shown in the Mexican war, by any American officer or soldier, would have given him renown and high honours.

" A slave named Edmonds escaped from Kentucky into Canada some time in 1850. After a few months' stay, he returned to Kentucky, much to the surprise of his old companions. They eagerly listened to his tales of the 'land of liberty,' the 'home of the oppressed,' which he had found, and which now, in their minds, suddenly rose from a dim and doubtful dream to a bright reality. Their hearts leaped at the thought of a home within its charmed borders, where no kidnapper nor bloodhound could ever come, where the driver's lash would never be heard, where the sacred circle of home would be inviolate, and they might live in the consciousness of manhood, 'with none to molest or make them afraid.'

" They needed no eloquent appeals from colonization agents, no flattering offers, nor fictitious pictures of wealth, honour, power, and national glory, no appropriations of government, nor any degree of banishment, to encourage or drive them into emigration. A deeper chord was touched, a stronger motive stirred within their hearts. Slavery was the woe they would fly—liberty the hope which beckoned them on. Twenty-five new emigrants soon volunteered for the hazardous flight, and engaged Edmonds as their pilot.

" The time and place of embarkation were fixed. The night arrived; and, while gathering his companions for the journey,

Sold by W. and F. G. CASH, 5, Bishopsgate Street, London; and by JANE JOWETT, Friends' Meeting-Yard, Leeds, at 7d. per 100.

Edmonds overheard a conversation between one of the party and his master, betraying the plot, and planning the capture of all engaged in it. The treacherous slave was to go to the place of rendezvous, while the master gathered an armed company of whites to surround the spot; and, at a signal from the betrayer, they were to rush upon, and seize or destroy the runaways.

" This betrayal might have cast down an ordinary man, and have defeated his scheme. It only gave energy to Edmonds. He was the man for the hour. Withdrawing unperceived from the hiding-place where he had overheard this conversation, he hurried to a few of his friends, made known his plan to escape the fatal snare laid for them all, and readily engaged them in it.

" They waylaid the traitor in a dark skirt of the woods; seized and bound him, threatened instant death to him if he attempted an alarm; then, gathering all their band, they took a different route for the Ohio from the one contemplated, marching their betrayer, closely guarded, with them. That night they reached Ohio, and so marched, without interruption, to Canada, never releasing their prisoner, nor relaxing their vigilance over him, till they reached the British line.

" Here, having won their own liberty, they gave him his —thus rewarding his baseness with the richest of blessings. It is said that he has since repented of his crime, and gratefully accepts the freedom forced upon him. Edmonds and his companions are engaged in such honest avocations as offer to them the means of an honourable livelihood, happy in their peace and security. We doubt, however, dearly as they love liberty, whether they feel any reproaches for their act of kidnapping.

" What man, who honours courage and military heroism, will not say that these brave fellows deserve the liberty they won for themselves and gave to their enemy? Whatever we may think of their course, we must confess that in one point it was particularly Christian, namely, in its return of good for evil."—*Pennsylvania Freeman*, May 22, 1851.

Leeds Anti-slavery Series. No. 28.

Sold by W. and F. G. CASH, 5, Bishopsgate Street, London; and by JANE JOWETT, Friends' Meeting-Yard, Leeds, at 7d. per 100.

Leeds Anti-slavery Series. No. 29.

MAN-STEALING AND RELIGION.

"The American Church is the bulwark of American Slavery."

THE connection of religious organizations with slavery has constituted one of the strongest supports to that inhuman system. Political parties, with all their base subserviency to the slave power, have been unable to render any such service as the church has rendered to slavery. The power of a political party is as inferior to that of the church, as time is to eternity. Important as it is to watch the movements of political parties, it is of still more importance to observe well the movements of *religious bodies.*

Wendell Phillips said truly, many years ago, " That the key of the slave's dungeon is in the hand of the church !" The power to abolish slavery rests with the church. They alone can, successfully, stamp the system as one of sin, and divest it of the garb of innocence and respectability by which it gets leave to live. The whole system would fall to pieces under the thunders of the pulpit. No earthly arm could save it against the arm of the church—and its destruction is to be despaired of without the aid of the church. Every sign of the coming up to this work, on the part of the church, must be hailed by the friends of freedom with joy and gratitude.

Happily for the poor soul-crushed bondman, these signs are multiplying of late. Religious bodies are becoming more and more sensible of their duties, and are evincing a stronger disposition to reform them. It is stated that movements are on foot in several denominations for the separation of the slaveholding, or slave-upholding part and the anti-slavery. In the success of these measures, incalculable advantage will ac-

Sold by W. and F. G. CASH, 5, Bishopsgate Street, London; and by JANE JOWETT, Friends' Meeting-Yard, Leeds, at 7d. per 100.

crue to the cause of freedom. It will remove all motive of a denominational character for standing aloof from the anti-slavery movement. It will throw open the doors of their churches, in America, to the advocates of emancipation, bring the untrammelled testimony of their press to bear upon the subject, and will greatly swell the vote for liberty at the ballet-box.

It is in vain to think of banishing the works of the devil from the world, while we admit those who do them to be disciples of Christ. To preach against slaveholding, and yet embrace as a Christian the slaveholder, is practically giving the lie to such preaching. When the church buys, sells, and heathenizes God's children, and blasphemously appeals to the name of Christ as its sanction, no language is strong enough to describe it. Talk of their piety! Though their prayers were longer than the Pharisees, and their praises were solemn and unceasing, they are all a mockery while they trample on God's image. Judge ye therefore what is Christianity, and give not the holy name to that which violates its laws, and has none of its spirit.

It is deeply to be lamented that professing Christians should have given the right hand of fellowship to such a system, by joining in communion with its upholders, by assisting to throw the mantle of Christianity over the iniquity of slavery, and, in so doing, rivetting the fetters on the limbs of the slave, and stifling the cries of his distress. Let us unite in every effort to withdraw the veil, to expose the horrors underneath, and to proclaim the right throughout our land and yours. If we are members of churches whose teachers attempt to screen slavery; if their prayers make mention of the slaveholder, forgetting the *slave;* if our fellow-members join in these acts—then let us lift up *our* voices for the oppressed, let us protest against such unchristian distinctions. Should our remonstrances prove unavailing, then let us obey the command, "Come out from among them, and be ye separate;" thus bearing our testimony to the honour of Christianity, and the cause of humanity.

Leeds Anti-slavery Series. No. 29.

Sold by W. and F. G. CASH, 5, Bishopsgate Street, London; and by JANE JOWETT, Friends' Meeting-Yard, Leeds, at 7*d.* per 100.

Leeds Anti-slavery Series. No. 30.

PARADISE OF NEGRO SLAVES

A DREAM, BY DR. RUSH.

Dr. Benjamin Rush, of Philadelphia, a member of the Presbyterian church, is well known to the literary world from his *Medical Dissertations, Treatises on the Discipline of Schools, Criminal Law,* &c. He was a great opposer of the slave-trade; and, at the instigation of Anthony Benezet, boldly vindicated the cause of the oppressed negroes. The following dream is related by this excellent man.

Soon after reading Mr. Clarkson's ingenious and pathetic essay on the *Slavery and Commerce of the Human Species,* says Dr. Rush, the subject made so deep an impression upon my mind, that it followed me in my sleep, and produced a dream of so extraordinary a nature, that I have yielded to the importunities of some of my friends, by communicating it to the public. I thought I was conducted to a country, which, in point of cultivation and scenery, far surpassed anything I had ever heard or read in my life. This country, I found, was inhabited only by negroes. They appeared cheerful and happy. Upon my approaching a beautiful grove, where a number of them were assembled for religious purposes, I perceived at once a pause in their exercises, and an appearance of general perturbation. They fixed their eyes upon me, while one of them, a venerable looking man, came forward, and, in the name of the whole assembly, addressed me in the following language:—
" Excuse the panic which you have spread through this peaceful and happy company. We perceive that you are a white man. That colour, which is the emblem of innocence in every other creature of God, is, to us, a sign of guilt in man. The persons whom you see here, were once dragged by the men of your colour from their native country, and consigned by them to labour, punishment, and death. We are here collected

Sold by W. and F. G. Cash, 5, Bishopsgate Street, London; and by Jane Jowett, Friends' Meeting Yard, Leeds, at 1s. 2d. per 100.

together, and enjoy an ample compensation, in our present employments, for all the miseries we endured on earth. We know that we are secured by the Being whom we worship, from injury and oppression. Our appearance of terror, therefore, was entirely the sudden effect of habits which have not yet been eradicated from our minds." "Your apprehensions of danger from the sight of a white man," said I, "are natural. But in me you behold a friend. I have been your advocate—and"—here he interrupted me, and said, "Is not your name *Rush?*" I answered in the affirmative. Upon this he ran up and embraced me in his arms, and afterwards conducted me into the midst of the assembly, where, after being introduced to the principal characters, I was seated upon a bank of moss; and the following account was delivered to me by the venerable person who first accosted me:—

"The place we now occupy is called the Paradise of Negro Slaves. It is destined to be our place of residence till the general judgment; after which time, we expect to be admitted into higher and more perfect degrees of happiness.* Here we derive great pleasure from contemplating the infinite goodness of God, in allotting to us our full proportion of misery on earth; by which means we have escaped the punishments, to which the free and happy part of mankind too often expose themselves and endure after death. Here we have learned to thank God for all the afflictions our taskmasters heaped on us; inasmuch as they were the means of our present happiness. Pain and distress are the unavoidable portions of all mankind. They are the only possible avenues that can conduct them to peace and felicity. Happy are they who partake of their proportion of both upon the earth!" Here he ended.

After a silence of a few minutes, a young man, who bore on his head the mark of a wound, came up to me, and asked, "If I knew anything of Mr. ——, of the Island of ——?" I told him "I did not." " Mr. ——," said he, "was my master. One day I mistook his orders, and saddled his mare instead of his horse, which provoked him so much, that he took up an axe, and with a stroke on my head dismissed me from life. I long to hear whether he has repented of this unkind action. Do,

* The reader should note that these sentiments are not given as those of the author; but simply as what was expressed to him in his dream.

Sir, write to him, and tell him his sin is not too great to be forgiven; tell him his once miserable slave, Scipio, is not angry at him; he longs to bear his prayers to the offended Majesty of Heaven, and, when he dies, Scipio will apply to be one of the convoy that shall conduct his spirit to the regions of bliss, appointed for those who repent of their iniquities."

Before I could reply to this speech, an old man came and sat down by my side. His hair was white as snow. With a low, but gentle voice, he thus addressed me: "Sir, I was the slave of Mr. ——, in the Island of ——. I served him faithfully upwards of sixty years. No rising sun ever caught me in my cabin; no setting sun ever saw me out of the sugar-field, except on Sundays and holidays. My whole subsistence never cost my master more than forty shillings a-year. Herrings and roots were my only food. One day, in the eightieth year of my age, the overseer saw me stop to rest myself while I was at work. He came up to me, and beat me, till he could endure the heat and fatigue, occasioned by the blows he gave me, no longer. Nor was this all, he complained of me to my master, who instantly set me up at public vendue, and sold me for two guineas, to a tavern-keeper, in a distant parish. The distress I felt in leaving my children and grandchildren (twenty-eight of whom I left on my old master's plantation), soon put an end to my existence, and landed me on these happy shores. I have now no wish to gratify but one, and that is, to be permitted to visit my old master's family. I long to tell my master that his wealth cannot make him happy; that the sufferings of a single hour in the world of misery, for which he is preparing himself, will overbalance all the pleasures he ever enjoyed in this life; and that for every act of unnecessary severity he inflicts upon his slaves, he shall suffer tenfold in the world to come."

He had hardly finished his tale, when a decent-looking woman came forward, and addressed me in the following language—"Sir, I was once the slave of Mr. ——, in the State of ——. From the healthiness of my constitution, I was called upon to suckle my master's eldest son. To enable me to perform this office more effectually, my own child was taken from my breast, and soon afterwards died. My affections, in the first emotions of my grief, fastened themselves upon my infant master. He thrived under my care, and grew up a handsome young man. Upon the death of his father, I became his property. Soon after this event, he lost £100 at cards. To raise this money I was sold to a planter in a neighbouring state. I can never forget the anguish, with which my aged father and mother followed me to the end of the lane, when I left my master's house, and hung upon me, when they bade me farewell. My new master obliged me to work in the field, which in a few weeks ended my life. Say, my friend, is my first young master still alive? If he is, go to him, and tell him his unkind behaviour to me is upon record against him. The gentle spirits in heaven, whose happiness consists in expressions of gratitude and love, will have no fellowship with him. His soul must be melted with pity, or he can never escape the punishment which awaits the hard-hearted equally with the impenitent, in the regions of misery."

As soon as she had finished her story, a middle-aged woman approached me, and, after a low and respectful curtsey, thus addressed me—" Sir, I was born and educated in a Christian family, in one of the Southern States of America. In the thirty-third year of my age I applied to my master to purchase my freedom. Instead of granting my request, he conveyed me by force on board a vessel, and sold me to a planter in Hispaniola. Here it pleased God"—upon pronouncing these words she paused, and a general silence ensued. All at once, the eyes of the whole assembly were turned from me, and directed to a little white man who advanced towards them, on the opposite side of the grove, in which we were seated. His face was grave, placid, and full of benignity. In one hand he carried a subscription paper and a petition; in the other, he carried a small pamphlet on the unlawfulness of the African slave-trade, and a letter, directed to the King of Prussia, upon the unlawfulness of war. While I was employed in contemplating the venerable figure, suddenly I beheld the whole assembly running to meet him; the air resounded with the clapping of hands, and I awoke from my dream by the noise of a general acclamation of —Anthony Benezet!

Leeds Anti-slavery Series. No. 30.

Sold by W. and F. G. CASH, 5, Bishopsgate Street, London; and by JANE JOWETT, Friends' Meeting Yard, Leeds, at 1s. 2d. per 100.

Leeds Anti-slavery Series. No. 31.

SLAVEHOLDING

WEIGHED IN THE BALANCE OF TRUTH

AND ITS

COMPARATIVE GUILT ILLUSTRATED.

BY AN AMERICAN PASTOR.

THAT we may understand the duties we owe to God and our fellow-men, relative to the subject of Slavery, it is necessary to examine the institution, in all its bearings, upon the temporal and eternal interests of the enslaved; and ascertain, as far as we are able, the extent of the injuries which it inflicts. To aid my readers in doing this is now my object.

I do not propose, however, to gauge this mammoth evil, and show you its exact dimensions; I fully confess to you, in the outset, that I am not able so to do. That it is greater, in some of its bearings at least, than any other evil that ever existed among men, and involves more guilt than any other crime ever committed by men, I fully believe, and shall endeavour to show; still the evil has a magnitude which my powers cannot describe; and the guilt a blackness which can never be painted, except by a pencil dipped in the midnight of the bottomless pit.

I am aware that great complaint has often been made of those who have endeavoured to rouse the indignation of their fellow-men against the wrongs inflicted on the poor slave, that they deal in unjust severity of language. That they have at any time spoken more than the truth, I do not believe—nor can I admit that they have dealt out severity and pointed rebuke in more unmeasured terms than they have received them from their opponents.

Sold by W. and F. G. CASH, 5, Bishopsgate Street, London; and by JANE JOWETT, Friends' Meeting Yard, Leeds, at 6s. 6d. per 100; 11d. per doz.; or 1d. each.

When I remember, too, the long and profound slumberings, even of Christians, on this subject, while their brethren were groaning under all the injuries and cruelties of iron-handed and steel-hearted oppression, I cannot suppress the feeling, that it was necessary that those who would arouse them should break forth as in thunder-tones, and gird up all their energies to shake off the sloth in which their fellow-men were bound. They had themselves but just awoke as from a dream, and found that they had long been sleeping as on the overhanging brink of a burning crater; and when they saw the whole multitude of their fellow-countrymen still asleep in the same situation of fearful peril, who can wonder that they should cry out, at the top of their voice, and resort to every possible expedient to awaken those around them before it was too late? They heard the suppressed and terrific mutterings of the incipient earthquake below, and felt the ground beneath them already giving way, what less could they do than to lay about them, with all their strength, in the use of the first expedient that seemed calculated to awaken and save? They had no time to devise a multitude of measures, and then choose from among them such as would be most likely to satisfy those who were unwilling to be awakened. They *must do something*, and do it *then*. Previous measures, though entered upon ostensibly for the purpose of arousing men from sleep, had only served as a lullaby. The oppressors of their fellow-men were but becoming more secure in their claims of property in God's image; the chains of the slave were getting more and more firmly rivetted; and the whole nation were fast binding themselves in a willing bondage to those who found it conducive to their ease, and interest, and shameful indulgence, to be permitted to inflict all the wrongs they pleased on their fellow-men, with none to utter a single note of remonstrance or rebuke. It was seen that the press was bribed, and the pulpit gagged, and the lips of the multitude padlocked, and nearly the whole population of the free States bound, by the chains either of prejudice, or interest, or ignorance, to the tremendous car of Slavery; and those who loved to have it so had mounted the engine, and were driving at railroad speed whithersoever they would; and when a few awoke, and saw the nation thus hastening to the precipice of ruin, to be dashed in the abyss below, what less could they do than to cry STOP?—and that, too, even at a pitch of remonstrance, which should subject them to the imputation of fanaticism or madness.

It is not unlikely that some of my readers may regard the language which I shall use as unreasonably severe; and yet I do not believe, nor can I think that any man, after looking candidly at the subject, will believe that it expresses more than the truth. My design is to draw a parallel between slavery and the evils which stand connected with it, and some of the worst evils, and vices, and crimes which are ever found among men, that we may see where slavery ought to be placed in the catalogue of sins.

I. Let us look at the Roman Catholic Church. Much has been said during the last few years of the efforts made to bring this country under subjection to the Pope of Rome. But what are the evils which the Romish Church inflicts upon such as are brought under her control?

She takes away the Bible from them, and gives them no opportunity to learn for themselves the way to heaven. All the religious instruction which the people can receive must come orally from the lips of the priest. Slavery does the same thing precisely to all who come under its control. They may not read the Bible, nor possess it; and can receive no religious instruction but what comes orally from the lips of the priest. The Roman Catholic Church depends for its perpetuity upon the ignorance of the common people. Slavery depends for its perpetuity upon the ignorance of the enslaved. Hence the great effort to shut out all *knowledge*. The Romish Church robs the labouring-classes of large sums of money to support its pope, and its cardinals, its bishops, and its priests in idleness, and luxury, and profligacy. Slavery robs the labouring-class of their earnings to support another set of men in the same mode of life. The Romish Church confiscates the property, and confines, and tortures, and puts to death, such as will not submit to her rule, whenever she has the power of doing so. Slavery does the same things. Not only the property, the whole earnings, but the wife and children, the hands, and feet, and head—the whole body and soul of the enslaved—are confiscated and appropriated to the use of men in power. Slavery also has tortures for its victims. It applies the scourge, until the blood runs down their lacerated bodies in streams, and in a multitude of ways inflicts its cruelties upon such as will not yield an entire submission to its rule. If any refuse to submit longer to their sufferings, and flee, they are followed into their hiding-places, and put to death. Others are whipped until death ensues; others are driven to hard labour, without proper food or rest, until they sink down and die.

But the Romish Church does not, ordinarily, strip the whole multitude of its victims of everything that bears the name of property, and take the ownership of themselves out of their hands, and drive them by the scourge to hard labour from the beginning to the end of the year. She does not measure out to them their scanty pittance of food, nor name every rag of clothing which they are permitted to put on, nor mock at all the relations of social life—stealing the child out of the father's arms, or off the mother's breast, and the wife out of the bosom of her husband, and separating them for life; depriving them of all the protection of law, and subjecting them daily to every injury and suffering which avarice, and passion, and lust can load upon them. Nor are men, women, and children, under her influence, like cattle, raised to sell. Such enormities as these are left to be practised by slavery; and to be legalized in the statute-books of a people who have boastingly regarded themselves as the most thoroughly christianized nation on which the sun ever shines. I say, then, there are points in which Slavery far outdoes the Romish Church in cruelty and guilt; binds heavier burdens, and more grievous to be borne, and lays them on men's shoulders, and will not touch them with a finger. Slavery also, like Romanism, cries out against free discussion, and the liberty of the press, and does not hesitate to silence both, so far as she has the power, and to make every possible advance toward it where the power is not possessed. Hence the outrages committed on peaceful citizens travelling in slaveholding States, and the efforts to put down discussion in almost all the States which call themselves free. Hence the destruction of Birney's press in Cincinnati, and the stones cast in the streets of Troy at the hero Weld, who, like his Master, goes about doing good. Hence all the shameful outrages by which that place has been disgraced, and the still more shameful neglect of the proper authorities to protect peaceful, respectable, high-minded, and pious men, in the exercise of the most noble of all their rights, that of publicly expressing and defending their own opinions. Hence all the excesses practised in this and several adjoining States to lay the heaven-born spirit of liberty asleep, even among her own New England hills. Hence the long, loud, and repeated threats of dissolving the Union which Southern men have sent up on our ears, and which even some of our governors have echoed back, in declarations that it is felony for a man to speak what he thinks on a particular subject. Who doubts that Slavery, if she could, would go as far in locking up the opinions of men within their own breasts as ever Popery went in the height of her power? She had already well nigh taken away the power of free discussion from those who dare to assert the rights of their fellow-men, and would soon have completed the *work*.

II. Let us look at Infidelity. The evil arising from this source is, that it blinds men respecting their duty to God and their own souls, and thus leads them down to hell. It urges itself, however, on no man by force. A spark of honest desire to know the truth and walk in its light is, at all times, abundantly sufficient to show a man the sophistry and wilful unbelief by which such doctrines are supported, and to warn him of all their snares, and to guide his feet into the path of life. A spark of honesty in the admission of the plainest principles of common sense will show a man that there is a God, that the Bible is a revelation of his will, and that he will not let the wicked go unpunished who refuse to repent. He, therefore, who suffers himself to be borne upon the shoals and rocks, and down the cataracts, or into the whirlpools of wilful unbelief, goes there warned of his danger, and with abundant means and opportunities for escape. But slavery wrests the Bible out of the hands of immortal men by force. In the midst of a Christian land, with the clear light of heaven shining all around them, they are shut out from this light, and left to grope their way in darkness down to hell. That I may not be suspected of declaring more than the truth on this point, I will just give a specimen of the laws of slave States touching this point:—

"A law of South Carolina, authorizes the infliction of twenty lashes on every slave, found in an assembly, convened for mental instruction, held in a confined or secret place, although in presence of a white." That this cuts them off, and was designed to cut them off, from all means of mental instruction, nobody doubts; for who in that State is permitted to give slaves mental instruction in a public place? "Another law imposes a fine of a hundred pounds on any person who may teach a slave to write." "In North Carolina, to teach a slave to read or write, or to sell or give him any book [the Bible not excepted], or pamphlet, is punished with thirty-nine lashes, or imprisonment if the offender be a free negro, but if a white, then with a fine of three hundred dollars. In Georgia, if a white teach a free negro or a slave to read or write, he is fined five hundred dollars, and imprisoned at the discretion of the Court. If the offender be a coloured man, bond or free, he may be fined, or whipped, at the discretion of the Court. A father, therefore, may not teach his own children, on penalty of being flogged." This was enacted in 1829. "In Louisiana, the penalty for teaching slaves to read or write is one year's imprisonment. In Georgia, also, any justice may, at his discretion, break up any religious assembly of slaves, and may order each slave present to be corrected, without trial, by receiving, on the bare back, twenty-five stripes with a whip, switch, or cowskin." "In South Carolina, slaves may not meet together before sunrise, or after sunset,.for the purpose of religious instruction, unless a majority of the meeting be of whites, on penalty of twenty lashes well laid on. In Virginia, all *evening* meetings of slaves, at any meeting-house, are unequivocally forbidden." Of course they may not meet in the day-time, for then they must labour. Possibly they may on the Sabbath, but their opportunities of doing it even then are few and far between.

You see, therefore, the strenuous efforts which are made by legislative enactments, to shut out all light from the mind of the slave, and surround him with a thick, impenetrable darkness, in the midst of which he must live and die; and from which his eye can never open, till death frees him from the grasp of his oppressor. I am aware, that the privilege of giving oral religious instruction to slaves is, to some extent, granted, and that some slave-masters do pretend to teach their slaves the truths of religion. But what is the amount of all this? A writer for the *New York Evangelist* has, some months since, given us what he terms "sketches of slavery from a year's residence in Florida," in one number of which he speaks on this very point. He had conversed with slaveholders on the subject. One man thought it a very fine thing to give slaves religious instruction. " I called my slaves together," said he, "one Sabbath-day, *the only time which I have been able to get this season ! ! !* and read to them the account of Abraham's servant going to seek a wife for Isaac. I took occasion from this to speak to them of the integrity of this servant—what an amount of property was committed to his care, how faithfully he watched over it, how careful not to purloin any of the rich jewels for himself, how anxious to return at the appointed time." " I think," said this slaveholder, "that religious instruction must be decidedly beneficial." Another master with whom I conversed, continues the writer, believed nothing about giving religious instruction to slaves. He regarded it as all a farce. " There is no man," said the slaveholder, " who will read the whole Bible to his slaves. If I recollect right, there is something in the Bible which speaks of *breaking every yoke, and letting the oppressed go free ;* and there is no master," continued he, " who will read *that* to his slaves, not even your good Methodists ; and if we must not read the whole Bible, we may as well read none at all." Such are the views of slaveholders.

I have somewhere read the following: whether authentic or not, it illustrates my point, and expresses, I am fully persuaded, very much of truth. It was the remark of a slave, after the master had been reading the Bible to him and his companion:—" Massa bery *good* Christian ; him bery *good* Christian *indeed*. Read de Bible to us ; but him always read de same chapter, what says, servants obey your massas in all tings."

Here, unquestionably we have just about the truth on the subject of giving religious instruction to slaves. Multitudes never attempt it, and those who do are sure to do it for their own interest, rather than for the good of the slave. That there are exceptions, I am willing to admit ; but all that I have said exists unquestionably to a wide extent, and to an extent provided for by law. I am aware that the gospel is preached to some extent, and that some truly embrace it ; but these are the exceptions, and not the general rule. My claim is, that slavery destroys more souls among the slaves, by keeping the Bible away from them, than infidelity could do in its place if they were permitted to have the Bible and read for themselves ; and it seems to me that this is a position which no honest man will dispute. Slavery also destroys souls by force, when infidelity could only decoy, and therefore leave an opportunity for escape.

III. Let us compare slavery with the making and vending of ardent spirits. Do not suspect me of a wish to palliate, or extenuate the evils, or the guilt of this abominable business. I have often dwelt on these until my soul has been pained within me, and until I am well persuaded that all, and far more than all which has ever been said or *dreamed* on that subject, is strictly true. I am aware too, that a highly-gifted mind has, some years since, drawn a parallel between intemperance and the slave-trade, in which he has endeavoured to show that the latter is an evil of the least magnitude. But I am comparing now the business of making and vending ardent spirits, with slavery as it exists at this time in our country.

It has often been said with unquestionable truth, that from three to five hundred thousand miserable men in our nation are confirmed drunkards, and that from thirty to fifty thousand go down every year to a drunkard's grave; and, inasmuch as the drunkard cannot inherit the kingdom of God, they must go down to the depths of hell. A most fearful destruction this indeed ! But instead of five hundred thousand, there are not less than three millions four hundred and forty-five thousand in our country held in the darkness of slavery! How many of these, think you, have sufficient light to guide their feet to heaven ? Shall we say one-half ? Who can believe it ? But if this be admitted, there are still more than three times the number shut up by slavery, in a state of darkness that leads to hell, than have ever, by any man, been estimated in the ranks of intemperance. Is it not most clearly a truth, then, that slavery destroys more souls than the making and vending of ardent spirits ? When we consider, too, that slavery seizes its victims by force, and binds and rivets chains upon them which they cannot throw off, and thus leaves their souls unprovided with any of the means of grace, to die without hope ; and that strong drink leaves men abundant opportunities to escape if they will ; who will not say that slavery is unspeakably more to be dreaded ; that it is an evil of far greater magnitude than the other ? The intemperate man may, at any time, break away from his bondage, give up his cups, enjoy the means of grace, embrace the truth and live. But the victim of slavery, shut out from all true knowledge of God, deprived by law of all opportunity of learning his Maker's will, or of studying the way of salvation by Christ ; what can he do, but remain in his darkness and sin, until the darkness of eternal night closes in upon his benighted soul, and he is left for eternity to suffer the consequences of unpardoned sin. True, the guilt of him who dies the willing victim of intemperance, must be greater than that of the poor benighted slave, and his future punishment consequently more severe; but if slavery holds three times the number of victims exposed to hopeless reprobation, then it destroys three times the number of souls, and is therefore the greatest evil.

IV. Let us compare slavery with theft and robbery. Let me give a case for illustration:—You are a husband and a father. You commenced the world a poor man, but, by hard labour and economy, you have collected together a sum of money, which you believe, if well invested, will place you and your family in circumstances of respectability and comfort. From statements made to you, or from your own observation, by going upon the ground, you come to the conclusion that your money can be more profitably appropriated by removing to a distant country. Accordingly you convert everything you possess into cash, and make all the necessary arrangements for a removal with your family. On the night previous to your intended departure, a thief enters your dwelling-house, takes possession of all you have, and makes off, and you never hear of it more. Or suppose you are already on your journey, and after many days of fatiguing travel, find yourself near the place of your destination ; when you are met by the highwayman, who, with a pistol at your breast, robs you of your last farthing. Now I suppose this would be a case where theft and robbery would stand out in their worst features. It would be a trying case indeed. After years of toil to gain something for yourself and household, you are in a moment penniless, with your destitute, needy family upon your hands. All you can do, is again to betake yourself to hard labour, to provide for those you love.

But suppose, after all this, you were doomed to see your children torn from you, one after another, and sold under the hammer, to go you know not where; to be subjected to the cruelty, and abuse, and outrage of any monster into whose hands they might chance to fall; where you could never see or hear from them more; and you left with no means of redress; to sit down beside your broken-hearted wife, and mingle your tears, and sighs, and sobs with hers, with no prospect of relief until death. But in the midst of it all, even the wife of your bosom, dear as your own heart's-blood, is sundered from you, and sold for ever from your embrace, and you at last go off under the hammer, to the highest bidder, and are driven by the lash, to groan, and sweat, under long, long days of unrequited toil, with no relief till you die. This is Slavery. It robs a man of all his earnings during his whole life. Labour as he may, sweat as he may, he can never have a farthing to call his own. Just hear the laws on this subject : " In South Carolina a slave is not permitted to keep a boat, or raise and breed for his own benefit, any horses, cattle, sheep, or hogs, under pain of forfeiture, and *any person may take them from him.*" I ask, what is that but robbery—except it is unspeakably worse, because it is legalized—and the poor man has no means of redress? It is made lawful for *any person* to rob him by the letter of the statute.

" In Georgia, the master is fined thirty dollars for suffering a slave to hire himself to another for his own benefit. In Maryland, the master forfeits thirteen dollars for each month that his slave is permitted to receive wages on his own account. In Virginia, every master is finable who permits a slave to work for himself at wages. In North Carolina, all horses, cattle, hogs, or sheep, that shall belong to any slave, or be of any slave's mark in this State, shall be seized and sold by the county wardens. In Mississippi, the master is forbidden, under the penalty of fifty dollars, to let a slave raise cotton for himself, or to keep stock of any description." Now where is the man under heaven, who would not say that such a system of legalized oppression was infinitely worse than theft or robbery, when practised towards himself? And what, I ask, makes the crime any less heinous, when practised towards a coloured man, than it would be if practised towards either of us? The poor slave feels such wrongs as deeply as we could, and groans under them as loudly, and sheds tears as profusely as we would do; but there he is, without means of redress. And in addition to all this robbery of everything in the shape of property, the poor slave is robbed of his children, and his wife, and robbed of himself—and has nothing left him but a miserable existence, subjected to the most cruel, heart-withering tyranny, that was ever practised by man on his fellow-man since this world has borne the curse of its God. When the thief or the robber takes your property, you can repossess it whenever you can find it; or if not, you can acquire more, and your wife, and children, and yourself, are still your own. Theft and robbery are nothing compared with the wickedness of slavery. Make them as bad as you please, and they do not deserve to be named the same week. The difference between them is too great to be described, too wide to be measured, too deep to be fathomed. The slaveholder who goes impenitent to hell, will find himself loaded down with a weight of guilt and damnation, that will sink him out of sight of the worst highway robber that ever walked the earth. But you will say the highway robber is often guilty of murder. Well, and so is the slaveholder often guilty of murder—and this brings me to my next point.

V. Let us now compare slavery with murder. Who does not know that oftentimes, when the poor slave can no longer endure the outrages practised upon him, and flies, and takes to the wood, he is hunted down by dogs and guns, and thus put to death, just for trying to escape? Everybody knows that it is a thing of frequent occurrence. Put to death just for trying to escape from his sufferings and his wrongs! Again, it is a maxim with them, that, at particular seasons, they can afford to work a set of hands to death, for the purpose of getting their crops early to market, and thereby securing a much greater price. The writer of *Sketches of Slavery*, from a year's residence in Florida, speaks of this particularly, as coming under his observation while there; and I have seen this fact referred to by other writers in public print. They do not hesitate to sacrifice the lives of their slaves to hard labour, when it will increase their profits. Besides, the poor slave is often whipped until the result is death. Is not my point made clear, abundantly clear, that slavery is worse than murder? Would you not prefer to be met by a highwayman, and shot dead, rather than have your life worn out on a slave plantation, toiling to enrich the hard-hearted wretch who had stripped you of all your rights? Would you not prefer this to being whipped, and then laid away to die under the effect? And is not the wretch who inflicts death by such means, to enrich himself, more guilty than he who blows out the traveller's brains, and seizes his money to enrich himself? Surely my point needs no more illustration. Slavery *is worse* than murder. But there is still this point to be taken into account. If a man shoots you dead by the way-side, it is your own fault if you do not go to heaven. You have the Bible and the gospel. You know that there is a Saviour; and if you have not repented of your sins, and believed in him for salvation, you are without excuse. If you lose your soul, the fault is your own. Though murdered, you might, if you would, have been saved. But the poor slave is prevented from learning the way of salvation while he lives, and then, worn out with toil, he dies, and may be lost for ever. Surely I need say no more: what honest man is not prepared to say that slavery is worse than murder?

VI. I come now to a point, which, in the estimation of some, perhaps, ought to be suppressed. But I am a servant of the Most High God, and to him accountable; and as such, placed under solemn obligation to cry aloud and spare not, and show this guilty nation its sins. This, with the Lord's help, I will do. It is high time, also, that our mothers and our wives, our sisters and our daughters, knew the sufferings and the wrongs of the poor defenceless female slave, that they may lift up their strong cries to Heaven in her behalf.

I wish, therefore, to compare slavery with fornication and adultery, and the violation of female purity by force. And, my hearer, I do not ask you to believe my bare assertion on this point; I will show you proof, as it has been my endeavour to do on every point previously considered.

Look again at the laws. In Kentucky—" any negro, mulatto,

or Indian, *bond or free, who shall at any time lift his hand in opposition to any white person* (mark the language), shall receive thirty lashes on his or her bare back, *well laid on,* by order of the justice."

This regulation, or something very much like it, is believed to be in force in all the slaveholding States. Look now at the condition in which this places the poor female. She is at the uncontrolled will of the master. He may order her, by fear of the lash, into any secret place where he pleases ; the same fear of the lash enables him to accomplish all the hellish purposes of his heart; and then, by the same means, he can seal her lips in silence, that the crime be never divulged. During all this time, if she lift a hand against him, he can procure thirty lashes for her, to be well laid on, by order of the justice, in addition to all he pleases to inflict himself. Let us now just remember, that, in addition to such a regulation, no person of colour can be a witness against a white man in a court of justice, and you see the exact condition of the poor female slave. There is nothing so foul in pollution, nothing so horrid in crime, but she may be driven, by the lash, to be the victim of it, and she must not lift a hand in self-defence ; and then she dare not divulge her wrongs, or if she does, there is no power on earth from whom she can gain any redress, or even protection, against a repeated infliction of the same evils.

If slaveholders had framed laws for the express purpose of placing the purity and virtue of their females entirely in their own power, they could not have done it *more* effectually than it is now done. It would seem to be a system, framed for the very purpose of giving them full power to pollute, by force, just as many as they pleased. At any rate, they know the power is in their hands, and there are developments enough which show that they are not slow to use it. * There is a multitude of facts on this subject ; and I will just relate one or two, because I know them to be authentic.

A particular friend of mine, who spent several years in a slave state, gave me the following as an occurrence which transpired in the place where he resided, and at the very time of his residence there. A man—I will not say gentleman,

* Read Bourne's *Picture of Slavery.*

and, in truth, I ought to say monster—who had a wife and a family of grown-up daughters residing with him, had also in his house a young female slave. This slave became the mother of a child; and it was a matter of public notoriety that the head of the family was the father of it. So barefaced had the thing become, that the man found it necessary to take some measures to get his shame, and the extreme mortification of his wife and daughters, out of his mind.* He accordingly sold her for the southern market; and though it was with some difficulty that he could persuade the purchaser to take the infant, he at length did so; and the wretched mother, the victim of the master's beastliness and abominable crime, was taken, or rather torn, from the house, and borne away literally uttering cries and shrieks of distress. Now, I would like to know whether there is any language under heaven that will sufficiently set forth the guilt of such a wretch?

The following fact was related by a pious physician, who resides in the city of Washington. It came to me in such a way that I know it to be a fact:—

"There is," said this physician, "residing in this city, a young female slave, who is pious, and a member of the same church to which I belong. She is a mulatto, and her complexion nearly white. One day she came to me in great trouble and distress, and wished me to tell her what she could do. She stated to me that her master's son was in the practice of compelling her, whenever he pleased, to go with him to his bed. She had been obliged to submit to it; and she knew of no way to obtain any relief. She could not appeal to her master for protection, for he was guilty of like practices himself. She wished to know what she could do? Poor girl! what could she do? She could not lift a hand in self-defence. She could not flee; for she was a slave. She would be brought back and beaten, and be placed perhaps in a worse condition than before. And there she was, a pious girl, with all the feelings of her heart alive to the woes of her condition, the victim of the brutal lusts of a dissolute young man; with no means of defence or escape, and no prospect before her but that of being

---

* This occurrence was not very far south, otherwise there would have been no shame.

again and again polluted whenever his unbridled passions should chance to dictate."

Perhaps there is a mother here who has a pious daughter; and I would like to come into her heart, and ask what would be her feelings if that daughter were placed in such circumstances as these? or what would be the feelings of that daughter, if she were thus bound down to a condition so much worse than death? I do solemnly believe that there is no adulterer under heaven, no fornicator, covered with a guilt so deep and damning as the wretch that will pursue such a course of conduct as that. Even the victim of seduction is but decoyed from the paths of virtue; but here is a disciple of Christ bound, and that, too, by the laws of the land, and laid, a helpless victim, on the altar of prostitution.

Here, then, is a crime, punishable under most governments with death, and the victim has the power of redress, and certainly of escape, from a repetition of the outrage; but Slavery places its victims where there is no redress, and no deliverance, and gives the slaveholder full power to roll and riot upon the virtue and innocence of as many defenceless females as he pleases, with no power under heaven to call him to account. I say again, if they had made their laws for the express purpose of securing to themselves this power, they could not have done the thing more effectually; and no man who has ever seen or heard much of southern practices, is ignorant of the truth, that such things as I have been relating are the common occurrences of every day. O! when I reflect on this subject, I could almost pray for a voice like a volcano, and for words that would scorch and burn like drops of melted lava, that I might thunder the guilt of the slaveholder in his ears, and talk to him in language which he *would* feel. Who will say that this system of slavery, under which no female who has a drop of African blood in her veins has any defence for her virtue against any white man, even for an hour, and no possibility of escaping from pollution, is not unspeakably worse than fornication and adultery, or even the violation of purity by force, where there are laws to apprehend and punish for such a crime? Do not suspect me of a wish to palliate these vices. They were never painted in colourings too foul and loathsome, nor was their guilt ever portrayed in a blackness deeper than the reality;

but I say the system of slavery is a thing fouler, blacker, guiltier still.

VII. But let us look again, and compare slavery with treason. Benedict Arnold was a traitor. At a time when his country was in great distress and difficulties, he formed the mad purpose of delivering her over to the will of her enemies; and did what he could to accomplish his end. Every breast in the land burned with indignation against him—and, but for his flight, he would have ended his days on a gallows.

But, suppose he had accomplished his end, and the unjust laws, against which our fathers fought and bled, had remained in full force upon us until now; I am bold to say that we should not have suffered wrongs that ought to be mentioned in comparison with the wrongs of the slave. There was a heavy and unjust taxation, but it was not stripping us of all our earnings for life. There was a refusal to give us a just representation in framing the laws by which we were to be governed; but it was not stripping us from all protection of law, and reducing us in that respect to the condition of cattle or swine. It was not stripping us of all our rights, and robbing us of our children, and subjecting our wives, our sisters, and our daughters to wanton and promiscuous violation, with no power to lift a hand in self-defence, and depriving us of the power of giving them protection. The husband or father, if he be a slave, may look on and see his wife or daughter polluted before his eyes, and all the laws of the land are against his lifting a finger for their deliverance. He may toil ever so hard during his whole life, and he cannot be worth a farthing. The treason of Arnold, had it prospered, would never have subjected us to such evils as these. Besides, had we remained until this British colonies, other things being as they now *are,* this evil of slavery would now have been done away, and perhaps years ago. When I think of this, if I had not confidence in the overruling providence of God, I could almost weep that it did not seem best to the God of armies to leave us under the control of a power that would have uprooted this destructive Bohon Upas, which is still throwing its broad branches of death and desolation over such wide-spreading portions of our otherwise happy land. Sure I am that Arnold's treason would never have made our land groan under such woes, and sent up to heaven such cries of distress as are wrung daily from the breasts of the helpless millions whom our nation now enslaves. I say again, therefore, that the system of slavery is unspeakably worse than treason. But I cannot pursue this parallel further. I have glanced at what men regard as the worst of evils and crimes; but when weighing the guilt of slavery, we find that everything which we can place in the opposite scale at once kicks the beam. It has a weight of guilt attached to it that can be balanced by the guilt of no other *crime*.

There is one more point to the thing which I wish to name, as giving blackness and aggravation to its guilt, and then I have done. It is, that multitudes of the professed disciples of Christ come forward to justify the system of slavery, and to claim for it sanction from the Bible. Yes, this system of slavery, red as it is with crime, black as it is with guilt, and foul as it is with impurity, is called, even by professed Christians and ministers, an institution of the Bible! O, it seems to me, that if the long-suffering patience of a forbearing God was ever insulted beyond endurance, it must be when the protection of his authority is claimed for the perpetuity of such a system as this. There is no crime which it does not legalize—no sin which it does not protect—no depth of impurity which it does not dig, and in which it does not permit vile men to wallow. And yet there are not wanting men, Christian men, and ministers who wait at the altar of God, who call this an institution of Heaven, and claim for it the authority of the Most High! I know that they would plead for slavery, without the abominations which I have named, and claim to look upon such crimes and vices with as deep an abhorrence as we.

But who cannot see that slavery is the common mother of all this brood of hellish ills; in whose frightfully prolific womb they are conceived, and by whom they are brought forth. Slavery *itself* is the thing to be reprobated. You must put the odious dam to death, or she will continue to multiply her infernal progeny, and send them abroad among us, prolific in woes. You cannot have slavery without its concomitant evils. I know men may be found whose hearts have felt the power of the religion of Christ, but whose moral sensibilities are not sufficiently awake to lead them to obey God on this subject; to break every yoke and let the oppressed go free; who claim that *they* treat their slaves kindly, and that under such circumstances slavery is justifiable; and that, moreover, they are not accountable for the crimes which other men commit among their slaves, or for the wrongs which they practise upon them. Kindness to an enslaved man! It is a contradiction in terms. You might as well rob him of his all on earth, cut off his hands and feet, and bore out his eyes, and then take him into your house and treat him kindly to make up for the wrong.

The slave, under the best circumstances, is the victim of robbery every day. Day by day, all his life, he is robbed of the fruits of his labour, that it may go to enrich another. He has hands, indeed, but he may not use them for his own benefit. Feet he has, but they may not bear him where *he* would go. They must go and come at the master's bidding, and not his. He has eyes, but he may not look on the light of science, or on the clearer, purer light of God's revealed truth. Even the sun shines not for him, as it only serves to light him to his unwilling and unrequited toil. Of what use, then, are hands, and feet, and eyes to him? He can no more use them for his own benefit than if he had none—and yet you think to make up to him by kindness what you have taken away; and call yourself a disciple of Christ, and think that Heaven will reward you for being so kind to your poor, oppressed, downtrodden victim, whom you compel to labour unrewarded for your good. Is that the religion of Christ? Is that loving your neighbour as yourself?

But the most kind-hearted, and upright, and pious slaveholder in the land, so far as he approves of the system of slavery, and pleads for its perpetuity, is at best accessory to all the evils to which the system gives rise. He is therefore a partaker in its guilt, and will hereafter find his hands stained and polluted with its vices and its crimes. He who has said in his Bible, "Be not partaker of other men's sins," has also said, "Come out from among them, and be ye separate, and touch not the unclean thing;" *and no man can be guiltless who refuses to do this.*

But perhaps it will be asked, admitting that slavery is everything that you claim it to be, what right have you to interfere? I claim no right of interference based on the existing laws of our country; for these, as we have seen, are so abominably wicked and oppressive, as fully to sanction all the evils and crimes which we have been considering. Still, I claim that I have a right to interfere,* and to do all in my power, by every possible means, for the extinction of slavery. Do any ask on what that right is based ? I answer, on the statute-book of Almighty God—on the pillars of Heaven's eternal throne; and better authority than this, to sanction my interference, I do not ask. "Thou shalt love thy neighbour as thyself." "Who is my neighbour?" Let Jesus Christ answer. "A certain man," no matter who, "went down from Jerusalem to Jericho, and fell among thieves, who stripped him of his raiment, and wounding him, departed, leaving him half dead. And by chance, there came down a certain priest that way; and when he saw him, he passed by on the other side." How exactly like the conduct of many ministers of the gospel towards the slave ! They just look on his sufferings, and pass by, making no effort to give him relief. "And likewise a Levite, when he was at the place, came and looked on him, and passed by on the other side." Just so multitudes of professing Christians' conduct towards the slave. They look on him, pass by, and leave him alone in his woes. "But a certain Samaritan, as he journeyed, came where he was, and when *he* saw him, he had compassion on him, and went to him and bound up his wounds, pouring in oil and wine, and set him on his own beast, and brought him to an inn, and took care of him. And on the morrow, when he departed, he took out money and gave it to the host, and said unto him, Take care of him, and whatsoever thou spendest more, when I come again I will repay thee." Here our Saviour has shown us what it is to act the part of a neighbour. This Samaritan found a fellow-being in distress. He stopped not to inquire who he was, but proceeded at once to do as he would like to have others do to him in like circumstances. And now the command of Christ is, "Go thou and do likewise." Wherever, therefore, we find a fellow-being in distress, we find in him a neighbour, one whom we are bound to love as we love ourselves. We are to identify ourselves with him, and feel for his wrongs and his woes, as we would for our own in like circumstances, and are to do for him, so far as lies in our power, everything which, in like circumstances, we could wish others to do for us. Tell me not, then, that I have no right to interfere, when I see more

---

* The author disapproves of interference at the expense of human life, but believes that all possible means, short of the shedding of blood, are justifiable.

than three millions of my neighbours, yes, of my brethren, my own fellow-countrymen, groaning, and toiling, and dying under the unparalleled wrongs of slavery: I have no right *not* to interfere. I am a traitor to my neighbour, and a rebel against my God, if I forbear to interfere—if I fail to use the last power which my Maker has given me, in pleading for the immediate deliverance of my fellow-men from their sufferings and their chains. I trample on the universal law of the infinite Jehovah, if I leave undone anything in my power, which I would wish to have done for me, if all the miseries of slavery were mine.

But it is not merely by looking at the general principles of God's government that I earn my duty toward the toil-worn, agonized, suffering slave. I find positive direction for this specific case. Jer. xxi. 12:—"Thus saith the Lord, Execute judgment in the morning, and deliver him that is spoiled out of the hand of the oppressor, lest my fury go forth like fire, and burn that none can quench it, because of the evil of your doings." Who is spoiled, if it be not the slave? Is he not spoiled of everything? Spoiled of all his earnings—spoiled of the child whom he loves—spoiled of the wife that is bone of his bone, and flesh of his flesh—spoiled even of the ownership of himself, and spoiled of his immortal soul, by being robbed of the light that would guide his feet to heaven? And the poor suffering female slave—of what is she not spoiled? Spoiled of all that protection which the innocent and helpless have a right to claim, even of the savage. Spoiled of all the affectionate tenderness which woman everywhere has a right to expect; spoiled even of her virtue, and that by law, for we have seen that the laws have placed her where she cannot preserve it if she would.

Who then, I ask again, is spoiled, if it be not the slave? And who is an oppressor, if it be not the man who holds him in bondage, and inflicts all these wrongs upon him? While, therefore, I hear the God of heaven saying, "Deliver him that is spoiled out of the hand of the oppressor, lest my fury go forth like fire, and burn, that none can quench it," can I expect to escape the fury of that fire, if I shut my ears against the mandate, which thunders upon me from the presence-chamber, and from the lips of Him, who declares himself King of kings and Lord of lords? Tell me not that I have no right to interfere— no right to plead for the deliverance " of the spoiled out of the hand of the oppressor." I may not fail to do it, lest the fire of God's fury kindle upon me for my disregard of his high command. And the same is true of all my readers. Unless you have a right to disobey Almighty God, you have no right to leave anything undone, which you might do, for the deliverance of the slave.

But who is the slave? He is a man—made in the image of God—and bears as much of God's image, remember, as though he had the complexion, and the features, and the limbs of the white man. Where is the man with a pale face, even among slaveholders, who will stand up, before the face of Heaven, and claim that he bears more of God's image than his slave? He would show the image of the devil large as life, had he the pride and effrontery to do such a deed of daring impiety. The slave is made in the image of his God, and to him God gave dominion over the works of his hand, as much as to the white man. For him God lighted up the sun and moon, and made the heavens resplendent with stars, as much as for us. For him God made the breath of morning, and the calm stillness of the summer eve. For him the deep blue sky was spread a canopy, and for him puts on alternate tints of purple and of gold. For him the landscape smiles in green, and flowers spring up to beautify his path, and trees hang out their foliage, and bend beneath their burdens of delicious fruit. For him the fields wave with their ripening grain—for him the valleys yield their corn—for him the flocks and herds lay down their treasures, and the sea sends up its inexhaustible supplies. For him the limpid stream, the clear, pure fountain were provided, and for him the balmy air, echoing with melody of birds. Ah, and for him, remember it, ye who dare withhold it from him, for him the Bible was given. Who dare say that God provided these things for the master, more than for the man whom he enslaves.

But what is more than all, for him the Son of God came down and died. The blood gushed from his heart as freely, and in streams as pure, for the oppressed and broken-hearted slave, as for us, or for the man who dares enslave God's image—for him the river of the water of life proceedeth, clear as crystal, from the throne of God and the Lamb—for him the streets of the New Jerusalem are paved with gold, and for him the glory of God and the Lamb shall pour forth its light, in beams that shall for ever hide the brightness of the noonday sun—and for him are made ready the joys of an eternal heaven. Yes, this is the being whom slavery binds in chains, and robs of all the richest gifts of heaven, and sinks in ignorance and pollution down to hell. O, if the whole arch of heaven above us ever echoed with the loud threatenings of an indignant God, it may now be heard to echo with the fearful interrogation—"Shall I not visit for these things, saith the Lord? Shall not my soul be avenged on such a nation as this?"

And now, will you look on, and seal your lips in silence, and say that you have no right to interfere for the deliverance of the slave? Do you not hear the God of heaven saying, "Deliver him that is spoiled out of the hand of the oppressor, lest my fury go forth like fire, and burn that none can quench it?" and dare you disobey? Do you ask what shall be done for his deliverance? I answer, let every pulpit thunder forth this mandate of the Most High God—let every minister at the altar cry aloud, and spare not, and lift up his voice like a trumpet, and show this people their transgressions, this guilty people their sins. Let every press groan to be delivered of its obligation to make known the Almighty's will; and let such as can pray, pray *now*, that God would break every yoke, and let the oppressed go free. Especially, let woman—woman, the last to linger around the cross, and the first to find the sepulchre of God's crucified Son—linger long at the altar of prayer, and be found early upon her knees wrestling at the throne of grace; and let all who fear God or love man, resolve before high heaven, that they will not rest till every chain is broken, every yoke buried, every scourge and fetter burned.

But I seem to hear some one ask, must we think only of the slave, must we not regard the master's rights? Rights! What rights? Right to hold his fellow-man in bondage for one hour? He might as well claim a right to sit on the throne of God. He has no such right. But must he relinquish all the property he now holds in slaves? He has no such property. He has no more right to call them his property, than he has to call the angels in heaven his property. God gave man dominion over the beasts of the field, but over God's own image he never gave him dominion. The wicked, heaven-daring laws of men confer the *power* of enslaving man, but the *right* they never gave, for it was never theirs to give. There is no such thing as property in man—there never can be. We do not ask the slaveholder to relinquish any right. We call upon him, on the authority of God, to break every yoke and let the oppressed go free. We do not ask them to give up their property. We tell them that God declares them to be "like wolves ravening the prey, to shed blood and to destroy souls, to get dishonest gain; and that the prophets have daubed them with untempered mortar, seeing vanity and divining lies unto them, saying, Thus saith the Lord, when the Lord hath not spoken. That the people of the land have used oppression, and exercised robbery, and have vexed the poor and needy, and have oppressed the stranger wrongfully, and that God now threatens to pour out his indignation upon them, and to consume them with the fire of his wrath, and to recompense their way upon their own heads." No, we do not ask the slaveholder to give up his property; we ask him "to cease beating God's people to pieces, to cease grinding the face of the poor;" and when the slaveholder has done that, the lost slave will have his freedom.

But you say it would make great changes in society, to free every slave at once; and many a man, who now lives in affluence, would instantly become poor. We doubt it not. We doubt not that many a wretch, who has rolled in profusion, by robbing his fellow-men of their earnings, would be obliged to go to work with his own hands to earn his bread; and this is just what he ought to have done long ago. He is made of no better clay than the lowliest of all God's creatures whom he enslaves; and there is no more reason why he should be exempted from eating his bread in the sweat of his brow. Let us arise then, with one heart, and with united voice, and with ready hands, do our utmost to deliver the oppressed from their wrongs.

But it may still be asked, what do you expect to accomplish? We expect to make the slaveholder feel, that when he crushes an immortal soul down to the depths of hell, to gratify his own abominable selfishness, God will hold him accountable for that soul at the judgment-day. We expect to make him see, that the short-lived gratification, which he can have derived from enslaving his fellow-man, will but poorly compensate him for the eternal damnation which he must hereafter endure, if he does not repent of his abominable sin. We expect to open to him the broad claims of the infinite God, and to make him see that, in his present course of conduct, he is holding himself in open exposure to the Almighty's wrath; and having thus bared his conscience to the arrows of truth, we expect to call down the Holy Spirit by our prayers, to fix these arrows deep in his heart; to reprove him of sin, of righteousness, and of judgment, and thus to bring him to unfeigned repentance before God. We expect not to accomplish what we aim at with our unaided strength; but we believe that the Lord of hosts is with us, and trusting in His strength we cannot fail. Christians of every name, shall we not have your aid? Lovers of your fellow-men, look at the wrongs of the slave, and weep and toil for him, that he may go free. Open your hearts and your hands to him, and remember that "He that hath pity on the poor, lendeth to the Lord, and that which he hath given he will pay him again."

Let no one think to rid himself of obligation on this momentous subject. Every man has a tongue, and he can use it; he has influence, and he can exert it; he has moral power, and he can put it forth; and this is all the power we need. Our efforts are aimed, not at the life of the slaveholder, but at his conscience—his moral feelings, and with the help of God, we do expect them to prevail. But perhaps you will say that slaveholders have no conscience on this subject. Doubtless their conscience may be dead and buried; it may have been sleeping these fifty years in its grave; but come on, one and all, let us raise the trump of truth, and blow a resurrection-blast above it, that shall call it forth from its dust, to take up its whip of scorpions, and scourge the guilty men into obedience to the commands of God. Slavery cannot long live among them. "Behold, the hire of the labourers, who have reaped down their fields, which is of them kept back by fraud, crieth; and the cries of them which have reaped are entered into the ears of the Lord of Sabaoth." The Lord of armies is the fearful signification of that term; and if they cease not from their oppression, they may well expect that the Lord of armies will not long withhold his hand. Up, my friends, and do your duty, to deliver the spoiled out of the hand of the oppressor, lest the fire of God's fury kindle ere long upon you.

Leeds Anti-slavery Series. No. 31.

Sold by W. and F. G. CASH, 5, Bishopsgate Street, London; and by JANE JOWETT, Friends' Meeting Yard, Leeds, at 6s. 6d. per 100; 11d. per doz.; or 1d. each.

Leeds Anti-slavery Series. No. 32.

THE FUGITIVE SLAVE BILL, AND ITS EFFECTS.

SLAVE-OWNER SHOOTING A FUGITIVE SLAVE.

IN the autumn of 1850, the American Congress passed the Fugitive Slave Bill. Previously to the passing of that measure, the slave who could manage to escape from the Southern States found shelter and refuge in the North. There he was safe. Public opinion guarded him. Now the case is altered. The slave may be tracked, and claimed, and sent back to slavery. The bill denies the privilege of a trial by jury. By the law of the United States, a trial by jury is granted in all cases where the value in controversy exceeds twenty dollars. By the slave law this privilege is denied. "A human being," says Judge Jay, in commenting upon this law, "is stripped of every right, and reduced to the condition of a vendible beast of burden, with less ceremony and more celerity than one neighbour can recover of another the value of a pig in any court of justice."

Sold by W. and F. G. CASH, 5, Bishopsgate Street, London; and by JANE JOWETT Friends' Meeting-Yard, Leeds, at 6s. 6d. per 100, or 11d. per dozen.

The American Constitution declares that no person shall be deprived of life or property, without due process of law. Also, it provides, that in criminal prosecutions the accused shall enjoy a speedy and public trial by jury, and be confronted with the witnesses against him. The Fugitive Slave Bill sets aside these provisions, it suspends the Habeas Corpus Act. It makes an *ex parte* judgment of a court in one state conclusive against the alleged fugitive in the state where arrested; and not satisfied with this, no appeal from the decision of the commissioner or court is allowed. Besides this, as was said by the Hon. Horace Mann, the proofs which the law provides for, and declares *conclusive*, are abhorrent to reason, to common sense, and to the common law. It provides that evidence taken in a southern state, at any time or place which a claimant may select, without any notice or the possibility of knowledge on the part of the person to be robbed and enslaved by it, may be clandestinely carried or sent to any place where it is to be used, and there sprung upon its victim, as a wild beast springs from its jungle upon the passer-by; and it provides that this evidence, thus surreptitiously taken and used, shall be *conclusive* proof of the fact of slavery and of escape from slavery. It does not submit the sufficiency of the evidence to the judgment of the tribunal, but it arbitrarily makes it conclusive, whether sufficient or not. It abolishes the common law distinction between competency and credibility.

The cruel fruits of this law have been such as might be expected to grow on so wicked a stock. *The first man sent into slavery under it, Adam Gibson, was a free man.* When the claimant's agent brought Gibson to him, he refused to receive him, for he knew that all his household and neighbours would know that Gibson had never been his slave; and so, after this free man had been seized and sentenced as a slave, and dragged forcibly away from home to Maryland, as a slave, he was set adrift, and left to find his way back as best he could. Of the first *eight* persons doomed to slavery under this law, *four were free men.* In the case of Daniel, who was tried before Mr. Commissioner Smith, at Buffalo, the slave-claimant never carried a single witness before the court that made the record of slavery and escape. In another case, in Philadelphia, Mr. Commissioner Ingraham decided some points directly against law and authority ; and when a decision of a judge of the United States Court was produced against him, he coolly said he differed from the Judge, made out the certificate, pocketed the ten dollars, and sent a human being to bondage. And yet, with all these abominations, we find the Democratic Convention, which met at Baltimore last year, resolved to—" Abide by, and adhere to, a faithful execution of the Act known as the compromise measures settled by the last Congress—the Act for reclaiming from fugitive slaves service or labour, included." And further, that they—" Will resist all attempts at renewing, in Congress or out of it, the agitation of the slavery question, under whatever shape or colour the attempt may be made."

Nor were the Democrats alone; the Whigs at the same place agreed to a resolution almost equally infamous.

But we give an outline of the Bill. From that it will appear how it tramples on human rights, how it arms the slave-owner with terrible and irresponsible power, and deprives the slave of all chance of escape:—

" Marshals and deputies are required to execute all warrants and precepts, or other process, for the arrest and detention of fugitives, under penalty of a fine of 1000 dollars for the use of the claimant of such fugitive; and in case of the escape of such fugitive from the custody of a marshal, whether with or without his knowledge and connivance, the said marshal is to be liable to a prosecution for the full value of the said fugitive.

" Any person who shall knowingly hinder the arrest of a fugitive, or attempt to rescue him after arrest, or assist such fugitive, directly or indirectly, to escape, or harbour or conceal him, after notice or knowledge of the fact that he was a fugitive, shall be liable to a fine of 1000 dollars, and six months' imprisonment, by conviction before the proper district or territorial courts, and to a suit for damages of 1000 dollars for each fugitive lost to his owner by said obstruction or rescue, the same to be recovered by action of debt in any of the courts aforesaid."

Such are the provisions of the bill. Yet actually infamous as they are, President Fillmore, in the annual presidential message, could thus speak respecting it:—

"It is deeply to be regretted that, in several instances, officers of the Government, in attempting to execute the law for the return of fugitives from labour, have been openly resisted, and their efforts frustrated and defeated by lawless and violent mobs; that in one case such resistance resulted in the death of an estimable citizen, and in others serious injury ensued to those officers and to individuals who were using their endeavours to sustain the laws. Prosecutions have been instituted against the alleged offenders, so far as they could be identified, and are still pending. I have regarded it as my duty, in these cases, to give all aid legally in my power to the enforcement of the laws, and I shall continue to do so, wherever and whenever their execution may be resisted."

After this we cannot be surprised to find ministers of religion sanctioning the Fugitive Slave Bill.

It is supposed there are 50,000 fugitive slaves in the various free states of the Union. It is easy to imagine the terror which the passing of such a measure created. How families were broken up—churches disorganized—joy turned into mourning, and laughter into tears. We propose to illustrate the workings of this law. We have tales of misery enough to fill a volume—but we make a few selections. We will begin with—

THE BREAKING UP OF A CHURCH.

The Rev. James Abbot, whose writings have made him popular on both sides of the Atlantic, says :—" In one of the cities of New England, there was a small Baptist church of coloured people. It consisted of 120 members. Of these, 60 had escaped from Southern bondage, and were consequently on the list of the proscribed by the Fugitive Slave Law. The old law had become a dead letter. Unconscious of danger, they were pursuing, industriously and cheerfully, their several avocations, when this dreadful edict was announced. The panic was terrible. Fathers were in danger of being torn from their wives and children. Mothers were liable, at any moment, to be hurried away from their families. As it is the law of slavery, that the child is to follow the womb which bore it, the children of these mothers, born of free fathers, baptized in free churches, and educated in free schools, were liable at any time to be manacled and sold to Southern taskmasters. In consternation the little church met, and with prayers and tears implored the aid of God.

"The slave-hunter was immediately after them. Writs were out for their arrest. They trembled by day and by night. They dared not appear in the street. They dared not enter the shops. They dared not go forth to labour. They hid in garrets and cellars. Affectionate daughters conveyed food to the father, whom the slave-hunter, like a bloodhound, was tracking out. The church, poor and feeble as it was, raised 500 dollars to aid their brethren in their helplessness and terror. The alternative before the victims was terrible. They must either be dragged back into slavery; or, abandoning their families, exile themselves alone, in poverty and friendlessness, to Canada; or, selling out, at any sacrifice, all their little concerns, trudge their weary way, with their wives and their little ones, to the cold north, where there was no home to receive them, no friends to greet them, and where, perhaps, starvation was to be their lot. But any doom was preferable to the doom of slavery."

A SCENE IN BOSTON.

The following sketch exhibits the misery the Fugitive Slave Law produces by the disruption of social ties, and the annihilation of the domestic hearth:—

"A coloured girl, eighteen years of age, a few years ago escaped from slavery at the South. Through scenes of adventure and peril, almost more strange than fiction can create, she found her way to Boston. She obtained employment, secured friends, and became a consistent member of a Methodist church. She became interested in a very worthy young man of her own complexion, who was a member of the same church. They were soon married. Their home, though humble, was the abode of piety and contentment. Industrious, temperate, and frugal, all their wants were supplied. Seven years passed away. They had two little boys, one six and the other four years of age. These children, the sons of a free father, but of a mother who had been a slave, by the laws of our Southern states, were doomed to their mother's fate. These Boston boys, born beneath the shadow of Fanueil Hall, the sons of a free citizen of Boston, and educated in the Boston free schools, were, by the compromises of the Constitution, admitted to be slaves, the property of a South Carolinian planter. The Boston father had no right to his own sons. The law, however, had long been considered a dead letter. The Christian mother, as she morning and evening bowed with her children in prayer, felt that they were safe from the slave-hunter, surrounded as they were by the churches, the schools, and the free institutions of Massachusetts; but no—the Fugitive Slave Law was enacted, and the hopes of the slave-owners revived. A young, healthy, energetic mother, with two fine boys, was a rich prize. The poor woman was panic-struck. She was afraid to go out of doors, lest some from the South should see her. One day she recognised a man prowling, whom she knew came from the place from which she had fled. She was hid in a garret. Immediately after, the officer came with a writ for her arrest. It was a dark and stormy day. The rain, freezing as it fell, swept in floods through the streets of Boston. Night came, cold, black, and tempestuous. At midnight her friends took her in a hack, and conveyed her, with her children, to the house of her pastor. A prayer-meeting had been appointed there, at that hour, in behalf of their suffering sister. A small group of stricken hearts were there assembled. They knelt in prayer. The poor mother, thus hunted from her home, her husband far away, sobbed, in the bitterness of her anguish, as though her heart would break. Her little children, trembling before a doom, the enormity of which they were incapable of appreciating, cried loudly and uncontrollably. The humble minister caught the contagion. His voice became inarticulate through emotion. Bowing his head he ceased to pray, and yielded himself to the sobbings of sympathy and grief. After an hour of weeping, for the voice of prayer had passed away into the sublimity of unutterable anguish, they took this Christian mother and her children in a hack, and conveyed them to one of the Cunard steamers, which fortunately was to sail for Halifax the next day. They took them in the gloom of midnight, through the tempest-swept streets, lest the slave-hunter should meet them. Her brethren and sisters of the church raised a little money from their scanty means to pay her passage, and to save her, for a few days, from starving, after her first arrival in the cold land of strangers. Her husband soon returned to Boston, to find his home desolate, his wife and his children exiles in a foreign land."

RACHEL PARKER'S CASE.

Rachel Parker, a coloured woman, was recently torn away from her home in West Nottingham, Pennsylvania, as the alleged chattel of a Mr. Schoolfield, a lottery dealer, of Baltimore. J. C. Miller, with whom the woman had been residing, followed the slave-taker and his victim in hot pursuit, accompanied by several other residents in the township. M'Creary, the slave-taker, was arrested on the charge of kidnapping. The evidence of Mr. Miller went to prove that he had known the girl from her earliest infancy, and that she was not a slave.

This latter most important and seemingly conclusive testimony the Justice was not willing to receive as satisfactory, and accordingly continued the case. The woman was committed to the city prison, and Miller and M'Creary held for appearance in the sum of 300 dollars! The parties immediately took the Philadelphia cars for their homes, the friends of the woman entering the Havre de Grace station, M'Creary for Elkton. Miller was missing. His travelling companions returned to Stemmer's Run, a watering place about eleven miles from the city, where it was ascertained Miller was seen to leave the cars. There they inquired and searched in vain, with the worst apprehensions as to his possible fate. A night of suspense passed away, without tidings from the missed one. Next morning, while some workmen, in the neighbourhood of Stemmer's Run, were going to their work, they were startled by the appalling sight of the stiffened body of poor Miller, suspended to a sapling, with a handkerchief fastened to the tree, and another round his neck, the latter of which was recognised as his own. Efforts at resuscitation were made, but in vain. An inquest was held, and a verdict of "Death by *Suicide*" (?) was made up. A *post mortem* examination ended in the discovery of arsenic in the stomach of the deceased, and the appearance of the wrists plainly showed that they had been handcuffed.

THE CASE OF HENRY LONG.

Henry Long was a fugitive from slavery. He had escaped to New York, where he was leading an industrious life, when he was seen by his master's brother-in-law, and claimed. The judge ordered him to be given up, hardly considering worth his notice the point strongly urged by the defence, that the claimant was under obligation to produce the recent existence of his title to the slave, having shown that such exists. A Richmond paper contained an advertisement of his sale, and the sequel is thus told by a Richmond correspondent of the *Evening Post* :

"It was announced, in the daily papers of yesterday, that Henry Long would be sold this morning, at ten o'clock, at an auction mart near the City Hotel. At that hour the people began to assemble. A few minutes after ten, Henry Long was brought into the auction-room, and seated near two women having infant children—two boys about ten years of age, and two smaller children—all to be sold.

" Long maintained, evidently, a forced smile, and was much agitated. It was only when spoken to that he appeared relieved. There were many soon gathered about him, together with myself, who put various questions to him. I shall detail the conversation in a categorical form, as the truest and shortest mode of conveying all that is necessary in regard to such speculations as have been made about him. His manner, throughout, was modest and civil, and his replies to questions, which were very much the same, repeated over to him by the different parties coming to see him, were sensible. There was no disposition to use taunting language to him. On the contrary, soft and persuasive language was adopted, such as the slave-dealers use to make them believe they are going to glory.

" Long, are you glad to get back to Virginia? They say you played the fiddle ! Didn't you sing or play ' Carry me back to old Virginny ?' Have you got a wife ? She is a white woman, said some one, isn't she, Long ? Long, said one man, in a meek and beneficent tone, were the abolitionists good to you ? why didn't they come to you when you was sick, and take care of you ? Now, Long, hadn't you rather be back here, a slave in Virginia, than be free in New York, where they don't care anything about you, you know; now, do they ?

" Such is, literally, the conversation, as far as it goes, with Long.

" After being thus, with others, participating in the conversation with Long, until about half-past ten o'clock, when probably two hundred persons had collected within the room and about the doors, the auctioneer called out, ' Whoever is going to buy niggers will come down to the other office.' A large number followed on to several doors beyond, where it was understood that the sale of Long would not take place until that was over.

"I returned to where Long was awaiting *his* execution. By that time, about eleven o'clock, a number of the members of the Convention and of the Legislature congregated about, and hundreds were coming and going, thus contributing to a large number permanently there. All continued in that manner until after twelve, when the sale was finished at the corner, and another announcement was made at the door, that another sale would take place across the way, where there were about twenty more small boys and girls. That sale occupied until two o'clock.

"From twelve to one o'clock, the President of the Senate stood close by the side of the auctioneer, whilst many of the members of each of the bodies of the Legislature, *which was then in session*—as well as of the Convention, *which was also in session*—were scattered about, waiting the demonstration. Many left between ten and twelve; others arriving to keep up the pressing crowd within. All passed on quietly, with no *noisy* expressions—some saying 'the damned nigger ought to be strung up;' another, that he was not to be blamed for trying to get away, if he could; another, that very likely some abolitionist was then watching their movements.

"Amongst the crowd was one young man, who, from his dress and expressions, appeared as if he might have suddenly come into possession of some property, which he was not accustomed to, and had, in consequence, become suddenly elevated in his own estimation. He swaggered about, to the merriment and approving smiles of a few, but met with no encouragement from the mass, swearing that he was about to buy the 'nigger,' so that he could give him thirteen every morning before breakfast; he would fix him, he would lay it on him, whilst flourishing his cane to show how he would do it.

"About two o'clock the auctioneer came in, and Henry Long was immediately placed on the stand. The auctioneer, turning to him, and taking his hat off, asked him, in a low tone, about his health, strength, soundness, &c., to all of which questions Henry responded favourably.

"The auctioneer then said, 'There is one condition about

this sale. Bonds are to be given by the purchaser that this man shall be carried south, and that he shall be sold and kept south;' then clenching his hand, with a very energetic gesture, and in emphatic language, declared that before Long left his possession he would see that the terms were fully complied with, and he would know his man well, before he gave Long up or received the money. That drew forth a round of applause.

"The auctioneer continued—' This man is in good health and sound mind. (Doubtful if he is, on the slavery question). I need not give you his history, that is known; and now, how much shall I have bid?'—Starting the bid himself, he said, ' I have only 700 dollars bid. Will nobody bid more?" I'll give twenty-five dollars more,' said a man standing in front, who bore a very strong resemblance to what the Peter Funks call a ' Dummy.' ' He is a good barber, good hotel waiter, and can work in the field, or do anything. He is worth a fortune to any man: he can be taken around and exhibited at the south—turned to advantage in that way; or he would be invaluable to a slave-dealer who has other slaves to sell, by advertising that Henry Long is at his place.' (This is the game that was played to-day. The crowd was kept together at the other sales, by putting off the sale of Long until all the others were disposed of.) ' Seven hundred and fifty dollars I have bid, will nobody say more?' After dwelling and repeating the usual slang-whang of the auctioneer, occupying, altogether, not five minutes, Long was knocked off to David Clopton, of Georgia—a slave-dealer of that state, where there is not a verdant field—not a yard square of green grass. The auctioneer himself was empowered to make the purchase, and, immediately after knocking off the bid, he gave assurance that Long should now be taken care of, when the audience gave a vociferous round of applause, leaving the room exultingly, one man crying out ' damn the North.'"

CASE OF WILLIAM HARRIS.

A slave named William Harris, and his wife and child, succeeded, a few weeks since, in escaping from their master, in South Carolina. At Philadelphia they came under the notice of the friends of the fugitive, who aided them northward. At Albany some friends paid their passage to Rochester, where they were to cross the lake to Canada. The crew of the boat on which they were, learned that they were fugitives, and immediately devised a plan to trouble and terrify them, probably thereby finding amusement. At night, some of the human fiends, in prosecution of their plans, went to the berth of the man Harris, and awakening him, informed him that his master was on board the boat, and that they would surrender him and his family into his hands. Harris drew a dirk, with which he was armed for self-defence, drove the scoundrels on deck, and by his decisive manner and actions kept them at bay till morning. In the morning he was informed that his master had left the boat and gone on to Syracuse, but would there meet him on the arrival of the boat. The boat came to a stopping-place at the first Lodi Lock, about a mile east of the city. As is often the case, a number of persons went aboard the boat. Harris supposed they came to take him, being so informed by some of the crew. In his desperation, he seized his razor, and drawing it forcibly across his throat, jumped into the canal. His wife, with their child in her arms, leaped after him; all determined to die rather than again come under the slaveholder's power. Efforts were then made to rescue the drowning family. Harris and his wife were got out, but the child was drowned. We are, however, happy to state that Harris and his wife are now in good hands, that they will be suitably cared for, and as soon as possible put beyond the danger of the slave-catcher's grasp.

Murder was also committed in the following case:—On November 24, 1851, in the United States Circuit Court, at Philadelphia, Castner Hanaway was tried for alleged treason, arising from the disturbances which took place at a place called Christiana, in Lancaster County, during the progress of which a man named Gorsuch was killed, and his nephew wounded. The statement of a witness named Kline shows the scenes rendered common in America by the Fugitive Slave Act. The witness said—" These are the warrants placed in my hands on the 9th of September last. I went to execute these warrants. Several persons were to meet me at Penningtonville. These were Mr. Gorsuch, and his son and nephew. About a mile from Christiana we met the guide. Old Mr. Gorsuch and the guide. walked ahead. We went about a mile, and then stopped. Mr.

Gorsuch proposed to divide the party. I objected, and said we wanted all, and more too. The guide then took us back through a corn field. We went on to a creek, where we sat down and ate something. I told them we had better not stop, as it was near daylight. We then went on; I was a little ahead until we came near Parker's house. When we got within forty yards of the house I saw a black man. The moment he saw us he took to his heels, and I after him. This was Nelson or Josh, I should say. A couple of bars were across the lane; I fell over them; this was in the short lane to the house; as near as I can tell, about fifteen or twenty yards from the long lane. I ran up to the house; Nelson got in before me; old Mr. Gorsuch and another got up a little before me. I went into the house, and called up stairs for the landlord; I told them who I was. I told them, and said I was an officer, and had warrants for Nelson and Josh. They called out there were no such persons there. They then pushed a sharp instrument down stairs at me. I then went out and told old Mr. Gorsuch he had better talk to them through the window. One of the blacks then fired, and I fired my revolver. I took out a piece of paper as if to write to the sheriff for a hundred men. I did this to intimidate them. I read my warrant three times—once in the house, and twice out. I remonstrated with the men; spoke to Parker, the landlord, a coloured man. Mr. Hanaway then came up to the bars, and Mr. Gorsuch told me to ask him to help us. I did so. I showed him my warrants. I asked him his name; he replied it was none of my business. I asked him if he lived in the neighbourhood, and he made the same reply. I told him I had come to arrest Nelson and Josh. He said he would not assist me; that the blacks had a right to defend themselves. I asked him if he would speak to them, and keep them off. He said, no; he would not interfere. There were a number of blacks in and around the house then, with guns, and were loading them. The negroes were armed with guns, scythes, &c. A few only were without something. Harvey Scott had nothing in his hands. Some fifteen or twenty negroes came up in the same direction and across the fields, after Mr. Hanaway. One came up immediately after he did, with a scythe in one hand and a revolver in the other. A man named Elijah Lewis came up shortly after Hanaway, in his shirt-sleeves. I showed him my warrant.

He read it, handed it to Hanaway, who read it again, and handed it to me. Lewis said the blacks had a right to defend themselves, and I had better go away, as blood would be spilt. I saw that a good many blacks were coming up, and I began to beg. I asked them to prevent the blacks from firing, and I would withdraw my men, but hold them responsible for the slaves. I followed Hanaway and Lewis up several yards, and begged them, for God's sake, not to let the blacks fire, I would withdraw my men."

Some years since, a slaveholder held a mulatto woman as a slave, who was his own daughter. Familiarity with the system had not obliterated all traces of human feeling in his bosom, and he desired that his daughter should be made free. Years passed on, and she became a wife after the slave-law mode, and the mother of children. For the purpose of attaining his cherished object, the mother and children were sent into Ohio, where, of course, they became free by Ohio law, as having been sent there for the purpose by the master. One of these children, a daughter, was at the time but eighteen months old. The slaveholder died; and his wife, as was stated in the settlement of the estate, paid 1300 dollars as a compensation to the heirs for those slaves who had been sent away. This woman also died, and no legal evidence of the transaction remained. The children of the woman sent into Ohio grew up to womanhood, and were married. The little girl, only eighteen months old when she came to Ohio, has been a resident in Cincinnati for fifteen years, living as unsuspecting of danger as any woman of our city. She is nearly white, it requiring a practised eye to detect her colour; is the mother of two children; and she with her family were pleasantly situated, with the comforts and conveniences of life around them. A few days since a message from a distant spot was sent to them in breathless haste, that the heirs of the father of this woman's mother had made a claim to all the children of the woman sent into Ohio so many years ago, and it was supposed a warrant was already in the city for the seizure of the woman and her children here, while the other branches of the family had just been hurried away for the North. Consternation seized this household. True, the woman was legally free, but once in the grasp of the slaveholder, she knew that nothing could save her. Not a moment was to be lost. The officers were probably already on her track. As the only resource, she, with her babes, were hurried instantly from their home, and with such comforts as could be hurriedly gathered, she bade her husband farewell (who could not at the time accompany her), left her pleasant home to desolation, and fled to Canada, where, thanks to the great Protector of the oppressed, and to the humane policy of the British Government, she is safe.

The scenes of bloodshed, in consequence of the attempt to carry out the Fugitive Slave Law, are of the most distressing character. The following extracts from the *Wytheville Republican* corroborates this, though the writer evidently thinks that slaves ought to remain slaves, and that the abolitionists are the most dangerous of men. The writer says:—

"Four negro men, the property of John Rives and David Cox, two citizens of that county, seduced by the advice of that notorious and infamous abolition emissary, Bacon, who has been prowling about through that county, and Russel in this State, and in Ashe and other counties in North Carolina, on the Virginia border, ran away from their masters, intending, no doubt, to make for Ohio, or some other lawless and forsworn State of the confederacy, there to be harboured and worked, and worked and harboured, as occasion might allow or require. They took the course of New River, intending, it is believed, to pursue that river to its mouth, there to meet the colleagues, hypocrites, and villains, of Bacon, Crooks, and M'Bride. It turned out, however, that as they travelled, and while yet in Grayson County, eight or ten miles from the Wythe line, they were fallen in with by five or six white men of Grayson, who undertook to stop and arrest them. The negroes were armed with knives, spears, and with one or two weapons made of broken English scythes. The white men had one or two guns.

"We are not prepared to give the particulars of the combat. The negroes assailed the whites, and the scythes were used with terrible effect. Samuel Bartlett was struck in the forehead and his head split open, cutting into the brain an inch or two the whole length of the head. He lived about eight hours. Alfred Bartlett, his brother, who had a gun, and who fired it foolishly, merely to wound, in attempting to relieve his brother, had his left wrist and hand badly cut, almost severed from the arm. Yet, after this he knocked two of the negroes down, and left them for dead. One of the negroes thus knocked down, had stabbed a Mr. Wilcox, whom he had under him on the ground, through the neck, and was in the act of inflicting a more deadly wound, when thus prevented by the wounded Bartlett. Mr. John Clemmonts was struck by one of the negroes, who used a scythe, across the head, and his skull was cloven from temple to temple, the brain cut in upon the whole way from one to two inches, and yet there are hopes of his recovery. Mr. Wm. B. Hale was severely injured with rocks thrown by the negroes. Notwithstanding the terrible wounds inflicted upon the white men, two of the negroes were secured, the other two (both believed to be wounded with gun shots) made their escape, and so far as we know, are yet out, though hotly pursued. The two taken are in Grayson jail, and will be tried for their lives, for insurrection and murder."

In a former number, says the *Richmond Standard*, we gave an account of the last slave-hunt in Pennsylvania, when a man of the name of Phillips, who had for years been an industrious and respectable citizen of Harrisburg, in that State, was brutally knocked on the head, to render his capture certain, and then taken, in a state of insensibility, before Commissioner M'Allister, who mocked and insulted him with a sham trial, and delivered him over to his captors, as a slave for life. His case excited a deep feeling of indignation among the people of Harrisburg, from the manner of his capture, and the character of the pretended trial which was awarded him, and also moved their sympathies for his probable fate, and for the sudden desolation which had thus fallen on his wife. The man-stealer, regardless of the misery he creates, enters a happy family, drags away the father to a felon's jail, deprives the members of that family of their natural guardian and head, and all this is done in a land that boasts that all are free.

We read in an American paper, in the beginning of May, that the town of Columbia was thrown into an extreme excitement by the report that a cold-blooded murder had been committed. The particulars of the terrible tragedy are as follow: Deputy-Marshal Snyder, of Harrisburg, and police-officer Ridgely, from Baltimore, came to Columbia to arrest an alleged fugitive slave, by the name of William Smith, who was engaged in piling lumber at Mr. Gotleib Sener's yard. The first witness, who testified before the coroner's jury, says, that he was standing on the steps at Parson's Hotel, when Ridgely called him out, and stated to him that they were going to take a slave, and wanted him to go with them and assist. He accompanied them, and saw Snyder touch William Smith on the shoulder. The witness then ran away immediately to some distance. In a very short time he heard the report of a pistol. Snyder and Ridgely, a moment afterward, made their appearance, the former very much frightened, and exclaiming that "Ridgely had shot the man." Another witness testifies that he saw Snyder and Ridgely have hold of the coloured man— Snyder of the left, and Ridgely the right shoulder. The deceased was pulling away, when Ridgely placed a pistol against his neck and fired. Poor Smith fell dead instantly. There was no effort made to rescue William Smith, though he was within one hundred feet of at least a dozen coloured men, who were at work in the lumber-yard. The perpetrator of the murder was allowed to escape. In America the slave may be murdered with impunity under the sanction of law.

Another illustration of the law, and of the demoralization of American society is from a New York paper:—" A few weeks since, a southern gentleman arrived in the city, and made known to a confidential friend that he had come in pursuit of a runaway slave, his own property; and from the fact of the slave being a beautiful young woman, and nearly white, he thought it advisable not to attempt to recover her by making application in any quarter where the fact of his pursuit would be likely to be made known to the public, as his object might thereby be frustrated. His friend advised him, therefore, to offer a reward of two thousand dollars to some intelligent police-officer, for the arrest of the fugitive, and trust to his prudence and discretion. The advice was taken, and after a while a clue was got to the whereabouts of the beautiful fugitive; but before she could be arrested, she was 'up and gone, the graceless girl,' and away down east, where the sun rises, and beyond the reach of her legal proprietor. There was nothing unusual or marvellous in all this, but it was discovered, during the time that the search for the fugitive was being made, that the 'fair she' was not only the legal property of the pursuer, but his natural property also; she was, in fact, his own daughter, and had escaped from the man to whom her father and owner had hired her. Since her arrival in this city she had captivated the heart of a white gentleman, who did not suspect her origin, and been 'woo'd and wedded, and a';' and her husband, having by some means or other, got scent of the danger, instead of playing the part of *Inkle* to his *Yarico*, had the manliness to bear her off to a place of safety."

The following incident is related by the Washington correspondent of the *Ashtabula Sentinel*:—Yesterday, a servant woman came to my room, saying a coloured woman wished to speak with me. I told her to show her up. She soon returned with her. She was sobbing, and evidently in great agony of mind. I asked the cause of her grief. It was sometime before she could so far compose her mind as to relate to me her misfortune; which consisted in living under the barbarous laws enacted by Congress for the government of this district. She said her husband had just been sold to a slave-dealer, and taken to the barracoons of Alexandria; that his purchaser was intending to take him to Alabama in two or three days; that she had four children at home. At this point she burst out into a loud expression of her grief. Her sobbings were interrupted occasionally with exclamations of "O God! O, my dear children! O, my husband!" Then appealing to me, "O, master, for God's sake, do try to get back the father of my babes." I learned that her husband's name is George Tooman. His former owner is a female, named Martha Johnwood, living east of the Capitol some half a mile. George went to work this morning in the barn, at husking corn, without any suspicion of the fate which awaited him. The slave-dealer and an assistant came to the barn, seized him, placed handcuffs upon him, and hurried him off to the slave-pen in Alexandria. The woman hearing of it, followed him there on foot, and returned, and then sought me, in the vain hope that I should be able to assist her. The day is said by many to be the coldest known here for years; yet she has been exposed to the keen piercing winds, although I think she was thinly clad. She had not seen her children since morning, when she left them without firewood. I endeavoured to soothe her feelings by expressing some faint hope that her husband might yet be redeemed—that I would make inquiry, and ascertain if I could find some one who would re-purchase him, and permit him to remain in the district. It was dark when she left my room to return to her home, rendered bitter by the fate of the husband and father. The cold winds rocked the building, and howled mournfully about the corners. I reflected upon the barbarous law by which Congress had authorized and encouraged such crimes, and inflicted such misery upon the down-trodden of God's poor. I trembled for my country, when I reflected that God was just, and that his justice will not sleep for ever. I asked myself the question, Will Heaven permit such wickedness, such barbarous cruelty, to go unpunished? Yet Mr. Fillmore, in his message, advises Congress to abide by the compromise as a final settlement of the slave question, and leave the coloured women who are wives and mothers in this district to the operations of this savage law—would leave fathers here to be sold in the manner above related—leave children here to be robbed of their parents. And the Whig caucus resolve substantially that they will lend their aid to sustain this law, which would disgrace the tyrant of Austria, and would add a deeper infamy to Haynau, the butcher of the Hungarians.

These cases are sufficient to show the abominable nature of the law, which has made American legislation a reproach and a shame. In a speech recently delivered in the senate of the United States, the Hon. Charles Sumner, of Massachusetts, stated, "That the slavemasters, few in number, amounting to about 300,000, according to the recent census, have succeeded in dictating the policy of the national government, and have written slavery on its front. And now an arrogant and unrelenting ostracism is applied, not only to all who express themselves against slavery, but to every man who is unwilling to be the menial of slavery. A novel test for office is introduced, which would have excluded all the fathers of the Republic—even Washington, Jefferson, Franklin. Yes, Sir. Startling it may be, but indisputable. Could these revered demi-gods of history once again descend upon the earth and mingle in our affairs—not one of them could receive a nomination from the National Convention of either of the two old political parties. Out of the convictions of their hearts and the utterances of their lips against slavery they would be condemned. This single fact reveals the extent to which the national government has departed from its true course, and its great examples. For myself, I know no better aim under the constitution, than to bring the government back to the precise position on this question which it occupied on the auspicious morning of its first organization under Washington—

<blockquote>' Cursus iterare relictos.'</blockquote>

That the sentiments of the fathers may again prevail with our rulers, and that the national flag may nowhere shelter slavery!" So powerful has been the effect of the speech, that it has created an echo even on this side the Atlantic. That graceful and eloquent advocate of the slave, the Earl of Carlisle, has written with reference to it :—

" In our past hours of friendly intercourse, in our frequent walks by the sparkling estuary of Boston, or upon the sunny brow of Bunker's Hill, how little did I, how little did he, I feel well assured, dream of such an opening upon his quiet and unostentatious career! and now, while I have been writing these lines, I have received the speech he has lately delivered in Congress on the bearings of the Fugitive Slave Law, which, by the closeness of its logic, and the masculine vigour of its eloquence, proves to me how all the perfections of his mind have grown up to, and been dilated with, the inspiration of the cause which he has now made his own. Indeed, when I rise from reading such a speech as his, or such a book as this to which I have now ventured to prefix this hurried prelude, I feel constrained at once to temper and to dignify my own sentiments by clothing them with appropriate accents borrowed from our own drama—

<blockquote>
' Reward them for the noble deed, just Heavens!
For this one action, guard them and distinguish them
With signal mercies and with great deliverance;
Guard them from wrong, adversity, and shame.
          The poor, forsaken ones!
Shall they be left a prey to savage power?
Can they lift up their harmless hands in vain,
Or cry to Heaven for help, and not be heard?
Go on! pursue, assert the sacred cause;
Stand forth, ye proxies of all-ruling Providence,
And save the friendless captives from oppression.
Saints shall assist ye with prevailing prayers,
And warring angels combat on your side.' "
</blockquote>

Another protest against the law has also reached us. It is the speech of Charles Durkee, in the House of Representatives, August 6, 1852. Mr. Durkee described the bill in the following striking terms. He said—"History proves that the most galling oppression the people have ever suffered has been inflicted by cruel and tyrannical governments under the name and forms of law. But in the long catalogue of public crimes among civilised nations, there is none more cruel and barbarous than the Fugitive Slave Law now in force in the United States. This law was called by its friends a healing and peaceful measure; yet time has proved it, what every candid mind knew it to be at the time of its passage, a *war* measure, in some instances even more cruel in its operation than the guillotine itself. Jefferson says, 'by the law of nature, man is at peace with man until some aggression is committed.' Here aggression exists in savage form. This law, in its operation, disregards every principle of justice, and tramples under foot the very objects for which government was instituted. The tendency of the Federal Government to consolidation and oppression was apprehended by our revolutionary fathers, and so great was their opposition to the Constitution, that it could only be overcome by the strongest assurances that the amendments now incorporated in that instrument should be immediately thereafter adopted. These amendments were designed as additional checks against an unlawful exercise of Federal power. But alas, how futile are paper constitutions, in the day of profligacy and usurpation! Who could have imagined, four years ago, that this great Republic, boasting of its intelligence and of its sentiments of equality, would be now engaged in performing the drudgery of slave-traders—kidnapping men, women, and children, for a slave-market! Who would have believed this government could ever be capable of waging a piratical war against an innocent, unoffending people, for the sole purpose of enriching the pockets of those who manufacture, and those who use, thumb-screws, chains, and fetters, and construct prisons in the maintenance of this horrid traffic? Good Heavens! can it be possible that the government established by Washington, Jefferson, and their compatriots, has engaged, in the middle of the nineteenth century, in what our own statute-book declares, in certain latitudes, piracy! Strange as it may seem, it is true. It remains to be seen how far the people are bound by the claims of party slavery to sustain and continue this unrelenting war against the African race."

Mr. Charles Durkee proceeds to say—and we would fain hope that he expresses the truth—" I do not believe that the Fugitive Slave Law of 1850 is approved of by the country generally. No, Sir. If it were submitted to-day, directly to the people, I have no doubt that it would receive the condemnation of *three-fourths* of the popular vote. It is the measure, alone, of a few strong partisan politicians, exceedingly ambitious of public notoriety and political power, who make politics a trade, and claim the control of Whig and Democratic organizations as a 'patent right' during life. It was enacted by influences not very complimentary to Congress or to the country. I need only to refer to the fact that Daniel Webster and Mr. Fillmore abandoned the ground they had previously occupied on the slave question, and gave their influence for this measure. Several members of the House of Representatives, elected by free soil votes, and who were supposed to be true to liberty, were also persuaded to abandon the cause of freedom in New Mexico and Utah, and subject that immense tract of country to the control of slavery. These recreant Representatives, now holding office in the government (in my candid opinion, as a reward of their treachery), contributed largely to bring about this humiliating and disgraceful state of things. But, though the minority has triumphed over the majority, as usual, through the treachery of Northern Representatives, thus widening the sphere of slavery, yet I look upon it only as an incident in a war still waging in behalf of the poor and oppressed; a war that must, sooner or later, bring triumph to freedom. I say it is but an *incident*. Our enemies, in 1812, gained a like temporary victory when they took possession of this city, and burned the public buildings. But their triumph was of short duration; and so, in my opinion, it will be with this high-handed piracy, now, under the name of law, engrafted on our statute-books. True, there is a dissimilarity in the manner of conducting these two wars, but a striking parallel in their origin and character."

We shall conclude these facts and observations with

THE CASE OF HORACE PRESTON.

The particulars from the *New York Tribune*.—A black man, named Horace Preston, residing in Williamsburgh, and earning an honest living by his own work, married to a woman most devotedly attached to him, was arrested the other day by a member of our Sixth Ward Police, named James Martin. Thĕ arrest was made on an utterly frivolous pretext; it was charged that he had committed a larceny; that the witnesses against him would be forthcoming; and accordingly he was incarcerated until they might be produced. But that nothing might occur to render imperfect this illustration of American equality before the law, and American respect for personal rights, he was hustled into the lock-up of the Sixth Ward Station in the lower part of the Tombs, not under the control of the regular warden of that prison, and kept there in a manner which might not disgrace the justice of Persia or Tartary, but is a foul blot on New York. The offence charged was a bailable one; ample bail was offered, but it was refused. The worst of criminals—a pirate, a murderer, a violator of helpless woman—is allowed to see counsel and prepare for his defence. A legal gentleman of the highest respectability having, after long search, discovered the place of this man's sequestration, went there and demanded to see him as counsel, but was turned away from the door, and was not even allowed to see the warrant upon which he was immured. The active agents in this business were a lawyer and a policeman, who had tracked out the fugitive, and informed his *owner*, Mr. Rees, of Baltimore.

It appears that after the preliminary steps above noted had taken place, the claimant's son arrived, when the following infamous proceedings were gone through:—Preston was kept locked up in the Sixth Ward, as he says, till twelve or one o'clock *at night* (*mark the hour!*), then taken out and conducted to the Second Ward Station-house. There he was held till the claimant's son arrived, when, it appears, he, together with Busteed and Martin, held a consultation at the Second Ward Station-house. Preston's wife, his counsel, and several of his friends, had been untiring in their pursuit of, and inquiry for him, but could learn nothing whatever, until a man hallced to the wife in the Park that they had just taken her husband into the U. S. Court-room. Preston's counsel and wife hurried with all speed to the Court-room, but, on arriving, found a witness sworn and giving evidence. At this stage our reporter has taken up the case and kept our readers advised on the subject.

When the case was adjourned on Friday afternoon till Saturday morning, it was with the avowed understanding, on the part of Preston's counsel, and assented to by the Commissioner, that if the latter should deny the motion made and argued by Mr. Jay to quash or dismiss the proceedings, then the counsel should go into their defence on the merits. To that end, several witnesses were in attendance ; others had process out for them, to be served as soon as found. Some of these witnesses had known Preston in Baltimore, and were prepared to prove the declarations of his former mistress as to his freedom, and the provisions in her will to that effect. By others it was proposed to show the admission of the claimant, and others, to contradict Busteed's affidavit and prove a conspiracy.

The Commissioner, instead of deciding the preliminary motion of Mr. Jay, and then stopping, took the counsel, the prisoner, and the audience by surprise. He *decided the whole case*—had his certificate in his hand—delivered it over in the twinkling of an eye—gathered up his papers, and retreated towards the back-door of the room. Busteed hardly had time to kiss the Bible held out to him by the Commissioner. It was all in vain that Messrs. Jay, Emmet, and Culver jumped upon the floor, asking the Commissioner to hear them—urging their surprise, and the injustice done to their client. Their efforts were all fruitless. The Commissioner refused to hear anything further.

Thus, from freedom and industry, and all that made life dear, poor Preston was torn away, at the command of a ruthless judge. Had Preston been a white man, and committed some infamous crime—some crime that entailed ruin and disgrace on him in this life, he might have had bail. However, he was a black man. His crime was the atrocious one of attempting to be free—of dwelling where he might earn a living for himself and for another—where the toil of his hands, and the sweat of his brow, might benefit himself alone. For this he was a criminal before American law, and was delivered over to the revenge of a man-stealer; his prayer for justice was unheard; equally vain were the tears and entreaties of an agonized and distracted wife, about to lose the husband she had sworn to live with till torn from her by the rude hand of death; the husband she was never more again to see. Such a scene must make the victim doubt in Providence. It must make him doubt whether this earth of ours be not altogether the devil's own—whether right be not crushed out by might; it must make him look to

"————Heaven, with that frenzied air,
As if to ask if a God were there."

A more touching exhibition of the working of the Fugitive Slave Law can hardly be witnessed, notwithstanding the many infamous cases with which that law has filled the land. The case of Preston was one of great hardship. The stroke fell not on himself alone. This man's wife stood by her husband for three days, with a devotion and tenderness unparalleled. Whenever permitted to sit near him, she had fast hold of his hand in both of her's, wringing herself in the most intense, half-suppressed agony. Near the time of the final separation, Busteed, the lawyer, to console her, gave her an orange, or peeled one for her. What a delicate attention! But we dare say even that was too humane a deed for some.

COLUMBIA! shall thy honoured name,
Be as a by-word through the world?
Rouse! for as if to blast thy fame,
This keen reproach is at thee hurled;
The banner that above thee waves,
Is floating o'er three million slaves.

Arouse! and let each hill and glen
With prayer to the high heavens ring out;
Till all your land with freeborn men,
May join in one triumphant shout,
That freedom's banner does not wave
Its folds above a single slave.

Leeds Anti-slavery Series. No. 32.

Sold by W. and F. G. CASH, 5, Bishopsgate Street, London; and by JANE JOWETT, Friends' Meeting-Yard, Leeds, at 6s. 6d. per 100, or 11d. per dozen.

Leeds Anti-slavery Series. No. 33.

OPINIONS OF AMERICAN MINISTERS

ON SLAVERY AND THE FUGITIVE SLAVE BILL.

IN No. 32 of the present series we have given some account of the Fugitive Slave Bill and its calamitous effects. We now purpose giving the opinions of American ministers on this iniquitous law. While reading the following, let it be remembered that the "Fugitive Slave Law" requires, under heavy penalties, that the inhabitants of the *free* States should not only refuse food and shelter to a starving, hunted human being, but also should assist, if called upon by the authorities, to seize the unhappy fugitive and send him back to slavery.

And "to what am I required to send this man back?"— asks the Rev. R. S. Storrs, jun., of Brooklyn, in a recently published sermon—an honourable exception to the ordinary ones on this subject—"To the endurance of a system which no man can contemplate without shuddering—of a system which puts the man into the power of his master, to be used by him as he will, only his life being preserved: to be sold by him, whenever he will, and to whomsoever he pleases: to have his wife and children taken from him at the pleasure of another— the wife that is dear to him as yours is to you—the children that are as precious to him as yours are to you, or mine to me. It is a system that forbids its subjects to be taught to read or write; that debars him from accumulation and progress, making all he acquires the property of his master; that takes away the Bible by legislative authority. It is to this system that I am to send the man back; and it will be administered to him with double rigour, because he has once escaped its grasp. The man implores me not to restore him. Why should I do him this mortal injury? He is my brother by creation—my

---

Sold by W. and F. G. CASH, 5, Bishopsgate Street, London; and by JANE JOWETT, Friends' Meeting Yard, Leeds, at 1s. 2d. per 100.

brother by redemption. God made that man in His own image, a sharer of that nature which Christ has glorified. How then can any other have *property* in him? Why should I send the man back to this unjust bondage? The fact that he has suffered it so long already, is a reason why I should NOT. God tells me to love him, and to do to him what I would, in turn, he should do to me. Why should I not HELP him in his struggle for the rights which God gave him indelibly when he made him a man? NAY, NAY! my friends, I cannot do this essential injustice; though the commands of the law were a hundredfold more stringent, I would not touch a hair of that man's head!"

Let it be remembered, that assisting to send a fugitive back to slavery is equally criminal with helping to steal a man from England and enslave him for life. The " Fugitive Slave Bill," then, forces this question upon the individual conscience of every inhabitant of the United States—" Am I to obey the laws of the government, or the laws of God?" Mark the answer by the following clergymen:—

The Rev. Dr. GARDINER SPRING, an eminent Presbyterian clergyman of New York, well known in this country by his religious publications, lately declared from the pulpit that, " if by one prayer he could liberate every slave in the world he would not dare to offer it."

Rev. Dr. JOEL PARKER, of Philadelphia, asks, " What are the evils inseparable from slavery? There is not one that is not equally inseparable from depraved human nature in other lawful relations."

Rev. MOSES STUART, D.D., (Professor in the Theological College of Andover), reminds us "many Southern slaveholders are true *Christians.*" That " though we may *pity* the fugitive, yet the Mosaic Law does not authorize the rejection of the claims of the slaveholders to their stolen or strayed *property.*"

Rev. Dr. SPENCER of Brooklyn, New York, has come forward in support of the " Fugitive Slave Bill," by publishing a Sermon entitled the *Religious Duty of Obedience to the Laws*, which has elicited the highest encomiums from Dr. SAMUEL H. COX, the Presbyterian minister of Brooklyn (notorious both in this country and America for his sympathy with the slaveholder), and also from the Hon. DANIEL WEBSTER, who says that "It is quite refreshing to read a production which, founding itself upon the express injunctions of the Holy Scriptures, goes back from theory to commandment—from human hypothesis and speculation to the declared will of God."

Rev. W. M. ROGERS, an orthodox minister of Boston, delivered on the last Thanksgiving-day a sermon in which he says, "When the slave asks me to stand between him and his master, what does he ask? He asks me to murder a nation's life; and I will not do it, because I have a conscience—because there is a God." He proceeds to affirm that if this resistance to the carrying out of the "Fugitive Slave Law" should lead the magistracy to call the citizens to arms, their duty was to obey, and "if ordered to take human life, in the name of God to take it; and he admonishes fugitives to "hearken to the Word of God, and to count their own masters worthy of all honour."

Rev. WM. CROWELL, of Waterfield, State of Maine, has printed a Thanksgiving Sermon of the same kind, in which he calls upon his hearers not to allow "excessive sympathies for a few hundred fugitives, to blind them so as that they may risk increased suffering to the millions already in chains."

Rev. Dr. TAYLOR, an Episcopal clergyman, of New Haven, deprecates the agitation on the new law, and urges obedience to it, asking—"Is that article in the constitution contrary to the law of nature, of nations, or to the will of God? Is it so? Is there a shadow of reason for saying it? I have not been able to discover it. Have I not shown you it is lawful to deliver up, in compliance with their laws, fugitive slaves, for the high, the great, the momentous interests of those [Southern] States?"

BISHOP HOPKINS, of Vermont, in a lecture, at Lockport, while admitting that slavery from *its inherent nature*, had in every age been a curse and a blight to the nation which cherished it, throws the sacred mantle of the Scriptures over it. He says, "It was warranted by the Old Testament;" and inquires, "What effect had the gospel in doing away with slavery? None whatever." Therefore he argues, as it is expressly permitted by the Bible, it does not in itself involve any sin; but that every Christian is authorised by the Divine law to own slaves, provided they be not treated with unnecessary cruelty.

Widely different from these are the "Teachings" of Dr. ADAM CLARKE, who in his commentary upon Isa. xxxviii. 6, says,—" HOW CAN ANY NATION PRETEND TO FAST OR WORSHIP GOD AT ALL, OR DARE PROFESS THAT THEY BELIEVE IN THE EXISTENCE OF SUCH A BEING, WHILE THEY CARRY ON WHAT IS CALLED THE SLAVE-TRADE, AND TRAFFIC IN THE SOULS AND BLOOD AND BODIES OF MEN? OH, YE MOST FLAGITIOUS OF KNAVES AND WORST OF HYPOCRITES! CAST OFF AT ONCE THE MASK OF RELIGION, AND DEEPEN NOT YOUR ENDLESS PERDITION BY PROFESSING THE FAITH OF OUR LORD JESUS CHRIST WHILE YE CONTINUE IN THIS TRAFFIC!"

JUDGE JAY'S OPINION OF THE FUGITIVE SLAVE LAW.

"If you ask my opinion of the 'binding force' of this law in a *moral sense*, I answer that its binding force is precisely the same as was that of the law of Nebuchadnezzar, commanding the multitudes on the plain of Dura to fall down and worship his golden image—of the decree of Darius forbidding prayer to God for thirty days—of the order of the Jewish magistrates to Peter and Paul 'not to speak at all nor to teach in the name of Jesus'—of the commands of the Roman emperors, that Christians should cast incense on the altars of idols—of the edicts of Louis XIV. requiring Huguenots to embrace the faith and practise the rights of the Church of Rome. This accursed statute requires us to become *active* instruments of treachery, cruelty, and oppression, to the persecuted but innocent fugitive—to set at nought the law of Jehovah, to do justice and love mercy—to trample under foot the great commandment of our blessed Redeemer, to love our neighbour—and, regardless of His authority, to do to others what would fill our souls with anguish if done to ourselves. Let us, with our families, enter the dungeons which Northern politicians have prepared, rather than hazard our souls by rendering obedience to the requirements of this wicked law."—*Reply of Judge Jay to a Deputation of Coloured Citizens, dated 2d October*, 1850.

Leeds Anti-slavery Series. No. 33.

Sold by W. and F. G. CASH, 5, Bishopsgate Street, London; and by JANE JOWETT, Friends' Meeting Yard, Leeds, at 1s. 2d. per 100.

Leeds Anti-slavery Series. No. 34.

FUGITIVE SLAVES:

DOUGLASS, PENNINGTON, WELLS BROWN, GARNETT, BIBB, AND OTHERS.

"America has the mournful honour of adding a new department to the literature of civilization—the autobiography of escaped slaves."—EPHRAIM PEABODY, D.D.

FREDERICK DOUGLASS.

THAT slavery exists in this, the nineteenth century, is a great fact, for which we have too much of mournful and affecting testimony. That it should be found amongst the degraded tribes that people the continent of Africa is not surprising—in a low state of society it always *has* existed ; but that in America—the boasted land of liberty and light—the young republic, by whom the old worn-out nations of the East are to be taught how to reign and to rule—that *her* soil should be thus fearfully polluted is one of the most melancholy facts the lover of his kind can learn. It is true efforts have been made to wipe away the foul stain by which America has become a stumbling-block and a reproach, the world's wonder and shame ; but hitherto with but little success. Slavery, in its most hideous forms, still disgraces the Southern States. Every year the number of its victims increases, and every year their doom seems more hopeless. Since the passing of the Fugitive Slave Act, America has published to the world that, in all her broad dominion, there is not one single inch of ground where the slave can find refuge, and in which he can be free.

Yet, if any men deserve freedom, these slaves do. In spite of the curse, many of them have still the attributes of men. They can think, and feel, and hope. God has given them the breath of life. On them, as well as the white, He has conferred the living soul. Such a one was Frederick Douglass. The

Sold by W. and F. G. CASH, 5, Bishopsgate Street, London; and by JANE JOWETT, Friends' Meeting Yard, Leeds, at 3s. 6d. per 100; or 6d. per doz.

English public have some recollection of him. A few years since he came to our shores, and spoke with power of the wrongs of the coloured race. Many of our readers, we presume, have listened to the heart-stirring eloquence of his public appeals. Many of them have read, we trust, the book in which he told the moving story of his life. We intend here to give an outline of it. It will teach that slavery is the curse it ever was; that, in spite of the outcry of indignant humanity, and the protest of religion against it, it remains unchanging and unchanged. It will teach, also, that slavery is not the omnipotent thing it seems; that it will bow and become weak when a strong man resolves to trample it under foot.

Frederick Douglass was born on an estate in Talbot County, Maryland. Slaves seldom know their birth-days, nor their father, and Douglass's case was no exception to the general rule. His mother he never saw, to know, but three or four times in his life. His father was said to have been his master —a white man. Masters in America often sustain the paternal relation to their slaves. These slaves invariably suffer greater hardships, and have more to contend with than others. They are a perpetual offence to the mistress. This class threatens to be an instrument for the removal of the very ills of which it is the effect. Every year increases its number. It was the knowledge of this fact that has already induced one American statesman to predict the fall of slavery by the inevitable laws of population. At any rate, the increase of this class will put a stop in America to the Scriptural argument for slavery. If the lineal descendants of Ham alone are to be Scripturally enslaved, then it must be soon admitted by the American slaveholders themselves, that American slavery is unscriptural, for the case of Douglass is that of an increasing number. Every year swells the number of white men, who are not ashamed to be the fathers of slaves.

Douglass's first master's name was Anthony. He was not considered a rich slaveholder. He owned two or three farms, and about thirty slaves. These were under the care of an overseer, who was a miserable drunkard, a profane swearer, and a savage monster. His master was equally savage, if we may judge from the following anecdote. One day a slave, named Aunt Rester, excited his displeasure; Douglass tells how he punished her :—" Before he commenced whipping Aunt Rester, he took her into the kitchen and stripped her from neck to waist, leaving her neck, shoulders, and back, entirely naked. He then told her to cross her hands, calling her, at the same time, a d—d b—h. After crossing her hands, he tied them with a strong rope, and led her to a stool under a large hook in the joist, put in for that purpose. He made her get upon the stool, and tied her hands to the hook. She now stood fair for his infernal purpose. Her arms were stretched out at her full length, so that she stood upon the ends of her toes. He then said to her, ' Now you d—d b—h, I'll learn you how to disobey my orders!' and, after rolling up his sleeves, he commenced to lay on the heavy cow-skin, and soon the warm red blood (amid heart-rending shrieks from her, and horrid oaths from him) came dripping to the floor. I was so terrified and horror-stricken at the sight, I hid myself in a closet, and dare not venture out till long after the bloody transaction." Nor was such horror unnatural. Till then Douglass had lived with his grandmother on the outskirts of the plantation. Consequently, to his young eyes, such scenes were sickening and strange.

Douglass's master lived on the home plantation of Colonel Edward Lloyd, and was the colonel's clerk and superintendent. The colonel kept from three to four hundred slaves on his home plantation, and owned a large number more on the farms belonging to him. The overseer, when first Douglass knew the place, was a man rightly named Severe. He seemed to take pleasure in manifesting his fiendish barbarity. Scarcely a sentence escaped his lips that was not commenced or concluded with a horrid oath. He filled the fields with blasphemy and blood. "From the rising to the going down of the sun he was cursing, raving, cutting, and slashing among slaves of the field in the most frightful manner. The next overseer, a Mr. Hopkins, was too humane, and did not stop long. The slaves called him the good overseer ; and goodness is a quality the slave-owner could well dispense with. He was succeeded by a wretch, of whom one anecdote will be enough. This Gore once undertook to whip one of Colonel Lloyd's slaves by the name of Demby. He had given Demby but a few stripes, when, to get rid of the scourging, he ran and plunged himself into a creek, and stood there at the depth of his shoulders, refusing to come out. Mr. Gore told him he would give him three calls, and that, if he did not come out at the third call, he would shoot him. The first call was given: Demby made no response, but stood his ground. The second and third calls were given with the same results. Mr. Gore then, without consultation or deliberation with any one, not even giving Demby an additional call, raised his musket to his face, taking deadly aim at his standing victim, and in an instant poor Demby was no more; his mangled body sank out of sight, and blood and brains marked the water where he had stood." No punishment was awarded this man for the foul murder done. He was continued in his office notwithstanding. It was only a slave; and, when they are concerned, in America the laws of God and man are alike set aside. On this plantation, then, grew up Douglass, till he was seven or eight years old. To most, childhood is a happy period of life; brightened by a mother's love, sheltered by a father's care. Of these the slave knows nothing. Douglass suffered from hunger and cold. His food was of the coarsest fare, and rudely served up. The children were all fed from a trough, like pigs. No wonder, then, that he heard with joy that he was to live with his master's son-in-law. It was an era in his life. He was cleaned and fresh clothed. A heavier heart than his might have been cheered by the change.

At Baltimore, Douglass learned the value of learning. His mistress began by teaching him the A B C. He then advanced to spelling words of three or four letters; but here his master interfered, and put a veto on all further progress. "If," said he, "you give a nigger an inch, he will take an ell. A nigger should know nothing but to obey his master—to do as he is told to do. Now, if you teach that nigger (pointing to Douglass) how to read, there will be no keeping him; it will for ever unfit him to be a slave; he will at once become unmanageable, and of no value to his master. As to himself, it can do him no good, but a great deal of harm. It will make him discontented and unhappy." This was enough. A new train of thought came into existence. The secret of the white man's power was at once perceived. Douglass silently resolved that he would win it and be free. During the seven years he lived in this family he kept firmly to his resolution. He got learning from children in the streets, from men in the docks—in fact, wherever he could; and as he grew in knowledge, so he grew in high hope and noble aim. A book called the *Columbian Orator* taught him the arguments against slavery. Sheridan's speeches on behalf of Catholic Emancipation, in the same book, furnished him with a bold denunciation of slavery, and a powerful vindication of human rights. His eyes were opened. The silver trump of freedom had spoken to his soul, and had there found an enduring response. But difficulties beset him on every side. It was long before he could even learn what was meant by an abolitionist. Still hope had been aroused, and henceforth Douglass had but one aim in life.

The death of Douglass's master led to his return, for a short time, to the place of his birth. It was necessary there should be a valuation of the property, for the purpose of division, and Douglass was sent for, to see what he would fetch. Douglass says, "We were all ranked together at the valuation. Men and women, old and young, married and single, were ranked with horses, sheep, and swine. There were horses and men, cattle and women, pigs and children, all holding the same rank in the scale of being, and were all subjected to the same narrow examination. Silvery-headed age and sprightly youth, maids and matrons, had to undergo the same indelicate inspection. At this moment I saw more clearly than ever the brutalising effects of slavery upon both slave and slaveholder." Such a conclusion was a very obvious one. Nor was it removed when the division of the property took place. To the unfortunate slave, such an event is a serious crisis. He may be torn from old associations and haunts—from kindred and from friends; he may be transferred from a master that he loves, to one he hates; and yet he must bear all in silence;—no words, no prayers, no tears of his are of any avail. So far as Douglass was affected, the distribution of the property mattered but little. He again went back to Orleans, and stopped there till 1832. He then returned to St. Michael's, to live with Master Thomas Auld. There are few slave-owners but have some good points. This man, however, had none. He and his wife were alike unforgiving, and cruel, and mean. Yet this man was a religious man. He was a professor of religion, and, what is more wonderful still, of the religion of Jesus of Nazareth. In 1832 this man attended a Methodist camp meeting, and there experienced religion. "I indulged," says Douglass, "a faint hope that his conversion would lead him to emancipate his slaves, and that, if it did not do this, it would, at any rate, make him more kind and humane." It did, however, nothing of the kind; he was worse than ever. Before he was converted —if such a phrase may be used with reference to him—he relied upon his own depravity to shield and sustain him in his savage barbarity. But after that he brought religion to his aid. Yet he made the greatest pretensions to piety. His house was the house of prayer. He prayed morning, noon, and night. He was a class-leader, a revivalist, and an exhorter. Many were made converts by him, and ministers of that Saviour who came to loose the prisoner, and set the captive free, ate at this man's table, and slept under this man's roof. "I have seen him," says Douglass, "tie up a lame young woman, and whip her with a heavy cow-skin upon her naked shoulders, causing the warm red blood to drip; and, in justification of the bloody deed, he would quote this passage of Scripture :—' He that knoweth his master's will, and doeth it not, shall be beaten with many stripes.' " This reminds us of

"The devil quoting Scripture
Like a very learned clerk."

Bad as all this is, yet worse follows. In the neighbourhood there lived a man named Covey—" a nigger breaker "—a professor of religion, and a class leader in the Methodist Church! To this man Douglass was sent to be broken in. Strange as it may seem, few men, at times, were more devotional than he. Family devotions were always commenced with singing, and it generally devolved upon Douglass to set the tune. Though like those who wept as they remembered Zion, at times Douglass refused to sing the Lord's song in a strange land. At such times the man prayed with more than ordinary fervour. Indeed, this man was a very pillar in the church, yet actually he was compelling his woman slave to commit the sin of adultery. The facts of the case were these. Mr. Covey was a poor man, and, just commencing life, he was only able to buy one slave; and he bought her, as he said, for a *breeder*. She had already given birth to one child, which proved to be just what he wanted. After buying her, he hired a married man to live with him one year; and him he used to fasten up with her every night. The consequence was, in twelve months' time, the miserable woman gave birth to twins, much to the delight of this Christian professor, who, if Douglass be an authority, succeeded in breaking him in, in body and soul. He felt himself transformed into a brute, and led the life of one. And yet there were times when the man within him would arise and put forth its powers. On Sabbath mornings he would stand gazing on Chesapeake Bay, whose broad bosom was ever white with sails from every quarter of the habitable globe, and would long that he like them could fly away and be at rest. Every day the cruelty of Covey became more unendurable. Douglass ran away, and appealed to his master, but in vain. However, the final struggle drew near. One morning, while he was feeding the horses, "Mr. Covey entered the stable with a long rope, and, just as I was half out of the loft, he caught hold of my legs, and was about tying me. As soon as I found what he was up to, I gave a sudden spring, and, as I did so, he holding to my legs, I was brought sprawling on the stable floor. Mr. Covey seemed now to think he had me, and could do what he pleased; but at this moment—from whence came the spirit I don't know—I resolved to fight, and suiting my action to the resolution, I seized Covey hard by the throat, and, as I did so, I rose. He held on to me, and I to him. My resistance was so entirely unexpected, that Covey seemed taken all aback. He trembled like a leaf. This gave me assurance, and I held him uneasy, causing the blood to run where I touched him with the ends of my fingers. Mr. Covey soon called out to Hughes for help. Hughes came, and, while Covey held me, attempted to tie my right hand. While he was in the act of doing so, I watched my opportunity, and gave him a heavy kick close under the ribs. This kick fairly sickened Hughes, so that he left me in the hands of Mr. Covey. This kick had the effect of weakening Hughes, but Covey also, when he saw Hughes bending over with pain, his courage quailed. He asked me if I meant to persist in that resistance. I told him I did, come what might; that he had used me like a brute for six months, and that I was determined to be used so no longer. With that, he strove to drag me to a stick that was lying just out of the stable door; he meant to knock me down. But just as he was leaning over to get the stick, I seized him with both hands by the collar, and brought him by a sudden smash to the ground. By this time Bill came. Covey called upon him for assistance. Bill wanted to know what he could do. Covey said, ' Take hold of him— take hold of him!' Bill said his master hired him out to work, and not to help to whip me, so he left Covey and myself to fight our battle out. We were at it for nearly two hours. Covey at length let me go, puffing and blowing at a great rate, saying, 'That if I had not resisted, he would not have whipped me half so much.' " This battle was the turning point in Douglass's career as a slave. The whole six months he spent after that, with his master, he never laid the weight of his finger upon him in anger. It recalled departed self-confidence. It re-inspired the determination to be free. From that hour Douglass felt that however he might be a slave in form, he had ceased to be a slave in fact. A new era commenced now for him—old things passed away, all things became new.

In 1834, Douglass was transferred to a new master, who had the merit of being open and frank, and not a professor of that religion which, in the Southern States of America, is a covering for the most horrid crimes, and a pretext for the commission of the foulest wrongs. Can we wonder that any man should loathe the society and the religion of such men! Religion has often been wronged—often has her fair name been loaded with disgrace; but never is she so wronged or disgraced as when she is worn as a cloak by men who dare, in direct violation of her precepts, to traffic in human flesh and blood— to sell their fellow-men as they do the beasts of the field.

In this new service again Douglass nursed thoughts of freedom. Nor did he labour for himself alone. His fellow-sufferers shared his sympathies, his hopes, and his labours. He held a Sabbath-school; and, that they might be fitted for freedom, he filled their breasts with thoughts similar to his own. They planned, decided, and acted together; but, alas for poor human nature, in that band there was a traitor; the plot was discovered, and, of course, suppressed. The discovery was not so disastrous as at first anticipated; so far as Douglass was concerned, it ended in sending him back to Baltimore, where, after working diligently and saving a little money, he managed to effect his escape. His feelings after the event he thus describes in his own graphic language :—

"I have been frequently asked how I felt when I found myself in a free State. I have never been able to answer the question with any satisfaction to myself. It was a moment of the highest excitement I ever experienced. I suppose I felt as one may imagine the unarmed mariner to feel, when he is rescued by a friendly man-of-war from the pursuit of a pirate. In writing to a dear friend, immediately after my arrival at New York, I said I felt like one who had escaped a den of hungry lions. This state of mind, however, very soon subsided; and I was again seized with a feeling of great insecurity and loneliness. I was yet liable to be taken back, and subjected to all the tortures of slavery. This in itself was enough to damp the ardour of my enthusiasm. But the loneliness overcame me. There I was in the midst of thousands, and yet a perfect stranger; without home and without friends, in the midst of thousands of my own brethren—children of a common father—and yet I dared not unfold to any one of them my sad condition. I was afraid to speak to any one, for fear of speaking to the wrong one, and thereby falling into the hands of money-loving kidnappers, whose business it was to lie in wait for the panting fugitive, as the ferocious beasts of the forest lie in wait for their prey. The motto which I adopted when I started from slavery was this—'Trust no man!' I saw in every white man an enemy, and in almost every coloured man cause for distrust. It was a most painful situation; and to understand it one must needs experience it, or imagine himself in similar circumstances."

In New York, whither Douglass fled, he found kind friends, by whose assistance he removed to New Bedford, where he married, and for some time lived by any kind of labour that came within his reach. So long as he was free, he cared not how lowly the labour was. He was resolved bravely to fight the battle of life for himself. One evening in August, 1841, an anti-slavery convention was held at Nantucket—the leading abolitionists were there. The excitement was great and growing. In the midst of it all there rose a noble-looking mulatto, whose appearance denoted no common intellectual power. At first he spoke tremblingly. He had never addressed a public audience; but he spoke of the wrongs of his race—of what he had seen, and heard, and felt—of the triumph of the oppressor —of might victorious over right—of life turned into a curse— of manhood degraded and undone—of a God of love defied. Words came swift and full of power. Men listened with wonder and delight. The name of the speaker was Frederick Douglass. That night witnessed his consecration to the sacred cause that aims to break the fetters of the slave. He put his hand to the plough, and since then he has never looked back. That night decided the destiny of his life. Ever since he has pleaded the cause which, as surely as there is a God in heaven, will triumph on the earth. Some time Frederick Douglass spent in England on an anti-slavery mission. He returned to America, where he edits a paper, established to carry out the object of his life. Comparatively speaking a young man, we may hope for him many years of noble and self-rewarding toil. The narrative of his life is calculated to do much in this respect, for he who can read it without indignation against slavery—without resolving as far as he can to extinguish it—without denouncing the American Church and American society, till that accursed thing be put down, must have indeed a flinty heart, and be something less than man.

THE REV. JAMES W. C. PENNINGTON, D.D.

Is another fugitive from American slavery, whose history is well known, and whose character is highly appreciated in England. The ancient and renowned University of Heidelberg, from whose venerable halls have gone forth masters in the loftiest departments of human lore, conferred an honorary degree upon Pennington for his abilities and reputation. The work which he has done in England, on behalf of his enslaved brethren, and the interest he has aroused on their behalf has been very great. Nor is this surprising. Despite what he says in reference to the painful defects of his education, it must be conceded that his amiable and gentlemanly deportment, his pliant and elegant mind, the culture and the power which he possesses, have won for him the esteem of very many; while his eloquence and pathos have touched the hearts of multitudes who have been privileged to hear him.

WILLIAM WELLS BROWN,

An intelligent, good-looking coloured man, is now in England, a fugitive slave, legally the property of another man, and cannot return to his native country for fear of being taken back into slavery. His narrative is replete with painful interest. In 1849, Brown was a delegate to the Peace Congress at Paris, where he spoke with much effect. His address is eloquent and impressive. He has delivered nearly five hundred lectures in England on slavery, twenty to thirty on temperance, and has addressed nearly one hundred public meetings, having travelled through Great Britain about 12,000 miles. He intended returning to America, but the passing of the Fugitive Slave Law prevented it.

William Wells Brown has recently published a work, entitled *Three Years in Europe*, &c., affording additional evidence of the falsity of the long-cherished notion, that the black man is mentally inferior to his white brethren. Yet, in the land of his birth, there is no spot on which Brown may not be claimed as a fugitive, and carried back to chains and bondage. Thank God! in England we do not recognise the right of any to hold a property in the flesh and blood of their fellow-men.

THE REV. HENRY H. GARNETT

Is another noble specimen of the negro race, a man who dares not return to the United States for fear of the fugitive slave-law. He was in England recently, and is well known, having addressed many public meetings. He has recently gone to the West Indies as a missionary.

The names of Henry Bibb, the Rev. Josiah Henson, Henry Box Brown, and William and Ellen Craft, and many others, might also be brought forward as illustrations of the accursed evils of slavery, and the blessings of freedom. Often has the indignation of those who hate slavery found expression in burning words and almost superhuman eloquence; but never yet has there been a mind which has *fully* comprehended all its vast enormity, a heart that has been *adequately* impressed by its horrors, or a tongue which could not exclaim—as it sounded forth its loftiest periods, and thrilled the deepest by its terrible recitals—"THE HALF HAS NOT BEEN TOLD!"

We have only mentioned a few of the fugitive slaves with whom we are best acquainted; those who have visited Great Britain, or taken up their residence in it to escape the dangers of the Fugitive Slave Law. Most, or all of these have written and published narratives of their lives in slavery, and how they were fortunate enough to escape from its horrors. To these works, which may be had through all booksellers on application, the reader is referred for realities exceeding any romance.

The *Chronotype,* an American paper, has the following remarks on this kind of publications :—" This fugitive slave literature is destined to be a powerful lever. We have the most profound conviction of its potency. We see in it the easy and infallible means of abolitionizing the free states. Argument provokes argument, reason is met by sophistry; but narratives of slaves go right to the hearts of men. We defy any man to think with any patience or tolerance of slavery after reading Bibb's narrative, unless he is one of those infidels to nature who float on the race as monsters, from it, but not of it. Put a dozen copies of this book into every school, district, or neighbourhood in the free states, and you might sweep the whole north on a thorough-going liberty platform for abolishing slavery, everywhere and everyhow. Stir up honest men's souls with such a book, and they won't set much by *disclaimers;* they won't be squeamish how radically they vote against a system which surpasses any hell which theology has ever been able to conjure up."

One conclusion forced upon the philosophical reader of such narratives of runaway slaves is this, that however tolerable chattel-slavery may be as an institution for savage and babarous life, when you bring it into the purlieus of civilization and Christianity, it becomes unspeakably iniquitous and intolerable. If the Americans really mean to uphold slavery, they *must*—there is no help for it—abolish Christianity, printing, art, science, and take their victims back to the standard of Central Africa, or the days of Shem, Ham, and Japhet.

Leeds Anti-slavery Series. No. 34.

Sold by W. and F. G. CASH, 5, Bishopsgate Street, London; and by JANE JOWETT, Friends' Meeting Yard, Leeds, at 3*s.* 6*d.* per 100; or 6*d.* per doz.

Leeds Anti-slavery Series. No. 35.

SINGULAR ESCAPES FROM SLAVERY.

THE MYSTERIOUS BOX.

THERE are many remarkable incidents in the history of fugitive slaves, which at once mark their ingenuity and the desperate determination of the victims of this cruel system to escape from it.

"A few weeks ago," says the *Burlington Courier* of April, 1849, "a slave in a Southern city managed to open a correspondence with a gentleman in a Northern city, with a view of effecting an escape from bondage. Having arranged the preliminaries, he paid somebody forty dollars to box him up, and mark him, 'This side up with care,' and take him to the express office, consigned to his friend at the North. On the passage, being on board a steam-boat, he was accidentally turned head downwards, and almost died with the rush of blood to the head. At the next change of transportation, however, he was

---

Sold by W. and F. G. CASH, 5, Bishopsgate Street, London; and by JANE JOWETT, Friends' Meeting Yard, Leeds, at 2s. 3d. per 100.

turned right side up again, and, after twenty-six hours' confinement, arrived safely at his destination. On receiving the box, the gentleman had doubts whether he should find a corpse or a free man. He tapped lightly on the box, with the question, 'All right?' and was delighted to hear the response, 'All right, Sir.' The poor fellow was immediately liberated from his place of living burial, and forwarded to a wealthy abolitionist in a city of New England, *where he now is*.

"When did Spartan intrepidity show greater firmness or fortitude under bodily suffering, than did this poor slave, when animated by the inspiring hope of freedom? We are glad to have assurance that this story is no flight of fancy, but is absolutely true. The fugitive, upon whose track the two-legged blood-hounds are coursing, will never go back to slavery, if the whole South should come after him."

The following account of the remarkable escape of this slave, from his own lips, may be relied on as strictly correct:—

"At the meeting on Wednesday evening, a fugitive slave, newly named Henry *Box* Brown, came on the platform, and related his adventures while escaping from the house of bondage.

"Henry was a slave in Virginia. He had a wife and three children, for whom their master asked 650 dollars. The husband and father made incredible exertions to purchase them, and succeeded in raising 600 dollars. The remaining fifty dollars were advanced by his own master, who had a lien upon the wife and children. After buying his family, Henry rented a house for them; but he soon became involved, as his master claimed the largest portion of his earnings. One morning, he went off to his work, but, on returning, found that his wife and children had been seized, sold upon the auction-block to the slave-traders, and were to be transported out of the state. They were sold for 1050 dollars. After this sad event, his master seized upon the furniture provided for the slave wife, sold it, and pocketed the proceeds.

"Henry remarked, with the deepest pathos, that after his wife and children were stolen, his heart was broken. He had learned to sing, to lighten the tedium of his labour, and for the gratification of his fellow-captives; but now he could not sing. His thoughts were far away in the rice-swamps of Carolina, or the cotton plantations of Georgia. His wife was not, and his children were not, and he refused to be comforted. When his master, noticing his despondency, told him he could get another wife (Southern morality!), Brown shook his head; the wife of his affections, and the children of his love, or none at all.

"Thoughts of liberty now began to spring up in his bosom. He had heard of the abolitionists, and determined to escape to them if it was possible. He became frugal, saved with more than a miser's eagerness every cent he could lay claim to, until he had amassed a sufficient sum for his purpose. The means used for escape were of the most unprecedented character. With the assistance of a friend, arrangements were made for him to escape in a box, which was to be forwarded to friends of the slave in Philadelphia, carefully marked as a valuable package.

"The *friend* who assisted him in this plot, took all his money, about forty dollars, and his clothes. Brown could offer no objections, though it left him penniless. Yet with a Roman heart, he was true to the fixed purpose of his soul; he was on his way to liberty. The box used for this extraordinary flight was only *three feet one inch long, two feet wide, and two feet six inches deep.* In this diminutive box he was transported from Richmond to Philadelphia, by railroad and steam-boat, a distance of 300 miles, amid perils so great, that the mind shudders when they are contemplated.

"On board of the steam-boat, while going up the Potomac, the box was set on end, which placed Brown *head downwards.* How long he remained in this fearful position, he does not know; but he mentally resolved to die, if die he must, without making a sign which might involve those who had been assisting him.

"The next great peril which he encountered was at the Baltimore depôt, at Washington. The box was roughly tumbled out of the transportation waggon, and it rolled over two or three times. This the unhappy fugitive thought was bad enough; but he was horror-stricken when it was proposed not to forward the box until the next day. In that event, he would die. But he bethought him to pray; and while yet praying, a superior officer ordered it to be forwarded. When put into the baggage car, he was again placed on his head, in which position he remained for the space of half an hour. His eyes became swollen nearly out of his head; his veins were filled to bursting, and he must have died, had not the position been providentially changed.

"The box arrived safely in Philadelphia at its destination. The friends who were anxiously waiting for it, were assembled in a room with the door locked. They were afraid to move. They feared that the inmate was dead, as he made no noise. Finally, one, more firm than the rest, rapped on the box, 'Is all right here?' in a friendly tone. 'All right,' was the brief response from within. The friends were overcome by their emotions; and one of them, finding speech, exclaimed, 'You are the greatest man in America!'

"As for Brown, he was joyful, his fatigues were nothing, his sufferings were forgotten. He was free; he breathed the air of liberty. That one thought swallowed up all others. After stretching himself for a moment, he breathed forth the feelings of his soul in a song of solemn praise for his deliverance. Without premeditation, he burst out, in a singularly melodious voice, this appropriate anthem:—

'I waited patiently, and the Lord my God delivered me.'

"What heroism, what self-denial, what energy of purpose are here manifested! The sincerity and strength of faith in the providence of God we must admire and respect. Such is the man who has been added to the freemen of the north. Let him be received as a brother beloved."—*Boston Paper, June,* 1849.

Since the passing of the Fugitive Slave Law, Box Brown has been obliged to leave his country, and has found a safe asylum in England. What a disgrace to a professedly free and Christian country as America, that such an acknowledgment should have to be made! That it should be published to all the world that *America's own born citizens are driven to seek refuge in a foreign clime from the man-stealer, and from the horrors of Slavery!*

Amongst the other refugees from Slavery, now in England, are William and Ellen Craft, whose escape was of the most romantic character; we shall, therefore, endeavour briefly to narrate the leading features of the case.

William and Ellen Craft were reared in Georgia, under different masters, but living near to each other they became eventually man and wife. Though their lot as slaves was not of

ELLEN CRAFT,
The fugitive Slave.

the worst kind, they nevertheless desired to escape from unjust bondage, in which they were at last successful. Their narrative comprises a most singular adventure, and forms a curious contrast to the usages of a civilized country. It is related in the pages of a contemporary nearly as follows:—

"William Craft is a black man, but his wife Ellen is nearly white, so much so, that the tyrannical lady to whom she belonged being annoyed at finding her often mistaken for a child of the family, gave her, when she was eleven years old, as a wedding-gift to her daughter. In the care of that lady she was better treated; but she nevertheless longed for freedom. Whenever she and William met after their marriage, they contrived and discussed plans of escape. At length, in 1848, they resolved on the ingenious expedient of disguising Ellen as a white young gentleman, while William should act as his servant, or rather slave. By cautious degrees they procured the necessary articles, buying one at one place, and another at another. Ellen then asked leave to go to see a sick aunt, and, after much entreaty, received the necessary permission. William, with much difficulty, obtained a similar permission to accompany his wife; and they lost no time in availing themselves of the liberty granted, that they might extend it to a point little thought of by the master and mistress. William cut off his wife's hair, and provided her with a pair of green spectacles. There was one difficulty which for a while puzzled them; this was, that at the railway offices, &c., they might be asked [as is customary in the Southern States] to write their names, and neither of them could read a letter, much less write one. So it was fixed that Ellen should pass for a very sickly young gentleman suffering from inflammatory rheumatism, which required the right hand to be kept poulticed, and her arm in a sling.

"This ignorance of being able to read, on more than one occasion nearly betrayed Ellen. Once a very kind-hearted gentleman, pitying her delicacy, presented her with a receipt for rheumatism, for which she thanked him politely, and, folding it carefully up, put it in her pocket, lest, in pretending to read it, she might hold it upside down.

"They first travelled to Savannah, and then took the steamboat to Charleston in South Carolina. On arriving there they went to the first hotel. William took care to secure a good room for his master, and to provide two hot poultices for the rheumatic hand and face. These, however, were not used till the poor invalid had tried to get some rest; the faithful slave then went to blacken the master's boots, and to perform all the usual necessary services; after which, dinner being served, the master with all honour was seated at the guest-table, and treated with the best viands, while the slave was sent off to the kitchen with a rusty knife and fork and broken plate, to get a few rough scraps. These, however, suited him as well as daintier fare, for appetite failed him at the moment, and he returned to the side of his master, who soon finished the repast, and, leaning on his slave for support, returned to the steamer. When they reached the office, the master asked for tickets for himself and servant to Philadelphia. The clerk requested him to write his name, to which he replied by pointing to his poulticed arm, and requesting the clerk to write the name. He declined, saying such was not his duty; but the difficulty was met by the captain of the steamer offering to do it, and William Johnston's name was entered on the books.

"On arriving at Wilmington, they took the railway, and travelled through Virginia. At Petersburg an old gentleman with two nice daughters got into the car along with the master. The old gentleman soon entered into conversation, and expressing much sympathy with the poor young man on his ill health, invited him to recline on the couch (which in the American railway cars stretches across one end of the saloon-like apartment), and also to take off his boots. These attentions were suffered, in the hope that further conversation would be avoided. The interesting young gentleman seemed to excite much sympathy in the young ladies, who were overheard expressing their interest in warm terms: they handed him refreshments, and vied with each other in attentions till they reached Richmond, Virginia, where the old gentleman and his daughters left the train, but not before warmly inviting their fellow-passenger to visit them whenever he went that way again.

"The fugitives proceeded in the same way, with many terrors excited by various incidents on the road, but in safety, to Fredericksburg, thence to Washington, and thence to Baltimore, which place they reached on the third day after leaving Macon. Here a great danger awaited them. The slave was accosted, and asked where he was going? He said he belonged to a sick young gentleman, and was going to Philadelphia. They were then informed that no negro was allowed to pass from the slave into the free states, between which this was the boundary, without a certificate to prove that all was right, and that they must go to the office to be examined. The clerk asked the master, 'Is this your servant?' to which he replied in the affirmative. 'Well, then,' said the clerk, 'it is against our rules to allow any slaves to pass, unless we have security that all is right. You must get some gentleman who knows you, to certify that you have a right to take this fellow with you.' The master replied, with more energy than could have been expected from a person of such delicate appearance, 'that he had bought tickets in Charleston to take both to Philadelphia; that he knew several gentlemen there, but that he did not know it was necessary to bring them along with him to certify that he was master of his own slave.' 'Well,' said the clerk, 'you must stay here then, as it is against our rules to let you pass.' But in the end, after some minutes' deliberation and consultation, he said—'I don't know what to do about it; but he is a sick young fellow, and I suppose I must tell the conductor to let him and his slave go on.' So the two fugitives, with trepidation which can scarcely be conceived, but with thankfulness of heart, resumed their seats in the train, and entered the free states.

"Here the coloured man had to be parted from his master, and to take his seat in the negro car, where he made inquiries as to lodging-houses in Philadelphia, and being satisfied as to the character of one for the coloured people, he repaired to it with his wearied but thankful wife, who concurred with him in thinking the effort well repaid by their being free; and though not a penny almost was left them, they considered the hard savings of all their previous lives well spent in securing the blessed boon of liberty. They made their case known to the lodging-house keeper, who introduced them to several friends, who thought it best for them to remove to Boston, where their safety was less liable to be endangered. Accordingly they repaired to that city, where they settled down, William to pursue his trade of cabinet-making, and Ellen to work with her needle.

"In this way they maintained themselves respectably, and

procured a little education, so as to enable them to read and write. They had formed pleasant plans for the winter of 1850 and 1851, of working in the day, and going to evening-schools to obtain what they so much prized—a little more learning—when the Fugitive Slave Law came into operation; and on the very first evening they attended the school, the warrant was issued for their apprehension, and the slave-catchers were abroad in Boston. William Craft lost no time in placing his beloved Ellen in a situation of concealment, and, as he hoped, safety, and then he left her, thinking at the time he would never see her again; for although he had resolved never to go back to slavery again, he fully contemplated that he should die in the attempt to resist his captors. The excitement and agitation of the three or four days' hunt in Boston were extreme; but William and Ellen ultimately succeeded in getting on board a British vessel, while the kidnappers were at New York."

These fugitives arrived in England about two years ago, when, for the first time, they set foot on really free soil. They are very interesting and intelligent persons. Ellen is a gentle, refined-looking young creature of twenty-four years, as fair as most of her British sisters, and in mental qualifications their equal too. William is very dark, but of a reflective, intelligent countenance, and of manly and dignified deportment. They have both been received as pupils into the Ockham Schools, near Ripley, in Surrey. These schools, which are partly industrial, were established by Lady Byron, for giving useful education to children residing in the rural districts. William Craft is cultivating his taste for drawing, under an able master. He renders himself useful by giving the boys instruction in carpentering and cabinet-making; while Ellen Craft exerts herself in communicating some of her varied mental acquirements to the girls. The children are greatly attached to her; and both she and her husband are happy, industrious, and making progress in their pursuits. The Ockham Schools are kindly and carefully superintended by the daughters of Dr. Lushington, of Ockham Park, which adjoins.

Leeds Anti-slavery Series. No. 35.

Sold by W. and F. G. CASH, 5, Bishopsgate Street, London; and by JANE JOWETT, Friends' Meeting Yard, Leeds, at 2s. 3d. per 100.

Leeds Anti-slavery Series. No. 36.

FUGITIVE SETTLEMENTS IN CANADA.

SINCE the passing of the Fugitive Slave Bill, by the Congress of the United States, fugitive slaves have arrived in large numbers in Canada, which, thank God, is a refuge for the poor hunted negro. There they have formed numerous settlements, and, assisted by kind friends, are making efforts to meet their destitute circumstances. The following are the principal locations of this kind :—

The *Dawn Settlement* was commenced twenty-five years since; but is not composed wholly of coloured persons. Scattered in various directions around the Educational Institute, established on a commanding point on the banks of the river Sydenham, about twelve years ago, by the late James Cannings Fuller, are five hundred refugees or more, mostly settled on farms. The lands are undulating, well wooded, producing in abundance the oak, the elm, the maple, the beach, the black walnut, the hickory, the sycamore, and other timber, well adapted for house-building and agricultural purposes. The cleared lands are found to be extremely fertile, and yield luxuriant crops of wheat, Indian corn, and oats. Owing to the mildness of the climate there is no difficulty in raising, in addition to the usual vegetables and fruits of this country, the sweet potato and tobacco, in any quantities required. Most of the farms of the settlers are sufficiently stocked with cattle and sheep, and with an abundant supply of pigs and poultry. What is most wanted is a near and profitable market for surplus produce. Around the land belonging to the Institute, three hundred acres in extent, on both sides of the river, are large tracts of land, which may be purchased, and which we yet hope to see mainly in the possession of coloured men of character and enterprise. In this settlement is found a large amount of in-

---

Sold by W. and F. G. CASH, 5, Bishopsgate Street, London; and by JANE JOWETT, Friends' Meeting Yard, Leeds, at 1s. 2*d*. per 100.

telligence, a more elevated moral tone, and broader views of what the refugees should be and should do, than in any other part of Canada. This is to be attributed to the advantages resulting from the school founded among them.

The *Elgin Settlement* is situated in the township of Raleigh, between the Lakes Erie and St. Clair, and consists of a block of land composed of nine thousand acres. It is held by an Association, under a special act of the provincial legislature, for the purpose of promoting the social and moral improvement of the coloured people in the province, by providing them with a home, and their children with a Christian education. It is under the direction of a gentleman well qualified, by his superior intelligence, and the deep interest he takes in the welfare of the refugees, for the office which he fills. Under his able direction, it promises to become one of the most flourishing and beautiful settlements in the country, and demonstrates the ability of the coloured man to place himself on a level with the whites. The first settler entered upon the land in 1849. Since then, a few families of superior character have been dropping in every month; and there are forty-five actual settlers, who have taken up two thousand five hundred acres of land at a fixed price, to be paid for by annual instalments. In 1852 they had cleared 230 acres of land, of which 194 were planted with Indian corn and other grain, and twenty-four acres in wheat. The houses are built uniformly, after an improved model. The gardens and the fronts of the houses are surrounded by picket fences, which give them a neat and snug appearance. The families settled at Buxton, for so the village is now called, are cheerful and happy, and a spirit of industry pervades the whole settlement. Some of the fugitives who entered it in 1850, without means, have earned enough to take up fifty acres of land on their own account, by payment of the first instalment. "I had the pleasure of meeting these interesting people," says John Scoble, " and learning from their own lips the perfect satisfaction they enjoyed in their new circumstances. The Rev. William King preaches to the refugees, and others, in a log-house chapel, which he has erected, and with assistance conducts a school, of a superior class, for the benefit of the children. A post-office has been established in the village; and when all the improvements which are designed are fully carried out,

Buxton will be a place of much interest to the philanthropist, and a real ornament to the province."

New Canaan is situated in the north part of the township of Colchester, seven miles east of Amherstburgh, in the western district, Canada West. The first families of coloured persons, two or three in number, settled there about five years ago. Since that time the settlement has gradually increased, until there are now twenty resident families, sixteen of which have taken lots, by paying the first instalment. The land not being of the first quality, is low in price, not exceeding two dollars per acre, and ten years are allowed the settlers to pay for the amount of land they may respectively take up, with the legal interest thereon. Nearly all the settlers are fugitive slaves, few of whom can read. There are nineteen children between the ages of five and sixteen. For the benefit of the settlement, a free school has been established, at which some of the parents attend with their children. Besides the day-school there is a Sabbath-school, and religious worship is regularly kept up by an agent of the Wesleyan Methodist Connection. The people are generally industrious and temperate, and in their general features and habits resemble the fugitives generally. Their present prospect is, that, with a little aid and encouragement, they will be able to secure themselves, at New Canaan, permanent homes. In other parts of the township of Colchester, there are a considerable number of coloured families.

Colchester Village Settlement comprises two villages, supposed to contain from 1200 to 1500 coloured people, mostly in the occupation of land, which many of them have already paid for. This is said to be the oldest coloured settlement in Canada, having commenced upwards of thirty years since. The land originally obtained by the settlers was very extensive in quantity, but partly for want of funds and advice, a considerable portion of it has gone into other hands; nevertheless those who are there, at the present moment, are said to be doing well. There appears, however, to be great need of good schools and teachers among these people. The settlement is about twelve miles from Malden, near the head of Lake Erie. Under judicious arrangements this would become a very flourishing part of the country.

Malden.—Around this town, now called Amherstburgh,

there is a large agricultural population, say from 1500 to 2000, composed of coloured persons. It is said that the people of this settlement have cleared the land for upwards of thirty miles up and down Lake Erie for the occupiers, and that whilst they have enriched others, they have done but little for themselves. There are, however, many among them who possess land, and others are desirous of doing so, whenever a favourable opportunity presents itself. The remarks respecting education, made in relation to Colchester, apply to Malden, and indeed to all the coloured settlements in West Canada.

Sandwich.—At this settlement there is computed to be about 300 coloured persons, increasing, however, in number from day to day, in consequence of its proximity to Detroit. From this point they draft themselves off to the larger settlements, further in the country, in many instances from fear of being captured. Many attempts of that kind have been made, and some of them have been successful. There are, however, a considerable number of respectable families settled there, on their own land, and doing as well as could be expected under their circumstances. At this settlement, Henry Bibb, a fugitive slave, resides, and edits with much ability the *Voice of the Fugitive,* an excellent little paper, issued once a fortnight, and deserves to be well supported. Henry Bibb is a man of great native talent, a good speaker, a man of business, and, above all, a sincere Christian. He is devoting himself to the improvement of his less gifted and less educated brethren, in various ways, and in this good work is ably assisted by his amiable and cultivated wife.

Wilberforce, about fifteen miles from London, and *Queensbush,* in the Huron tract, may also be mentioned, though not in a very flourishing state. There are other small settlements of coloured people in various parts of Canada. The possession of property by individuals, and the education of the coloured people, are two great means of elevating that oppressed and degraded race to a participation in the blessings of civilization.

Leeds Anti-slavery Series. No. 36.

Sold by W. and F. G. CASH, 5, Bishopsgate Street, London; and by JANE JOWETT, Friends' Meeting Yard, Leeds, at 1s. 2d. per 100.

Leeds Anti-slavery Series. No. 37.

PRAYER FOR THE NEGRO.

It is our duty ever to "remember them that are in bonds as bound with them." Let us prove that we *do* remember them, by endeavouring to do something towards rescuing so many unhappy beings from the miserable thraldom to which they have long been subjected by slavery. Let us not rest satisfied until the doors of the prison-house of bondage are broken down, liberty to the captive is effected, and "the oppressed go free!" until "the princes shall come forth from Egypt, and Ethiopia stretch out her hand unto God!"

May the fervent prayers of all those who are interested in the welfare of their fellow-men, and sympathize with the suffering African, ascend to the throne of heaven. It is the all-wise and all-merciful Disposer of events, the Lord Omnipotent alone, that can bless our efforts, and He will assuredly crown them with success, if we place our full confidence in Him, and faint not. To His name be ascribed all the praise and all the glory!

> Jesus! from thy dwelling-place,
> Look on Afric's captive race;
> While their bitter groans ascend,
> Let thy willing ear attend;
> Thou who never didst deny
> Pity to the mourner's cry,
> Hear the prayer we send to Thee,
> Set the injured negro free.
> Lo! in faith we turn to Thee,
> Set the injured negro free.

"Let the sighing of the prisoner come before Thee; according to the greatness of thy power preserve them that are appointed to die."—Psal. lxxix. 11.

Leeds Anti-slavery Series. No. 37.

Sold by W. and F. G. Cash, 5, Bishopsgate Street, London; and by Jane Jowett, Friends' Meeting Yard, Leeds, at 6d. per. 100.

Leeds Anti-slavery Series. No. 38.

A VOICE FROM OLD ENGLAND.

AMERICANS, will you regard a voice,
   That comes across the sea from Britain's shore?
How would it make a stranger's heart rejoice,
   To win to Freedom's cause one friend the more!

You hold the truth of man's equality,
   That none to be oppressive have a right;
Then how can you so inconsistent be,
   As to enslave because you have the might?

If all are equal, and if none have right
   To be unjust or cause another pain,
How then can you God's laws eternal blight,
   And round the negro throw vile Slavery's chain?

Is not the negro human? Is his heart
   Incapable of love, his mind of thought?
Do you not fear instruction to impart
   To him? Or cannot he be taught?

You know, you also know that Slavery,
   In which you hold three millions of your kind,
Has, of necessity, invariably,
   A tendency to brutalize the mind.

The noblest creatures exercise their power
   To bless the wretched and support the weak;
But you upon the weak and wretched lower;
   The "bruised reed" you scruple not to break.

How will you answer at the bar of God,
   For having made a fellow-man a slave?
Can you endure the terrors of his rod,
   His deep, determined anger can you brave?

Arise! to captive myriads freedom speak!
   Gladden the spirit of each abject slave!
Nought is more fiendlike than to oppress the weak,
   Nor aught more Godlike than to bless and save.

Leeds Anti-slavery Series. No. 38.

Sold by W. and F. G. CASH, 5, Bishopsgate Street, London; and by JANE JOWETT, Friends' Meeting Yard, Leeds, at 6d. per 100.

Leeds Anti-slavery Series. No. 39.

MURDEROUS TREATMENT OF A SLAVE GIRL.

THE *St. Louis Republican* gives an account of the death of a young slave, in consequence of cruel treatment. Some of our exchanges wonder that the matter is not investigated. They don't seem to know that the slave has no redress for wrongs inflicted—that the whole system of slavery is a system of cruelty, and that the laws which sustain it, authorize the taking of life even, to secure obedience. Read the account.

" On Friday last, the coroner held an inquest, at the house of Judge Dunica, a few miles south of the city, over the body of a negro girl, about eight years of age, belonging to Mr. Cordell. The body exhibited evidence of the most cruel whipping and beating we ever heard of. The flesh on the back and limbs was beaten to a jelly—one shoulder-bone was laid bare—there were several cuts, apparently from a club, on the head—and around the neck was the indentation of a cord, by which it was supposed she had been confined to a tree. She had been hired by a man named Tanner, residing in the neighbourhood, and was sent home in this condition. After coming home, her constant request, until her death, was for bread; by which it would seem that she had been starved as well as unmercifully whipped. The jury returned a verdict, that she came to her death by blows inflicted by some person unknown, while she was in the employ of Mr. Tanner."

OUTRAGE ON PUBLIC DECENCY.—The *St. Louis Organ* says that a shocking outrage on public decency was perpetrated on Tuesday, in Third Street, near the market. " A man, it appeared, had caught a negro girl who was a runaway. He carried her into an open lot, and in the presence of a crowd of men and boys, stripped her naked, tied her feet and hands, and in this condition chastised her with a horsewhip."—How long shall such atrocities be tolerated ?

Leeds Anti-slavery Series. No. 39.
Sold by W. and F. G. CASH, 5, Bishopsgate Street, London; and by JANE JOWETT, Friends' Meeting Yard, Leeds, at 6*d* per 100.

Leeds Anti-slavery Series. No. 40.

PLANTATION SCENES.

FEW know what slavery really is. Its atrocities are so horrible that the relation of them seems to be a most wicked exaggeration. The following was related by a lady of the highest respectability, as having occurred a few months since on a plantation where she was temporarily residing.

The planter, with whose family she was then staying, held about two hundred slaves on a plantation a few miles distant from his dwelling. The slaves, as usual, were under the charge of an overseer or driver. The planter had, among his house-servants, a bright boy about seventeen, a special favourite with the whole household, who was tenderly reared. He presented one of those cases often held up by the advocates of slavery, to show its mild and patriarchal character; and certainly this boy possessed all but one thing which is essential to humanity.

He was sent one day to the plantation on an errand, and having in some manner offended the overseer, was tied up and severely whipped. Not having had his spirit crushed by *field practice*, he felt and expressed an indignation natural to one nurtured as he had been. The driver ordered a pair of spirited horses to be fastened to a plough, and having so tied the boy to it that he could not guard himself from injury, he set them in rapid motion round the field, with the body of the poor boy now dragging across roots, now rebounding as it struck the ground, and finally, his head hitting a stump, he was instantly killed. Great consternation and sorrow seized the family when the account of Henry's murder reached the house. They felt it almost as keenly as if he had been a child or a brother.

What now was done? Was the murderer arrested? Was the blood avenged? Was he even dismissed? Nothing of this. He was secreted a few days, until a coroner's verdict covered up the deed as a *casualty*, and then returned to his place, with his heart harder than ever, and all things went on as before. A hole in the corner hides the corpse of the murdered boy, and justice sleeps till God shall deal with his murderer.—*Christian Press.*

Leeds Anti-slavery Series. No. 40.

Sold by W. and F. G. CASH, 5, Bishopsgate Street, London; and by JANE JOWETT, Friends' Meeting Yard, Leeds, at 6d. per 100.

Leeds Anti-slavery Series.   No. 41.

SALE AND SEPARATION OF A FAMILY.

A LATE traveller at the Cape of Good Hope, says, in a letter to a friend, "Having learned that there was to be a sale of cattle, farm-stock, &c., by auction, at a veld-cornet's in the vicinity, we halted our waggon for the purpose of procuring fresh oxen. Among the stock of the farm was a female slave and her three children. The farmers examined them, as if they had been so many head of cattle. They were sold separately, and to different purchasers. The tears, the anxiety, the anguish of the mother, while she met the gaze of the multitude, eyed the different countenances of the bidders, or cast a heart-rending look upon the children; and the simplicity and touching sorrow of the poor young ones, while they clung to their distracted parent, wiping their eyes, and half-concealing their faces, contrasted with the marked insensibility, and jocular countenances of the spectators, furnished a striking commentary on the miseries of slavery, and its debasing effects upon the hearts of its abettors. While the woman was in this distressed situation, she was asked, 'Can you feed sheep?' Her reply was so indistinct, that it escaped me, but it was probably in the negative, for her purchaser rejoined, in a loud and harsh voice, 'Then I will teach you with the *sjamboe*,' a whip made of the rhinoceros hide. The mother and her three children were literally torn from each other."—*New Monthly Magazine.*

No matter, under whatever specious term it disguises itself, slavery is hideous. Man held as a thing, and sold with as little concern, and often in the same lot as a Berkshire sow, or a Sussex boar! This is the indignity put upon our kind—an outrage committed on the world's liberty, which no sophistry can disguise, no expediency can palliate, and no language can hold up to sufficient execration.

Leeds Anti-slavery Series.   No. 41.
Sold by W. and F. G. CASH, 5, Bishopsgate Street, London; and by JANE JOWETT, Friends' Meeting Yard, Leeds, at 6*d*. per 100.

Leeds Anti-slavery Series. No. 42.

MURDER OF AN INFANT.

ON board a slave-ship, a child of about ten months old took *sulk* (as they term it), and would not eat. The captain took up the child and flogged it with a cat, saying, with an oath, "I'll make you eat, or I'll kill you." From this, and other ill treatment, the child's legs swelled, and the captain ordered some water to be made hot, for abating the swelling. But even his tender-mercies were cruel; for the cook, putting his hand into the water, said it was too hot. The captain, with another oath, said, " Put his feet in." The child was put into the water, and the nails and skin came all off his feet. Oiled cloths were then put round them. The child was then tied to a heavy log, and two or three days afterwards, the captain caught it up again, and said, "I will make you eat, or I will be the death of you." He immediately flogged the child again, and in a quarter of an hour it died. After the infant was dead, he would not suffer any of the people on deck to throw the body overboard, but called the *mother*, the wretched *mother*, to perform this last sad office to her murdered child. He beat her, regardless of the indignant murmurs of her fettered countrymen, (whom, in the barbarous plenitude of secure tyranny, he permitted to be spectators of this horrible scene), he beat her till he made her take up the child, and carry it to the side of the vessel, and then she dropped it into the sea, turning her head the other way, that she might not see it.—*Evidence before the House of Commons.*

"A few days ago, a young female was arrested at New Buffalo, where she had resided some time. She had been married but a short time before she was torn away from her husband by the cruel slave-hunter, and hurried off into Kentucky slavery, never more to see her husband; for the laws would not permit him to visit her."—*Voice of the Fugitive.*

Leeds Anti-slavery Series. No. 42

Sold by W. and F. G. CASH, 5, Bishopsgate Street, London; and by JANE JOWETT, Friends' Meeting Yard, Leeds, at 6d. per 100.

Leeds Anti-slavery Series. No. 43.

THE SLAVE-SHIP.

THE French ship, *Le Rodeur*, with a crew of 22 men, and with 160 negro slaves, sailed from Bonny, in Africa, April, 1819. On approaching the line, a terrible malady broke out—an obstinate disease of the eyes—contagious, and altogether beyond the resources of medicine. It was aggravated by a scarcity of water among the slaves (only half a wine-glass per day being allowed to each), and by the extreme impurity of the air in which they breathed. By the advice of the physician, they were brought on deck occasionally; but some of the poor wretches, locking themselves in each other's arms, leaped overboard, in the hope, which so universally prevails among them, of being swiftly transported to their own homes in Africa. To check this, the captain ordered several, who were stopped in the attempt, to be shot or hung before their companions. The disease extended to the crew; and one after another was smitten with it, until only one remained unaffected. Yet even this dreadful condition did not preclude calculation: to save the expense of supporting slaves rendered unsaleable, and to obtain grounds for a claim against the underwriters, 36 *of the negroes, having become blind, were thrown into the sea and drowned.*

In the midst of their dreadful fears, lest the solitary individual whose sight remained unaffected, should also be seized with the malady, a sail was discovered. It was the Spanish slaver, *Leon.* The same disease had been there; and, horrible to tell, all the crew had become blind! Unable to assist each other, the vessels parted. The Spanish ship was never after heard of. *Le Rodeur* reached Guadaloupe in June; the only man who escaped the disease, and was thus enabled to steer the slaver into port, caught it in three days after its arrival.—*Speech in French Chamber of Deputies, June* 17, 1820.

"All ready?" cried the captain;
"Ay, ay!" the seamen said;
"Heave up the worthless lubbers—
  The dying and the dead."
Up from the slave-ship's prison
  Fierce, bearded heads were thrust—
"Now let the sharks look to it—
  Toss up the dead ones first!"

Corpse after corpse came up,—
  Death had been busy there;
Where every blow is mercy,
  Why should the spoiler spare?

Sold by W. and F. G. CASH, 5, Bishopsgate Street, London; and by JANE JOWETT Friends' Meeting Yard, Leeds, at 1*s.* 2*d.* per 100.

Corpse after corpse they cast
   Sullenly from the ship,
Yet bloody with the traces
   Of fetter-link and whip.

Gloomily stood the captain,
   With his arms upon his breast,
With his cold brow sternly knotted,
   And his iron-lip compress'd.
"Are all the dead dogs over?"
   Growl'd through that matted lip—
"The blind ones are no better,
   Let's lighten the good ship."

Hark! from the ship's dark bosom,
   The very sounds of hell!
The ringing clank of iron—
   The maniac's short, sharp yell!—
The hoarse, low curse, throat-stifled—
   The starving infant's moan—
The horror of a breaking heart
   Pour'd through a mother's groan!

Up from that loathsome prison
   The stricken blind ones came:
Below, had all been darkness—
   Above, was still the same.
Yet the holy breath of heaven
   Was sweetly breathing there,
And the heated brow of fever
   Cool'd in the soft sea air.

"Overboard with them, shipmates!"
   Cutlass and dirk were plied;
Fetter'd and blind, one after one,
   Plunged down the vessel's side.
The sabre smote above—
   Beneath, the lean shark lay,
Waiting with wide and bloody jaw,
   His quick and human prey.

God of the earth! what cries
   Rang upwards unto Thee?
Voices of agony and blood,
   From ship-deck and from sea.

The last dull plunge was heard—
  The last wave caught its stain—
And the unsated sharks looked up
  For human hearts in vain.

Red glowed the Western waters—
  The setting sun was there,
Scattering alike on wave and cloud
  His fiery mesh of hair.
Amidst a group in blindness,
  A solitary eye
Gazed, from the burden'd slaver's deck,
  Into that burning sky.

"A storm," spoke out the gazer,
  "Is gathering and at hand—
Curse on't—I'd give my other eye
  For one firm rood of land."
And then he laughed—but only
  His echo'd laugh replied—
For the blinded and the suffering
  Alone were at his side.

Night settled on the waters,
  And on a stormy heaven,
While fiercely on that lone ship's track
  The thunder-gust was driven.
"A sail!—thank God, a sail!"
  And, as the helmsman spoke,
Up through the stormy murmur
  A shout of gladness broke.

Down came the stranger vessel
  Unheeding on her way,
So near, that on the slaver's deck
  Fell off her driven spray.
"Ho! for the love of mercy—
  We're perishing and blind!"
A wail of utter agony
  Came back upon the wind.

"Help *us!* for we are stricken
  With blindness every one;
Ten days we've floated fearfully
  Unnoting star or sun.

Our ship's the slaver *Leon*—
   We've but a score on board—
Our slaves are all gone over—
   Help—for the love of God!"

On livid brows of agony
   The broad red lightning shone—
But the roar of wind and thunder
   Stifled the answering groan.
Wailed from the broken waters
   A last despairing cry,
As, kindling in the stormy light,
   The stranger ship went by.

In the sunny Guadaloupe
   A dark-hulled vessel lay,
With a crew who noted never
   The night-fall or the day.
The blossom of the orange
   Waved white by every stream,
And tropic leaf, and flower, and bird,
   Were in the warm sunbeam.

And the sky was bright as ever,
   And the moonlight slept as well,
On the palm-trees by the hill-side,
   And the streamlet of the dell;
And the glances of the Creole
   Were still as archly deep,
And her smiles as full as ever
   Of passion and of sleep.

But vain were bird and blossom,
   The green earth and the sky,
And the smile of human faces,
   To the ever-darken'd eye;
For, amidst a world of beauty,
   The slaver went abroad,
With his ghastly visage written
   By the awful curse of God!

Leeds Anti-slavery Series. No. 43.

Sold by W. and F. G. CASH, 5, Bishopsgate Street, London; and by JANE JOWETT, Friends' Meeting Yard, Leeds, at 1s. 2d. per 100.

Leeds Anti-slavery Series. No. 44.

THE ENGLISHMAN'S DUTY

TO

THE FREE AND THE ENSLAVED AMERICAN.

A Lecture by the Rev. Charles Wicksteed, B.A. ;—Twice Delivered at Leeds in 1853.

" Blush ye not
To boast your equal laws, your just restraints,
Your rights defined, your liberties secured ;
Whilst, with an iron hand, ye crush to earth
The helpless African, and bid him drink
That cup of sorrow which yourselves have dashed,
Indignant, from oppression's fainting grasp?"

WILLIAM ROSCOE.

THE highest human liberty consists in the unrestrained power of obeying the law of God. The law of God is manifested in creation, in our own hearts, and, more plainly still, in the Spirit and Doctrine of our Lord Jesus Christ. The highest and best human law is that which is based upon these three manifestations of the Divine Law. That legislative code which, most firmly based upon great natural truths and great Christian principles, best avails itself also, in a practical form, of the results of human experience in all time, is the best of all codes.

Speaking generally, there can be no worthy liberty apart from the enjoyment of the privileges conceded, and acquiescence in the restraints enjoined, by these forms of the Divine Law. For I am denied my liberty if I am prevented, by a power outside myself, from obeying any great natural law. I am denied my liberty if I am prevented, by a power outside myself, from

---

Sold by W. and F. G. CASH, 5, Bishopsgate Street, London; and by JANE JOWETT, Friends' Meeting Yard, Leeds, at 5s. 3d. per 100; or 9d. per doz.

subjecting myself to the moral restraints or the religious guidance of any great Christian law. I am denied my liberty, in fine, if I am deprived, by a power outside myself, of my life, my possessions, the command of my own person, the culture of my own mind, and the exercise of my own faith. On the other hand, that person is not denied his liberty who is *prevented* from *preventing me* from obeying a great natural law, or a great Christian law; or who is prevented from depriving me, by his own will and superior strength, of my life, my limbs, or my possessions.

The law of liberty, then, is, after all, a law of personal and mutual restraint, and therefore, there is no liberty where there is no law. Where there is no law a man is not secure of his liberty to obey God, to follow Christ, or to possess his own. Now I believe that to be under the highest results of the best study and fulfilment of the combined natural, and Christian, and political laws, which the nation or the quarter of the globe in which he lives, has been able to reach, is the privilege and the right of every human being. It is only the race of man that lives subject to this combination of law, and it is only that race, therefore, that can enjoy the liberty which is the result. The human race is easily and markedly defined. No other animal was ever deliberately taken for a human being, and no human being was ever deliberately taken for any other animal. Man, wherever found, can, in more or less time, be made to understand these laws, and to feel himself the subject of them. This can be said of no other breathing thing upon the earth. Man—man, I say, wherever found, of whatsoever stock, of whatsoever climate, of whatsoever condition, whether of civilization or of barbarism, is found to have a *conscience* capable of being awakened to the knowledge of an all-mighty, all-righteous, and ever-present God, and the obligations of duty ; is found to have a *soul* capable of receiving, appreciating, enjoying, and fulfilling the hopes, commands, and privileges of the holy Christian faith; is found to have a *mental and social nature*, capable of rendering him a citizen in a state where order and liberty are secured by law.

And yet, in a country within ten days' sail of us; in a country inhabited by a race that has been in the possession of our blessed faith twelve centuries ; in a country which, by every imaginable relation of commerce, religion, literature, laws, and kindred, may be said to touch ours ; there are at this moment existing three million human creatures, systematically, knowingly, designedly *kept back by force* from obeying that law which God made for them; *kept back by force* from the full improvement of which their nature is capable (and shown, in spite of all obstructions, to be capable, were they permitted to obey God) ; *kept back by force* from sharing in those results which human study of the natural, the Christian, and the social law has secured to the country and the age in which their lot has also been cast ; *kept back by force* from breathing the moral atmosphere which all these influences united have raised around them, and which God intends for all his creatures, and compelled to breathe the air of a lower religion, morality, and civilization; *kept back by force* from the holiest truths; *kept back by force* from the most sacred relations ; *kept back by force* from the proved and acknowledged blessings of the highest human laws. This is a blasphemy and a crime unparalleled in human history. A race of slaves, where the principles of freedom have not been worked out and acknowledged ; a race of compelled victims to lust where Christianity has not shed its holy moral light, but where heathen pollution reigns around; a race of men deprived of the means of knowledge, where all around is ignorance, and where it is not felt for the soul to be without knowledge is not good—these things have been, these things are bad. But to put all this into the very midst of Christian faith, and love, and knowledge, and culture—to stab this into the very heart of Jesus Christ—to have all this, and to insist upon the continuance of all this, in an age and a country in which every confessed principle of law and justice around stamp it with infamy ; in which every avowed sentiment of the moral worth, and holy influence of the relations of domestic life, point to the sanctity of marriage ; every experience of the salutary effects of freedom upon human character and social life point to the duty of extending liberty and the final necessity of allowing it; in which every principle of religion and faith gather together, to pronounce the relation of man-owner and man-owned as morally and materially blighting to both; in such an age and country, in such a state of individual culture, and social and religious conviction, to vindicate and maintain, and strengthen this fatal institution, covers, from the contrast between the light and the darkness, the omissions and commissions prescribed by it—covers the spot in the earth and the age of the world in which it is done with a peculiar and unparalleled blackness.

And this state of things, I say, is realized by the existence of negro slavery in the midst of a land whose whole history, experience, religion, and sentiment is one prolonged and unmitigated condemnation and antithesis to it. For in such a state of things we are presented with the picture of a people throwing off the ordinary political rule of their mother country, because they did not choose to pay taxes without representation, erecting themselves into an independent state, and declaring all men free and equal (thus realizing the very ideal and abstract extreme of popular liberty), and holding three millions of their fellow-creatures not only in the denial of all rights of *citizenship*, but of all rights of humanity; making " representation" to them the *inversion of itself;* making them elect their oppressors as their representatives, and increasing the power of the latter in proportion to the multitude of the wronged ones; making them belong to any man who chooses to own them—the picture of a country professing Christianity, and inculcating, in the most earnest and convinced spirit, the duty and necessity of purity of mind, the sanctity of marriage and all the domestic relations, and depriving three millions of its inhabitants by law of the possibility of such relations; denying that there is or shall be such an institution among them as that which says, "what God hath joined together, let no man put asunder;" making purity of life—to wife, mother, daughter, and sister—by law impossible in certain circumstances, and its violation without redress and punishment, or reproof, in that unparalleledly pagan code. I say, savage life is heroic, manly, virtuous, holy, in comparison with this Christian heathenism, this instructed ignorance, this pure impurity, this freedom-loving tyranny, this humane inhumanity.

To the dark and frightful nature of this anomaly, as existing in their own dominions, the conscience of the English people began to awake in the latter part of the last century, so that in the beginning of the present, in 1807, after a parliamentary struggle of thirty years, the entire abolition of the slave-trade was carried throughout the British dominions. This was followed by another enactment, at again an interval of some thirty years, by which, in 1834, not only the slave-trade but slavery itself was abolished in like manner throughout the British dominions. We allow another interval of thirty years from that time, for the completion of the work of conscience among our brethren of the United States of America; and I cannot myself believe, that if the friends of the slave are faithful to their work or duty, more will be required, but that, before the year 1870 arrives, the step will be matured, by which slavery shall be made to cease in the United States.

The dead period—the deaf and dumb period of this question —the period when the opponents of slavery speak not out, and the friends of slavery hear not, is happily passed. We are at the beginning of that period which, in the achievement of all great objects (in reference to which human interests and human prejudices are bitterly opposed), precedes immediate victory— the period of fear on one side and courage on the other—of rage and opposition on one side, and persevering resolution and combat on the other. The indifferent period, the laughing and ridiculing period, are passed—the alarmed defying period is come—and in all human history, that has been the stage immediately antecedent to the last battle, and the triumph of God and right, of man and truth.

There are some here too young to recollect the time of that struggle in this country; but I trust that no one who does remember it, still more, that no one who took a part in it, has *gone back* upon the question, or fallen under the moral degradation of becoming indifferent to it. From my earliest years I remember the appeal for the slave as the watchword of the noblest, loftiest, humanest, and devoutest natures in our country; and what was done and suffered by them, was done and suffered not for our own age and country only, but for all the world and all time. Still—the struggle over, and the victory achieved—there was certainly, as was natural, a pause in English emotion and English action on the general subject for a time. We had done our duty, all that it appeared to us at the time, perhaps, it was our duty to do. We had purged our own dominions of the curse and crime. We had set an example to the world, and we were content, as it were, to wait the world's time for following it. And truly conscience was not dead in the United States, encouraged by the good example of this country, as unhappily they had previously been influenced by its evil example. Some firm and resolute men began to apply the lesson conveyed in it to their own condition. Few, and despised, and hated were the voices raised in the States to accomplish the same cause which in this country had just been placed in the car of victory, amidst the rejoicings of sovereign, and nobles, and people—the elevated, the learned, and the good—the patriot, the politician, and the philanthropist. These few prophets of the wilderness appealed to England for its sympathies. They said, "You have spoken by example, and this entitles you to speak by persuasion, remonstrance, and entreaty. We greatly need your aid."

In the most determined wills, convictions are often of the slowest growth. Those who will act with most energy when they do act, are often very deliberate in deciding when it is their duty to act. A not unnatural dislike to interfere with another country, on a matter in which we ourselves had only just had courage and wisdom enough, under less trying circumstances, to do the right thing, a hope and belief that the cause of liberty was advancing, and an unwillingness to complicate, by injudicious interference, the difficulties which America must experience in settling this question—a not entire accordance with the violent and dictatorial tone sometimes assumed by the friends of immediate and total abolition—not against the iniquity itself alone, but against all those who did not go to the full extent with themselves, in their modes of combating and opposing the iniquity—united with the languor which always succeeds a long-protracted struggle, in many minds indisposing them to renew it—all combined to make the response, even of English philanthropy and religion, not so strong and earnest as we now see it ought to have been.

We believed in human nature, we placed trust in the omnipotence of a good example, we were unwilling to hasten other men's arrangements, which we were assured they in good faith were making. A whisper rose within us of—Who art thou that judgest another in that thing which thou hast so recently allowed, and which, if thou wert placed in the circumstances thou condemnest, thou wouldst perhaps still allow. In the meantime, the native anti-slavery movement was every year acquiring fresh force and influence, and the free states were gaining a numerical ascendancy in Congress.

But alas for those dreams and hopes! In September, 1850, there was introduced into Congress the Fugitive Slave Bill, lauded and defended by representative, senator, and clergyman; and universal acquiescence in it urged as the peculiar duty of the Christian patriot. Our eyes were opened and we did see! A cry more indignant, more widely extended, more sorrowful and rebukeful, than had been raised by her since her own struggle, was sent by England across the Atlantic waters in return. In that cry, thank God, we too joined. The coldest felt moved, the feeblest thought he must do something, the advocate of slavery, here at least, was silenced and ashamed. At first, men could not believe it, they required the very Act itself to satisfy them that it could be true. A more melancholy disgrace has not fallen upon a Christian people in our age.

I carefully read and re-read that Act in the very form and the very words in which it was passed in Congress ; and I found that it was an amendment upon the former fugitive slave law, the amendment being to make the new law more cruel and tyrannical than the old one. This amendment provided a great multiplication of magistrates and persons authorized to act, for the express purposes of this law; it authorized any man to seize on any negro whom he might declare or fancy to be his, and bring him before a magistrate without warrant; it empowered that man or his agent to call the bystanders to assist him in the seizure. When brought before the magistrate, the testimony of the fugitive was not to be received in evidence, the exhibition of a general description was to be regarded as full and conclusive evidence against the fugitive; but if not convenient (for example, if it did not fit), the transcript of this record need not be produced, but some other satisfactory evidence in its place. Any person obstructing or resisting the claimant, or directly or indirectly aiding the fugitive to escape, or harbouring or concealing him, is subject to a fine not exceeding 2000 dollars, and imprisonment not exceeding six months ; and finally, every person assisting in the arrest, whether the claim be proved or not, is to be rewarded, *and the magistrate is to have a fee of five dollars if he decide in favour of the slave, and of* TEN *if he decides against him.*

Do you wonder at the alarm and trouble of a land where justice was still revered? But this excitement, like all other excitements where the perpetual food of an ever-present evil is not at hand to feed it, in time abated; but it left, I believe, an ineradicable impression, such as we never had before, of the inveteracy of the slave-holding spirit in the United States, of the convulsive firmness of its grasp, and the hopelessness of looking to it for any self-reform. And now has come this wonderful book, which is not a fiction but a parable*—the voice of one crying, "Repent, prepare ye the way of the Lord, make straight his paths." I have not met with any person who has read that true tale, without being moved to the heart's most sorrowful and most sympathizing depths—those depths where the voice of God, and goodness, and conscience is heard; and I hope I never may meet with such a person, for I should then assuredly know that I had met with one who had lost the feeling of humanity, and still more the feelings of piety and Christianity, and was buried in the degradation of an utter and immoral selfishness.

Under the circumstances of this new excitement, the national heart beats to do something again in the cause of the slave; yes, beats to do it, and will do it in defiance of that great daily power by which its faculties are daily taken captive and entranced, and whose too frequent province it seems to be to resist and ridicule the cause of good and right, while it is young and humble, but to confess and bow before it when it has become mature and great.

It is objected indeed to this earnest but sometimes perplexed desire, that the evils it seeks to remedy are greatly exaggerated. Greatly exaggerated! it is possible they may be, *and greatly extenuated too;* but, exaggeration and extenuation laid aside (and I certainly take the last to be quite as great as the first), our business is with the certain, notorious, necessary, uncontroverted facts that remain. But even these some are inclined

---

* *Uncle Tom's Cabin; or Negro Life in the Slave States of America;* by Mrs. H. B. Stowe.

to doubt. They reason from the feelings with which persons return from seeing the system in actual operation, and who have not found it so bad as it was represented to them to be. No! because perhaps an exaggeration had taken place in their own imaginations, and they had supposed that they should find every slave being flogged all day and kept in chains all night. And because they have seen many of them, on many estates, free from the constant infliction of these sufferings, they think that a mild admixture of them, and the constant exposure to them, is a very moderate evil indeed.

But further, do all these travellers *know*, not the exaggerated but the actual facts of the case, when they do come back? Travelling as birds of passage through the Southern States, visiting the planters and the clergy possibly, who will make the best of the system, the existence of which is their condemnation and disgrace; having no opportunity of observing the actual daily lives, knowing the actual secret hearts of these poor slaves, how are they in a position to know what are the facts of the case? Had these travellers spent as many hours in the huts of the negroes as they have at the tables of their masters, their account might be worth something more. What should we think of the inquirer into the condition of the mining population of this country, who took a mid-day stroll through the mines with the owner, and dined with him on the surface on his return?

We are told, therefore, on the testimony of such travellers, that the system is greatly improved, and that its evils are much exaggerated. But there are other travellers who are not content without getting a little nearer the facts, and these travellers are speaking every day now. In the travels of Mr. Sullivan, an English gentleman, just published, he tells us of a slave who was sold, but pacified by the assurance that his wife should accompany him the next day; the assurance was a falsehood, and the man, when he found it was, watching his opportunity, seized a hatchet, and chopped his right hand off at the wrist. Some humane persons wanted to buy him, but the owner would not sell him; he wished to have his revenge in the life-long torture of his victim, and for that victim there shall be no redress, or remedy, or compensation, till the day of God's holy judgment, when the master and the slave shall stand together at His bar.

A mother purchased her freedom, and redeemed part of her children from slavery, by her own industry and the liberality of friends; she hears that her daughter is sold and going to be sent to the south; her friend, Mr. Harned, of New York, writes to Bruin and Hill, of Alexandria, who hold the girl, relating the distress of the mother, and asking at what price she may purchase her freedom. Messrs. Bruin and Hill write back that her price is 1800 dollars. So much comfort for a poor slave mother who wants to buy her child! * Their letter is dated in 1851.

But I had in my possession, last week, a letter from a gentleman, who is well known to many here, the Rev. Francis Bishop, the respected minister to the poor in Liverpool, who has lately been travelling in the States, and who posts his letter from St. Louis, on August 28, 1852, not four months since. In that letter he writes, "I saw a large number of men, women, and children sold in Richmond; I saw families scattered in the most merciless manner, husband and wife, mother and daughter, brother and sister torn from each other, and sold in opposite directions." He went behind the auction-screen and witnessed exposure and insult, such as, even as described by himself, I cannot quote, and such as seen by himself he dared not even describe.

"I received," he says, "the entreaties of a mother and a daughter as I was looking round, the latter about nineteen years of age, of great personal attractions, and quite as white as Ellen Craft, to buy them together; and I afterwards saw the mother sold to a person from Alabama, in the extreme south, whilst the daughter was bought by a man near Richmond." "I saw a woman suffering from illness, and scarcely able to support herself with a staff, sold amid the jeers and ridicule of the assembled dealers for fifteen dollars, by order of the Circuit Court of Chancery, to pay the debts of her owner." He saw an old man on the block clasp his hands in agony, when he observed a stranger bid for him, and heard him exclaim that he could not work, he would be of no use, he would be whipped, he would die if taken from his wife and family in Richmond. He saw the marks of the lash on the naked backs of men,

* This girl died just afterwards, on her way south. She was described by her owners as the finest woman in the country. This was the reason they could not part with her for less than 1800 dollars. But God took her!

women, and children, in the examinations (above referred to) behind the screen. Mr. Bishop rushed, in the excitement of his feelings, to the Baptist Book Depository across the way, and said to the person who kept it, "What does the Christian church say to all this?" "Sir," replies the man, "you will be less moved by these things when you have been a little longer here." This, in last August, four months since! The system is improved! its evil is exaggerated! Let us at least, as worshippers of God, and disciples of Jesus Christ, beware of the more heinous sin, in our case, of "extenuation!"

But it is objected that there is danger connected with this object. Yes, there is gigantic danger—and it is a continually growing danger. It is greater this year than it was last; it will be greater next year than it is this; it will be greater the year after than it will be next. It becomes darker and more alarming every year. But the danger lies, not in the cessation of the evil, but in its continuance; for man's lust is working its own bitter and fearful punishment. The blood of liberty, of hatred, of a sense of wrong, of revenge, is gathering in fuller and fuller tides under the dark skin of the meeker and milder African. The white man is mingling the fire of his own ungoverned passions—of his own lawless freedom, of his own thirst of power—in the veins of the poor African, and that which, if done now, may be done in peace and safety, will, if delayed a century longer, be accomplished by outburst, slaughter, and a servile war. There would be danger, we were told, in the total emancipation of the negroes of our own West Indian colonies; and though they were far *more* numerous there than the whites, instead of being far *less* numerous, as in the States, the hour during which they passed from the remains of captivity to the first breath of liberty, was spent by those slaves in prayer, in exhortation, and in hymns of thanksgiving, and praise to God. Danger! danger from three million slaves against twenty million freemen!

But there is danger that there will not be so much produce created in the States for the employment of our mills and work-people in England, if labour be set free. Dr. Channing, in his address at Lennox, said, when celebrating the anniversary of the West Indian Emancipation, "Perhaps you will say that we are bound to wait for the fruits of emancipation before we celebrate it as a great event in history. I think not so. We ought to rejoice immediately without delay, whenever an act of justice is done, especially a grand public act, subverting the oppression of ages." And now, what has come to light in vindication of this noble trust of Channing, and in rebuke of this ignoble fear on the part of many in this country? The late Chancellor of the Exchequer's statement that already, where emancipation is not fourteen years old, the free labour of our West Indies is driving the slave labour out of the sugar market of the world; and that the produce of emancipated labour is largely and rapidly increasing, while that of enslaved labour is yearly and largely diminishing.*

That announcement ought to be printed and circulated over the whole earth, to re-assure the timid, the selfish, and the worldly, who are numerous everywhere, that the right course is ever the *safest*.

But it is objected—that we have enough to do at home, without concerning ourselves with other nations. We have; but we are not to neglect the cure of gigantic evils, and wide-spread curses among our fellow-creatures within ten days' reach of us, until every tittle of the undesirable is removed among ourselves. A man shall not be justified to the world in leaving his city in squalor and filth, a prey to the epidemic and the cholera, because, if he went back to his own house, he might find in it a dusty cupboard, or a soiled cloth. No! when there is a nation that has freed every slave it possesses, and fined itself twenty millions sterling to do so with a better grace; when there is a nation which raises itself up, and puts into action all its machinery of inquiry, punishment, and remedial caution, if a single old man or woman, among its 26,000,000 of souls, is turned away in want from his parish workhouse; when there is a nation which rings from end to end with indignation when a parish apprentice has been discovered to have been ill used, and commits the master and the mistress of a comparatively high station in

* As a great deal of the impression of such statements depends upon their exactness, it may not be amiss to give the figures in which the results were added up. In 1851 there were admitted 4,126,000 cwt. of British or free-grown sugar, against 1,487,000 cwt. of foreign, or for the most part, if not entirely, slave-grown sugar. In 1852 there were admitted 5,378,000 cwt. of free-grown sugar, against 814,000 cwt. of foreign or slave-produced sugar.

society, to prison for two years, for their undue severity; when the most laborious inquiries are instituted immediately whenever there is said to be an oppression, a cruelty, or a neglect, to protect even the free from the encounter of wrong ; that nation has the right to speak for humanity in other quarters of the globe, and to implore attention to its claims.

Besides, I think it is open to every one's observation, that they who are most earnest to redress the wrongs of the slave are among the most earnest advocates of every other means of elevating and improving the moral and social position of those nearer to them. Indeed, to the eye of humanity, the whole earth is kin. The ignorant, and degraded, and brutal man, the wronged and persecuted woman, the neglected and hard-used child, are objects of the profoundest and most painful interest, and of the most earnest efforts here at home, with the very same class of people who have sympathy with the wrongs and sufferings of the slave. I believe, for the most part, were you to analyse their elements, you would find that the same people who advocate the cause of the liberty of the slave, advocate the cause of liberty, civil and religious, human improvement, intellectual and moral, among every other class of persons. I believe you would find the friends of the slave among the signers of the petition for poor Francisco Madiai and his wife, and the friends of religious freedom ; among the advocates of representative institutions and reforms of government, and the friends of political freedom; among the anxious labourers for the religious improvement, and the social and moral amelioration of the people, and the friends of churches and chapels, schools, mechanics' institutions, temperance societies, saving societies, charities of help and aid, public baths, wash-houses, model lodging-houses, improvements in the dwellings of the poor, reformatory schools, and amendments in the civil and the criminal law. In short, it strikes me on a general survey, and it stands to reason that it should be so, that for the most part those who feel for the slave, are also found among those most willing to do something in some one or more of these various forms of good nearer home ; for it is the heart of sympathy that is wanted, and where that is present there will be feeling and exertion for the near as well as the distant, and the *distant* and forgotten as well as the *near* and forgotten.

If, therefore, our friends in the United States should answer, or, as it is reported, should have answered, the address from this country, and should do so in a similar spirit of earnest sorrow for the evils and the wrongs which exist in the old and crowded countries of Europe—(where there is not, as in America, open room and space whither the poor, and discontented, and disorderly, and adventurous can retire to find a new home, wheresoever they desire, but where they are almost necessarily pent up together in narrow space, and with limited means of support— a very trying state of life, and forming a problem far more difficult to solve, than any that America has yet had to grapple with—even than her own slavery question)—if, I say, such an address, in such a spirit, is sent us from the States, it would greatly strengthen our hands; it would stimulate our exertions, it would excite and shame the indifferent and the selfish to help the work of reformation, and would exercise an influence in showing that the eye of humanity was upon us in other nations, and opening our own eyes more widely to our own evils—which we should greatly value—and for which, I am confident, every sincere labourer in the removal of those evils would be grateful.

I believe we should be able to say, in reply to such addresses, that we agreed with them entirely ; that we were already doing something by parliamentary inquiries and legislative enactments, and the efforts of religious and philanthropic bodies, and the exertions of individuals, to check and cure these evils, and that, thus encouraged and stimulated, we should try to do more.

God grant that we may, ere long, receive similar replies from the United States upon this subject ! God grant that they may soon be able to tell us, in like manner, that they agree with us on the sin and misery of this institution, that they are heartily sorry for its existence, that they are giving it every possible consideration, private and public, and are taking steps to remove it ; that with them too, whenever any wrong or injustice is done one of the humblest of their negro population, an inquiry is immediately instituted, and the offender punished ; that they are giving the subject the fullest and gravest consideration and discussion in Congress, and devising means for its removal ; that they are publishing the reports which contain the results of these inquiries; that they are moulding and training, in all good and holy influences, their negro population, improving their dwellings and social condition, establishing schools and institutions for them, and making justice and kindness more accessible to them.

But lastly, we may be asked—supposing these objections removed—and the duty of doing something established, *what* are we to do, and *how* are we to do it?

When the affair is our own, the reply is easy—work to get the thing that ought to be done—done. But when the evil to be remedied is not among ourselves—when we cannot take action, as it were upon it, legislate upon it, or directly interfere in it—then what can we do? I believe that we may exercise the most powerful and salutary influence, by sympathy with the labours of those on whom the task of removing the evil immediately rests. They are poor, they need our aid; they are persecuted, they require our sympathy; they are doubted, they need our confidence. Every year a message goes from this town in which every one who now hears me may, and in which many who now hear me, for many years have borne a part. There are annual bazaars held in some of the principal towns of the Northern States to raise funds for prosecuting this object, to which all may contribute in money or articles; and at this moment there is in course of signature, throughout our land, an address of earnest and affectionate remonstrance to a portion of the United States people upon this subject.* I believe that every sincere, hearty, and well-timed expression of opinion on any subject, especially when it is on the side of truth, has its effect. It was recently and tauntingly said by the leading journal of this country, "When Mr. Fry's opinions become those of the majority, we can discontinue our insurance against attack, and disband our army and our navy." We believe in the literal truth of this principle, and apply it to every other question. This *is* a work of *conviction*; we wish to strengthen the *conviction* of the evil of slavery, of the duty and wisdom of emancipation, where it already exists, and to create it where it does not. The only possible mode of doing this is by representation, argument, and persuasion, untiring and continuous. This is

---

* A copy of this address, which has been signed by many hundred thousands of the women of England, and forwarded to the women of America, is inserted at page 17.

the method by which *every* great, moral, and social reform, every great change of conviction and opinion, is effected. It may seem little to sign an address. But it is *your voice*, it is that by which you *speak*, and will be heard three thousand miles off. If it be little, and you feel it little, do more: but do not withhold it because it is little. I do not regard it as little. I regard it as a great thing. Whenever in my life I have set my hand to a petition or an address advocating a great principle of truth, or right, or humanity, I have felt that I was doing a solemn act, and exercising a privilege, the opportunity of exercising which, so far from avoiding or neglecting, I most gladly and gratefully embraced. I have thought, the world is full of voices, let me swell by one the number of those that are uplifted in the cause of God and man, and thus far neutralize some voice that is raised upon the other side—yea! and by the grace and mercy of God, perhaps help to change that voice, and wean a wrong-doer from the evil of his ways. If no one spake, who should be heard? If none but the blinded of interest and prejudice offer guidance, how shall those who are seeking for truth and light be led? We have now put our hands to many a petition on various subjects; and on looking back we shall find, in the great majority of cases, the cause in which such a petition was signed, has since been victorious. I rejoice in it, and believe in the power of many voices. If each one, being by himself insignificant, withholds from the duty, how could be gathered that multitude of witnesses for truth, in which the history of the world has shown there is a victorious significance?

And when I ask every mother, wife, sister, daughter, in this place, who has not already signed it, to sign the address which I shall presently read to them, I only ask them to use that influence which God has given them, through these blessed relationships, in behalf of the mothers, wives, sisters, daughters, of their own stock in another country, who are gloriously labouring for, or miserably wronging, the mothers, wives, sisters, daughters, of another and a humbler race; who have the fewest friends and the heaviest wrongs of any creatures on the face of God's earth; who are in bonds, and have none to free them; in sorrow, and none to comfort them; in a compelled subservience to the imperious passions of absolute and irresponsible owners and possessors, and made by law incapable of the highest religion, and have none to vindicate their cause.

Do not believe, as you are falsely told, that you are doing mischief by this. The public eye fixed upon an evil, the public voice lifted up against an evil, never did mischief yet. It may exasperate the doers of the evil for a moment, but it exasperates them because they can no longer do it as they have hitherto done it, without disgrace and dishonour, and public rebuke. The cry that has been raised for the slave, has kept off many a blow for which the arm was uplifted, from descending upon him. It is making the evil known, awakening the perpetrators of it to the consciousness of it, and gigantic as it still is, is lessening it.

There will be a volume in your voice which shall roll over the Atlantic, and spread over the Northern States, nor utterly die, until, in the lower notes of its sympathy and love, it reaches the secret ear of the captive in the south. In the inscrutable ways of God, I believe that the young girl here to-night, and the loving mother, shall, by the writing of their names, and the prayer of their souls, speak into the very ear, shed comfort into the very heart of the young weeping girl, and the bereaved and loving mother, in those lands of the dark deed and the unknown oppression!

The following is the affectionate remonstrance alluded to at page 15:—

"'The affectionate and Christian Address of many thousands of the Women of England to their Sisters, the Women of the United States of America:—

"A common origin, a common faith, and, we sincerely believe, a common cause, urge us at this present moment to address you on the subject of that system of slavery which still prevails so extensively, and with such frightful results, in some of the vast regions of the western world.

"We will not dwell on the ordinary topics; on the progress of civilization; on the advance of freedom in various directions; on the requirements of the nineteenth century; but we appeal to you very seriously to reflect, and to ask counsel of God, how far such a state of things is in accordance with His holy Word, the inalienable rights of immortal souls, and the pure and merciful spirit of the Christian religion.

" We are not insensible to the difficulties that the abolition of slavery in your country may encounter from supposed pecuniary interests and long-cherished prejudices, but whatever difficulties may exist, we believe it to be a Christian duty to terminate, without delay, a system which deprives man of his rightful freedom; withholds from him the just reward of his labour; and which, both by law and in practice, in direct contravention of God's law, 'instituted in the time of man's innocency, denies, in effect, to the slave, the sanctity of marriage, with all its joys, rights, and obligations; which separates, at the will of the master, the wife from the husband, and the children from the parents. Nor can we be silent on that awful system, which, either by statute or by custom, interdicts to any race of man, or any portion of the human family, education in the truths of the gospel and the ordinances of Christianity.

" We appeal, then, to you as sisters, as wives, and as mothers, to raise your voices to your fellow-citizens, and your prayers to Almighty God, for the removal of these calamities and crimes from the Christian world. We do not say these things in a spirit of self-complacency, as though our nation had been free from the guilt it perceives in others. We acknowledge with grief the heavy share we have had in this great sin. We acknowledge that our forefathers introduced, if they did not compel the adoption of slavery in some of your states. We humbly confess this before Almighty God; and it is because we so deeply feel the share which our ancestors have had in this iniquity, and on account of the deep injury to the interests of humanity and Christianity involved in its continuance, that we now venture to implore your aid to wipe away that which has been our common guilt and our common dishonour."

O liberty! thou choicest treasure,
Seal of virtue, source of pleasure,
Life without thee knows no blessing,
No endearment worth caressing.

Leeds Anti-slavery Series. No. 44.

Sold by W. and F. G. CASH, 5, Bishopsgate Street, London; and by JANE JOWETT, Friends' Meeting Yard, Leeds, at 5s. 3d. per 100; or 9d. per doz.

Leeds Anti-slavery Series. No. 45.

SLAVERY HOSTILE TO RELIGION,
TEACHES BLASPHEMY,
AND IS A SCHOOL FOR ATHEISM.

"A NUMBER of coloured persons, both free and slave, were arrested in New Orleans on Sunday, the 8th ultimo, for the crime of assembling to worship God! A New Orleans paper mentions, as an evidence of their criminality, that one of them had a Bible and three prayer-books."—*North Star*, March 3, 1848.

"The Rev. Mr. Dowal, agent of the Virginian Bible Society, stated, in a discourse at Charleston, on Sunday last, that there are upwards of *fifteen thousand* families in Virginia without the Scriptures."—*Burritt's Christian Citizen.*

"A woman has been tried and convicted, in Virginia, for teaching a slave to read the Bible, and sentenced to two years' imprisonment in the penitentiary. According to the indictment, she, 'not having the fear of God before her eyes, but moved and instigated by the devil, wickedly, maliciously, and feloniously, did teach a certain negro woman to *read the Bible*, to the great displeasure of Almighty God.'"—*Investigator.*

"Rev. Dr. Taylor, at the head of the Theological School of Yale College, stated, in a lecture before the theological class, that he had no doubt, *if Jesus Christ was now on earth, that he would, under certain circumstances, become a slaveholder!* I have this from students who heard it, some of them agreeing with him in opinion, and some not."—*Boston Emancipator*, 1846.

Dr. E. D. Hudson, reporting a recent tour, in a letter published in the *New York Anti-Slavery Standard*, of September 23, 1847, describes a conversation with an avowed atheist, an old man of about seventy years of age. The latter kindled up with indignation as he gave vent to his feelings of hatred against slavery and slaveholding professors. He made use of language absolutely blasphemous, declaring the Bible to be a

Sold by W. and F. G. CASH, 5, Bishopsgate Street, London; and by JANE JOWETT, Friends' Meeting-Yard, Leeds, at 7*d.* per 100.

"fiction got up by bloody-minded human butchers and slave-holders," and proceeded to get *Taylor's Diegesis* and *Volney's Ruins* to sustain his opinion "that Jesus Christ was an ideality, and his history plagiarism from heathen descriptions of Bacchus and Prometheus."

The following is Dr. Hudson's account of the origin of this fearful case of infidelity:—

"This old man was formerly a prominent member of the Baptist Church, at a time when slavery existed in this State. The church then, as now, was full of *practical atheists*, saying, in her *deeds*, 'Who is God, that we should obey him?' It was full of *practical infidels*, as it is now, who practically deny the brotherhood of mankind. Priests then defended slavery as they do now, 'divining lies for hire.' It was such atheism, infidelity, antichrist, that drove this old man out of the church, and into his present frame of mind.

"One of the most exemplary members of the church (held and used as a piece of merchandise by another brother), by the name of Jethro, was compelled to toil six days in the week, and then go to church on Sunday, without shoes, though the season was cold and frosty. Jethro felt that he had a right to so much of the proceeds of his labour as would purchase him a pair of shoes, and accordingly took enough corn from the crib to purchase a pair. For this he was severely flogged, then led on foot, by his Christian claimant on horseback, with a large hay rope round his neck, to the neighbours to make confession, and then excommunicated from the church. The old man (on whom we called), after protesting in vain against slavery, and such brutality on the part of the slave-owner, and the church in its endorsement of such an impious outrage against God and man, fled from such a cage of unclean birds, and has, in consequence of the continued impiety and pharisaism of the church, been made what he is."

READER! How long shall these things continue to be so—contributing, as they do, so largely to the spread of infidelity, by bringing our holy religion into disrepute?

Leeds Anti-slavery Series. No. 45.

Sold by W. and F. G. CASH, 5, Bishopsgate Street, London; and by JANE JOWETT, Friends' Meeting-Yard, Leeds, at 7*d.* per 100.

Leeds Anti-slavery Series. No. 46.

APPALLING FEATURES OF SLAVERY.

"THERE was a planter named Anthony Williams, who lived upon the Red River. This Williams tied up a poor slave, and gave him a THOUSAND lashes on the bare back. I saw it done myself. About six weeks after that time, said Williams came out to the field where the slaves were at work, and brought with him his double-barrelled hunting-piece. He leaned the gun in the crotch of an apple-tree, and stepped forward to the head of the gang to speak to the overseer, who was on horseback. In the meantime, the above-mentioned slave lagged behind; and, as Williams came back, the slave caught up the gun, and fired at Williams. The first shot shattered his master's arm only; but the slave fired the second charge directly into his head, and sent him to his own place.

"I well remember a circumstance of inhuman cruelty and brutality that I witnessed near Natchez, when I was only about seven years of age. 1 went out one morning, in company with some other little boys, to hunt monkeys. These animals abounded in that country at that time; and we climbed on a rail fence near by, and there sat, for some little time, to see the 'hands' hoe cotton. One of these 'hands' was a black woman, who had a child at her breast, aged about six or seven months. The slaves are in the habit of taking their children out to the fields, and leaving them in the shade, or bushes alongside the fence, giving the child nutriment occasionally, as the overseer may order.

"The 'hands,' in this case, were each hoeing their row of cotton, and were some twenty yards from the fence, when, all at once, the babe began to scream as though its little heart-strings would break. No slaves are allowed to leave their work, in that country, without leave of the overseer; but, in this case, the maternal feelings of the frantic mother rose beyond

Sold by W. and F. G. CASH, 5, Bishopsgate Street, London; and by JANE JOWETT, Friends' Meeting-Yard, Leeds, at 7d. per 100.

the fear of orders, and she rushed to the rescue of her child, which was struggling with a huge snake. The overseer (John Manning was his infamous name) cried out, 'Stick to your work, or I'll cut you in pieces!' But that poor trembling mother kept on her maternal errand of mercy, snatched up the little one, the snake wound around it: the overseer followed on close at her heels, with his curses and imprecations upon the woman for leaving her work without orders. He stripped her as naked as the day she was born, fastened a rope round her two hands, and ordered two other slaves to climb a tree with the other end of the rope, and to pull this woman up so that her extremities would be about two feet from the ground; and this overseer, with his terrible lash, whipped this poor ill-fated creature to the extent of three hundred lashes. He literally 'cut her to pieces,' as he had said he would do.

"I distinctly recollect the language of this victim, until she got so faint that she could no longer speak, but hung to the rope as a dead person, without any living motion whatever.

" She screamed, as the lash went into her flesh, in these words, namely, 'Pray, massa! pray, massa! O, pray massa! Snake bite chile, massa, O, massa; forgive me, massa! Snake bite my chile, massa! Lord, make massa have little feeling for poor nigger! Lord, massa, you kill me, massa! Snake bite chile, massa!' &c., &c. And her voice became more and more faint, till the faculty of speech was whipped out of her, so that she hung in the lifeless manner to which I have alluded above.

"Now, I declare, in the face of God and man, that my two eyes beheld this sight; for the proof of which I can produce living witnesses even at this distant day.

"And I am commanded to obey the Fugitive-slave Law in the face of these things, am I? No! I will obey the injunctions of Jesus Christ, who has commanded me 'to let the captive go free.' And may this hand become withered, and this soul of mine for ever cursed, when I cease to recognise the inspiring precepts of Jesus, rather than to follow those of Millard Fillmore."—*Albany Busy Bee.*

Leeds Anti-slavery Series. No. 46

Sold by W. and F. G. CASH, 5, Bishopsgate Street, London; and by JANE JOWETT Friends' Meeting-Yard, Leeds, at 7*d.* per 100.

Leeds Anti-slavery Series. No. 47.

THINK OF THE SLAVE.

LET us never forget the obligations we are under towards our suffering fellow-creatures, wherever they are found. Let us remember we have a sacred duty to perform to the oppressed slave, inasmuch as he is our brother, and in chains. Long, *long*, are the arrears of compassion, of justice, and of love, due to the descendants of Afric's bleeding soil.

> PITY the negro, lady! hers is not,
> Like thine, a blessed and most happy lot!
> Thou, shelter'd 'neath a parent's tireless care,
> The fondly loved, the theme of many a prayer;
> Blessing and blest, amidst thy circling friends,
> Whose love repays the joys thy presence lends,
> Tread'st gaily onward, o'er thy path of flowers,
> With ceaseless summer lingering round thy bowers.
> But her—the outcast of a frowning fate,
> Long, weary years of servile bondage wait.
> Her lot uncheer'd by hope's reviving gale,
> The lowest in life's graduated scale—
> The few poor hours of bliss that cheer her still,
> Uncertain pensioners on a master's will—
> 'Midst ceaseless toils, renewed from day to day,
> She wears in bitter tears her life away.
> She is thy sister, woman! shall her cry,
> Uncared for, and unheeded, pass thee by?
> Wilt thou not weep to see her rank so low,
> And seek to raise her from her place of woe?
> Or has thy heart grown selfish in its bliss,
> That thou should'st view unmoved a fate like this?

May we daily feel a stronger conviction, that no life can be acceptable to God which is not beneficial to man, and thus be

---

Sold by W. and F. G. CASH, 5, Bishopsgate Street, London; and by JANE JOWETT Friends' Meeting Yard, Leeds, at 7*d.* per 100.

led to seek diligently for opportunities of active usefulness. Where suffering and wrong-doing are near, may we be quick to relieve, and unhesitating to reprove. Where they are remote, may we still feel that the suffering man is our neighbour, though at the farthest pole. May the wrongs endured by the seven millions of our fellow-creatures in the chains of slavery, at all times have our remembrance and sympathy.

> THINK of the slave in your hours of glee,
>   Ye who are treading life's flowery way;
> Nought but its rankling thorns has he,
>   Nought but the gloom of its wintry day.
>
> Think of the slave in your hours of woe:
>   What are your sorrows, to those he bears?
> Quenching the light of his bosom's glow,
>   With a life-long stream of gushing tears.
>
> Think of the slave in your hours of prayer,
>   When worldly thoughts in your hearts are dim;
> Offer your thanks for the bliss you share,
>   But pray for a brighter lot for him.

Merciful Father! we would especially bear upon our hearts before thee, that injured portion of thy family, who are bound in fetters by their fellow-men. Thou suppliest us largely and freely with gentle and benevolent emotions, when with genuine tenderness of heart, we entreat thy aid in the performance of kind offices towards our brethren and sisters. May we, therefore, always perceive it to be our duty to sympathize with, and pray for the slave, as a man and a brother. O break, speedily break, if it please Thee, that brother's bonds by sending out thy light and thy truth, that so they should shine in every Christian land more and more unto the perfect day. May we clearly see, that thy richest gift, the gospel, was bestowed upon us, not only that the spirit of its Founder might lead individuals to the steady practice of all holiness, but that it might gradually reform every earthly institution, which does not bear the impress of Divine purity and love. May the oppressor no longer oppress!

Leeds Anti-slavery Series. No. 47.

Sold by W. and F. G. CASH, 5, Bishopsgate Street, London; and by JA E JOWETT, Friends' Meeting Yard, Leeds, at 7d. per. 100.

Leeds Anti-slavery Series. No. 48.

THE GENTLEMEN FARMERS OF VIRGINIA ATTENDING THEIR CATTLE-MARKET.

"The following letter from Dr. Harvie may be relied on for its truthfulness. He resides in the neighbourhood of Philadelphia, and is a worthy man. What monsters of inhumanity—what unequalled pirates—are slaveholders! Buying and selling men, women, and children! Tearing from each other those bound together in the closest and dearest relations! Unutterable crimes! GERRIT SMITH.
"Peterborough, March 16, 1847."

"MYSELF and two others lately visited eastern Virginia, and there saw a slave auction. My friends, not abolitionists before, pitied my credulity when I told them the horrors of slavery; but one week in the Old Dominion has added two stanch adherents to our cause. I wish every pro-slavery man and woman in the North could witness one slave auction.

"We attended a sale of land and other property near Petersburg, and unexpectedly saw slaves sold at public auction. The slaves were told they would not be sold, and were collected in front of the quarters, gazing on the assembled multitude. The land being sold, the auctioneer's loud voice was heard, 'Bring up the *niggers.*' A shade of astonishment and affright passed over their faces, as they stared first at each other and then at the crowd of purchasers, whose attention was now directed to them. When the horrible truth was revealed to their minds that they were to be sold, and nearest relations and dearest friends parted for ever, the effect was indescribably agonizing. Women snatched up their babes, and ran screaming into the huts. Children hid behind the huts and trees, and the men stood in mute despair. The auctioneer stood on the portico of the house, and the men and boys were ranged in the yard for inspection. It was announced that no warrants of *soundness* were given, and purchasers must examine for themselves. A few old men were sold at prices from 13 to 25 dollars; and it was painful to see old men, with beards white with years of toil

Sold by W. and F. G. CASH, 5, Bishopsgate Street, London; and by JANE JOWETT, Friends' Meeting-Yard, Leeds, at 7*d.* per 100.

and suffering, stand up to be the jests of brutal tyrants, and to hear them tell of their diseases and worthlessness, fearing they would be bought by traders for the Southern market.

"A *white boy*, about 12 years old, was placed on the stand. His hair was brown and straight; his skin exactly the same hue as other white persons, and no discoverable trace of negro feature in his countenance.

"Some coarse and vulgar jests were passed on his colour, and 5 dollars were bid for him, but the auctioneer said 'That is not enough to begin on for such a likely young nigger!' Several remarked 'they would not have him as a gift.' Some said a white nigger was more trouble than he was worth. One man said it was wrong to sell white people. I asked if it was not wrong then to sell black people? He made no reply. Before he was sold, his mother rushed from the house upon the portico, crying in frantic grief, 'My son, O my boy, they will take away my dear ——.' Her voice was lost, and she was rudely pushed back and the door closed. The sale was not for a moment interrupted, and none of that crowd of ruthless tyrants appeared to be in the least degree affected by the scene. The poor boy, afraid to cry before so many strangers, who showed no sign of sympathy or pity, trembled and wiped the tears from his cheeks with his sleeve. He was sold for about 25 dollars. The monsters who tore this child from his mother would sell your child and mine if they had the power. During the sale, the quarters resounded with cries and lamentations that made my heart ache. A woman was next called by name. She gave her infant one wild embrace before leaving it with an old woman, and hastened mechanically to obey the call, but stopped, threw her arms aloft, screamed, and was unable to move.

"One of my companions touched my shoulder and said, 'Come, let us leave here, I can bear no more.' We left the ground. The man who drove our carriage from Petersburg had two sons belonging to the estate—small boys. He was asked if they were his own children? He answered, all that's left of eight. The others had been sold to the South, and he would never see or hear from them again."

Leeds Anti-slavery Series. No. 48.

Sold by W. and F. G. CASH, 5, Bishopsgate Street, London; and by JANE JOWETT, Friends' Meeting-Yard, Leeds, at 7*d.* per 100.

Leeds Anti-slavery Series. No. 49.

A SLAVE AUCTION IN VIRGINIA.

THE following very recent account of a slave auction in Virginia is from a letter in the *New York Tribune*, by a young citizen of New York, dated, Richmond (Virginia), March 3, 1853:—
"Since I left New York I have seen the original Declaration of Independence, and I have seen it "illustrated" here in this place. O, my God! O, my country! I have been an eye-witness to scenes such as never can be described. You and I have been told by some of the dough-faces of the north that the evils of slavery are exaggerated. But they have not been half told, and I have neither the ability nor the heart to describe the scenes I have this moment come from witnessing.
"I have spent two hours at the public sales of slaves. There are four of them, and all in the same street, not more than two blocks from the Exchange Hotel, where we are staying. These slave depots are in one of the most frequented streets of the place, and the sales are conducted in the building on the first floor, and within view of the passers-by. There are small screens, behind which the women of mature years are taken for inspection : but the men and the boys are publicly examined in the open store, before an audience of full one hundred. These examinations are carried on by various persons interested, and are enough to shock the feelings of the most hardened. You really cannot conceive that men in human form could conduct themselves so brutally ; each scar or mark is dwelt upon with great minuteness—its cause, its age, its general effect upon the health, &c., are questions asked and readily answered. I saw full twenty men stripped this morning, and not more than three or four had what they termed "clean backs," and some of them—I should think full one quarter of them—were scarred with the whip to such an extent as to present a frightful appearance ; one in particular was so cut that I am sure you could not lay your finger on any part of his back without coming in contact with a scar. These

scars were from the whip, and were from two inches to one foot in length. These marks damaged his sale; although only about 45 to 50 years old, he only brought 460 dollars; but for these marks he would have brought 750 to 800 dollars. I saw several children sold; the girls brought the highest price. Girls from 12 to 18 years old brought from 500 to 800 dollars.

"The slaves did not display as much feeling as I had expected, as a general thing—but there was one noble exception—God bless her! and save her too!! as I hope He will in some way, for if He does not interpose, there were no men there that would. She was a fine looking woman, about twenty-five years old, with three beautiful children; who, as well as herself, were neatly dressed. She attracted my attention at once on entering the room, and I took my stand near her to learn her answers to various questions put to her by the traders. One of these traders asked her what was the matter with her eyes? Wiping away the tears, she replied, 'I s'pose I have been crying.' 'Why do you cry?' 'Because I have left my man behind, and his master won't let him come along.' 'O, if I buy you, I will furnish you with a better husband, or man, as you call him, than your old one.' 'I don't want any better, and won't have any other as long as he lives.' 'O, but you will though, if I buy you.' 'No, massa, God helping me, I never will.'

"Did Mrs. Stowe exaggerate the spirit in the slave? No no. I saw 'Cassie's' character in this woman fully and fairly sticking out. Her answers to other inquiries put by another man were quite as 'liberty loving' as these indicated. The most indecent questions were put to her, all of which, after a little hesitation, she answered. But when asked if she thought she could turn out a child a-year, she replied, 'No, massa, I never have any more, and I sorry I got these.'

"Just before she was put up I left the room, for I could not have stood the scene. I should have betrayed myself. I cannot go further. I don't tell half the truth. I have said nothing of the brutality of the audience I saw at four of these auctions. I saw one hundred Legrees, and even worse than he. These auctions are held daily."

Leeds Anti-slavery Series. No. 49.

Sold by W. and F. G. CASH, 5, Bishopsgate Street, London; and by JANE JOWETT, Friends' Meeting Yard, Leeds, at 7d. per 100.

Leeds Anti-slavery Series. No. 50.

THE QUADROON GIRL.

A *Quadroon* (or quarter white) is the offspring of a Mulatto woman by a white man. Other odious distinctions are sometimes made in regard to shades of complexion; as, the offspring of a black woman by a Mulatto man is denominated a *Sambo*, that of a black woman by a white man, a *Mulatto*.

The fate of the Negro is not nearly so morally offensive as that of the Quadroon, the offspring of the white man and his Mulatto slave. Many of them are tenderly brought up and carefully educated, whilst others are sold as slaves. Here is a revolting, yet true picture of that accursed traffic, resulting in complicated crime, at which humanity shudders. In the following lines a slave captain, on the coast, is described, by the poet, Longfellow, as bargaining with a planter for the purchase of a young female slave, *his own child!*

"Maria was the daughter of a wealthy, titled father, who had not intended her for market, and so educated her; but debt, and a tempting offer from a bachelor merchant, induced him to dispose of her. . . . She was represented as tall and commanding in figure, of uncommon beauty, and nearly white."—Pittsburg paper, 1839.

The above shows that the Quadroon girl's story is by no means a mere fancy-sketch, but a fearful tale, of very frequent occurrence.

THE Slaver in the broad lagoon
Lay moored, with idle sail;
He waited for the rising moon,
And for the evening gale.

Under the shore his boat was tied,
And all her listless crew
Watched the gray alligator slide
Into the still bayou.

Odours of orange-flowers, and spice,
Reached them from time to time,
Like airs that breathe from Paradise
Upon a world of crime.

The Planter, under his roof of thatch,
Smoked thoughtfully and slow;
The Slaver's thumb was on the latch,
He seemed in haste to go.

Sold by W. and F. G. Cash, 5, Bishopsgate Street, London; and by Jane Jowett, Friends' Meeting Yard, Leeds, at 7d. per 100.

He said, "My ship at anchor rides
　　In yonder broad lagoon;
I only wait the evening tides,
　　And the rising of the moon."

Before them, with her face upraised,
　　In timid attitude,
Like one half-curious, half-amazed,
　　A Quadroon maiden stood.

Her eyes were, like a falcon's, gray,
　　Her arms and neck were bare;
No garment she wore, save a kirtle gay,
　　And her own long, raven hair.

And on her lips there played a smile
　　As holy, meek, and faint,
As lights in some cathedral aisle,
　　The features of a saint.

"The soil is barren—the farm is old,"
　　The thoughtful Planter said;
Then looked upon the Slaver's gold,
　　And then upon the maid.

His heart within him was at strife
　　With such accursed gains;
For he knew whose passions gave her life,
　　Whose blood ran in her veins.

But the voice of nature was too weak,
　　He took the glittering gold!
Then pale as death grew the maiden's cheek,
　　Her hands as icy cold.

The Slaver led her from the door,
　　He led her by the hand,
To be his slave and paramour
　　In a strange and distant land!

Leeds Anti-slavery Series.　No. 50.

Sold by W. and F. G. CASH, 5, Bishopsgate Street, London; and by JANE JOWETT, Friends' Meeting Yard, Leeds, at 7d. per 100.;

Leeds Anti-slavery Series. No. 51.

AN AUCTION SALE OF A YOUNG WOMAN,
WITH REFLECTIONS.

"WHILE travelling at the South, a short time since, one day as I was passing through a noted city, my attention was arrested by a concourse of people upon the public square.

"Soon I saw two men coming through the crowd attended by a female. They entered the ring around the stand. The sequel showed them to be an auctioneer, the unfortunate merchant, and the more unfortunate young lady—for slave she could not be. The auctioneer stepped upon the stand and ordered her to follow. She dropped her head upon her heaving bosom, but she moved not. Neither did she weep—her emotions were too deep for tears. The merchant stood near me. I attentively watched his countenance. 'Twas that of a father for the loss of an only daughter. Daughter he had not ; but I understand that he had intended to adopt her, who, instead of being now free, was doomed to perpetual slavery. He appeared to have a humane heart. With tears in his eyes, he said, 'Helen, you must obey—I can protect you no longer.' I could bear no more—my heart struggled to free itself from the human form. I turned my eyes upwards—the flag lay listlessly by the pole, for not a breeze had leave to stir. I thought I could almost see the spirits of the liberty-martyrs, whose blood had once stained that soil, and hear them sigh over the now desecrated spot.

"I turned to look for the doomed. She stood upon the auction-stand. In stature she was of the middle size ; slim and delicately built. Her skin was lighter than many a

Sold by W. and F. G. CASH, 5, Bishopsgate Street, London; and by JANE JOWETT, Friends' Meeting Yard, Leeds, at 1s. 2d. per 100.

Northern *brunette*, and her features were round, with thin lips. Indeed, many thought no black blood coursed in her veins. Now despair sat on her countenance. O ! I shall never forget that look. ' Good heavens!' ejaculated one of the two fathers, as he beheld the features of Helen, ' is that beautiful lady to be sold?'

" Then fell upon my ear the auctioneer's cry, ' How much is said for this beautiful healthy slave girl—a real albino—a fancy girl for any gentleman ? (!) How much ? How much ? Who bids ?' ' Five hundred dollars,' ' eight hundred,' ' one thousand,' were soon bid by different purchasers. The last was made by the friends of the merchant, as they wished to assist him to retain her. At first no one seemed disposed to raise the bid. The crier then read from a paper in his hand, ' She is intelligent, well-informed, easy to communicate, a first-rate instructress. Who raises the bid ?' This had the desired effect—' Twelve hundred'—' fourteen'—' sixteen,' quickly followed. He read again—' She is a devoted Christian, sustains the best of morals, and is perfectly trusty.' This raised the bids to two thousand dollars, at which she was struck off to the gentleman in favour of whom was the prosecution. Here closed one of the darkest scenes in the book of time. This was a Southern auction—an auction at which the bones, muscles, sinews, blood, and nerves of a young lady of nineteen, sold for one thousand dollars ; her improved intellect for six hundred more ; and her Christianity—the person of Christ in his follower—four hundred more."—*Liberty Press.*

"A CHRISTIAN! going, gone!
Who bids for God's own image ?—for His grace,
Which that poor victim of the market-place
  Hath in her suffering won?

My God! can such things be ?
Hast Thou not said that whatsoe'er is done
Unto Thy weakest, and Thy humblest one,
  Is even done to Thee ?

In that sad victim, then,
Child of Thy pitying love, I see Thee stand—
Once more the jest-word of a mocking band,
  Bound, sold, and scourged again!"

[REFLECTIONS ON THE ABOVE FACT, INTENDED FOR YOUNG MEN.]

Shame to the youth whose best blood does not stir within him, as he reads such a tale of wrong and suffering. Shame to him whose reverence for chastity does not lead him to censure, with strong indignation, the utter indelicacy of the whole scene. Dead should I be to the emotions of a manly tenderness, and to the holy throbbings of a virtuous sympathy, if I could behold the iron enter the soul of my lovely sister, woman, and not feel with her and for her. She has a right to expect a generous determination on our part to protect her from insult, and this determination it is man's best glory to form and to manifest. Slavery! thou low, mean, vile detestable thing—die! die under the deep loathing of an enlightened and improving world. Emancipation! thou fair friend to virtue, all hail to thy onward step, to thy benign and humanizing influences! How shall I, then, promote its progress?

One thing is certain—that for the young to be indifferent to the sufferings caused by great social evils, it is not well: it is not as it should be; it is trifling with the advantages, neglecting the duties, and forgetting the responsibilities of youth. Can I spend this hour more profitably than in briefly considering what these are? Among the *first*, may be classed (supposing the average degree of health) great capacity of endurance, ("youth by long toil incurring short fatigue,") and lively, strong emotions, which, in a young man morally well trained, powerfully aid in the formation of a permanently virtuous character. To these may be added that elastic buoyancy of hope, and that undaunted ardour of expectation, which supply a substratum for noble *effort*. Among the *second*, the first and greatest is, to keep the passions in check, and to obey the voice of reason and religion (for without doing this, youth will not only be indifferent to downward tendencies in society, but will manifest a downward tendency itself), *then*, to cultivate virtuous friendships, and to listen with a becoming and engaging modesty to the wisdom and experience of age. Lastly, among the *third*, a great point is, to bear in mind that the responsibilities of youth are many and weighty. The rising generation of any age or country gives the impress of its character to the generation which succeeds. Are the young men serious and earnest in the pursuit of truth and virtue? It would be strange, indeed, that their sons should be trifling and thoughtless. Are they dissolute and religious? it would be equally strange that their successors should be devout and self-governed. Are they watching with anxiety every onward and upward movement? who would expect to find their children looking with a heedless unconcern upon a guilty yet improvable world, and shrouding their dormant energies in a languid and inglorious self-indulgence?

My heart and understanding cannot but assent to the truth of the above imperfect outline of the position of youth, as respects his duty to himself, to his race, and to God. The thoughtful, serious, and vigorous discharge of these duties, furnishes, as it were, those "weapons of immortal temper," assailed by which, corrupt institutions *have* fallen in ages gone by, and by which they ever *must* fall. And what more pleasing subject for the mind to dwell upon, is there, than that of those master spirits whom we have seen blessed and guarded by Providence to a happy maturity, whose youthful powers were devoted to suffering humanity. To return to the consideration of that specific form of wrong-doing which has just been presented to my mind, in the unmanly and revolting treatment of a pure, sensitive, and lovely young woman.

I am young, and should not youth sympathize with youth! If *my* morning of life is unclouded, should I not grieve when the tempest of sorrow overcasts that of one youthful as myself, and equally alive to youth's innocent and varied gratifications. If *my* affections are suffered to flow unrestrained in those calm and holy channels, to which nature has destined them, should I not mourn over those, who are violently deprived of the tender care of cherished friends, or of near and dear relatives; and when the peace of a gentle heart is cruelly broken in the very spring-tide of womanhood, should not the remembrance of its harsh rupture fill the generous heart of youth with compassion, and with an ardent wish to subjugate the unlimited power and unjust control which inflicts such wounds, to the dominion of equity, and the law of righteousness?

Leeds Anti-slavery Series. No. 51.

Sold by W. and F. G. CASH, 5, Bishopsgate Street, London; and by JANE JOWETT, Friends' Meeting Yard, Leeds, at 1s. 2d. per 100.

Leeds Anti-slavery Series.   No. 52.

THE CHRISTIAN SLAVE.

THERE is in Georgia an association for the religious instruction of the negroes. From their seventh annual report, we extract the following:—" There is a growing interest in the community in the religious instruction of the negroes. There is a conviction that religious instruction promotes the *quiet* and *order* of the people, and the pecuniary interest of the owners."

This instruction is given without teaching them to read, and the doctrines of non-resistance, forgiveness of injuries, &c., which form a prominent part of it, are thought well calculated for the great ends above alluded to.

Conformable to this, we see, in the Southern papers, advertisements recommending individual slaves, or sometimes a lot, as *pious*, or *members of churches*. Lately we saw one advertised who, among other qualifications, was described as a Baptist preacher. In Mahometan countries, a slave, by embracing the religion of his master, becomes by law a free man. In America, the *Christian* slaveholder proclaims the religion of his bondsman in order to increase his value in the auction mart.

Two very striking illustrations of the fact, that Christian brotherhood purchases no immunity for the bondsman, are presented in this country at the present time.

Two ministers of the gospel, whose pulpit services have been acceptable both here and in the Northern United States, are fugitives from Southern slavery. One of them, the Rev. H. H. Garnett, is still *legally the slave* of an owner in Maryland; should he now return to his congregation in the state of New York, according to the recent Fugitive Slave Law, his master could seize him in his very pulpit, or while ministering at the table of the Lord; could drag him before a commissioner, prove his identity, and then put him up at auction in a

Sold by W. and F. G. CASH, 5, Bishopsgate Street, London; and by JANE JOWETT Friends' Meeting Yard, Leeds, at 1s. 2d. per 100.

Southern mart, or work him under the lash, far away from wife, family, church, and Christian friends; denying him even the reading of the Word of God, if his cruelty or caprice so dictated.

The second illustration is the Rev. Dr. Pennington, on whom a degree in divinity was lately conferred by a German university.

Happily, English gold has purchased for this gentleman the privilege of using his own faculties of mind and body, both of which are made over to him by a bill of sale of a doctor of divinity!

Should such things be? not if such sale concedes to the owner the right of holding property in *man*.

Thus saith the Lord:—" For the transgression of Israel, I will not turn away the punishment thereof; because they sold the righteous for silver."

A CHRISTIAN! going, gone!
Who bids for God's own image? for His grace,
Which that poor victim of the market-place,
 Hath in her suffering won?

My God! can such things be!
Hast thou not said that whatsoe'er is done
Unto Thy weaker and Thy humblest one,
 Is even done to Thee?

In that sad victim, then,
Child of thy pitying love I see thee stand,
Once more the jest-word of a mocking band
 Bound, sold, and scourged again!

A Christian up for sale!
Wet with her blood your whips, o'ertask her frame,
Make her life loathsome with your wrong and shame,
 Her patience shall not fail!

A *heathen* hand might deal
Back on your heads the gathered wrong of years,
But *her* low, broken prayer, and nightly tears,
 Ye neither heed nor feel.

Con well thy lesson o'er,
Thou *prudent* teacher—tell the toiling slave
No dangerous tale of Him who came to seek and save
    The outcast and the poor.

    But wisely shut the ray
Of God's *free* gospel from her simple heart,
And to her darkened mind alone impart
    One stern command, "OBEY."

    So shalt thou deftly raise
The market-price of human flesh; and while
On thee, their pampered guest, the planters smile,
    Thy church shall praise.

    Grave, reverend men shall tell,
From northern pulpits, how the work was blest,
While in that vile south Sodom, first and last,
    Thy poor disciples sell!

    O, shame! the Moslem thrall,
Who with his master to the prophet kneels,
While turning to the sacred Kebla feels
    His fetters break and fall.

    Cheers for the turbaned Bey
Of robber-peopled Tunis! he hath torn
The dark slave-dungeons open, and hath borne
    Their inmates into day.

    But *our* poor slave in vain
Turns to the Christian shrine his aching eyes—
Its rights will only swell his market-price,
    And rivet on his chain.

    God of all right! how long
Shall priestly robbers at thine altar stand,
Lifting, in prayer to Thee, the bloody hand
    And haughty brow of wrong!

    O, from the fields of cane,
From the low rice-swamp, from the trader's cell—
From the black slave-ship's foul and loathsome hell,
    And coffle's weary chain,

Hoarse, horrible, and strong,
Rises to heaven that agonizing cry,
Filling the arches of the hollow sky,
How long—O God, how long?

Well, indeed, did the great John Wesley designate slavery "the sum of all villanies!" Is it not amazing, that at a time when the rights of humanity are defined with precision, in a country above all others fond of liberty, that in such an age, and in such a country, we should find men, professing a religion the most humane and gentle, adopting principles so repugnant to humanity, inconsistent with the Bible, and destructive to liberty?

HORRIBLE TRAGEDY.—A telegraphic despatch from Cincinnati, May 19, says—

"A slave-trader from the South, purchased a negro man, wife, and child yesterday, in Covington, Kentucky, and placed them in jail for safe keeping. Last night, the woman, in the excitement of despair, we suppose, murdered her child, by cutting its throat—after which the man cut the woman's, and then his own. The former are dead—the latter is living, with but faint hope of his recovery."—*New York Evening Post*, 1848.

THE GOOD SAMARITAN IN JAIL.—"We learn by a letter from Tazewell county, says the *Western Citizen*, Chicago, that Geo. Kearn, an old gray-haired Christian, a local preacher in the Methodist denomination (not a Seceder), has been imprisoned in Tazewell county, on a charge of feeding the hungry, clothing the naked, and giving aid to the hunted fugitive! He is a resident of Woodford county; but as there is no jail there, he is confined at Tremont. How long shall wicked men, under the sanction of the law, be permitted to insult God, and mock his mercy and loving-kindness?"—*New York Evangelist*, May, 1846.

Leeds Anti-slavery Series. No. 52

Sold by W. and F. G. CASH, 5, Bishopsgate Street, London; and by JANE JOWETT, Friends' Meeting Yard, Leeds, at 1s. 2d. per 100.

Leeds Anti-slavery Series. No. 53.

TENDER MERCIES OF THE DOMESTIC INSTITUTION.

"THE crying injustice and cruelty of slavery had frequently engaged my attention during the course of this journey; but never more than while I was in this place, where this oppressed race are very numerous, and frequently sold at auction like cattle. At one of these sales, I was much affected in hearing a young coloured man pleading his cause. His aged father and mother, and his wife and child were all mounted upon a stage, so that they might be seen by the bidders, they being about to be sold. The young man stepped forward, and stood by them; but was soon ordered down. He said he wanted to be sold with them; but was told that he could not, as it was a sale to satisfy a mortgage upon the others, in which he was not included. He pleaded with very affecting and moving language, to show how hard it was to be separated from his family; but it was all to no purpose. When he saw that his prayers were unheeded, and that the others would be sold without him, he burst into a flood of tears, and, in the anguish of his feelings, besought them rather to kill him; 'For,' said he, ' I would rather die than be separated from my family.' Upon which he was dragged off the scaffold, and driven away. The company went on bidding, apparently as unconcerned as though the auctioneer had been selling a sheep; while the screams and prayers of the aged parents and the bereaved wife, with her infant in her arms, went up to heaven in behalf of themselves, and especially for the poor young man who had been so inhumanly torn from them. Besides these victims of cruel and unchristian avarice, there was a large number more confined in a cellar, who were brought out and sold to different purchasers. Thus it is that near relatives are violently separated, never to see each other in this world!"
—*Extract of a Letter received by Nathan Hinshaw, of Randolph County, Indiana, from a Correspondent in the South.*

Leeds Anti-slavery Series. No. 53.
Sold by W. and F. G. CASH, 5, Bishopsgate Street, London; and by JANE JOWETT, Friends' Meeting Yard, Leeds, at 6d. per 100.

Leeds Anti-slavery Series. No. 54.

CONVERSATION ON SLAVERY,

BETWEEN A LADY IN SCOTLAND, AND A RELATIVE OF HERS, WHO HAD LATELY RETURNED FROM BALTIMORE.

ON the subject of slavery being mentioned, the American lady became greatly excited. She said she had one slave, and nothing should induce her to give him up. He was very well off. "Did you ever see a slave beaten?" asked her friend. "O! very frequently; I often do it myself. I just take my shoe whenever I need it. But the slaves are better off than the servants of this country." "O, you are mistaken," rejoined the lady; "if a mistress strike a servant, she may appeal to a magistrate, and generally has the verdict in her favour. The mistress has no such power over her servant." "Poor things! how I pity them, then, not to be able to do as they please with their servants." The name of Frederick Douglass being mentioned, the American lady exclaimed against him in the most violent language, saying, if she had him in Baltimore, he should be tarred and feathered. And on a remonstrance being made, she remarked to her relative, "And you would be tarred and feathered too, if you were in the slave states."

Thus the sensibilities are blunted, and the mind is vitiated by the poisonous contamination of slavery. Another instance of these effects was exhibited in the conduct of the little daughter of this lady, a child of seven years old. She was on a visit to her cousin, who had a favourite canary, which hopped in and out of its cage with the greatest familiarity. One day, this canary came too near the little visitor, who seized it, and with savage pleasure, held it in a tub of water with its head downwards, till the life of the pretty little pet was extinct; and then, upon being questioned, she laughingly, related the occurrence, as if something clever had been done.—Such are the hardening effects of slavery, upon even a young and tender mind!

Leeds Anti-slavery Series. No. 54.
Sold by W. and F. G. CASH, 5, Bishopsgate Street, London; and by JANE JOWETT, Friend's Meeting Yard, Leeds, at 6d. per 100.

Leeds Anti-slavery Series. No. 55.

THE BIBLE AGAINST SLAVERY.

THE spirit of slavery never seeks refuge in the Bible of its own accord. The horns of the altar are its last resort—seized only in desperation, as it rushes from the terror of the avenger's arm. Like other unclean spirits, it "hateth the light, neither cometh to the light, lest its deeds should be reproved." Goaded to frenzy, in its conflicts with conscience and common sense denied all quarter, and hunted from every covert, it vaults over the sacred inclosure, and courses up and down the Bible, "seeking rest and finding none." THE LAW OF LOVE, glowing on every page, flashes around it an omnipresent anguish and despair. It shrinks from the hated light, and howls under the consuming torch, as demons quailed before the Son of God, and shrieked, "Torment us not." At last it slinks away under the types of the Mosaic system, and seeks to burrow out of sight among their shadows. Vain hope! Its asylum is its sepulchre; its city of refuge, the city of destruction. It flies from light into the sun, from heat into devouring fire; and from the voice of God into the thickness of His thunders.—*Weld*.

"He that stealeth a man, and selleth him, or if he be found in his hand, he shall surely be put to death."—Ex. xxi. 16; 1 Tim. i. 9, 10.

"Woe unto him that buildeth his house by unrighteousness, and his chambers by wrong; that useth his neighbour's service without wages, and giveth him not for his work."—Jer. xxii. 13; James v. 1-5.

"Therefore all things whatsoever ye would that men should do to you, do ye even so to them: for this is the law and the prophets."—*Jesus Christ*.

God "hath sent me to bind up the broken-hearted, *to proclaim liberty to the captives*."—*Jesus Christ*.

Leeds Anti-slavery Series. No. 55.
Sold by W. and F. G. CASH, 5, Bishopsgate Street, London; and by JANE JOWETT, Friends' Meeting Yard, Leeds, at 6*d*. per 100.

Leeds Anti-slavery Series. No. 56.

"THE ORDER OF THE FAMILY REQUIRED IT."

"A CHRISTIAN woman from one of the slave states, a lady who, although a large slaveholder, sustains at this moment a reputation for piety such as few enjoy, and who, in most of the relations of life, discharges every duty as in the fear of God—this lady holds now as a slave a Christian sister, who also is of irreproachable character, and holding for many years in the household the place of cook, is highly valued as a servant. This cook was one day so unwell, that she was unable to leave her bed without help; and yet, as a carriage-load of company had just arrived, Southern hospitality required that a good dinner should be prepared. None but the sick woman could be allowed to take the responsibility; but a Northern woman, then one of the family, volunteered to aid, so far as she could, in getting dinner. When it was upon the table, the mistress of the family called for an extra plate, and before cutting into a fine chicken-pie placed before her, she carefully cut off and put aside a few crumbs of the crust which was slightly burned on one side. After the company departed, this lady brought out the pieces of burnt crust, and, charging the mishap upon the cook, sent for the constable, and had the sick slave most severely whipped. She did this, although the lady who aided in preparing the dinner petitioned for her, and said she was herself most to blame; and although the woman was so ill that her husband had to lift her out of bed to take her whipping. And why did she do it? Because, as the mistress herself said, *the order of the family required it*, and she had told the cook what she might expect if guilty of such carelessness!! If this be Christian slaveholding, what may not the poor slave suffer under ungodly men? Alas! we know but too well what some suffer."—*Letter from W. E. Whiting, Esq., Merchant, of New York, dated May*, 1847.

Leeds Anti-slavery Series. No. 56.
Sold by W. and F. G. CASH, 5, Bishopsgate Street, London; and by JANE JOWETT, Friends' Meeting Yard, Leeds, at 6*d*. per 100.

Leeds Anti-slavery Series. No. 57.

SONG OF HUMANITY.

"Remember them that are in bonds."

In the God of truth be strong!
 For the truth shall perish never,
 Nor the weak be crushed for ever—
Right shall triumph over *wrong!*
 Cherish, then, our bond of union—
 Live in brotherly communion—
 Love our neighbour—help our brother—
 With our watchword cheer each other—
 "BE STRONG!"
In the God of truth be strong!

In the cause of man press on!
 Let new sympathy be kindled
 In the breast where love hath dwindled,
Until warmth of soul be won!
 Here upon our common altar,
 With true hearts that ne'er shall falter,
 Let us pledge our life's devotion
 To humanity's promotion—
 Press on!
In the cause of man press on!

Man is destined to be free!
 Free from slavery's aggression—
 Free from tyranny's oppression—
And from cheerless poverty;
 Free from prejudice and error—
 Free from vice, the greatest terror:
 Fear not!
Man is destined to be free!

Leeds Anti-slavery Series. No. 57.
Sold by W. and F. G. CASH, 5, Bishopsgate Street, London; and by JANE JOWETT, Friends' Meeting Yard, Leeds, at 6d. per 100.

Leeds Anti-slavery Series. No. 58.

THE AMERICAN SLAVE-SHIP.

"WHAT interested us most deeply, was his description of the extent and horrors of slavery and the slave-trade on the coast of Brazil. Not less than thirty or forty thousand slaves are brought there annually, and the mass of them in American vessels, under the American flag on the African coast, disguised elsewhere.

"And what is worse, these vessels are owned and controlled by *Americans! citizens of New England!* Aye, and what is worse than all, *by profession, Christians of New England!* Yes, I write with shame and sorrow, one vessel, which we saw and named, was owned and controlled by the Rev. Mr. ———, *a Baptist minister in the village of* ———, *in Massachusetts.*"—Published in the *Cleveland True Democrat,* from the testimony of Thomas C. M'Donald. Esq., bearer of despatches from the American Legation at Rio-de-Janeiro to the Government at Washington.

No breeze the dark pine-wood can wave,
  In your proud country of the free,
But fans the bosom of a slave—
  Slave of the "sons of liberty!"

Though brightly foams the feathery spray,
  A gloom is on the sunny sea;
For the pirate slave-ship wings her way,
  Manned by the "sons of liberty!"

The stars and stripes are at her mast,
  But crimson must their shadow be;
For the shark hath tracked her as she passed,
  And hailed the "sons of liberty."

Look ye to Washington's lone grave,
  And blush that human eye may see
The turf polluted by a slave,
  That shrouds that "son of liberty."

Land of the West, one task is yours,
  Bid the proud waters of your sea
In triumph flow round happy shores,
  Trod but by "sons of liberty!"

Leeds Anti-slavery Series. No. 58.

Sold by W. and F. G. CASH, 5, Bishopsgate Street, London; and by JANE JOWETT Friends' Meeting Yard, Leeds, at 6*d.* per 100.

Leeds Anti-Slavery Series. No. 59.

HUNTING SLAVES WITH BLOOD-HOUNDS.

FUGITIVE SLAVE ESCAPING THE PURSUIT OF BLOOD-HOUNDS.

AN article, recently published in *Household Words*, speaks of American Slavery in far milder terms than we should have expected in a work edited by so genial and humane a writer as Charles Dickens. William Craft, the fugitive slave, remarks on this, in the *Morning Advertiser* :—" The writer of *Household Words* implies that the American slaves are not hunted down with blood-hounds, as is the case in Cuba. But I am fully prepared to deny that incorrect assertion; for I have frequently seen the blood-hounds on the chase of slaves, and have seen the poor trembling victims, after they were caught and handcuffed, come limping through the streets of Macon ; yes—limping, because they were so badly bitten and bruised, in the combat with the dogs and hunters, that they could scarcely hobble

Sold by W. and F. G. CASH, 5, Bishopsgate Street, London; and by JANE JOWETT, Friends' Meeting Yard, Leeds, at 1s. 2d. per 100.

along to jail ; and if the master was not present to pay expenses, and take the slave in custody, he, or she, as the case might be, were put in close confinement, and an advertisement inserted in the papers, something like the following, from the *Milledgeville Recorder*, November 6, 1838 :—' A negro man has been lodged in the common jail of this county, who says his name is Jupiter. He has lost all his front teeth, above and below ; speaks very indistinctly ; is very lame, so that he can hardly walk.—J. B. Randall, jailor, Cobb Co., Georgia.' "

Some persons in America make it their business to catch runaway negroes, with blood-hounds trained for the purpose. Their profession is openly carried on, assisted by advertisements. The following is from the *Sumner County Whig*, an Alabama paper :—

"NEGRO DOGS.

"The undersigned having bought the entire pack of negro dogs (of the Hay and Allen stock), he now proposes to catch runaway negroes. His charges will be three dollars, per day, for hunting, and fifteen dollars for catching a runaway. He resides 3½ miles north of Livingston, near the lower Jone's Bluff Road.

"Nov. 6, 1845 ; 6 m.   WILLIAM GAMBREL."

Take another advertisement from the *Madison Journal*, published at Richmond, in Louisiana, Nov. 26, 1847 :—

" NOTICE.—The subscriber, living on Carroway Lake, on Hoe's Bayou, in Carroll Parish, sixteen miles on the road leading from Bayou Mason to Lake Providence, is ready, with a pack of dogs, to hunt runaway negroes at any time. These dogs are well trained, and are known throughout the parish. Letters addressed to me, at Providence, will secure immediate attention.

" My terms are five dollars, per day, for hunting the trails, whether the negro is caught or not. Where a twelve hours' trail is shown, and the negro not taken, no charge is made. For taking a negro, twenty-five dollars, and no charge made for hunting.

" JAMES W. HALL."

A VISIT TO A KENNEL OF BLOOD-HOUNDS, KEPT FOR THE PURPOSE OF HUNTING SLAVES.

"WHEN I was travelling through the southern portion of the United States, I remained for a few days at Columbia, South Carolina, the seat of the State legislature. One evening, I was much surprised to see a great number of men on horseback, accompanied by dogs. Upon inquiring who they were, I was informed that they were negro-hunters, whose horrible business consisted in tracking and catching runaway slaves. They came into the yard attached to the boarding-house at which I was stopping. When they had kennelled their dogs, and were about to feed them, I felt a curiosity to go out and see them. The dogs were of a species between the blood-hound and fox-hound, and were ferocious, gaunt, and savage-looking animals. Their masters fed them exclusively on Indian cornbread. This kind of food, they told me, made the dogs eager and lively for their business. It is the practice, when these wretches come to a town, for any white person, who has lost slaves, to go to the 'nigger-catchers,' as they term them, and as nearly as they can to put them on the track; of course giving a sufficient remuneration for their trouble. Even in this slaveholding community, such is the odium and contempt with which these creatures are regarded, that none but the very scum of society can be found to pursue so inhuman an occupation."
—*Testimony of a respectable English Traveller.*

HUNTING SCENE IN A LAND OF FREEDOM.

"A FEMALE runaway slave had been missed some days by her master. He employed some 'nigger-catchers' to take her, putting them, as near as he was able, on her track. After a short time, the hounds scented her, and opened mouth in full cry. They tracked her to a house which was nearly finished, but not occupied, in which the poor woman had taken shelter, and was lying secreted in a chimney. The dogs leaped in at a window, and discovered a foot protruding from the chimney. The leading dog seized her by her foot, and dragging her down, the rest tore her to pieces, before their masters could come up to prevent it. I received this account from a person of respecta-

bility at Columbia, in whose veracity I have every confidence."
—*Report of an English Traveller.*

THREE CHILDREN EATEN BY BLOOD-HOUNDS IN PURSUIT OF NEGROES.

THE *Wilkinson* (Louisiana) *Whig*, of August 1, records the following horrible event:—

"During the last few days, a report has been in circulation in our vicinity to the following effect:—It is stated that on Friday last, as three children were returning to their homes from school, near Liberty, in Amite County, they were overtaken by a pack of dogs in pursuit of runaway negroes. The dogs fell in upon them, and before assistance could be rendered, killed and nearly devoured every one of them. The father of the children hearing their screams, and the barking of the dogs, ran out with his gun, and succeeded in killing two of them. At this time, the owner of the dogs rode up, and threatened to shoot the father, if he shot any more of his dogs. The distressed father reloaded his gun, and deliberately shot the owner of the dogs through the heart; after which he gave himself up, was tried, and discharged. We have not heard the names of any of the parties."

Such are the cruelties to which American slavery gives birth; such the horrors to which the human mind is capable of being reconciled! From the testimony of the Southern journals, there are slave-hunts with muskets and blood-hounds. With a full knowledge of these facts—nay, under the hardening effects of familiarity with them, the leading statesmen, and religious teachers of America, affect to believe, and would fain make others believe, that the slaves are contented and happy in their present condition. In almost the same breath they exhort the people to the patriotic and Christian duty of enforcing the infamous Fugitive Slave Bill; quote the Bible and the Constitution to sustain their exhortations, and then complain of being slandered if accounted pro-slavery!

Leeds Anti-Slavery Series. No. 59.

Sold by W. and F. G. CASH, 5, Bishopsgate Street, London; and by JANE JOWETT Friends' Meeting Yard, Leeds, at 1s. 2d. per 100.

Leeds Anti-Slavery Series. No. 60.

TENDER MERCIES OF SLAVERY.

TREATMENT OF INFANTS IN A CHRISTIAN (?) COUNTRY.

"IN a tour a few years since through the State of Tennessee, the following scene presented itself, and although it had but little novelty about it to me, having witnessed the like before, yet its atrocious character is none the less on that account. On entering the city of Nashville, from the east, a steam-boat was ringing her bell, just ready to be off down the Cumberland. A company of slaves, men, women, and children, were driven up to the landing—some of them manacled together—as freight for the Southern market; and as they had been brought up in the neighbourhood, they were busy in taking leave, for the last time on earth, as they appeared conscious, of their friends and relations; and such a scene of bitter lamentation and weeping, I suppose, never was more than equalled in Rama. As if to heighten the climax of despair, the fiendish driver was running about with an infant in his arms, endeavouring to give it away from its mother, amid her shrieks and agonized wailings. Having staid a few moments to gaze upon this hard sight, and recollecting that hereabouts Dresser received his dressing, I urged my way forward about a mile, where I stopped for the night. And where should it be but at the father's-in-law of the same wretch of a slave-driver. You, perhaps, can imagine something of my feelings when I found myself in such company; but by remaining silent I learned several very important facts. One was, that the son-in-law did not succeed in getting any one to take the infant; but the consolation was, that he would not go far before he would succeed. Another one was, that some time previous, a man, a hundred miles off, had procured two infant children thus, and carried them all the way home in a wallet swung across his horse, with holes in the wallet for their heads, and after keeping them a few years, he sold one for six hundred dollars.

Sold by W. and F. G. CASH, 5, Bishopsgate Street, London; and by JANE JOWETT Friends' Meeting Yard, Leeds, at 7*d.* per 100.

We are told these are only rare cases, and therefore, not a fair representation of the workings of slavery. This idea is perfectly delusive. It is such a legitimate result of the system, that it attracts little or no attention or concern at the South."
W. M. ALLISON.

THE SLAVEHOLDER'S PRESENT.—Mr. Walker soon commenced purchasing to make up the third gang. We took steam-boat to Jefferson City, on the Missouri river. Here we landed, and took stage for the interior of the state. He bought a number of slaves, as he passed the different farms and villages. After getting twenty-two men and women, we arrived at St. Charles, a village on the Missouri. Here he purchased a woman who had a child in her arms, four or five weeks old. Soon after we left St. Charles, the child grew very cross, and kept up a noise during the greater part of the day. Mr. Walker complained of its crying several times, and told the mother to stop the child's noise, or he would. The woman tried to keep it from crying, but could not. We put up at night with an acquaintance of Mr. Walker; and in the morning, just as we were about to start, the child again commenced crying. Walker stepped up, and told her to give it to him. The mother tremblingly obeyed. He took the child by one arm, as you would a cat by the leg, walked into the house, and said to the lady, "Madam, I will make you a present of this little nigger; it keeps such a noise, I can't bear it." "Thank you, Sir," said the lady. The mother, as soon as she saw the child was to be left, ran up to Mr. Walker, and falling on her knees, begged him to let her have her child ; she clung round his legs, and cried, " O, my child ! my child ! master, do let me have my child ! O, do, do, do ! I will stop its crying if you will only let me have it again." When I saw this woman crying for her child so piteously, a shudder—a feeling akin to horror, shot through my frame. Mr. Walker commanded her to return into the ranks with the other slaves. Women who had children were not chained, but those that had none were. As soon as her child was disposed of, she was chained in the gang."—*Narrative of William W. Brown.*

Leeds Anti-Slavery Series. No. 60.

Sold by W. and F. G. CASH, 5, Bishopsgate Street, London; and by JANE JOWETT Friends' Meeting Yard, Leeds, at 7*d.* per 100.

Leeds Anti-Slavery Series. No. 61.

SLAVERY ALWAYS DIABOLICAL.

"THE same cause will produce the same effect," and, therefore, it excited no surprise in us to find Mrs. Stowe and Mr. Hildreth describing slavery in America exactly as it obtained among ourselves in the colonies five-and-twenty years ago. Scarcely a scene or an incident is given by either of them to which the *Anti-Slavery Reporter*, when under the editing of that able and truthful man, Zachary Macaulay, will not supply a parallel. Does the fiend Legree order 'two gigantic negroes to give this dog, Uncle Tom, such a breaking in as he won't get over this month,' which order is executed in blood? We can match it with a flogging yet more severe given to an old and faithful female slave for over-dressing a Turkey for a Christmas dinner! and in this case the flogging was directed by no slave-dealer, but by a reverend divine, distinguished by his literary talents no less than by his orthodoxy! Did the miscreant of Mrs. Stowe exultingly boast, 'I gave him the cussedest flogging I ever gave nigger yet. I b'lieve he is trying to die.' We can outdo him with the tale of a master who flogged his slave into insensibility, and anointed her eyes with Cayenne pepper to recover her to a sense of pain! Does the driver throw down a peck of corn before the famished labourer for a week's allowance, 'thar, nigger, grab; take care on't, ye won't get no more this yer week?' In an English colony, not five-and-thirty years ago, it is in evidence that slaves habitually dug up the buried carrion of diseased cattle to satisfy the cravings of hunger, and were flogged for the theft! It is in evidence that a young girl stole a few handfuls of rice to prevent death by starvation, and was sentenced by her inhuman mistress to carry a pitcher every morning to a river, half a mile off, fill it, and bring it home on her head, when it was emptied on the ground, to be thus refilled six times. After this whimsical preparation for the torture, she

Sold by W. and F. G. CASH, 5, Bishopsgate Street, London; and by JANE JOWETT Friends' Meeting-Yard, Leeds, at 7d. per 100.

daily received ten lashes. The punishment was to continue for three weeks; but long before the expiration of that time, the poor girl threw herself into the river and was drowned. If the case admits of aggravation it may be in this—that the punishment and suffering were daily witnessed by many officers and privates, but none dared to interfere! In a certain English colony there lived a female, by birth and courtesy received as a lady. She was admitted to the best colonial circles, left and received cards and invitations, and set as well as followed fashions; for she was well educated, well looking, and, as we have heard, attractive, even to fascination in her manners. Not a breath of scandal ever touched her fair fame; not a whisper to her prejudice was ever muttered, even over a tea-table within the tropics. A ball was a dull formality if she were not there to grace it; a party was stiff, tedious, and imperfect in her absence. What a romance might be raised upon the interesting charms and social inestimability of this bewitching widow! But how did she live? how sustain her high pretensions? how defray the cost of her elegant reunions, her gay equipage, and refined establishment? Nothing more easy in a slave colony. Her husband left no property, and fortunately no debts; but he had a small gang of good-looking mulattoes and quadroons, and they maintained his widow in decency and in comfort. It is true the whip was occasionally required; even slaves will not always submit to infamy without compulsion, or not be so unreasonable as to think that what is infamy in a white skin must be infamy in a brunette; but the whip or the cow-hide is a most efficient instructor in such cases, and in this case the military barracks being most conveniently situated near the lady's residence, the whip succeeded in procuring an average return of half a dollar per day per slave, from each of the miserable girls. If the authority for this anecdote is desired, it will be found stated in the evidence on the Mauritius inquiry, by several of the soldiers themselves, with the addition that the whip-compelled daily average (it was paid, however, weekly) was often raised by the humanity of the soldiers to secure the unfortunate from a flogging.

Leeds Anti-Slavery Series. No. 61.

Sold by W. and F. G. Cash, 5, Bishopsgate Street, London; and by Jane Jowett, Friends' Meeting-Yard, Leeds, at 7d. per 100.

Leeds Anti-Slavery Series, No. 62.

SCENE IN THE JAIL AT WASHINGTON.

REV. A. A. PHELPS visited this jail, and made the following statement :—

"There are in the prison sixteen solitary cells on the lower floor, the debtors' and criminals' rooms being above. These cells are mostly used for the confinement of slaves lodged there by the master as a punishment for some fault; of slaves 'suing for their freedom,' as they termed it, and of coloured persons, bond or free, arrested as runaways, or lodged there by the slave-dealers. We found not less than *thirteen* individuals in them at this time, every one of whom claimed that, on one ground or other, they were entitled to their freedom. In one cell we found a *Fanny Jackson*, with three little children, one of them an infant at her breast. Her husband, also in the prison, was in a separate cell. They were claimed by one Asa Buckner, of Loudon Co., Va., but having been in Washington several years, unclaimed by the master, they were suing for their freedom under some act which entitled them to it. They had lain in prison, awaiting their trial, *nine months*. We spoke to the mother about her little ones, and we found she had indeed a mother's heart. The scene cannot be described.

"*Rachel Turner* was the occupant of another cell. She was young—had been owned for a limited time by Lewis Bromley, of Baltimore, and was to have been free in a year. Mrs. Bromley [her husband being dead] sold her for that time, to a man, who either changed his name to that of Angt. de Nanteuil, or sold her a slave for life to another person of that name. He took her to Washington, and lodged her in the jail 'for safe keeping' till he should call for her. Nothing had been heard from him. Meanwhile the girl had been in the prison more than six months, and the keeper assured me that she would soon be sold, *for her jail fees*, as a *slave for life*. The whole affair was doubtless a mere trick, to evade the law, and make her a slave for life.

"On returning from the prison, the lady who had accompanied me, and who had often aided the poor outcasts, said that her attention was first called to the subject by the following incident. Some seven years before, a poor coloured man came to her door, walking on his knees—having lost his legs to the knee, and his arms also to the elbow. She asked him how it happened. He said he had been put in prison as a runaway, though he was free, and the winter was so cold, and his covering so scanty [having scarce a blanket to throw over him], that his limbs were frozen, and it *became necessary to take them off* TO SAVE HIS LIFE! Thus was a free American made a cripple for life, for the crime of having a coloured skin, and had to pay the United States for the expense of having suspected him to be a slave!"

In 1826 Congress appropriated out of the public treasury 5000 dollars "for the purpose of altering and repairing the jail in the city of Washington," and 10,000 dollars to build "a county jail for the city and county of Alexandria."

Congress in 1820 empowered the corporation of the city of Washington to "prescribe the terms and conditions upon which free negroes and mulattoes may reside in the city." In May, 1827, that corporation enacted that all negroes found residing in the city who shall not be able to establish their title to freedom [except such as may be hired] shall be committed to the jail, as absconding slaves. The result is, that free citizens are often arrested, plunged into prison, and then sold for the jail fees AS SLAVES FOR LIFE. In 1829, Mr. Miner, of Pennsylvania, declared in Congress, that in 1826-7, no less than *five persons* were thus sold. In July, 1834, in a Washington paper was the following notice:—"Was committed to the prison of Washington Co., D. C., on the 19th day of May, 1834, as a runaway, a negro man, who calls himself DAVID PECK. He is five feet eight inches high. Had on, when committed, a check shirt, linen pantaloons, and straw hat. *He says he is free.*"

How long shall this state of things continue to be?

Leeds Anti-slavery Series. No. 62.

Sold by W. and F. G. CASH, 5, Bishopsgate Street, London; and by JANE JOWETT, Friends' Meeting-Yard, Leeds, at 7d. per 100.

Leeds Anti-slavery Series. No. 63.

SLAVES HAPPY!

IT has often been alleged that slaves are happy in their state of thraldom. The following facts prove the contrary:—

THE DISMAL SWAMP A REFUGE FROM SLAVERY.—" This gloomy swamp is not without its interest; for it serves as a hiding-place, a 'city of refuge,' for the poor slave. I am told there are hundreds of fugitives who have sought an asylum from oppression in this damp and dreary region, and here they have hitherto been secure. But recently, parties of young men, with dogs, have hunted out these poor creatures; and, to use the expression of my informant, have 'shot them down like partridges.' A few weeks since, a company of them were discovered, and made resistance, as they were armed with pistols; they fired, without effect, and then were fired on by these man-hunters, with their longer and heavier guns, and four of them shot, and others wounded so, that they could not retreat. One of them, in particular, was shot in the knee, which was badly shattered. He was then brought out to the place near where I am now writing, when a surgeon dressed his wound, and placed it in a box, prepared to keep it straight and still. When his master arrived, he was so enraged at seeing him, that he stamped upon the poor man's face where he was lying, in a most shocking manner. My informant was a witness, and is a respectable man.

" So many of these poor wretched fugitives have been shot and wounded, others have become alarmed, and have come out and returned to their former masters. Query—If the slaves are happy in their present condition, would they prefer a residence in the Dismal Swamp to it?"—*Zion's Herald.*

THE NEGRO'S HORROR OF SLAVERY.—" On Saturday last, an affecting scene took place in the cars, about two miles below

Sold by W. and F. G. CASH, 5, Bishopsgate Street, London; and by JANE JOWETT, Friends' Meeting-Yard, Leeds, at 7*d.* per 100.

Newark, calculated to touch the heart of the most inhuman slaveholder in the country. It never fell to our lot to witness the horror and fear the poor negro has of slavery, as upon this occasion. Three free-coloured persons were in the cars, and should have got out at the Newark depot, but, on inquiring, were informed that the next station was the place. They kept their seats for about a mile, when they learned they were going at a rapid rate to Maryland—then a scene followed that we cannot find language to describe. One was a young woman, and the others a man, his wife, and child. The young woman was so frightened, that sooner than run the risk of going to Maryland, she jumped from the platform ; and next followed the man with his child, and were safe. His wife's turn came next ; but observing her great danger, we seized her by the arm and prevented her, assuring her that we would get her a pass to return when we arrived at Elkton. She implored us to let her go, that she would be arrested and sold into slavery. She fell on her knees and wrung her hands—a more painful or affecting sight we never beheld. We saw the poor woman provided for, and sent back as soon as the train from Baltimore arrived. We have witnessed many scenes ; but, in this instance, the poor negroes' fear of being sold into slavery, and their love of freedom, surpassed all."—*Blue Hen's Chicken* (Delaware Paper).

"We are told the slave is happy ;" says Dr. Channing, "that he is gay ; that he is not the wretched and miserable being he is represented to be. After his toil he sings and dances. The slave indeed has his pleasures. His animal nature survives the injury to his rational and moral powers ; and every animal has its enjoyments. The kindness of Providence allows no human being to be wholly divorced from good. The lamb frolics ; the dog leaps for joy ; the bird fills the air with cheerful harmony ; and the slave spends his holidays in laughter and the dance. He is gay, because he is too fallen to feel his wrongs — because he wants proper self-respect. There is a sadness in the gaiety of him whose lightness of heart would be turned into bitterness and indignation, were one ray of light to awaken in him the spirit of a man."

Leeds Anti-slavery Series. No. 63.

Sold by W. and F. G. Cash, 5, Bishopsgate Street, London ; and by Jane Jowett, Friends' Meeting-Yard, Leeds, at 7*d*. per 100.

Leeds Anti-slavery Series. No. 64.

SALE OF SLAVES IN VIRGINIA.

THE following advertisement, an account of a sale of slaves, is from a report of the American Anti-Slavery Society :—
"Monday next, at 9 A.M., at public sale, the slaves whose names follow, all negroes of the first quality—namely, Betsy, a negro woman, 23 years of age, with her child Cæsar, 3 years old, an excellent cook, washer, and ironer, warranted healthy; Julia a mulatto girl, aged 13, robust and active, a good field labourer—with the exception of a slight defect in the left eye, she is without fault."

"'Let us proceed, gentlemen,' cried the seller of human flesh, in a stentorian voice ; 'let us proceed. A woman for sale. An excellent woman—not a fault ; and a little boy in the bargain ! How much for the mother and child—250 dols. ? Very well, sir, 250 to begin. Some one has bid 250. Truly, gentlemen, they sell cattle for a larger price. Look at these eyes—examine these limbs ; shall I say 260 ? Thanks, gentlemen, some one has bid 260. It seems to me that I heard 275; go on gentlemen; I have never sold such a bargain. Haw! 280 for the best cook, the best washer, and best dressmaker in Virginia? Must I sell her for the miserable price of 280 ? 300 ; two gentlemen have said 300. Very well, gentlemen ; I am happy to see you begin to warm a little. Some one bids 310 ; 310, going—330—335—340—340 ; going. Upon my honour, gentlemen, it is indeed a sacrifice to lose so good a cook; a great bargain for 340 dollars. Reflect upon it a little, and do not forget there is a little boy in the bargain.'

"Here our auctioneer was interrupted in his harangue by one of his customers, a man whose appearance had inspired me, from the first moment, with a feeling of horror, and who, with the indifference and *sang froid* of an assassin, made to him the following observation :—

Sold by W. and F. G. CASH, 5, Bishopsgate Street, London; and by JANE JOWETT, Friends' Meeting Yard, Leeds, at 7d. per 100.

"'As to the negro child, it is good for nothing; it is not worth a day's nourishment; and if I have the mother, I will give away the child very quick : the first bidder will be able to have it a cheap bargain.'

"I glanced at the unfortunate mother, anxious to see what effect this barbarous proposal would have upon her. She did not speak, but a profound sadness was impressed on her countenance. The little innocent which she held in her arms fixed his large eyes upon her, as if saying, Mamma, why do you weep? Then he turned towards the witnesses of this heart-rending scene with an expression that seemed to ask—what they had done to his mother to make her weep so bitterly? No, never will this moment escape my memory! It has confirmed me for all my life in the horror that I already felt at this horrible traffic. The auction continued; and finally the crier, striking a heavy blow with the hammer, pronounced the award to Mr. —— for 360 dollars. The victim descended from the table, and was led away by the purchaser. The other slaves were sold in the same manner as poor Betsy. Julia was sold at 326 dollars; and Augustus, 105. They both fell to the same individual who had purchased the former lot.

In what a mean position in the scale of civilized nations do the Americans place themselves, by tolerating and legalizing such barbarities. Well may their poet Whittier exclaim,

"What! Ho! our countrymen in chains!
Americans to market driven,
And bartered as the brute for gold!"

SLAVERY AND THE BIBLE.

"The *Savannah* (Georgia) *Journal* has an advertisement running as follows :—' Wanted to exchange, a boy, ten years old, for a girl of equal value. Enquire at this office. March 22.' The same contains an advertisement of Bibles and Testaments beautifully bound."—*Investigator*.

Leeds Anti-slavery Series. No. 64.

Sold by W. and F. G. CASH, 5, Bishopsgate Street, London; and by JANE JOWETT, Friends' Meeting Yard, Leeds, at 7d. per 100.

Leeds Anti-Slavery Series. No. 65.

THE VIRGINIA SLAVE CROP.

The Virginia slave crop this season has proved an abundant one. The domestic consumption has been supplied, and a surplus remains for the Louisiana market.

We annex quotations from the *New Orleans Picayune* of the 20th of January, 1853 :—

" Maryland and Virginia Negroes for sale—Just arrived and for sale, at No. ·18, Esplanade Street, 100 negroes, consisting of a choice selection of field hands, house servants, cooks, washers, ironers, seamstresses, carpenters, blacksmiths, and a fine painter, all of which will be sold on the most accommodating terms by

" M. Wilson."

" Just received, at No. 156, Common Street, Creswell's old stand, from Virginia and North Carolina, a lot of 85 likely young negroes, consisting of field hands, house servants, No. 1 carpenters and blacksmiths, which will be sold cheap for cash or good city paper. Persons wishing to buy will find it to their advantage to call on the subscriber before purchasing elsewhere.

" C. Lamarque, Jr."

" One hundred and fifty Negroes for sale.—Just arrived and for sale, at my old stand, No. 7, Moreau Street, Third Municipality, 150 young and likely negroes, consisting of field hands, house servants, and mechanics. They will be sold on reasonable terms for good paper or cash. Persons wishing to purchase will find it to their advantage to give me a call.

" W. F. Talbott."

Sold by W. and F. G. Cash, 5, Bishopsgate Street, London; and by Jane Jowett, Friends' Meeting Yard, Leeds, at 1s. 2d. per 100.

"Just received, on consignment from Virginia, 64 young and likely negroes, comprising field hands, house servants, &c., all young and likely, and will be sold on liberal terms. Purchasers should call and see this gang before buying elsewhere.

"J. T. HATCHER, No. 157, Gravier Street,
in the rear of the St. Charles Hotel."

"Negroes Arrived Yesterday.—A choice lot of Virginia negroes, received yesterday. Among them are some pretty ploughboys and young girls; also, a superior blacksmith, accustomed to do all manner of plantation work, and has also worked in repairing machinery, &c.

"WALTER L. CAMPBELL, Esplanade Street,
Corner House, Slatter's Old Stand."

We congratulate the "gentlemen farmers" of Virginia that they are still able to réalise a handsome profit from a well-selected stock of "pretty ploughboys and young girls," and, by this judicious rotation of crops, turn their exhausted soil to a good account. Moreover, the constant cultivation of wheat and tobacco is destructive to the agriculture of any country. They do well to vary their productions.

Prime articles in the way of "Griffs," we notice, still command exorbitant prices :—

"For sale, a Griff boy named Jim, aged about 26 or 28 years, a first-rate steward, waiter, and barber, and a confidential servant, fully guaranteed, and sold for no fault whatever. He has been raised by one of the first physicians in Virginia. Can be seen in the barber's shop in Exchange Alley, opposite the Post-Office. Price 1500 dols., but will be sold to a master he is pleased with for less."

This must be, however, a very choice staple, and as it "was raised by one of the first physicians in Virginia," is probably equal to the best Richmond brands, or even to that of Sherwood Forest.

Choice articles like the following must, however, always be in demand for domestic purposes :—

"Negroes for Sale.—In addition to my large stock of negroes previously on hand, I have just received a negro woman of unequalled qualifications. She is a good seamstress, hairdresser, and first-rate shirtmaker, amiable, kind, and affectionate to children, very ladylike in her person, and can turn her hand to any kind of house work. Sold without a fault, and her owner wishes a good home for her.

"JAMES WHITE, 73, Baronne Street."

The market, we notice, is in some respects unsettled, and in many cases holders are unable to realise even upon their best purchasers :—

"Fifty Dollars' Reward.—Ran away, about the 25th ultimo, Allen, a bright mulatto, aged about 22 years, 6 feet high, very well dressed, has an extremely careless gait, of slender build, and wore a moustache when he left the property of J. P. Harrison, Esq., of this city. The above reward will be paid for his safe delivery at any safe place in the city. For further particulars, apply to No. 10, Bank Place."

"One Hundred Dollars' reward will be paid for the apprehension and delivery of the slave Edmund, who absented himself from the steam-boat *E. Howard*, on the 28th day of December, 1852. Edmund is about 20 years of age, 5 feet 10 inches high ; is a very bright mulatto, hair light and straight, and blue eyes. Had on, when last seen, pale yellow pants, white shirt, coat and hat not recollected. There is no doubt but he is lurking about the city, and will try to make his way up the river. Captains of steam-boats are cautioned against employing said slave. The above reward will be paid if apprehended out of this State, or 50 dollars if apprehended in the State, and delivered to No. 114, Camp Street, or to

"JAMES WHITE, No. 73, Baronne Street."

"One Hundred Dollars' Reward.—Ran away from the subscriber, living on Lafourche, a negro man named Adam, about 26 years old, a bricklayer and plasterer by trade, about 5 feet high, and weighs about 160 lbs., very black, one tooth missing, and has a small scar on his upper lip, large, full white eyes, rather dressy. He was seen in this city last month. I will give a reward of 100 dollars for his delivery to me on Lafourche, or to Thomas B. Lee, of this city.

"W. L. WYNN."

Instances like the above must still be very rare, and, from the constant consumption of the old stock, it may be expected that the market will soon recover a healthy tone.—*New York Tribune.*

A NOBLE-MINDED EDITOR.

"'Am I my brother's keeper?'—The *Gazette* must decline the publication of an advertisement, headed, A hundred dollars' reward. We are not aware that such a paltry sum would tempt a reader of the *Gazette* to catch a boy about 'ten years old, rather spare and delicately made, with black eyes, hair straight, though somewhat inclined to curl.' Nor would any proposition of that amount induce them to harm a woman twenty-six years old, who is said to be 'very respectful and pleasant when spoken to.' No one would harm her when we say she is the mother of the 'delicate made' boy, and of two other children also with her.

"It is to be hoped that no one who reads the *Gazette* is so poor that he can be tempted to gain his bread by money thus earned. Famine alone, in its most horrible form, could tempt a man thus to sell his manhood, by turning an informer. No man who reads the *Gazette* could eat bread which would be literally soaked in the bitter tears of a mother and her little ones; who, with their hopes of freedom blighted, would be, by his act, given once more into the hands of their task-masters. If this family are within the limits of free Pennsylvania, we hope, for the honour of the press, the state, and of humanity, that no trace of them will be found through the medium of 'the press.' We are sure the advertisement has been sent us from one who does not read the *Gazette*, for no one who does could thus insult its conductors and readers."—*Pittsburg Gazette.*

Leeds Anti-Slavery Series. No. 65.

Sold by W. and F. G. CASH, 5, Bishopsgate Street, London; and by JANE JOWETT, Friends' Meeting Yard, Leeds, at 1s. 2d. per 100.

Leeds Anti-slavery Series. No. 66.

VOICES FROM SLAVERY,

WRITTEN ON READING A PAPER BY JOSEPH STURGE ON THE AGGRAVATED HORRORS OF THE SLAVE-TRADE.—OCT., 1848.

I.—CAPTURE AND EMBARKATION.

HARK! to the cry from Afric's shore,
The mingled sound of strife and battle;
   The prisoners come,
   Behold their doom;
A wretched drove of *human cattle!*

Sold for a draught of liquid fire!
Bartered for toys, that hapless band!
   Oh, who can know
   The depth of woe
That fills each heart along the strand?

Now packed liked bales of senseless ware,
Within the vessel's murky hold;
   Close, closer still—
   They cram, they fill—
Oh guilt enormous! crimes untold!

II.—MISERIES AT SEA.

Hark! to the sound that comes from far,
Borne o'er the waves in utterance low;
   Deep stifled moans,
   And dying groans:
That living freight of human woe!

Sold by W. and F. G. CASH, 5, Bishopsgate Street, London; and by JANE JOWETT, Friends' Meeting Yard, Leeds, at 1s. 2d. per 100.

Now the full vessel courts the wind,
O'er swelling seas they swiftly go;
    And fever burns,
    And pity spurns
The palpitating mass below!

But death in mercy thins the ranks;
Pulse after pulse forgets to beat—
    They gasp, they die
    In agony—
In quenchless thirst, and maddening heat!

III.—LANDING IN THE WEST INDIES.

Hark! to the plaint from yonder shore,
A voice of woe, and helpless wailing—
    They land, they land
    On foreign strand,
Gaunt, trembling forms, in weakness failing!

And now a transient dream of rest,
Ere to the *human shambles* driven;
    They feed them well,
    To make them sell—
Oh, mockery of mercy given!

Soon as returning health appears,
To raise the feeble, nerve the strong,
    Away, away—
    In sad array—
With whip and menace urged along.

IV.—SLAVE-MARKET.

Hark! to the wail from yonder mart,
The tale of grief and anguish spoken;
    Heart torn from heart—
    Friends sold apart—
And every tie of Nature broken!

Husbands and wives to meet no more!
Children from parents forced to sever!
   For paltry gold,
   To bondage sold,
Beyond the reach of hope for ever!

Oh piteous sight! oh hapless throng!
Is there no mercy strong to save?
   Must thousands die
   In Slavery—
Their only freedom in the grave?

V.—SLAVE-LABOUR.

Hark! to the voice from yon fair land,
Where all the sweets of Nature grow:
   Who tills the soil
   With grief and toil?
The wretched Slave! the child of woe!

His *tyrant-master* goads him on—
He knows no sweets, he feels no rest;
   But whip and chains,
   And festering pains,
But mock the anguish of his breast!

Bowed down beneath the galling yoke,
Scorned and reviled, he longs to die;
   But months and years,
   'Mid groans and tears,
Drag on in sad captivity!

VI.—APPEAL TO CHRISTIANS.

For *whom* this labour, grief and sin?
Daughters of England, can it be,

That in your Isle
You sit and smile,
Yet *clad in fruits of Slavery ?*

" Oh, touch not, taste not, handle not,"
The produce raised on Freedom's grave !
 Else, while you sigh
 O'er Slavery,
You press the links upon the Slave.

For *you* that strife on Afric's shore—
For *you* that vessel fraught with death—
 The blood, the toil,
 That feed the soil,
The scourged limbs, the wasting breath!

VII.—FREEDOM OF THE GOSPEL.

Christians of England, haste, arise,
The Bond of Brotherhood proclaim ;
 Christ died to save
 The Negro-Slave—
Freedom for all in Jesus' name.

Spirit of Liberty, descend !
And make our hearts with joy forego
 Each tempting good,
 In clothes or food,
If purchased by a brother's woe.

Let every Nation, hand in hand,
In love, and peace, and strength combined,
 United be,
 One Family,
The Brotherhood of all Mankind.

Leeds Anti-slavery Series. No. 66.

Sold by W. and F. G. CASH, 5, Bishopsgate Street, London; and by JANE JOWETT Friends' Meeting Yard, Leeds, at 1s. 2d. per 100.

Leeds Anti-slavery Series. No. 69.

DREADFUL EFFECTS OF IRRESPONSIBLE POWER.

A BELOVED friend in South Carolina, the wife of a slaveholder, with whom I have often mingled my tears, when, helpless and hopeless, we deplored together the horrors of slavery, related to me, some years since, the following circumstances:—
" On the plantation adjoining her husband's, there was a slave of pre-eminent piety. His master was not a professor of religion; but the superior excellence of this disciple of Christ was not unmarked by him; and I believe he was so sensible of the good influence of his piety, that he did not deprive him of the few religious privileges within his reach. A planter was one day dining with the owner of this slave, and, in the course of conversation, observed that all professions of religion among slaves were mere hypocrisy. The other asserted a contrary opinion, adding, 'I have a slave, who, I believe, would rather die than deny his Saviour.' This was ridiculed, and the master urged to prove his assertion. He accordingly sent for the man of God, and peremptorily ordered him to deny his belief in the Lord Jesus Christ. The slave pleaded to be excused, constantly affirming that he would rather die than deny the Redeemer, whose blood was shed for him. His master, after vainly trying to induce obedience by threats, had him terribly whipped. The fortitude of the sufferer was not to be shaken; he nobly rejected the offer of exemption from further chastisement at the expense of destroying his soul; and this blessed martyr *died in consequence of this severe infliction.* O how bright a gem will this victim of irresponsible power be, in that crown which sparkles on the Redeemer's brow! and that many such will cluster there, I have not the shadow of a doubt.
"SARAH M. GRIMKE."
[Miss Grimke is a daughter of the late Judge Grimke, of the Supreme Court of South Carolina, and sister of the late Hon. Thomas S. Grimke.]

Leeds Anti-slavery Series. No. 69.
Sold by W. and F. G. CASH, 5, Bishopsgate Street, London; and by JANE JOWETT, Friends' Meeting-Yard, Leeds, at 6d. per 100.

Leeds Anti-slavery Series. No. 70.

THE SLAVE-TRADE IN COLUMBIA.

"YESTERDAY, a servant man came to my room, saying, a coloured woman wished to speak with me. I asked the cause of her grief. It was some time before she could so far compose her mind as to relate to me her misfortune. She said her husband had just been sold to a slave-driver, and taken to the barracoons of Alexandria—that his purchaser was intending to take him to Alabama in two or three days—that she had four children at home. At this point she burst into a loud expression of her grief. Her sobbings were interrupted occasionally with exclamations of 'O, God! O, my dear children! O, my husband!' Then, appealing to me, 'O, master, for God's sake, do try to get back the father of my babes!'

"I learned that her husband went to work this morning in the barn, husking corn, without any suspicion of the fate that awaited him. The slave-dealer and an assistant came and seized him, hurrying him off to the slave-pen in Alexandria.

"The woman, hearing of it, followed him here on foot, and sought me in the vain hope that I should be able to assist her. The day is the coldest known here for years; yet she has been exposed to the keen piercing winds, although thinly clad. She had not seen her children since morning, when she left them without firewood. I endeavoured to soothe her feelings by expressing some faint hope that her husband might yet be redeemed—that I would make inquiry, and ascertain if I could find some one who would repurchase him, and permit him to remain in the district. I reflected upon the barbarous law by which Congress has authorized and encouraged such crimes, inflicting such misery upon the down-trodden of God's poor. I trembled for my country, when I reflected that God was just, and that his justice will not sleep for ever. I asked myself the question, Will Heaven permit such wicked, barbarous cruelty to go unpunished?"—*Ashtabula Sentinel.*

Leeds Anti-slavery Series. No. 70.
Sold by W. and F. G. CASH, 5, Bishopsgate Street, London; and by JANE JOWETT Friends' Meeting Yard, Leeds, at 6d. per 100.

Leeds Anti-Slavery Series, No. 71.

OPINIONS OF EMINENT PERSONS
IN VARIOUS AGES
RESPECTING SLAVERY AND THE SLAVE-TRADE.

"WHATSOEVER ye would that men should do unto you, do ye even so unto them."—*Jesus Christ.*

God "hath sent me to bind up the broken-hearted, *to proclaim liberty to the captives.*"—*Jesus Christ.*

"Where the Spirit of the Lord is, *there* is liberty."—*St. Paul*, in 2 Cor. iii. 17.

"Is not this the fast that I have chosen? to loose the bands of wickedness, *to undo the heavy burdens, and to let the oppressed go free, and that ye break every yoke.*"—*Isaiah*, lviii. 6.

"He that stealeth a man, and selleth him, or if he be found in his hand, he shall surely be put to death."—*Exodus*, xxi. 16.

"A man loses half of his manhood by slavery."—*Homer,* about 900 B.C.

"Whatever is just, is always true law; nor can true law either be originated or abrogated by any written enactments."—*Cicero*, lived B.C. 107, to B.C. 43.

"To cultivate land by slaves is the worst of follies, for all work is badly done by people in despair."—*Pliny*, A.D. 23–79.

"The redeeming of captives enters not less into the obligations of justice and tender charity."—*Lactantius*, A.D. 250–325.

"Both religion and humanity make it a duty for us to work for the deliverance of the captive."—*St. Cyprian.*

Of evils similar to slavery Tertullian says—"One cannot argue from Scripture that it condemns such practices, but will it be argued from its silence that it does not condemn them?"—*Tertull. Lib. Cor.*, p. 121.

Sold by W. and F. G. CASH, 5, Bishopsgate Street, London; and by JANE JOWETT, Friends' Meeting Yard, Leeds, at 2s. 3d. per 100.

Wickliffe, "the morning star of the Reformation," taught "that it was contrary to the principles of the Christian religion that any one should be a slave."—1324-1384.

"Not only the Christian religion, but nature herself, cries out against slavery."—*Pope Leo X.*, 1475-1521.

Queen Elizabeth expressed her concern lest negroes be carried off without their own free consent, in which case she declared "*it would be detestable, and call down the vengeance of Heaven upon the undertakers.*"

"To steal a man is the highest kind of theft. In other instances, we only steal human property; but when we steal or retain a man in slavery, we seize those who, in common with ourselves, are constituted, by the original grant, lords of the earth."—*Hugo Grotius*, 1583-1645.

"O execrable man, so to aspire
Above his brethren, to himself assuming
Authority usurp'd from God, not given;
——————————Man over men
He made not lord, such title to himself
Reserving."—*Milton*, 1608-1674.

"Slave-traders are pirates; and those that buy men as beasts, for their own convenience, are *demons* rather than *Christians.*"—*Rev. R. Baxter*, 1615-1691.

"Slavery is not good in itself: it is neither useful to the master nor to the slave."—*Baron Montesquieu*, 1689-1755.

"The owners of slaves are *licensed robbers*, and not the just proprietors of what they claim."—*Rev. Jonathan Edwards*, 1703.

"Every human creature has a right to liberty, which cannot, with justice, be taken from him, unless he forfeits it by some crime."—*Lord Chesterfield*, 1694-1773.

"Slavery is of such a nature, that it is incapable of being introduced on any reasons moral or political, but only by positive law. It is so odious, that nothing can be suffered to support it but positive law."—Judgment in the great case of the slave Somersett.—*Lord Mansfield*, 1705-1793.

"O Freedom! first delight of human kind."—*Dryden.*

" Slavery is a state so improper, so degrading, and so ruinous to the feelings and capacities of human nature, that it ought not to be suffered to exist.

" He who makes a happy slave, makes a degraded man."—*Edmund Burke, M.P.*, 1730-1797.

" No man is, by nature, the property of another. The rights of nature must be some way forfeited, before they can be justly taken away."—*Dr. Samuel Johnson*, 1709-1784.

" Whitfield questions — " Whether it could be lawful for *Christians* to buy slaves, and thereby encourage the nations to maintain perpetual war with each other, in order to furnish them, and specially remonstrates against the sinfulness of treating them as if they were mere brutes, or even worse; and enjoying all the conveniences and luxuries of life, while the slaves, by whose indefatigable labour they were procured, were left in destitution, and exposed to hardship and cruelty."
—From a letter to America, by *Rev. George Whitfield*, 1714.

Slavery " is the sum and substance of all villanies."—*Rev. John Wesley*, 1703-1791.

" Those who traffic in human flesh and blood, and those who legalize or connive at such traffic, all these are *man-stealers*."—*Rev. Dr. Adam Clarke*, 1760-1832.

Anthony Benezet designates slavery " a mighty infringement of every human and sacred right."—1713-1784.

" That horrid traffic of selling negroes."—*Horace Walpole*, 1750.

" Slavery is a system made up of every crime that treachery, cruelty, and murder can invent."—*Rev. Rowland Hill*, 1744-1833.

" Slavery is sinful in its origin, sinful in its effects, sinful in its continuance, and sinful eternally."—*Rev. Dr. Andrew Thomson*, 1779-1831.

" The slave-trade is a gross violation of the law of nature, and attended with many aggravating circumstances of cruelty."
—*Moral and Political Philosophy, Archdeacon Paley*, 1743-1805.

"Slavery is an infringement on all laws—a law having a tendency to preserve slavery would be the grossest sacrilege."—*Bolivar* (a celebrated American General), 1783-1839.

"All who are concerned in bringing any of the human race into slavery, or in retaining them in it—all who bring off slaves or free men, and keep, sell, or buy them, are man-stealers, guilty of the highest kind of theft, and SINNERS OF THE FIRST RANK."—*Book of Discipline of the Presbyterian Church in the United States,* 1794.

"The slave-trade is an infamous traffic. Charity is the soul of religion; and that, while forbidding all cruelty, expressly prohibits that which is inflicted on the human race."—*Pope Gregory XVI.*, 1765-1846.

"Slavery is the greatest practical evil that can afflict the human race."—*Thomas Clarkson,* 1760-1847.

"No matter under whatever specious term it disguises itself, slavery is still hideous. It has a natural and inevitable tendency to brutalize every noble faculty in man."—*Daniel O'Connell, M.P.,* 1779-1847.

"Slavery is an unmixed evil, whether regarded in a moral or political point of view."—Historical and Moral Essay, by *Dr. Geo. Gregory,* 1754-1808. He early proposed that Parliament should abolish both the slave-trade and slavery.

"Slavery is a complicated system of iniquity."—*Granville Sharp,* 1735-1813.

President Jefferson says—"I tremble for my country [America], when I remember that God is just, and that his justice may not sleep for ever. A revolution is among possible events. The Almighty has no attribute which would side with us in such a struggle. Whatever is morally wrong cannot be politically right." Referring to the slaves, he adds:—"Nothing is more certainly written in the Book of Fate than that these people are to be free."—*Thomas Jefferson,* President of the United States, 1743-1826.

> "When the blood
> Thou pourest now, so warm along our veins,
> Shall westward flow, till Mississippi's flood
> Gives to our children's children his broad plains,
> Ne'er let them *wear*, O God, or forge a bondman's chains!"
> John Pierpont, 1840.

"Yonder, upon a throne made of the affections of the planters, in the face of an indignant and offended God, sits slavery horrible as a hag of hell. Her face is brass; her heart is stone; her head is iron, with which she wrings, from the multiplied sufferings and labours of the poor negroes, the wealth by which she is clothed in purple and fine linen, and fareth sumptuously every day; watching, with unslumbering jealousy, every ray that would enlighten the darkness of her kingdom, and frowning indignantly on every finger that would disturb the stability of her throne."—*Elihu Burritt*.

"It is the double curse of slavery to degrade all concerned with it, doing or suffering. The slave is the lowest in the scale of human beings, *except the slave-dealer*."—*Montgomery*.

"The whole tenor of the Christian system is so directly opposed to the very idea of slavery, that it is a matter of astonishment how any persons calling themselves Christian can suffer themselves to be participators in its support."—*J. S. Buckingham, M.P.*, 1825.

> "It is, in truth, a loathsome trade,
> A sordid traffic—to abhor;
> *Of* which one feels asham'd, afraid,
> *With* which our nature is at war;
> *For* which no prayer can soar above,
> Unto that God whose name is Love!"
> Bernard Burton.

"Slaveholding is a violation of natural justice."—*James G. Birney*.

"Slavery is a sin that includes all manner of iniquity."—*Rev. Thos. Swan*.

"Slavery is a heinous crime against the laws of God and man."—*Rev. Wm. James*.

"Modern slavery bears no analogy to the slavery of those

times (when Christ and the apostles were on earth). It is incompatible with Christianity."—*Rev. John Angell James.*

" Slavery is a system of the grossest injustice, of the most heathenish irreligion and immorality, of the most unprecedented degradation and unrelenting cruelty."—*Wilberforce, Bishop of Oxford.*

" Slavery is a sin against God, and that is a sinful church which sanctions it."—*Rev. J. Burnett.*

" Slavery is undoubtedly and confessedly one of the greatest evils that ever was inflicted on the human race, and has been considered as the greatest curse by all nations, in all ages of the world."—*Rev. R. Bickell, Naval Chaplain at Port-Royal.*

" By the law of God, unchangeable and eternal, while men despise fraud, and loathe rapine, and abhor bloodshed, they shall reject with indignation the wild and guilty phantasy, that man can hold property in man!"—*Lord Brougham in* 1830.

" Domestic slavery is contrary to the rights of mankind; opposed to the fundamental principles of free government; inconsistent with a state of sound morality; hostile to the prosperity of the commonwealth."—*R. J. Breckinridge, D.D.*

" Every effort should be made to put a stop to a trade so disgraceful to every human being or nation concerned in its encouragement."—*Bishop of Norwich,* 1848.

> " Come, justice, come! in glory drest,
> O come! the woe-worn negro's friend,—
> The fiend-delighting trade arrest,
> The negro's chains asunder rend."—*Amelia Opie.*

" That slavery is sinful, not only in its own abuse, but in its own nature, is evident from its practical results."—*Joseph John Gurney.*

" Persevere in representing, boldly and unceasingly, the right which the negro has to emancipation, and the utter unlawfulness of that system of spoliation and plunder which first made him a slave, and still continues him so—I say unlawfulness, in the most precise sense of that term. No law which man can enact can give one a right over the compulsory labour of another, except as the punishment of crime proved by evidence. I say it advisedly, no man has any lawful property in the labour of another, except by free compact."—*Lord Nugent,* 1830.

" The holding of human beings in a state of slavery, is in direct opposition to all the principles of natural right and the benign spirit of the gospel of Christ."—*Wesleyan Conference,* England.

" There is no vice too loathsome—no passion too cruel or remorseless, to be engendered by this horrid system (American slavery). It brutalizes all who administer it, and seeks to efface the likeness of God stamped on the brow of its victims. It makes the former class demons, and reduces the latter to the level of brutes."—*Rev. Thomas Price, Hackney,* 1837.

" American slavery is the greatest, foulest wrong which man ever did to man ; the most hideous and detested sin a nation has ever committed before the just, all-bounteous God—a wrong and a sin wholly without excuse."—*Theodore Parker,* 1848.

"Men-stealers are inserted among those daring criminals against whom the law of God directed its curses. These kidnapped men to sell them for slaves ; and this practice seems inseparable from the other iniquities and oppressions of slavery; nor can a slave-dealer keep free from this criminality, if ' the receiver be as bad as the thief.' "—*Rev. Thomas Scott* (author of the celebrated Family Bible).

" O ye heavens, be kind !
And feel, thou earth, for this afflicted race !"
Wordsworth, 1802.

" If there is a living being in the United States who does not lament and shudder at this scourge of humanity, he is dead not only to the voice of conscience and of patriotism, but to the sense of shame and the honour of his country."—*Geo. Combe,* 1845.

" The spectacle of an entire race of men crushed, basely, cruelly, by the men of a republic, is the most odious, the most fatal ever beheld.

"The oppression of a single man is a crime against the whole human race."—*Victor Schœlcher*, 1851.

"Gracious God! to talk of men as of herds of cattle, of property in rational creatures endowed with all our faculties, possessing all our qualities but that of colour, our brethren both by nature and by grace, shocks all the feelings of humanity, and the dictates of common sense! Nothing is more certain in itself and apparent to all, than that the infamous traffic in slaves directly infringes both Divine and human law. Nature created man free, and grace invites him to assert his freedom."—*Dr. Warburton*, Bishop of Gloucester.

"What! God's own image bought and sold!
And bartered, as the brute, for gold!"
John G. Whittier.

"We abhor and denounce that iniquitous system of slavery, which disgraces and desolates so many regions of the civilized world."—*Earl of Shaftesbury*, 1852.

"I reserve for the last topic of animadversion the crowning evil—the capital danger—the mortal plague-spot—slavery. Whilst it lasts, it must continue, in addition to the actual amount of suffering and wrong which it entails on the enslaved, to operate with terrible reaction on the dominant class, to blunt the moral sense, to sap domestic virtue, to degrade independent industry, to check the onward march of enterprise, to sow the seeds of suspicion, alarm, and vengeance, in both internal and external intercourse, to distract the national councils, to threaten the permanence of the union, and to leave a brand, a byeword, and a jest upon the name of Freedom."—*The Earl of Carlisle's Travels in America*, published in 1851.

☞ For further opinions on the foregoing subject the reader is referred to a small pamphlet issued with these tracts, entitled *A Cloud of Witnesses against Slavery and Oppression*, by Wilson Armistead; published by W. & F. G. Cash, London.

Leeds Anti-slavery Series. No. 71.

Sold by W. and F. G. CASH, 5, Bishopsgate Street, London; and by JANE JOWETT, Friends' Meeting Yard, Leeds, at 2s. 3d. per 100.

Leeds Anti-slavery Series. No. 72.

CONFESSIONS OF SLAVEHOLDERS;
OR OF THOSE LIVING IN THE MIDST OF SLAVERY.

"Out of thine own mouth will I judge thee."

WHAT can the defenders of slavery say in its favour, when such confessions as the following, are made by slaveholders themselves, or by those who, residing in the midst of slavery, know from experience what it really is?

" I consider slavery a curse—a curse to the master—a wrong, a grievous wrong to the slave. In the *abstract*, it is all wrong, and no possible contingency can make it right."—*Henry Clay* (slaveholder), Kentucky, in Colonization Speech, 1836.

" Avarice alone can drive, as it does drive, *this infernal traffic*, and the wretched victims of it, like so many post-horses, *whipped to death* in a mail-coach."—*Hon. John Randolph*, Roanoke (a slaveholder).

" The gentleman has appealed to the Christian religion in justification of slavery. I would ask him upon what part of those pure doctrines does he rely? to which of those sublime precepts does he advert to sustain his position? Is it that which teaches charity, justice, and good-will to all? Or is it that which teaches, ' Do ye unto others as ye would they should do unto you?' "—*Thomas J. Randolph*, Virginia.

" A slave population exercises the most pernicious influence upon the manners, habits, and character of those among whom it exists. Lisping infancy learns the vocabulary of abusive epithets, and struts the embryo tyrant of its little domain. The consciousness of superior destiny takes possession of his mind at its earliest dawning, and the love of power and rule ' grows with his growth, and strengthens with his strength.'

Sold by W. and F. G. CASH, 5, Bishopsgate Street, London; and by JANE JOWETT, Friends' Meeting Yard, Leeds, at 1s. 2d. per 100.

When, in the sublime lessons of Christianity, he is taught to do unto others as he would have others do unto him, he never dreams that the degraded negro is within the pale of that holy canon."—*Virginia Debates*, 1832; *Summers* (a slaveholder).

"It is in vain for me to plead that I have sanction of law for holding slaves, for this makes the injury the greater—it arms the community against the slave, and makes his case desperate. The owners of slaves are *licensed robbers*."—*J. Price, Kentucky.*

"Slavery is ruinous to the whites. The master has no capital but what is vested in HUMAN FLESH. The father, instead of being richer for his sons, is at a loss to provide for them. There is no diversity of occupations, no incentive to enterprise. *Labour of every species is disreputable*, because performed mostly by slaves. Our towns are stationary, our villages almost everywhere declining, and the general aspect of the country marks the curse of a wasteful, idle, reckless population, who have no interest in the soil, and care not how much it is impoverished." —*T. Marshall*, of Fauquier county, Virginia. Speech in Virginia Legislature, 1845.

"The deplorable error of our ancestors in copying a civil institution from savage Africa, has affixed upon their posterity a depressing burden, which nothing but the extraordinary benefits conferred by our happy climate could have enabled us to support."—*Governor Randolph's* Address to the Legislature of Virginia, in 1820.

"Slavery is an unnatural state, a dark cloud, *which obscures half the lustre of our free institutions*. I would hail that day as the most glorious in its dawning, which would behold, with safety to themselves and our citizens, the black population of the United States placed ubon the high eminence of equal rights."—*Mr. Read*, of Georgia, in the debate in Congress on the Missouri question.

"As a Virginian, I do not question the master's title to his slaves; but I put it to the gentleman as a *man*, as a *moral man*, as a *Christian man*, whether he has not some doubt of his claim being as absolute and unqualified as that of other property? I acknowledge I tremble for the fate of my country at some future day, unless we 'do something.' "—From the speech of *J. A. Chandler*, Virginia, United States.

"It is really matter of astonishment to me that the people of Maryland do not blush at the very name of freedom. Not content with exposing to the world, for near a century, a speaking picture of *abominable oppression*, they are still ingenious to prevent the hand of generosity from robbing it of half its horrors."—*William Pinckney*, Maryland House of Delegates, 1789.

Slavery, "the *dreadful calamity* which has so long afflicted our country, and filled so many with despair."—*Madison*, Letter to American Colonization Society, 1831.

"We have found that this evil (slavery) has preyed upon the very vitals of the community, and has been prejudicial to *all* the States in which it has existed."—*Monroe* (President of the United States), in Virginia Convention, 1765-1837.

Mr. Wirt, of Virginia, said that "slavery was contrary to the laws of nature and of nations."

"That slavery is an evil, and a transcendent evil, it would be more than idle for any human being to doubt or deny. It is a mildew, which has blighted every region it has touched, from the creation of the world. Illustrations from the history of other countries and other times might be instructive; but we have evidence nearer at hand, in the short histories of the different States of this great confederacy, which are impressive in their admonitions, and conclusive in their character."—Speech of *Mr. Brodnax*, in the Virginia Legislature, 1832.

"Sir, the evils of this system of slavery cannot be enumerated. They glare upon us at every step. When the owner looks to his wasted estate, he knows and feels them. When the statesman examines the condition of his country, and finds her moral influence gone, her physical strength diminished, her political power wanting, he sees and must confess them."—Speech of *Mr. Summers*, in the Legislature of Virginia, 1832.

Slavery.—"I tremble for my country," said president Jefferson, "when I remember that God is just, and that his justice may not sleep for ever. A revolution is among possible events. The Almighty has no attribute which would side with us in such a struggle. Whatever is morally wrong cannot be politically right." Referring to the slaves, he says:—"Nothing is more certainly written in the Book of Fate than that these people are to be free."

President Jefferson also said, "One hour of American slavery is fraught with more misery than ages of that which we rose in rebellion to oppose;" and as early as 1774, he declared that "the abolition of domestic slavery is the greatest object to be desired in these colonies."—*Thomas Jefferson*, President of the United States, 1743–1826.

"What! are thousands of our fellow-creatures within our State, destitute of every real protection afforded them by law, either in their persons or property—without any law to guard their marriage rights, or without the law's having any knowledge of marriage among them—(for such is the fact with regard to the whole slave population among us)—many of them under the control of cruel and relentless masters, from whom they receive much inhuman abuse—and yet are we told that all this needs no legislative interference! Monstrous, indeed, is the doctrine!"—Oration by *Amos Weaver*, of Guildford County, North Carolina, delivered in 1829.

"Slavery has been the foundation of that impiety and dissipation, which has been so much disseminated among our countrymen."—*Johnson* (a slaveholder).

"Slavery, as it exists among us, may be regarded as the heaviest calamity which has ever befallen any portion of the human race."—*Virginia Debates*, 1832; *Moore* (a slaveholder.)

"Slavery may be regarded as the *heaviest calamity* which has ever fallen to this portion of the human race."—*Mr Moore*, Speech in Virginia Legislature, 1832, (a slaveholder).

We forbear citing further testimonies. If such be the language of slaveholders themselves, we need no further witnesses, their own mouths uttering their own condemnation.

Leeds Anti-slavery Series. No. 72.

Sold by W. and F. G. CASH, 5, Bishopsgate Street, London; and by JANE JOWETT, Friends' Meeting Yard, Leeds, at 1s. 2d. per 100.

Leeds Anti-slavery Series. No. 73.

A FEW WORDS ON
ABSTINENCE FROM SLAVE PRODUCE.

It is now fully admitted, except by a comparatively few infatuated, though by a still greater number of interested persons, that for a man to hold property in his fellow-man is awfully opposed to the inalienable rights of our common nature, both human and Divine.

Africa is annually robbed, by fire and sword, of 400,000 of her native population, forcibly torn from their homes and their kindred, that those who survive the carnage and the pestilence of the middle passage may supply those colonies where slavery still exists. Besides a larger number in other parts, there are at this moment, in the United States of America alone, upwards of three millions of slaves (men, women, and children), held in cruel and hopeless bondage. These are not imported from Africa, but propagated on the soil; bought, and sold, and worked as the beasts which perish!! The innocent babe does not belong to the mother who bare it, and (by law) the father has no claim to his own offspring. Nevertheless Nature, true to its feelings, will weep, but without remedy, when the ruthless slave dealer, to increase his gains, parts husband from wife, and parents from their children, to sell them far away, never more to behold each other again.

There are very many abolitionists who lament the wrongs of the Negro race, but who are quite at a loss to imagine in what way they, as individuals, can do anything towards arresting the progress of these enormous evils. It is true every one is not able to do *much* for the cause, still *all can do something;* and "many hands make light work." The sugars of Cuba and the Brazils, and the cotton of the United States, are the chief products of slavery; and it is an admitted axiom of commerce, that so long as there is a demand for any particular commodity, so long there will be a supply; and whenever the demand ceases, the supply ceases with it. Now as we, the people of Great Britain, are by far the principal purchasers, merchants, and consumers of these blood-stained articles, it becomes a question whether we, as individuals, are not participating in the crime of shedding our brother's blood, by upholding, in any degree, so flagrant a species of iniquity. It has been computed that it requires the entire labour and toil of *one* slave to supply, on an average, every *six* Englishmen with their annual consumption of sugar and of cotton goods. The demand which exists for slave produce is the chief support of slavery; it is that which keeps open the slave markets. Slavery is certainly sustained by the purchase of its productions, and if there were no consumers of slave produce, there would be no slaves.

Channels are now open through which British philanthropists may steer clear of the sin of slavery, by making their purchases of sugar and of cotton manufactured goods in *the free labour market*, unstained with the blood and bondage of the slave; and we venture to assert, that if the people of these kingdoms would generally act upon this principle, and refuse to purchase slave-grown produce, slavery itself would quickly cease to be, for want of profitable occupation. The sons and daughters of Africa would then remain unmolested in their native homes; and the poor oppressed Negro slave be suffered to go forth a free man, no longer to be bought, and sold, and worked as a beast of the field. Christian friends! philanthropists! free-born fellow Britons! men, women, and young people! say not there is nothing for you to do in this great work; *all may do something* towards the abolition of Negro slavery. Small grains compose the earth itself, and drops of water fill the bosom of the ocean; every aggregrate is composed of units, and, with the Divine blessing, your united efforts, however small, will be crowned with a rich reward, and the taint of slavery will no longer lie at your door. Christianity and humanity demand your co-operation in this great and good work; will you not henceforward respond to the call, and avoid spending your money for those things which are bedewed with the tears of the slave, which bring reproach in the using?

If we would keep our hands clean from the spoils of oppression, we must, whenever and wherever we have opportunity, give preference to the productions of free labour, and abstain from the use of articles raised by slaves.

Leeds Anti-slavery Series. No. 73.

Sold by W. and F. G. CASH, 5, Bishopsgate Street, London; and by JANE JOWETT Friends' Meeting Yard, Leeds, at 7*d.* per 100.

Leeds Anti-slavery Series. No. 74.

PARTING OF A SLAVE-MOTHER AND HER SON

"At about ten o'clock in the morning, I went on board the boat, and found my mother there, in company with fifty or sixty other slaves. She was chained to another woman. On seeing me, she immediately dropped her head upon her heaving bosom. She moved not, neither did she weep. Her emotions were too deep for tears. I approached, threw my arms around her neck, kissed her, and fell upon my knees, begging her forgiveness, for I thought myself to blame for her sad condition; for if I had not persuaded her to accompany me, she would not then have been in chains.

"She finally raised her head, looked me in the face (and such a look, none but an angel can give!) and said, 'My dear son, you are not to blame for my being here. You have done nothing more nor less than your duty. Do not, I pray you, weep for me. *I cannot last long upon a cotton plantation.* I feel that my heavenly Master will soon call me home, and then I shall be out of the hands of the slaveholders!'

"I could bear no more—my heart struggled to free itself from the human form. In a moment, she saw Mr. Mansfield coming towards that part of the boat, and she whispered into my ear, 'My child, we must soon part to meet no more this side of the grave. You have ever said, that you would not die a slave; that you would be a free man. Now try to get your liberty! You will soon have no one to look after but yourself!' And just as she whispered the last sentence into my ear, Mansfield came up to me, and, with an oath, said, 'Leave here this instant; you have been the means of my losing one hundred dollars, to get this wench back;' at the same time, kicking me with a heavy pair of boots. As I left her, she gave one shriek, saying, 'God be with you!' It was the last time that I saw her, and the last word I heard her utter.

"I walked on shore. The bell was tolling. The boat was about to start. I stood with a heavy heart, waiting to see her leave the wharf. As I thought of my mother, I could but feel that I had lost

>   ———'The glory of my life,
>   My blessing, and my pride!
>   I half forgot the name of slave,
>   When she was by my side.'

The love of liberty, that had been burning in my bosom, had well nigh gone out. I felt as though I were ready to die. The boat moved gently from the wharf, and while she glided down the river, I realized that my mother was indeed

> 'Gone—gone—sold and gone,
>   To the rice-swamp, dank and lone!'

"After the boat was out of sight, I returned home; but my thoughts were so absorbed in what I had witnessed, that I knew not what I was about half of the time. Night came, but it brought no sleep to my eyes."—*Narrative of William W. Brown, a Fugitive Slave; Boston,* 1848.

A MOTHER'S AFFECTION.

"LAST evening, as the slave-hunters were arresting the fugitives from slavery, on the Mad River Dock, one of them seized hold of a young woman, with an infant child, eight or nine months old, in her arms. She jerked loose from him, ran some steps, threw the child upon the ground, and returned towards the slave-catcher. She was seized, and marched towards the mayor's office. The child was picked up by one of our citizens. One of the Kentuckians claimed to be the owner. Mr. B. refused to give up the child without evidence. The infant was taken to the mother, who, supposing herself doomed to slavery, disowned it: denied, in the most positive terms, that it was her child. To own her offspring, was to doom the child to slavery; to disown and desert it, she hoped, was to allow the dearest treasure of her heart to grow up, breathing the air of freedom. For this she stands nobly ready to dismember the ties of such affection as a mother only knows, and leave to chance, or other hands, the rearing of the infant, dearer than life itself. Truly a mother's love, though an ignorant and uncultivated slave-mother,

> 'Lives before life, with death dies not, but seems
>   The very substance of immortal dreams.'"

—*Sandusky Mirror.*

Leeds Anti-slavery Series. No. 74.

Sold by W. and F. G. CASH, 5, Bishopsgate Street, London; and by JANE JOWETT Friends' Meeting Yard, Leeds, at 7*d.* per 100.

Leeds Anti-slavery Series. No. 75.

A CONTRAST.

"I WAS breakfasting one morning," says a naval officer, "with Mr. M'C., who had charge of the slaves at Sierra Leone, after they had been landed from the slavers, or from the ships of war which had re-captured them. We had finished breakfast and were leaning over the balcony, looking at a cargo of slaves which had just arrived from the Gallinas, and were being brought into the yard. I ought to observe that Mr. M'C. had in his service an intelligent African youth, about sixteen years of age, whose name was Joe, who himself had been taken from his own country, and as a slave re-captured and landed at Sierra Leone. Mr. M'C., whilst looking at the arrival of slaves, called out to the boy, who was at work in the house, and said, 'Here, Joe, there's a cargo of slaves just come in from your old country, the Gallinas; go and see if you can find any one you know amongst them.' Joe did not require to be told twice; he was in the midst of the new-comers in a moment, and had not been long employed in making an examination of them, to see if there was any amongst them whom he knew, when a little girl rushed out of the crowd and seized hold of him, casting her arms around him. And who was the stranger? It was his sister! Thus they met after being separated in their own country at a considerable distance from Sierra Leone, and after both had been rescued from the cruel hands of the slave-traders by the English ships of war. Mr. M'C. was not an unaffected witness of the scene. Seeing what had taken place, he called out to his young black servant, 'There, Joe, take her in; you shall never be separated again.' Gladly did that happy brother take charge of his dear sister, and bring her into the house of that kind master, who was so interested in the welfare of poor Africans." So much for Englishmen.

Let us now turn to America. There we shall see a very different scene. From Mr. Clarke's narrative we take the following extract :—" Mr. Cyrus Clarke, a brother of the well-known Milton and Lewis Clarke (all of whom, till within a short time since, for some twenty-five years, were slaves in Kentucky), mildly but firmly presented his ballot at the town meeting board. Be it known that the said Cyrus, as well as his brothers, are *white*, with only a sprinkling of the African; just enough to make them bright, quick, and intelligent, and scarcely observable in the colour except by the keen and scenting slaveholder. Mr. Clarke had all the necessary qualifications of white men to vote.—Slave: Gentlemen, here is my ballot; I wish to vote. (Board and by-standers well knowing him, all were aghast; the waters were troubled; the slave legions were 'up in their might.')—Judge E. : You can't vote! Are you not, and have you not been, a slave?—Slave: I shall not *lie* to vote. I am and have been a slave, so called; but I wish to vote, and I believe it my right and duty.—Judge E. : Slaves can't vote.—Slave: Will you just show me in your books, constitution, or whatever you call them, where it says a slave can't vote?—Judge E. (pretending to look over the law, &c., well knowing he was 'used up'): Well, well, you are a coloured man, and can't vote without you are worth two hundred and fifty dollars.—Slave: I am as white as *you*, and don't *you* vote? (Mr. E. is well known to be very dark; indeed as dark or darker than Clarke. The current began to set against Mr. E. by murmurs, sneers, laughs, and many other demonstrations of dislike).—Judge E. : Are you not a coloured man? And is not your hair curly?—Slave: We are both coloured men; and all we differ in is, that you have not the handsome wavy curl; you raise *Goat's wool*, and I come, as you see, a little nearer *Saxony*. At this time the fire and fun was at its height, and was fast consuming the judge with public opprobrium.—Judge E.: I challenge this man's vote, he being a coloured man, and not worth two hundred and fifty dollars. Friends and foes warmly contested what constituted a coloured man by the New York statute. The board finally came to the honourable conclusion that, to be a coloured man, he must be at least one-half blood African. Mr. Clarke, the SLAVE, then voted, he being nearly full white."

Leeds Anti-slavery Series. No. 75.

Sold by W. and F. G. CASH, 5, Bishopsgate Street, London; and by JANE JOWETT, Friends' Meeting Yard, Leeds, at 7*d.* per 100.

Leeds Anti-slavery Series. No 76.

SLAVEHOLDING INCONSISTENCIES.

ADVERTISEMENT IN THE "RELIGIOUS HERALD," A VIRGINIA PAPER.—" Who wants 35,000 dollars in property?—I am desirous of spending the remainder of my life as a missionary, *if the Lord permit*, and therefore offer for sale my farm, and the vineyard, adjacent to Williamsburg, containing 600 acres, well watered, and abounding in marl; together with all the crops, stock, and utensils thereon. Also, my house and lot in town, fitted up as a boarding establishment, with all the furniture belonging to it. Also, about 40 servants [*slaves*], mostly young and likely, and rapidly increasing in number and value. To a kind master, I would put the whole property at the reduced price of 35,000 dollars, and arrange the payments to suit purchasers, provided the interest be annually paid.—S. JONES."

A RUNAWAY PREACHER.—" A late Kentucky paper contains an advertisement, offering a reward of 400 dollars for the recovery of 'a negro man named Richard,' who is 40 years old, reads and writes very well, is a preacher, and has a license to exhort, endorsed by the elder of Stone River Circuit or Murfreesborough Station. The advertisement states that he preaches and sings well, and it is supposed he will try to make a living in that way. The crime for which he is advertised is twofold—he is black, and was born contrary to the Declaration of Independence. Perhaps he has some wild notions of his responsibility as a preacher, and is inclined to give a too literal construction to the passage, *Go ye into all the world, &c.* Is not this a great country, where preachers of the Gospel are advertised like stray cattle?"—*New York Tribune.*

A PREACHER ON THE AUCTION BLOCK.—" At Louisville, Ky., on the 6th inst., Peter Roberts, a free man of colour, a regularly licensed Methodist Preacher, a member of the Indiana African Conference, and a Master Mason of the Philadelphia Lodge, was sold at public auction before the Court-house door in that city, for the term of one year. He was bought by J. L. Hyatt, for 75 dollars, 50 cents.—An act of the Kentucky Legislature prohibits the migration of free negroes to that State, under a penalty of three hundred dollars, on which charge he was arrested and sold."—*True Wesleyan, September,* 1848.

TARRING AND FEATHERING OF A BAPTIST MINISTER IN SOUTH CAROLINA.—An Englishman travelling through the town of Winnsboro', was one evening sitting at the outside of his hotel, according to American custom, and overheard a description by the landlord, to some parties present, of the treatment given a few months previous to a Baptist minister, who came to the town, and preached abolition sentiments. He was privately warned to leave the town forthwith, or take the consequences. He neglected the hint, and to his surprise and alarm, his chamber door was burst open, and he was unceremoniously dragged from his bed, and compelled to put on his trousers, and then, after being stripped to his waist, was besmeared with warm tar. They next ripped open one of the pillows and shook the feathers over him. In this disgusting and ridiculous costume the poor sufferer was conveyed down stairs, and setting him astride a three-sided rail, very sharp on the edges, they carried him with brutal violence and rapidity through the parish, a distance of about two miles. When they had sufficiently wreaked their vengeance upon him, they gave him up to his friends, with a very significant injunction to leave the State in twenty-four hours, or take the consequences. Under the influence of slavery, even the ministerial character, adorned as in this case with the Christian virtue of benevolence, was no security against violence in "the Free Republic."

A PRO-SLAVERY CHURCH.—" As a specimen of the tone of religious feeling in the Slave States, I would mention that, at a recent Methodist missionary conference in Tennessee, General Taylor, commander of the invading army, and a notorious slave breeder, was made a life member of the Missionary society; together with Captain Walker, of the Texas banditti, called ' Rangers,' and some score of other ' heroes.' "—*Letter from John G. Whittier, the American Poet.*

Leeds Anti-slavery Series. No. 76.

Sold by W. and F. G. CASH, 5, Bishopsgate Street, London; and by JANE JOWETT Friends' Meeting Yard, Leeds, at 7*d.* per 100.

Leeds Anti-slavery Series. No. 77.

PHOEBE MOREL

WAS the daughter of a wealthy planter in Georgia, who had imprudently contracted marriage with a beautiful Creole —a slave on his father's estate. The mother of Phoebe died during the infancy of the child, whose father had her educated and attended with the most affectionate solicitude. He had, however, omitted to execute the necessary forms for her manumission, and the sad consequence of his neglect was that, immediately after his death, his legal representatives claimed the unfortunate Phoebe as a portion of their property. She did not long survive the indignity; for within a few months of her father's decease, her lifeless body was discovered floating down the dark waters of the Savannah.

I HAD a dream, a happy dream,
   I thought that I was free—
That in my own bright land again
   A home there was for me;
Savannah's tide dashed bravely on,
   I saw wave roll o'er wave,
But in my full delight I woke,
   And found I was a slave.

I never knew a mother's love,
   Yet happy were my days,
For by my own dear father's side
   I sung my simple lays.
He died, and heartless strangers came
   Ere clos'd o'er him the grave,
They tore me, weeping, from his side,
   And claimed me as their slave.

And this was in a Christian land,
   Where men kneel oft to pray;
The vaunted home of liberty,
   Where lash and chain hold sway.
O, give me back my Georgian cot;
   It is not wealth I crave;
O, let me live in freedom's light,
   Or die if still a slave.

Sold by W. and F. G. CASH, 5, Bishopsgate Street, London; and by JANE JOWETT, Friends' Meeting-Yard, Leeds, at 6d. per 100.

Leeds Anti-slavery Series. No. 78.

THE WITNESSES.

In ocean's wide domains,
  Half buried in the sands,
Lie skeletons in chains,
  With shackled feet and hands.

Beyond the fall of dews,
  Deeper than plummet lies,
Float ships, with all their crews,
  No more to sink or rise.

There the black slave-ship swims,
  Freighted with human forms,
Whose fettered, fleshless limbs
  Are not the sport of storms.

These are the bones of slaves!
  They gleam from the abyss;
They cry, from yawning waves,
  "We are the witnesses!"

Within earth's wide domains
  Are markets for men's lives;
Their necks are galled with chains,
  Their wrists are cramped with gyves.

Dead bodies, that the kite
  In deserts makes its prey;
Murders, that with affright,
  Scare schoolboys from their play!

All evil thoughts and deeds;
  Anger, and lust, and pride;
The foulest, rankest weeds,
  That choke life's groaning tide!

These are the woes of slaves;
  They glare from the abyss;
They cry, from unknown graves,
  "We are the witnesses!"

Sold by W. and F. G. Cash, 5, Bishopsgate Street, London; and by Jane Jowett, Friends' Meeting Yard, Leeds, at 6d. per 100.

Leeds Anti-slavery Series. No. 79.

INTELLECT AND CAPABILITIES OF THE NEGRO RACE.

ARE the negroes men? Are they men capable of civilisation? Are they an immediately inferior race? The negroes are men, capable of civilisation, though now suffering under the degradation of centuries of complicated injustice, and trodden down under the iron heel of almost unmitigated oppression. That they are men, human beings like ourselves, possessed of capacities in kind the same as our own, is not doubted by any impartial person who has had intercourse with them. Admit a negro family into your home; treat them in a Christian spirit, let them eat of your bread and drink of your cup, you can no longer doubt of their essential equality with yourself. That intelligence which the members of the family display in conversation; that deep and lively affection of the husband toward the wife, and of the mother toward her children; that calm and earnest spirit with which the parents join in your domestic devotions—the fears, hopes, and longings they express or silently entertain, leave on your mind a feeling of wonder that any, at least any professors of religion, should have questioned their alliance with the great human family. Yes! negroes are men, and every now and then, such as Douglass or Pennington, rise up to show what the race can do when placed in favourable circumstances. History has several such instances. We propose to chronicle a few of them here. Our first shall be that of Ignatius Sancho, who is an illustration of what the negro can do in the way of letters. When he was but two years old, he was brought to England and presented to three young maiden ladies, sisters, who resided at Greenwich. On the death of his mistresses, the Duchess of Montague, who admired his character, admitted him into her household, where he remained till she died, when, through economy and a legacy she left him,

---

Sold by W. and F. G. CASH, 5, Bishopsgate Street, London; and by JANE JOWETT, Friends' Meeting Yard, Leeds, at 3s. 6d. per 100, or 6d. per dozen.

he was possessed of £70 and an annuity of £30. Having dissipated most of this, he was again taken into Montague House, where he remained till 1773, when, having married an interesting and deserving young woman of West Indian origin, he commenced business as a grocer, and reared a numerous family in a life of domestic virtue which gained the public esteem. But this was not the only reputation that he won. Ignatius Sancho devoted himself earnestly to the cause of negro freedom, and, amid the trivial interruptions of a shop, he also applied himself to study. He cultivated the muses with success, especially the sister arts of poetry and music. He wrote two pieces for the stage; he discussed the theory of music in a dissertation, which was published and dedicated to the Princess Royal; and painting was so much within the circle of his judgment and criticism that Mortimer came to consult him. His reputation as a wit and humourist were considerable, and his acquaintances were men remarkable in their way. Sancho corresponded with Sterne, and it is said Garrick was very fond of him. Two volumes of Sancho's letters were published, with a fine portrait of the author. They exhibited considerable epistolary talent—rapid and just conception, as well as universal philanthropy. They are all the more creditable from the fact that they were not written for publication, no such idea having ever been entertained by the writer. His appeal to Sterne, in order to engage the sympathies of the latter in behalf of his oppressed race, did honour alike to his head and heart. He died in 1780, having deservedly won public esteem. He who surveys the extent of culture to which Ignatius Sancho had attained by self-education, must be convinced that the perfection of the reasoning faculties does not altogether depend on a peculiar conformation of the skull or the colour of a common integument, in defiance of that wild opinion which, says a learned writer, "restrains the operations of the mind to particular regions, and supposes that a luckless mortal may be born in a degree of latitude too high or too low for wisdom or wit."

Gustavus Vassa is another well-known name. At one time his life was a very popular work, and deservedly so, for, says *Abbé Gregoire*, "the individual is to be pitied who, after having read the memoir of Vassa, does not feel for the author sen-

GUSTAVUS VASSA,
OR
Olaudah Equiano

MANCHESTER:
WILLIAM IRWIN, 39, OLDHAM ST

timents of affection and esteem." Gustavus was born in the year 1745, in a charming and fruitful vale called Essaka, in one of the most remote and fertile provinces of the kingdom of Benin. His father being a man of rank, his life was a happy one, till he had attained the age of eleven. At that age he was torn away from his free and happy home as follows:— "One day," he writes, "when our people were going to their work, and only my sister and myself were left to watch the house, two men and a woman came, and seeing us, stopped our mouths, that we should not make a noise, ran off with us into the woods, where they tied our hands, and took us some distance to a small house where the robbers halted for refreshment, and spent the night. We were then unbound, but were unable to take any food, and being quite overpowered by fatigue and grief, our only relief was some sleep, which allayed our misfortunes for a short time. The next morning, after keeping the woods some time, we came to an opening, where we saw some people at work. I began to cry out for their assistance, but my cries had no other effect than to make them tie us faster and again stop our mouths; and they put us into a sack until we were out of sight of these people. When they offered us food we could not eat, often bathing each other in tears—our only respite was sleep. But, alas! even the privilege of weeping together was soon denied us. The next day proved a day of greater sorrow than I had yet experienced, for my sister and I were torn asunder while clasped in each other's arms; it was in vain that we besought them not to part us; she was torn from me and immediately carried away, while I was left in a state of distraction not to be described. I wept and grieved continually, and for several days did not eat anything but what was forced into my mouth." Thus torn away, Gustavus Vassa was hurried to Barbadoes, from which he was sold and removed to America. There he was taken into the service of a Captain Pascal, from which, in 1757, he was removed by a press-gang, and carried on board a man-of-war. Amongst the English he was happy enough. His English mistress taught him to read. Many years were spent by Gustavus Vassa on board the same man-of-war. He served his master to the best of his power; but the Christian master's treatment was not what it ought to have been; for after having held out hopes of freedom, and having received his wages and his prize-money, he sent back poor Vassa to the West Indies. There he was bought by a Mr. Robert King, of Philadelphia, of whom he in time managed to buy his freedom. After a short interval of time we again find Gustavus Vassa in London; and when, in 1773, an expedition was fitted out to explore a north-west passage to India, conducted by the Honourable Constantine John Phipps, afterwards Lord Mulgrave, Vassa accompanied Dr. Irving in the expedition. On his return to London, Vassa became an altered man. He had gone through great dangers, and his life had been preserved. He felt also that he was a sinner before God. Under the mingled emotions of gratitude and fear his heart melted—he saw and felt what he had never seen and felt before. His conscience was touched; he experienced the great change, and, in the language of Scripture, he passed from death unto life. Once more Vassa went to the West Indies, but he suffered innumerable wrongs in consequence of so doing, and again with joy returned to London, where, however, he did not stop long, as he was sent out to Sierra Leone, as commissary to the colony then forming there. The situation, however, he did not long retain, in consequence of his integrity. He lifted up his voice against the peculation by which the government was robbed, and his poor brethren wronged, and in consequence was relieved of the duties devolving on him, and permitted to return to London, where he published, in 1794, an autobiography, from which we have taken the above particulars. We have only to add here that he married in London, and had a son Sancho, to whom he gave a good education, and who became assistant librarian to Sir Joseph Banks, and secretary to the committee for vaccination. His life shows that a negro may be a Christian man equally with the white; that in the one race as well as in the other may be found a high degree of purity, of goodness, and of moral worth.

Henry Garnett is another illustration of the abilities of the negro race. He was born in Maryland in 1815. His family escaped into the non-slaveholding states in 1822. Henry, with his father, mother, sister, and eight other fugitive slaves, found an asylum in New York. They belonged to a Colonel Spencer, at whose death the estate passed into the hands of his nephew

—a man-tyrant, from whose clutches they determined to escape. The escape was managed by the mother—a woman of great energy of character. Having on one occasion obtained permission to be absent two days to attend the funeral of a relative ten miles distant, they started about sunset, travelling all night towards the land of freedom, hiding themselves in the woods by day, till they found themselves safe in New Hope, a village in Pennsylvania. At last they reached New York city, where they remained about seven years. There, however, after a residence of seven years, they were detected by the man-stealers, who managed to seize the sister—the father and mother having previously made their escape, and Garnett himself being at the time a cabin-boy on board a schooner trading to Washington. The news came on him as a thunderbolt, and he would have revenged the wrongs he had received, had not his friends placed him in the African Free School, where he soon reached the highest class. In 1833 he was admitted into the Canal Street Collegiate School, with several other coloured youths, and commenced the study of the Latin language. In 1835, Henry Garnett removed to New Hampshire, and became a member of Canaan Academy. He was not there, however, three months before the inhabitants attacked and demolished the house. The same year Garnett experienced a religious change of mind, and united with the Frankfort Street Presbyterian Church, in New York, at that time under the pastoral charge of the Rev. T. J. Wright. There he gained the reputation of a courteous and accomplished man, an able and eloquent debater, and a good writer. His first public appearance was before the American Anti-slavery Society, in 1837, and his address at once secured for him a standing among the first class of speakers. In 1840, Henry Garnett graduated at the school at Whitesoun, and received his diploma. He then repaired to the city of Troy, State of New York, where, in 1841, he married, and where, in 1843, he was ordained pastor of the Presbyterian Church in that town. Garnett is an acceptable preacher, his discourses being evangelical and poetical. He usually speaks from notes, rarely appearing with written sermons. Having complete command of his voice, he uses it with skill, never failing to fill the largest houses with perfect ease. One of his most remarkable speeches was an address to the negroes, at a National Convention in Buffalo, in 1843, when, for the space of two hours, the mighty assembly was swayed as he pleased. He made another very remarkable speech at Old Fanueil Hall, Boston, and has also published a *Discourse upon the Past and Present Condition and Destiny of the Coloured Race.* He was for some time connected with the *National Watchman.* Garnett was recently in England on an anti-slavery mission, which was attended with considerable success. He is now a missionary in the West Indies.

Toussaint l'Ouverture, a negro slave, was born on the estate of the Count de Breda, then under the care of M. Bayou de Libertas, near Cape Français, in "the Queen of the Antilles" —that is, Hayti, or the Isle of St. Domingo, on May 20, 1743. Of feeble frame and health, his parents, whom family traditions represented to be of royal lineage, had for a long while great difficulty in rearing the child. Strengthened at length by a life of exposure and hardships, and baptized into the Christian church, Toussaint early manifested good intellectual capabilities, and, together with some first notions of religion, acquired skill to read and, in a humble way, to write. Prudently, for their own sordid purposes, have the slave-masters closed and barred the doors of knowledge to their wretched victims. In his learning, rudimental though it was, Toussaint found one, and the chief effectual means of his self-elevation and usefulness. Occupied in keeping cattle, the young slave was advanced first to the office of his master's coachman, and then to the more responsible post of foreman of sugar-works. Thus placed in a somewhat superior position, he took a wife, and in this showed the good sense which was one of his qualities, by preferring solid housewife qualities to mere personal charms. "We went," he said to a traveller, "we went to labour in our fields with hand clasped in hand, we returned in the same manner; scarcely did we feel the fatigues of the day. Heaven bestowed a blessing on our toil; not only we swam in abundance, but we had the pleasure of giving provisions to blacks who were in want. On the Sunday, and on holidays, my wife, my relatives, and myself, went to church. Returning to our cottage, after an agreeable repast, we spent the rest of the day in family intercourse, and we terminated it by a prayer in which we all joined."

At the time when Toussaint l'Ouverture began to make a public appearance, Hayti was occupied by two populations, the one of Spanish, the other of French extraction ; the former dwelling in the eastern, the latter in the northern and western part of the island. Besides these, a large number of persons, of African descent, lived partly in servitude, partly in a state of disqualification, among the whiter and more fortunate inhabitants. In the French district there were first colonists or planters, who, of Gallic origin, bore sway, and had all power in their hands. Below them were free persons of colour, having more or less white blood in their veins.

Lastly, black slaves formed a large portion of the inhabitants. The interests, real or fancied, of these several tribes were diverse and conflicting. The most ancient possessors of the soil, the Spanish races, regarded the French intruders with jealousy and dislike. The planters, who were intimately connected with France, their mother country, and monopolising nearly all power and privileges, despised the coloured population, and feared their negro slaves. Heart-burnings, divisions, and rivalries, universally prevailed.

Into the midst of these discordant elements the news of the first French Revolution threw firebrands. Hopes and alarms, the most intense and diversified, were awakened on every side. The proclamation in Paris, that " all men are equal" made the colonists tremble for their usurped ascendancy, agitated the freed men of colour with the hope of social equality, and awoke in the mind of superior individuals among the negroes, a dim idea and a faint hope of personal freedom. By no one of African blood was the new impulse felt more than by Toussaint l'Ouverture.

At this momentous crisis Toussaint was loved and respected by all on account of his character. The great planters held him in consideration. His intellectual faculties grew in strength in virtue of his habitual connection with persons who were in the enjoyment of liberty. Directing his thoughts to the degraded condition of his brethren, he could not comprehend on what grounds slavery existed side by side with freedom, nor how a difference in the hue of the skin could have caused so enormous a distance of one man from another. His ideas expanded under the influence of passages which he frequently heard cited from Raynal's *Philosophical History*. He succeeded in procuring the work, and the reading of it disclosed to him the nature of the evils which crushed his kindred. A great excitement of mind ensued; but the agitation was, in a measure, calmed by religious considerations. In the midst of social disparities, alarms, and agitations, the negroes rose in revolt. Fire and devastation began to prevail. The march of the incendiaries was so rapid, that within the space of a week, devouring flames covered all the plain of the north of the island, from west to east, from the sea to the foot of the central mountain ridges. Those rich houses, those superb and productive manufactories, which poured wealth into the lap of France, were utterly destroyed. The activity of the flames was such, that the smoke and the ashes, carried by the wind on to the mountains, made them appear like volcanoes. The air all on fire, and dried up, resembled a burning furnace. Dwellings half burned continually threw up a shower of sparks. Ruins, wrecks, rich plunder lay scattered everywhere. The earth ran with blood, and was loaded with dead bodies. At this time Toussaint was about forty-eight years of age, and still a slave; but, slave as he was, he saved his master and his master's property. Having done this, Toussaint, who had now no tie to detain him longer in servitude, perceiving both reason and justice in the struggle which his oppressed race were making to regain their liberty, attached himself to the body of the negroes, but to that body which was under royalist commanders, in the Spanish part of the island, and opposed to the French Republican planters. With this party, however, he did not act long. The decree of the French convention, of February 4, 1794, which confirmed and proclaimed the liberty of all slaves, and declared St. Domingo to be an integral part of France, opened his eyes, and immediately he joined the French forces under Laveaux, who made him brigadier-general. The power which Toussaint speedily obtained over the ignorant and barbarous soldiery was wonderful. To assist him in his military operations, we are told, " that imitating the example of the captains of antiquity —Lucullus, Pompey, Cæsar, and others—he constructed a topographical chart of that part of the island, marking accurately the position of the hills, the course of the streams, &c." So much did he harass the commissioners, that when the Spanish posts fell one after another into the hands of the French, one of them exclaimed, "Cet homme fait ouverture partout"— (This man makes an opening everywhere). This expression becoming public was the cause of his ever after being called Toussaint l'Ouverture. The French general becoming more and more convinced of Toussaint's integrity and skill, made him lieutenant-governor of the island; the consequence of this was, the establishement of order among the black population. Upon the French general's return to France, Toussaint became commander-in-chief of the French forces in St. Domingo. From this time he gradually advanced in power and splendour. The British, who retained a footing in the island, evacuated it, and he took possession of their posts with great pomp; but the mulattoes charged him with selling the island to the British, and raised a rebellion—one, however, very speedily crushed. In 1801, Toussaint was in the plenitude of his power. At that time, assisted by a council of his adherents, he prepared a colonial constitution, uniting the different inhabitants of the island under an impartial and uniform government. By this constitution all executive power was put into his hands, under the title of President for life, with power to choose his successor, and to nominate to all offices. The island then prospered, and everywhere order reigned—everywhere Toussaint was beloved. But this was not to last. Bonaparte formed the resolution of extinguishing Toussaint, and taking possession of St. Domingo. The French squadron reached the island early in 1802. In all quarters they were successful. But Toussaint was not defeated. After the French commander had left 5000 of his men dead on the battle-field, and 5000 more in the hospitals, he was willing to treat with Toussaint, who appeared before him for that purpose. But though the French commander was the nominal, Toussaint was the real, monarch of the island. And it was resolved that Toussaint should be seized and sent to France. By means of a stratagem this was done. Toussaint was seized and sent as a prisoner to Paris; and after ten months' confinement at the castle of Joux, in the east of France, among the Jura moutains—far from all who loved him, or whom he loved, the great negro chief was found dead; but not with his body did his memory die. So long as truth, and courage, and patriotism are held dear, will increasing reverence cluster round the honoured name. We may say as Wordsworth has beautifully said—

> "Thou hast left behind
> Powers that will work for thee—earth, air, and skies;
> There's not a breathing of the common wind
> That will forget thee—thou hast great allies—
> Thy friends are exultations, agonies,
> And love—and man's unconquerable mind."

Lott Carey, another intelligent negro, was born a slave in Virginia, but by repeated presents for his integrity, and subscriptions among merchants, by whom he was highly esteemed, he purchased his freedom. His intellectual ability, his firmness of purpose, unbending integrity, correct judgment, and disinterested benevolence, placed him in a conspicuous situation, and gave him wide and commanding influence.

Phillis Wheatley was stolen for a slave when a little girl from her parents in Africa. In sixteen months she acquired the English language so perfectly, that she could read any of the most difficult parts of Scripture, to the great astonishment of those who heard her; and this she learned without any instruction, except what was given her in the family. She wrote poems between the age of fourteen and nineteen, which were published in this country. The talented editors of the *Edinburgh Journal* in quoting a portion from one of her poems "On the Providence of God," observe, "it shows a very considerable reach of thought, and no mean powers of expression." Phillis visited England and was admired in the first circles of society.

Jasmin Thoumazeau was originally a slave of St. Domingo; the Philadelphia Society, and the Agricultural Society of Paris, both decreed medals to him.

Paul Cuffe presents us with an example of great energy of mind in the more common affairs of life. Born under peculiar disadvantages, notwithstanding the pressure of many difficulties, he qualified himself for any station of life. A sound understanding, united with indomitable energy and perseverance, mingled with a fervent but unaffected piety and benevolence, were the prominent features of his character. Religion, influencing his mind by its secret guidance, and silent reflection, added, in advancing manhood, to the brightness of his character, and confirmed his disposition to practical good. His exertions to promote the happiness of his fellow-men, and to relieve their sufferings, confer more honours upon him, than ever marble statue or monumental trophy could do.

J. E. J. Capitein was brought from Africa when about seven years old, and purchased by a slave-dealer. Of his early history but little is known, or by what means he became instructed in the elements of the Latin, Greek, Hebrew, and Chaldaic languages. He was a painter from taste. He published at the Hague an elegy in Latin verse, on the death of his instructor. From the Hague he went to the university of Leyden; on entering which he published a Latin dissertation on the calling of the Gentiles. He also published several sermons and letters at Leyden, one of which went through four editions very quickly. He took his degree at Leyden, and was ordained to the office of a Christian minister in Amsterdam. He went to Elmina on the Gold Coast, where it is probable he was either murdered or sold into slavery.

An instance occurred in the United States, during the last century, of a coloured man showing a remarkable skill in mathematical science. His name was Richard Banneker, and he belonged to the state of Maryland. He was altogether self-taught, and having directed his attention to the study of astronomy, his calculations were so thorough and exact, as to excite the approbation of Pitt, Fox, Wilberforce, and many other eminent persons. An almanac which he composed, was produced in the British House of Commons, as an argument in favour of the mental cultivation of the coloured people, and of their liberation from their wretched thraldom.

In 1734, Anthony William Amo, an African from the coast of Guinea, took the degree of Doctor in Philosophy at the university of Wittemberg. Two of his dissertations, according to Blumenbach, exhibit much well-digested knowledge of the best physiological works of the time. He was well versed in astronomy, and spoke the Latin, Hebrew, Greek, French, Dutch, and German languages. In an account of his life, published by the academic council of the university, his integrity, talents, industry, and erudition are highly commended.

Correa de Serra, a learned secretary of the academy of Portugal, informs us that several negroes and coloured persons have been learned lawyers, preachers, and professors; and that many in the Portuguese possessions have been signalized by their talents.

The Rev. James W. C. Pennington, D.D., is well known, and his character highly appreciated in England. The ancient and renowned University of Heidelberg, from whose venerable halls have gone forth masters in the loftiest departments of human lore, conferred upon him an honorary degree for his abilities and reputation.

The Rev. S. R. Ward, Wm. Wells Brown, James M'Cune Smith, M.D., and the Rev. Alexander Crummell, B.A., afford evidence of the mental qualities of the coloured man; and last, not least, Frederick Douglass, whose eloquence and thrilling accents speak for themselves.

Were it necessary, we could lengthen this list, but the few names we have given may suffice for our purpose. Those who wish for further evidence are referred to *A Tribute for the Negro; being a Vindication of the Moral, Intellectual, and Religious Capabilities of the African Race*, by Wilson Armistead; a work which contains a large mass of facts on this subject.

Here, on this side the Atlantic, with God's gospel in our hands, we have none bold enough to deny to the negro endowments similar to our own. In spite of colour, we see that they are men of like passions with ourselves—creatures of a common God, and born to the enjoyment of a common faith. Surely the time will come when this truth shall be universally felt—when the hour of Africa's regeneration shall arrive, and she shall be great, and glorious, and FREE.

Dr. Wright, a clergyman of the Church of England, who resided many years in Africa, states, " I am perfectly satisfied, from what I have both seen and heard, that the black man only wants the same opportunities which the white man enjoys, in order to raise himself to the highest degree to which intellect can conduct him."

Leeds Anti-slavery Series. No. 79.

Sold by W. and F. G. CASH, 5, Bishopsgate Street, London; and by JANE JOWETT, Friends' Meeting Yard, Leeds, at 3s. 6d. per 100; or 6d. per doz.

Leeds Anti-slavery Series. No. 80.

RESULTS OF IMMEDIATE EMANCIPATION;

FROM HISTORICAL EVIDENCE.

WHEN the question of immediate abolition was first started in England, the friends of slavery vociferated nothing more loudly, than the danger of universal insurrection and bloodshed; and nothing took stronger hold of the sympathies and conscientious fears of the people, than these repeated assertions. This is precisely the state of things in America at the present time. We all know that it is not according to human nature for men to turn upon their benefactors, and do violence, at the very moment they receive what they have long desired; but we are so repeatedly told the slaves *will* murder their masters, if they give them freedom, that we can hardly help believing that, in this peculiar case, the laws of human nature *must* be reversed. Let us try to divest ourselves of the fierce excitement now abroad in the community, and calmly inquire what is the testimony of history on this important subject.

In June, 1793, a civil war occurred between the aristocrats and republicans of St. Domingo; and the planters called in the aid of Great Britain. The opposing party proclaimed freedom to all slaves, and armed them against the British. It is generally supposed that the abolition of slavery in St. Domingo was *in consequence of insurrections* among the slaves; but this is not true. *It was entirely a measure of political expediency.* And what were the consequences of this sudden and universal emancipation? Whoever will take the pains to search the histories of that island, will find the whole coloured population remained faithful to the republican party which had given them freedom. The British were defeated, and obliged to evacuate the island. The sea being at that time full of British cruisers

---

Sold by W. and F. G. CASH, 5, Bishopsgate Street, London; and by JANE JOWETT Friends' Meeting Yard, Leeds, at 2s. 3d. per 100.

the French had no time to attend to St. Domingo, and the colonists were left to govern themselves. And what was the conduct of the emancipated slaves, under these circumstances? About 600,000 slaves had instantaneously ceased to be property, and were invested with the rights of men; yet there was a decrease of crime, and everything went on quietly and prosperously. Col. Malenfant, who resided on the island, says, in his historical memoir:—" After this public act of emancipation, the negroes remained quiet both in the south and west, and they continued to work upon all the plantations. Even upon those estates which had been abandoned by owners and managers, the negroes continued their labour where there were any agents to guide; and where no white men were left to direct them, they betook themselves to planting provisions. The colony was flourishing. The whites lived happy and in peace upon their estates, and the negroes continued to work for them."

General Lacroix, in his memoirs, speaking of the same period, says—" The colony marched, as by enchantment, towards its ancient splendour; cultivation prospered; every day produced perceptible proofs of its progress."

This prosperous state of things lasted about eight years; and would probably have continued to this day, had not Bonaparte, at the instigation of the old aristocratic French planters, sent an army to deprive the blacks of the freedom which they had used so well. It was the attempts to restore slavery, that produced all the bloody horrors of St. Domingo. *Emancipation produced the most blessed effects.*

In 1794, Victor Hugo, a French republican general, retook the island of Guadaloupe from the British, and immediately proclaimed freedom to all the slaves. They were 85,000 in number, and the whites only 13,000. *No disasters whatever occurred in consequence of this step.* Seven years after, the supreme council of Guadaloupe, in an official document, alluding to the tranquillity that reigned throughout the island, observed: —" We shall have the satisfaction of giving an example which will prove that all classes of people may live in perfect harmony with each other, under an administration which secures justice to all classes." In 1802, Bonaparte again reduced this island to slavery, at the cost of about 20,000 negro lives.

In 1821, the congress of Colombia emancipated all slaves who had borne arms in favour of the republic ; and provided for the emancipation in eighteen years of the whole slave population, amounting to 900,000.

In 1829, the government of Mexico granted immediate and unqualified freedom to every slave. *In all these cases, not one instance of insurrection or bloodshed has ever been heard of, as the result of emancipation.*

In 1823, 30,000 Hottentots in Cape Colony, were emancipated from their long and cruel bondage, and admitted by law to all the rights and privileges of the white colonists. Outrages were predicted, as the inevitable consequence of freeing human creatures so completely brutalized as the poor Hottentots ; but all went on peaceably ; and as a gentleman facetiously remarked, "Hottentots as they were, they worked better for Mr. *Cash*, than they had ever done for Mr. *Lash*."

In 1831, it is stated—" Three thousand prize negroes have received their freedom ; four hundred in one day ; but not the least difficulty or disaster occurred. *Servants found masters— masters hired servants—all gained homes, and at night scarcely an idler was to be seen.*—To state that sudden emancipation would create disorder and distress to those you mean to serve, is not reason, but the plea of all men adverse to abolition."

It is common to speak of the immediate abolition of slavery as being difficult and dangerous. It may, however, be remarked, that during the struggle for the abolition of British Colonial Slavery, the friends of the slave in this country, including all the most distinguished advocates of abolition, both in and out of Parliament, were brought to the conclusion that immediate emancipation was an act of Christian duty, and that difficulty and danger would arise from a measure of supposed preparation, instead of being counteracted by it. These opinions were embraced by them, although nearly all had previously held contrary views, and were forced upon them by a consideration of the nature of slavery ; its violation of human rights; its deplorable effects on the physical, intellectual, moral, and religious condition of its victims ; and by a knowledge of the vast number of instances in which the despotic power vested in the slaveholder was fearfully abused.

On the 1st of August, 1834, Great Britain emancipated the

slaves in all her colonies, of which she had twenty ; seventeen in the West Indies, and three in the East Indies. The measure was not carried in a manner completely satisfactory to the English abolitionists. Historical evidence, and their own knowledge of human nature, led them to the conclusion, that immediate and unqualified emancipation was the *safest* for the master, as well as the most just towards the slave. But the West India planters talked so loudly of the dangers of such a step, and of the necessity of time to fit the slaves for freedom, that the government resolved to conciliate them by a sort of compromise. The slaves were to continue to work six years longer without wages, under the name of apprentices ; but during this period, they could be punished only by the express orders of magistrates.

The legislatures of the several colonies had a right to dispense with the system of apprenticeship ; but Antigua and Bermuda were the only ones that adopted immediate and unconditional emancipation.

Public proclamation of freedom was made on the first of August, and was everywhere received in joy and peace. Mr. Cobbett, a missionary stationed at Montego Bay, Jamaica, writes thus :—" The first of August was a memorable day ! Our preaching place was crowded at an early hour. At the close of the services, I read the address of his excellency the governor to the negro population, made several remarks in reference to the change of their condition, and exhorted them to be obedient to their masters and to the powers that be. There was in every countenance an expression of satisfaction, and of gratitude to God and their benefactors. The conduct of the negroes during this eventful period has been such as will raise them, I should think, in the eyes of all their friends."

Mr. Wedlock, of the same place, writes thus :—" The first day of August, a day to which the attention of the wise, the good, and the philanthropic, of other countries besides our own, was directed, has arrived and passed by in the most peaceful and harmonious manner. Such congregations, such attention, such joys and grateful feelings as are depicted in every countenance, I never beheld !—Up to this time, peace and harmony prevail."

The marquis of Sligo, governor of Jamaica, in his speech to the assembly, after five months' trial of emancipation, declares

—"Not the slightest idea of any interruption of tranquillity exists in any quarter ; and those preparations which I have felt it my duty to make, might, without the slightest danger, have been dispensed with." In a recent address to the assembly, he states that the crops this year (1835), will fall short only about one-sixteenth ; and that this slight difference may be accounted for by the unfavourableness of the season.

The enemies of abolition predicted that the crops in Jamaica would perish for want of being gathered ; because the negroes could not possibly be induced to work an hour longer than the law or the whip compelled them. But as soon as the planters offered them *wages* for working extra hours, more work was offered than the planters were willing to pay for. Even the low price of a penny an hour operated like magic upon them, and inspired them to diligence!

The numerical superiority of the negroes in the West Indies is great. In Jamaica there were 331,000 slaves, and only 37,000 whites. By the clumsy apprenticeship system, the old stimulus of the whip was taken away, while the new and better stimulus of wages was not applied. The negroes were aware that if they worked well they should not be paid for it, and that if they worked ill they could not be flogged, as they had formerly been. Yet, even under these disadvantageous circumstances, no difficulties occurred except in three of the islands; and even there the difficulties were slight and temporary. Let us inquire candidly how these troubles originated. The act of parliament provided, that the apprentice should work for his master *forty and a half* hours per week, and have the remainder of the time for his own benefit ; but it did not provide that while they were apprentices (and of course worked without wages) they should enjoy all the privileges to which they had been accustomed while slaves. The planters availed themselves of this circumstance to put obstructions in the way of abolition ; with the hope likewise of coercing the apprentices to form individual contracts to work *fifty* hours in the week, instead of *forty and a half*. While the people had been slaves, they had always been allowed *cooks* to prepare their meals ; *nurses* to take care of the little children ; and a person to bring *water* to the gang, during the hot hours ; but when they became apprentices, these privileges were taken away. Each slave was obliged to quit his or her work to go to his own cabin (sometimes a great distance) to cook their meals, instead of having them served in the field; water was not allowed them; the aged and infirm, instead of being employed as formerly, to superintend the children in the shade, were driven to labour in the hot sun, and mothers were obliged to toil at the hoe with their infants strapped at their backs. In addition to this, the planters obtained from the governor a new proclamation, requiring the apprentices to labour extra hours for their masters, when they should deem it necessary *in the cultivation, gathering, or manufacture of the crop,* provided they repaid them an equal time " at a convenient season of the year." This was like taking from a New-England farmer the month of July to be repaid in January. Under these petty vexations, and unjust exactions, some of the apprentices stopped work in three of the colonies, out of seventeen. But even in these three their resistance was merely passive. THE WORST ENEMIES OF ABOLITION HAVE NOT YET BEEN ABLE TO SHOW THAT A SINGLE DROP OF BLOOD HAS BEEN SHED, OR A SINGLE PLANTATION FIRED, IN CONSEQUENCE OF EMANCIPATION, IN ALL THE BRITISH WEST INDIES!

In Jamaica they refused to work upon the terms which their masters endeavoured to impose. A very small military force was sent into one parish, and but on one occasion. Not a drop of blood was shed on either side.

In Demarara they refused to work on the prescribed terms, and marched about with a flag-staff, as "the ten hour men" have done in many American cities. But the worst thing they did was to strike a constable with their fists.

In St. Christopher's the resistance was likewise entirely passive. In two weeks the whole trouble was at an end; and it was ascertained that, out of twenty thousand apprentices, only *thirty* were absent from work; and some of these were supposed to be dead in the woods.

One apprentice, executed in Demarara for insubordination, is the only life that has yet been lost in this great experiment! and a few *fisty cuffs* with a constable, on one single occasion, has been the only violence offered to persons or property, by eight hundred thousand emancipated slaves.

Antigua and Bermuda did not try the apprenticeship system;

but *at once* gave the slaves the stimulus of wages. *In those islands not the slightest difficulties have occurred.* The journals of Antigua say—" The great doubt is solved ; and the highest hopes of the negroes' friends are fulfilled. Thirty thousand men have passed from slavery into freedom, not only without the slightest irregularity, but with the solemn and decorous tranquillity of a Sabbath ! "

In Antigua there are 2000 whites, 30,000 slaves, and 4500 free blacks.

Antigua and St. Christopher's are within gunshot of each other; both are sugar-growing colonies ; and the proportion of blacks is less in St. Christopher's than it is in Antigua: yet the former island has had some difficulty with the *gradual* system, while the quiet of the latter has not been disturbed for one hour by *immediate emancipation.* Do not these facts speak volumes ?

There are, in the West Indies, many men (planters, overseers, drivers, and book-keepers), who, from pride, licentiousness, and other motives, do not like a change which takes away from them uncontrolled power over men and women. These individuals try to create difficulties, and exaggerate the report of them. It is much to be regretted that the press has hitherto preferred their distorted stories, unsubstantiated by a particle of proof, to the well-authenticated evidence of magistrates and missionaries resident on the islands.

The following are recent well-authenticated reports :—

Sir Charles Grey, governor of Jamaica, as is stated in the *Parliamentary Report* for 1848, wrote to the British minister : "If the negro population are treated with thorough fairness and complete justice, they will make an admirable peasantry." "The negroes appear to me to be generally as free from rebellious tendencies, turbulent feelings, and malicious thoughts, as any race of labourers I ever saw or heard of. My impression is, indeed, that under a system of perfectly fair dealing, and of real justice, they will come to be an admirable peasantry and yeomanry ; able-bodied, industrious and hard working, frank and well disposed."

The governor says in reference to education—" The present moment (April, 1849) is unfavourable to the cause; but I have sanguine hopes that ere long Jamaica will be distinguished amongst the people of the Western world for her colleges, her schools, and her elementary institutions." "The hamlets, villages, and towns, as they are called, of the negroes, which have sprung up in the interior and amongst the mountains, and in which they live in great physical comfort, are a remarkable and interesting feature in the state of the island."

The governor of British Guiana reports, that "the labouring population are commonly quiet, peaceable, and industrious."

The governor of Barbadoes says—"The old system, under which the island depended for subsistence on imported provisions, has been abandoned, and the industry of the country has been directed to the raising of supplies on plantations—a system of husbandry which has also introduced a useful rotation of crops."

The governor of Antigua writes—"Rays of hope are discernible, both at home and abroad, which should incite the advocates of freedom throughout the world to persevere in the righteous cause in which they are engaged. Peace and order continue to reign uninterrupted throughout the land. Cheap food is abundant, and the means of earning it are readily obtained."

The governor of St. Kitt's thinks "it would be difficult to adduce, on the part of the working-classes in other countries, instances of more unexceptionable conduct."

Messrs. Alexander and Candler, of England, who have recently visited most of the West India Islands, to see the workings of emancipation, testify that notwithstanding the calamitous state of things, owing to bad legislation, improvident habits, the want of a social system, and the multifarious effects of long-continued slavery, the population of the Islands is increasing, the condition of the great mass of the people is one of much comfort, and that those planters who introduce improvements and practise economy, thrive.

Why are the friends of slavery so desirous to make it appear that the British experiment does *not* work well? It is because they are conscious that if it *does* work well, America has no excuse left to screen her from the strong disapprobation of the civilized world.

Leeds Anti-slavery Series. No. 80.

Sold by W. and F. G. CASH, 5, Bishopsgate Street, London; and by JANE JOWETT, Friends' Meeting Yard, Leeds, at 2s. 3d. per 100.

Leeds Anti-slavery Series. No. 81.

WHO ARE RESPONSIBLE FOR SLAVERY?

MOTIVES FOR ANTI-SLAVERY EFFORT.

WHO ARE RESPONSIBLE FOR SLAVERY?

Answer. 1. All slaveholders. 2. All who justify or excuse slaveholding. 3. All who make and who administer or execute the slave laws. 4. All legislators who do not wield their lawful powers for the abolition of slavery. 5. All who vote for such legislators, or for slaveholders. "He that ruleth over men must be just, ruling in the fear of God." 6. All who do not bear testimony against slavery, and conform their activities and their position to their testimony. 7. All who maintain a pro-slavery religion, or hold fellowship with it. 8. All who do not put forth self-denying exertions for the diffusion of anti-slavery sentiment, and the abolition of slavery. 9. All who live under pro-slavery constitutions, and do not demand their amendment.

MOTIVES FOR ANTI-SLAVERY EFFORT.

1. Efforts for the abolition of slavery are *right*. 2. They are in accordance with the will of God, who is the God of righteousness, the refuge of the oppressed. 3. *Not* to plead the cause of the oppressed is to fail of being God-like—to fail of forming a godly character—to fail of securing the Divine approbation and favour. 4. The cause of the oppressed is the cause of mercy and humanity, as well as the cause of justice and the cause of God. 5. Anti-slavery efforts are necessary for the preservation of civil and religious liberty. 6. They are necessary for the moral reformation of the community—for the suppression of lawlessness and vice, for the promotion of industry, purity, and virtue. 7. They are necessary for the purification of the churches, for the honour of Christianity, for the revival

Sold by W. and F. G. CASH, 5, Bishopsgate Street, London; and by JANE JOWETT Friends' Meeting Yard, Leeds, at 7*d.* per 100.

of pure and undefiled religion. They are necessary for the evangelizing of the heathen at home, and for the propagation of a pure and liberty-loving religion among the heathen abroad. 8. They form an essential link in the chain of connected efforts for the progressive enlightenment, civilization, elevation, and restored brotherhood of the family of man. 9. Anti-slavery efforts are necessary to the restored idea and correct apprehension not only of the rights of humanity, but of the rights of property, of the true relation between labour and wages, between capital and labour. 10. They are therefore necessary to a perfected science of domestic industry, of political economy, of commercial intercourse, a proper and healthful development of man, and of the elements and the riches of nature, created for man's benefit. We say not that *mere* anti-slavery efforts are sufficient to accomplish any one or all of these objects. We do say that they are essentially necessary to those ends, nevertheless.

There are questions affecting the highest interests of Man, on which it is criminal to be silent. We cannot plead ignorance as an excuse either for silence or inability in the anti-slavery cause. When we remember that there are now in the world upwards of SEVEN MILLIONS *of human beings detained in slavery;* who are held as goods and chattels, the property of other human beings having similar passions with themselves; that they are liable to be sold and transferred from hand to hand like the beasts that perish; that more than 400,000 are annually torn from the land of their birth, and sent into distant regions; and this not in families, the nearest connections of life being frequently torn asunder; and when we further reflect, that in several, if not in most of the slaveholding states, the slaves are systematically excluded from all means of improving their minds—that in some, even teaching them to read is treated as a crime. I say, when we know and remember all this, does not the question naturally arise in every bosom, "*Can I be an innocent,* and yet *a silent* spectator of this mighty infringement of every human and sacred right?"

Leeds Anti-slavery Series. No. 81.

Sold by W. and F. G. CASH, 5, Bishopsgate Street, London; and by JANE JOWETT Friends' Meeting Yard, Leeds, at 7*d*. per 100.

Leeds Anti-slavery Series. No. 82.

TO THE FRIENDS OF EMANCIPATION;

AN APPEAL TO CHRISTIANS OF ALL DENOMINATIONS.

THE deep conviction of religious duty that prompted the friends of the slave in the British colonies to seek and to secure their freedom, should impel them to similar zeal and exertion, in the use of all legitimate means, to attain the same end in every part of the world for those who are still held in bondage. SLAVERY, WHEREVER IT EXISTS, IS THE SAME MORAL DEFORMITY, THE SAME CRIME BEFORE GOD; and ought to be viewed with detestation by every one who professes to act on Christian principles.

To the accomplishment of this great work, CHRISTIANS OF ALL DENOMINATIONS are summoned. Will they not answer the appeal? It were injurious to their principles to question the course they will pursue. Surely Africa, ravished of her children, will not stretch out her hands in vain, to implore their assistance to deliver her sons from slavery, and her daughters from the hands of the spoiler. The promptings of humanity, the pleadings of benevolence, will lead to exertion; and cheered by the Divine promises, and animated by the glorious results of past labours in the same sacred cause, they will devote themselves to the UTTER EXTINCTION OF SLAVERY AND THE SLAVE-TRADE THROUGHOUT THE WORLD.

Among the means recently adopted to expose the dreadful iniquities of slavery, probably none has been more efficacious than the publication, *Uncle Tom's Cabin; or, Negro Life in the Slave States of America.* Nothing has ever argued better for the cause of emancipation, than the popularity of this work. Nothing could have been more opportune for the cause of

Sold by W. and F. G. CASH, 5, Bishopsgate Street, London; and by JANE JOWETT, Friends' Meeting Yard, Leeds, at 2s. 3d. per 100.

humanity. Already, by means of this touching but too truthful tale, the slumbering embers of anti-slavery zeal have been re-kindled into active power. Influence enough has been excited to move the world on this topic, and all that we require is cooperation and union. The pulpit, the press, and the platform must speak out on the subject of slavery once more, and by their thunders shake the whole world. We must appeal, instruct, and arouse. In America, we have a goodly number of abolitionists as our fellow-helpers, and they will be increased a thousandfold. We would as soon believe in the power of the planters to reverse the revolutions of the planets as to resist the present influence. The voice of humanity is the voice of God, and is essentially omnipotent. As a punishment for not having listened to this Divine oracle, the slaveholders must have the humiliation of being vanquished by a woman. And, after all, what more natural than that the woes of our race should owe their softest, sweetest, and consequently most powerful utterances to the heart of the sex which was created to bless the world with its tenderest sympathies?

> " Who can behold unheeding
> Life's holiest feelings crush'd ;—
> While *woman's* heart is bleeding
> Shall *woman's* voice be hush'd?"

The friends of emancipation are now placed on a vantage ground from which it would be base to retire, especially as we have been raised thus high by the talent and benevolence of a female. Christian chivalry has now open before it a race of glory, compared with which the tilts and tournaments of the olden time are the veriest trifles. The whole country is baptized with anti-slavery zeal, just ready to burst forth in every possible way to emancipate the slave. We must have public meetings everywhere. It is only for the friends of humanity once more to gird themselves for their work, and in a few years there will be another and more extensive triumph over the foes of liberty and the oppressors of the negro. We must continue to expostulate ; and the denunciations we utter against the rulers of the slave will be carried by the birds of the air to the ears of these tyrants, and make their hearts quiver and knees shake like those of Belshazzar. The words of justice require no patent from courts to render them authoritative. The stamp of Heaven is upon them; and, though spoken by a Paul in chains, they pierce the hearts of despots, and make them tremble. We mistake if we suppose that conscience is altogether dead in the souls of slaveholders. Heaven has decreed that the wretch who is deaf to the small still voice of duty and mercy, shall be horrified by the thunders of guilt, and feel a hell within. "Haley" hoping to cheat the devil when he has made his fortune; and "Legree" trembling for fear of ghosts and hobgoblins, are no creatures of fiction, but the truthful delineations of the conscious degradation and forebodings of the trader in human blood.

And further, cannot *consistency* utter a plea? There is nothing, perhaps, at which men labour more earnestly than to appear consistent. But what fellowship can there be between liberty and slavery? Slavery is a foul blot on the escutcheon of the United States; and every patriotic American feels it to be so. Here, in the land of liberty, freedom receives her deepest wound in the house of her vaunting friends. The enemies of tyranny over the world are taunted with the despotism of the American democrat. The infidel of our day draws his most potent arguments from the vices and faults of professing Christians; and the advocates of despotism act in the same manner, and procure their artillery from the barbarism of American slaveholders. We must, then, assail this inconsistency, until the guilty parties blush and are ashamed. The continual dropping of water will wear away stones, and the persevering reiterations of truth shall eventually prevail, and make even slaveholders relent and listen to the voice of consistency and humanity.

We have had among us glorious specimens of what the slave can be. To those who talk of his inferior powers and limited rights, we point to such men as Frederick Douglass, Wells Brown, Henson, Garnett, and Dr. Pennington. The academy at Heidelberg conferred on Dr. Pennington his diploma. And is this the man that the slaveholder would sell as he would a horse or bullock? What is the reply of humanity to this question? We need not dwell on the mind, talents, and piety of Brown, Henson, and Garnett. The country has long since borne witness to these. Exeter Hall has often resounded with the loftiest strains of eloquence, but never has it listened to a more intellectual, eloquent, and soul-stirring tongue than that of Frederick Douglass; and yet this is the man on whose head the planters have set a price, because he obeyed the voice of nature and of God in running away from the horrors of slavery. But why advance these examples? There is not a field of slaves, a slave-market, or a negro cabin, but proclaims the equality of the African with the rest of the human family. The tears, cries, and broken hearts which every separation by the dealer occasions, proclaim that the sympathies of the slave are equal to those of the rest of mankind. Every argument used by these sons and daughters of bondage, every prayer they offer, every speech they make, and every sermon they preach, prove that all the essentials of soul belong to them in as much native richness as to us. It is true everything has been done to degrade them. The cruelties practised by Simon the cobbler to deprave and demoralize the Dauphin of France, and which awakened the execration of the world, are every day being followed by the planters of America. What if any of us had had the sphere of our knowledge contracted to the smallest span, and our language confined to a few words of the most outlandish *patois*, is there one man among us that would surpass them in their present condition? Where would Milton, Shakspeare, or Newton have been under such training? Considering the debasing education to which they have been doomed, the slaves are our equals, if not our superiors; every part of their history shows the truth of the words of our poet:—

> " Fleecy locks and black complexion,
> Cannot forfeit Nature's claim;
> Skins may differ, but affection
> Dwells in black and white the same.
>
> Deem our nation brutes no longer,
> Till some reason ye shall find,
> Worthier of regard and stronger,
> Than the colour of our kind.
>
> Slaves of gold! whose sordid dealings
> Tarnish all your boasted powers,
> Prove that you have human feelings,
> Ere you proudly question ours."

The passing of the Fugitive Slave Bill adds strength to our cause. This measure has shocked every human heart; it has libelled humanity; it has sunk the republican below most of the tyrants that have ever scourged society; it has insulted the world, and blasphemed the Eternal. It commands and compels free men to become informers and kidnappers, and thus degrades them below the meanest of our race. It is an attempt to render freedom the slave of slavery. A viler law has never degraded any statute-book. However, its iniquity and its cruelty have aroused thousands to action who before were asleep; and when the history of the emancipation of American slaves shall be written, the narrator will triumphantly relate that the infamous Fugitive Slave Bill very greatly hastened this glorious consummation.

We have also another material aid in the clerical teachings of pro-slavery priests and preachers. We shall hereafter have to thank Dr. Spring, of New York; Dr. Parker, of Philadelphia; Dr. Stuart, of Andover; Dr. Spencer, of Brooklyn; the Right Rev. Bishop Hopkins, of Vermont; and a host of other reverends, for their advocacy of the cause of slavery. This outrage on Christianity, by its own ministers, has shocked the whole Christian world, and led to the inquiry,—

―――― "Just God, and holy!
Is that church, which lends
Strength to the spoiler, Thine?"

Even the planters despise these sycophants. To hear men at the sacred desk, and in the name of the Redeemer of the world, advocate a system which cherishes ignorance, vice, debauchery, dishonesty, and murder, out-Herods anything that was ever taught by the most depraved heathens and infidels. Even Pagans had their dark groves, and other midnight recesses, for their sensual orgies. No atheist or barbarian has yet taught that the infant should be torn from the breast of its mother, and sold like a swine to the murderous dealer in human flesh. It was left for the 19th century, and doctors of divinity in a Christian garb, to arrive at this degree of blasphemy, impiety, and immorality. Well, we thank them for their teachings, we congratulate them for their boldness in iniquity; and we will repeat their sayings until we make every ear in Christendom tingle with their presumption and inhumanity.

> "Just God!—and these are they
> Who minister at Thine altar, God of Right!
> Men who their hands with prayer and blessing l;
>   On Israel's Ark of light!
>
> What! preach and kidnap men?
> Give thanks—and rob Thy own afflicted poor?
> Talk of thy glorious liberty, and then
>   Bolt hard the captive's door?
>
> What! servants of Thy own
> Merciful Son, who came to seek and save
> The homeless and the outcast,—fettering down
>   The tasked and plundered slave!
>
> How long, O Lord! how long
> Shall such a priesthood barter truth away,
> And, in Thy name, for robbery and wrong
>   At Thy own altars pray?"

As far as England is concerned, the odium of anti-slavery movement has passed away. *Uncle Tom's Cabin* has re-kindled the zeal of the lukewarm, and baptized with holy fire myriads who before cared nothing for the suffering slave. Where is the heart it has not roused into indignation, or melted into tears? Mrs. Stowe's work has indeed come down upon the dark abodes of human bondage like the morning sun-light, unfolding to view the enormities of slavery in a manner which has fastened all eyes upon them, and awakened sympathy in hearts unused to feel. Day by day, and hour by hour, throughout the civilized world, sympathy is diminishing for the oppressor, and increasing for its victims. Never, since the abolition of West Indian slavery, has there existed so deep and powerful an anti-slavery feeling as at the present moment. Let each only do his duty, and this foul blot on humanity, and daring insult to the Deity, shall ere long become the history of a bygone age; and a few years hence the system shall be deemed too monstrous to be believed but as a myth of some misanthrope, who felt a malignant pleasure in libelling his species.

ENCOURAGEMENTS.

It is evident, on all hands, that the friends of the slave have everything on their side, and may now make a noble stand in the cause of liberty. Providence is remarkably appearing on their behalf, and pointing out the path of duty and of victory. " Is not the Lord gone up before us ?" God is on the side of justice and mercy—on the side of the oppressed—and " *how many shall* HE *be counted for ?*"

The tendencies of the age, so far as they favour improvement and progress, are in favour of abolition. Not a step can be taken for the diffusion of light, for the promotion of virtue, for the creation of an enlarged public spirit, for the downfall of antiquated barbarisms, for the establishment of free institutions, for the reformation of time-sanctioned abuses, that does not directly or indirectly tend to the abolition of slavery. Among the things evidently waxing old and tending to decay, the so-called "institution" of slavery is the most dilapidated and crazy. Its literary and theological defenders are already and evidently the stalking skeletons of a former age, awaiting their proper niche in some museum of petrifactions. Their ranks are constantly thinning, while the advocates of freedom constantly multiply There is nothing wanting to insure the success of the latter, but that their fidelity, consistency, courage, and energy should increase with their increasing *numbers*. The argument is already exhausted, and the logical defences and apologies of slaveholding are overturned. The pleas and objections against abolition, so formidable twenty years ago, are, for the most part, withdrawn or silenced. The dangers of emancipation, the disasters of freedom, the fear of vagrancy, of pauperism, of amalgamation, the inferiority of the negro, the happy and contented condition of the slave, the need of a preparatory process, the superior wisdom and prudence of gradualism—all these, and scores of similar allegations, are seldom repeated now, or mentioned, except in derision. Difficult as it may *still* be to carry forward the public sentiment to the proper degree of advancement, it would be *more* difficult—nay, impossible—to carry it back to where it was, fifteen or twenty years ago "Revolutions never go backward." The slave-power, once so invincible, has been seen to waver. Its courage begins to falter. Its policy reacts upon itself. Its missiles rebound. Its counsels are confounded; its unity of action is broken. Now is the right time for a renewed and a still bolder onset, for a more vigorous assault—for a more aggressive warfare against it; a campaign that shall carry the battle to its own gates—that shall dethrone the demon slavery, never to rise again. Let it not be said that the courage, the energy, and the self-denying labours of the friends of freedom have relaxed. "*Onward!*" still be the watchword. "*Excelsior!*" (higher, still higher) be our motto. LIBERTY MUST BE RESTORED AND SECURED. Till then, there must be no relaxation of effort.

CLEAR THE WAY.

MEN of thought! be up and stirring
 Night and day;
Sow the seed—withdraw the curtain,
 Clear the way!
Men of action! aid and cheer them
 As ye may.
There's a fount about to stream,
There's a light about to beam,
There's a warmth about to glow,
There's a flower about to blow,
There's a midnight blackness changing
 Into gray;
Men of thought, and men of action,
 Clear the way!

Once the welcome light has broken,
 Who shall say
What the unimagined glories
 Of the day—
What the evil that shall perish
 In its ray?
Aid the dawning, tongue and pen;
Aid it, hopes of honest men;
Aid it, paper—aid it, type—
Aid it, for the hour is ripe,
And our earnest must not slacken
 Into play.
Men of thought, and men of action,
 Clear the way!

Leeds Anti-slavery Series. No. 82.

Sold by W. and F. G. CASH, 5, Bishopsgate Street, London; and by JANE JOWETT, Friends' Meeting Yard, Leeds, at 2*s*. 3*d*. per 100.

ISSUE OF

HALF A MILLION ANTI-SLAVERY TRACTS.

"STRIKE THE IRON WHILE IT IS HOT."

AMONGST the means recently adopted to expose the dreadful iniquities of Slavery, none has been more efficacious than the well-known publication, *Uncle Tom's Cabin; or, Negro Life in the Slave States of America.* The gratitude of the Christian public is especially due to the gifted authoress for that production of her graphic pen. Her name will be chronicled amongst the most conspicuous benefactors of the human race, and recurred to with feelings of the highest admiration and esteem, when the memory of those who have soaked the earth with human gore will be remembered with abhorrence, or consigned to oblivion.

Mrs. Stowe's Work has come down upon the dark abodes of human bondage like the morning sunlight, unfolding to view the enormities of slavery in a manner which has fastened all eyes upon them, and awakened sympathy in hearts unused to feel. Day by day, and hour by hour, throughout the civilized world, sympathy is diminishing for the oppressor and increasing for his victims. Never since the abolition of Colonial Slavery, has there existed so deep and powerful an anti-slavery feeling as at the present moment.

The touching, but too truthful tale of *Uncle Tom's Cabin*, has re-kindled the slumbering embers of anti-slavery zeal into active flame. Its recitals have baptized with holy fire myriads who before cared nothing for the bleeding slave. Where is the heart it has not roused into indignation, or melted into tears? It is extremely desirable that this feeling should not be allowed to pass hastily away, without its leading to practical results. The old adage, "Strike the iron while it is hot," is especially applicable to the present moment. Some immediate means must be adopted to strengthen the impression, and fix it indelibly on the public mind, till slavery be eradicated. Now, it is the press we have to thank as the medium for calling forth much of this feeling, and as the press ever remains to be one of the mightiest instrumentalities that can be employed in the annihilation of systems of cruelty and despotism, the present favourable opportunity has been embraced for a general distribution of Anti-Slavery Tracts. Five hundred thousand have been printed, which can be supplied to the public at a very low cost; say 24 pages at 6s. 6d. per 100, 11d. per dozen; 12 pages, 3s. 6d. per 100, 6d. per dozen; 8 pages, 2s. 3d. per 100; 4 pages, 1s. 2d. per 100; 2 pages, 7d. per 100; and 1 page, 6d. per 100.

The series consists of 82 Tracts, varying from 1 page to 28 pages each, comprising the following subjects, specimens of which will be sent on application, and any other information supplied:—

No.		PAGES.
1.	Brief Definition of Negro Slavery	4
2.	Slavery Described. By a member of Congress . . .	1
3.	Startling Facts relative to Slavery	1
4.	Concise View of Slavery and the Slave-Trade . . .	8
5.	Statistics of the Coloured Race	2
6.	Workings of American Slavery, as regards Caste and Prejudice	4
7.	Slavery a System of Inherent Cruelty	12
8.	Slavery Considered in its various Relations and Consequences	28
9.	Auction Sales of Men, Women, and Children, with Houses, Cattle, &c.	4
10.	The Farewell of a Slave Mother to her Daughter (a Poem)	4
11.	Traffic in Human Affections	4
12.	Alleged Exaggeration of Slavery Considered . . .	2
13.	The Negro our Brother Man (a Poem)	1
14.	Death of the Slave (a Poem).	1
15.	Auctioneering Advertisements	1
16.	Slave Auction in a Southern City	1
17.	Sale of Aged Negroes: A Woman sold for a Jackass .	1

No.		PAGES.
18.	Business Letter from a Slave-trader	1
19.	Influence of American Churches on the Progress of Emancipation	8
20.	Expurgated Literature; Mutilation and Suppression of Works containing Anti-Slavery Sentiments	4
21.	Clerical Oppressors (a Poem)	4
22.	Reproof of the American Church. By the Bishop of Oxford	12
23.	Slave Branding	4
24.	Secrets of the Prison-house	2
25.	Boy Sold for a Watch (a Poem)	2
26.	The Blind Slave-Boy (a Poem)	2
27.	Scene on Board a Steam-Boat	2
28.	Kidnapping out of Slavery into Freedom	2
29.	Man-stealing and Religion	2
30.	Paradise of Negro Slaves: a Dream	4
31.	Slaveholding Weighed in the Balance	24
32.	Fugitive Slave-bill, and its Effects	24
33.	Opinions of American Ministers on the Fugitive Slave-bill	4
34.	Fugitive Slaves, Douglass, W. Wells Brown, Dr. Pennington, &c.	12
35.	Singular Escapes from Slavery. The Crafts, Box Brown	8
36.	Settlements of Coloured People in Canada	4
37.	Prayer for the Negro (a Poem)	1
38.	Voice from old England (a Poem)	1
39.	Murderous Treatment of a Slave-Girl; Outrage on Public Decency	1
40.	Plantation Scenes	1
41.	Sale and Separation of a Family	1
42.	Murder of an Infant	1
43.	The Slave-Ship (a Poem)	4
44.	The Englishman's Duty to the Free and Enslaved American	18
45.	Slavery Hostile to Religion, &c.	2
46.	Appalling Features of Slavery	2
47.	Think of the Slave	2
48.	The Gentlemen Farmers of Virginia attending their Cattle-market	2
49.	Slave-Auction in Virginia	2
50.	The Quadroon Girl (a Poem)	2
51.	Auction Sale of a Young Woman, with Reflections	4
52.	The Christian Slave (a Poem)	4
53.	Tender Mercies of the "Domestic Institution"	1
54.	Conversation between a Scotch Lady and a Baltimore Relative	1
55.	The Bible against Slavery	1
56.	The Order of the Family required it	1
57.	Song of Humanity (a Poem)	1
58.	The American Slave-Ship	1
59.	Hunting Slaves with Bloodhounds	4
60.	Tender Mercies of Slavery	2
61.	Slavery always Diabolical	2
62.	Scene in the Jail at Washington	2
63.	Slaves Happy!	2
64.	Sale of Slaves in Virginia	2

No.		PAGES.
65.	The Virginia Slave-Crop	4
66.	Voices from Slavery (a Poem)	4
67.	Slaveholding Piety	1
68.	Blasting Influence of Slavery on the Social Circle	1
69.	Dreadful Effects of Irresponsible Power	1
70.	Slave-trade in Columbia	1
71.	Authorities against Slavery	8
72.	Confessions of Slaveholders, &c.	4
73.	Abstinence from Slave Produce	2
74.	Parting of a Slave-Mother and her Son: Maternal Affection	2
75.	A Contrast	2
76.	Slaveholding Inconsistencies	2
77.	Phebe Morel (a Poem)	1
78.	The Witnesses (a Poem)	1
79.	Intellect and Capability of the Negro	12
80.	Results of immediate Emancipation. From Historical Evidence	8
81.	Who are responsible for Slavery; motives for Anti-Slavery effort	2
82.	To the Friends of Emancipation—an Earnest Appeal to Christians of all Denominations	8

There are also printed and issued with the foregoing series of Tracts, *The Garland of Freedom*, a collection of Anti-Slavery poems, in 3 parts, at 1s. 6d. each, and *A Cloud of Witnesses, in all Ages, against Oppression and Slavery*, comprising the sentiments of eminent persons on those subjects, 1s. 6d.; also a small series of JUVENILE ANTI-SLAVERY TRACTS.

Several of the Tracts are illustrated with woodcuts, expressly executed for them; some are also printed on superior paper, bound into volumes, for Libraries, Schools, and Public Institutions, with additional engravings.

The want of a cheap variety of well-written, judiciously-selected, and popular Anti-Slavery Tracts, has long been felt, for distribution after public meetings, lectures, and on all suitable opportunities; for, in the days in which we live, more is to be effected by public opinion, and by appeals to the great sympathies of mankind, than by force or by statute laws. We have abundance of Tracts on Peace and on Temperance, &c., in extensive circulation—*Olive Leaves* are scattered the wide world over. Why should we not have something equally cheap, for diffusing information on the question of slavery, when it is admitted to be one of the greatest calamities that afflict mankind?—something calculated to excite interest on a subject so intimately connected with the happiness or misery of a very large portion of the human family? What abundance of good might they effect, if packages of such tracts were distributed amongst emigrant ships, bound for foreign lands where slavery prevails, or is advocated. America should be deluged with these missiles. They should be wafted over the vast stronghold of slavery, like the leaves of autumn. Pamphlets, embodying facts, arguments, and appeals, calculated to arouse the reader to a sense of the sinfulness of slaveholding; exhibiting briefly, yet cogently, its enormous evils, its inherent cruelties, and its repugnance to Christianity; contrasting it with the benefits of emancipation, and showing that the holding of men in abject bondage, subjected every moment to all the liabilities attaching to any other description of property, is utterly opposed to those inalienable rights with which God has invested every human being—to all the principles of truth and justice—to the provisions of all righteous government—and to the laws of God —and that it therefore becomes our duty, as men and Christians, to seek its eternal overthrow.

If persons corresponding with, or sending goods to America, made a point of inclosing some of these Tracts, it would be like scattering seed in the now prepared soil. We ought also to endeavour to derive the full benefit from our cheap postage at home, by making up the weight prescribed with something likely to do good, thus "casting our bread upon the waters." Tracts might be inclosed in every letter, without increasing the postage. Let them be sent in faith, a blessing asked upon them, and we know not how many may take root, and what a fruitful harvest will result. We must not be silent or inactive so long as a single brother or sister bleeds in chains. So long as one man holds property in another, an anti-slavery feeling needs to be created and kept alive—society must be saturated with it; it must be preached everywhere, and to the great work of emancipation every assistance must be summoned.

To carry out the object proposed, the co-operation of all is requisite. Let none withhold assistance "for them that are in bonds," on account of the distance of the evil, remembering "the world is our country and every man our brother." The friends of humanity everywhere, are called upon to aid in endeavouring to banish for ever this foul blot on humanity from the face of the earth, and to assist in restoring to the millions of our fellow-creatures who still endure the toils and hardships of slavery, those rights and blessings designed for them by a beneficent Creator, of which they are unjustly deprived.

Those who are willing to promote this means of assisting to hasten the day of freedom to the slave, will oblige by forwarding their contributions, or orders for Tracts, to WILSON ARMISTEAD, WATER HALL, LEEDS; who will be glad to forward specimens, or any information required. Volumes, including the whole Series (about 450 pages), with Steel Engravings, will be sent, post-free, for 2s. 6d. in stamps; or, if preferred, a bundle of Tracts, of about a pound weight, will be forwarded free for the same amount.

The London Publishers of the Leeds Anti-Slavery Tracts are W. and F. G. CASH, 5, Bishopsgate Street; and WILLIAM TWEEDIE, 337, Strand—from whom they may be obtained through any country Bookseller.